Visual Models for Software Requirements

Joy Beatty
Anthony Chen

PUBLISHED BY
Microsoft Press
A Division of Microsoft Corporation
One Microsoft Way
Redmond, Washington 98052-6399

Library of Congress Control Number: 2012939549
ISBN: 978-0-7356-6772-3

Printed and bound in the United States of America.

3 16

Microsoft Press books are available through booksellers and distributors worldwide. If you need support related to this book, email Microsoft Press Book Support at mspinput@microsoft.com. Please tell us what you think of this book at http://www.microsoft.com/learning/booksurvey.

Acquisitions Editor: Devon Musgrave
Developmental Editor: Devon Musgrave
Project Editor: Carol Dillingham
Editorial Production: Online Training Solutions, Inc.
Copyeditor: Kathy Krause
Indexer: Jan Bednarczuk
Cover Illustration: John Hersey

We dedicate this book to all the unrecognized analysts who don't get the credit they deserve for making their projects successful.

Contents at a Glance

Contents

PART II OBJECTIVES MODELS

PART III PEOPLE MODELS

PART V DATA MODELS

Chapter 20 Data Flow Diagram 287

Chapter 21 Data Dictionary 299

Foreword

The most striking thing about requirements work is the enormous difference between what academics think it involves and what people in industry actually do.

The academics think they are far ahead, because they have a wide range of models and techniques, complete with experimental studies (done with specially tamed industrial tribespeople), theoretical analyses, and enormous textbooks full of excellent advice. They can't see why people in industry are being so slow to adopt their methods.

The people in industry think they are far ahead, because they have years of experience, software that works (after a bit of pushing and shoving), and proven methods of managing requirements with traceability matrices, reviews, configuration management, and attributes for priority and status. They can't see why people in academia are being so slow to catch up with reality.

It's like watching two cyclists on a circular racetrack, 180 degrees apart, endlessly circling.

That's why it is so good to see this book from Joy Beatty and Anthony Chen. They are practitioners who speak from their own experience. But—and this is the crucial thing—they are familiar with the range of models advocated by researchers, and even better, they have steadily incorporated more and more of these into their practice. Now they have reached the point where they can see that the models they are using enable them conveniently and effectively to analyse all the requirements they come across. They've seen and heard the academics talking about, say, goal modeling using KAOS or i*. They've seen challenged projects that only needed a context model to inject clarity, or the disaster that looms on projects that lack something as simple and traditional as a data dictionary. And they have a practical handle on the essential fact that you have to use all these things together.

They've arrived at a clear understanding that in a requirements process, as in any system or product, the whole is more than the sum of its parts. An airframe, a pair of powerful engines, an avionics system, and an aircrew do not make an aircraft until they are integrated. When they work together, something new emerges that none of the parts could achieve on their own: the ability to fly.

To make a requirements process "fly," the first step is to understand that there is more than one kind of requirements model. A shopping list of requirements is invaluable in a contract, but on its own, it's desperately difficult to check for correctness and completeness, and it doesn't offer any suggestions on how to discover requirements, either. Different requirements models are needed to assist with discovering, checking, and analyzing the requirements. The "shopping list" is an output, not the one-and-only input.

Joy and Anthony identify four major classes of requirements model: those dealing with objectives, people, systems, and data.

Their *objectives* come closest to traditional requirements, but starting at a much earlier and more tentative stage, looking at what a business's objectives are and from there working out how those needs can be met.

People, obviously, means looking at who has an interest in the system under design, how they will use it, and what they want from it.

Systems means exploring the context, interfaces, and events that govern what the new system will have to do. This is largely a traditional set of analysis techniques, often considered outmoded by those subject to the whims of software fashion, and it is creditably brave of Joy and Anthony to face up to this and to state clearly that old—even if incomplete—does not mean wrong. The point is, of course, that 1970s-style system analysis on its own was not enough—for example, it often failed for lack of proper attention to *objectives*.

Finally, *data* means defining the information that is needed by business users and exploring how it is used within the system. Again, much of this is very traditional, though it covers not only data analysis but state models and report analysis—a modern take on an old topic.

There is a necessary complexity here. Requirements models interlock. Objectives relate to features, which relate to processes, which relate to use cases, which relate to the user interface. Joy and Anthony show how this requirements architecture—you could call it a meta-model—can be tailored to the individual project. They have tried it, over and over, and it works.

The approach in this book is designed for software that supports business processes. Related but distinctively different requirements processes are needed for other kinds of projects, such as developing a family of mass-market products that include both hardware and software. Joy and Anthony focus specifically on one world: the world of software for businesses. The result is an innovative but compelling requirements approach.

- Ian Alexander, April 2012

Introduction

Visual requirements models are one of the most effective ways to identify software requirements. They help the analyst to ensure that all stakeholders—including subject matter experts, business stakeholders, executives, and technical teams—understand the proposed solution. Visualization keeps stakeholders interested and engaged, which is key to finding gaps in the requirements. Most importantly, visualization creates a picture of the solution that helps stakeholders understand what the solution will and will not deliver. Despite this fact, many business analysts and product managers continue to create nonvisual requirements using spreadsheets or documents listing thousands of line items. These unwieldy documents are overwhelming, boring to review, and extremely difficult to analyze for missing requirements. Such practices are a symptom of the state of current requirements training, which is often focused on how to write a good requirement rather than how to analyze an entire solution.

This book will help business analysts, product managers, and others in their organizations use visual models to elicit, model, and understand requirements. It describes a simple but comprehensive language of visual models for software requirements called RML (Requirements Modeling Language) that is a collection of best-practice models that have commonly been used in industry in an ad-hoc fashion.

Who Should Read This Book

Although this book is geared primarily toward business analysts and product managers, we think that project managers, developers, architects, and testers will get a tremendous amount of value out of the book because it can help them understand the standard of information that they should be receiving to make their jobs easier. Throughout the book, we commonly refer to the person doing the work as "the analyst," because this role has many different titles across organizations. When we refer to "you," we are also referring to "the analyst."

We want to be up front and mention that our experience has primarily been with projects that are geared toward building software that operates within an existing infrastructure, such as internally facing information technology (IT) systems, large-scale consumer-facing software as a service (SaaS) systems, and cloud systems. Although we have used RML on stand-alone ("packaged") software and embedded systems, those types of projects have not been our primary focus. However, based on our limited experience with these systems, we still think that readers working with those systems will find incredible value in RML, and we look forward to receiving feedback from those readers to improve it.

Assumptions

This book does not cover basic information on requirements; therefore, it assumes that you have existing foundational knowledge about how to write software requirements. It expects that you have a basic understanding of software development processes such as iterative, waterfall, and agile methods, and how requirements fit into those approaches.

Who Should Not Read This Book

If you are just starting out as a business analyst, you should probably read *Software Requirements* by Karl Wiegers (Microsoft Press, 2003) before reading this book, for an overview of requirements practices. If you are developing shrink-wrapped consumer software, some of the concepts will be useful, but you might find the business orientation distracting. If you are a product manager who focuses on the strategy or marketing aspect of software products rather than on software construction, then this book might not be a good fit, because it heavily emphasizes how to design features for high end-user adoption and satisfaction.

Organization of This Book

We have organized this book so that you can use it as a reference guide.

Part I, "An Introduction to Models," introduces models in general and then goes on to discuss RML and the four classifications of models: objectives models, people models, systems models, and data models (OPSD).

Each chapter in Parts II through V covers one RML model and has a consistent layout, including:

- A story that relates the model to the real world.
- A definition of the model.
- The model template.
- A suggestion of which tools to use to create the model.
- A fictional example.
- Explanations of how to create and use the model.
- An exercise so that you can practice using the model.

The exercise in each chapter is in the context of one sample project that is used throughout all chapters.

Part VI, "Models in the Big Picture," explains how to select the models and how to use models together to derive requirements.

Appendix A contains two quick lookup models grids as references for how to select models. Appendix B suggests general guidelines for creating models, including metadata for all models and template tips. Appendix C contains the answers to all of the exercises in the book. There is also a Glossary defining the terms that are used throughout the book.

Finding Your Best Starting Point in This Book

You can read the book straight through, but for some people, reading Part VI first might help create context before you delve into the details of each model. The following table provides more guidance.

If you are	Follow these steps
New to requirements modeling or visual modeling in general	Read the book from front to back so that you can get an introduction to requirements models, learn about the individual models, and finally put them all together.
Familiar with visual requirements modeling and are a business analyst who uses similar models already	We suggest that you look at all of the chapters to understand how RML treats the visual models differently than other modeling languages. However, you might find Part VI more useful to start with for understanding the more advanced topic of how to select models and use them together on projects. You can then refer to the specific model chapters as you need them on your project.

Models Quick Start

This book contains a tremendous amount of information to absorb about models. The prospect can be overwhelming, so we have developed a way for you to get started with models that uses as few models as possible but still creates significant value for projects. This quick-start method fits most IT-based projects. The following Process Flow provides an overview of this approach.

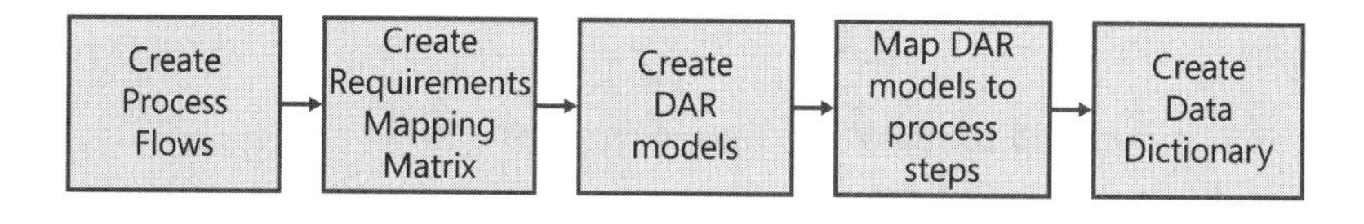

As shown in the diagram, you start by creating the Process Flows. Next, you create a Requirements Mapping Matrix (RMM) based on the Process Flow steps. Then you create Display-Action-Response (DAR) models for screens and map them against business processes. Finally, you create Data Dictionaries to ensure that all fields are covered and that the validation rules are known.

This leaves out a lot of the value of the other models, but it is a series of steps that can be adopted without major upheaval. The result is that your requirements will be organized by process steps and your screens will also be mapped to process steps to ensure that the key processes are satisfied by the user interface.

Conventions and Features in This Book

This book presents information by using conventions designed to make the information readable and easy to follow.

- Every chapter starts with a non-software story in italics to set context for the reader.
- All RML model names are capitalized throughout the book. Models from other modeling languages that are not part of RML are not capitalized.
- The building blocks of RML models are called elements, and those model elements are not capitalized so that they are not confused with model names.
- The glossary at the end of this book contains terms that we consider to be important terms for RML. These terms appear in italics throughout the book.
- Each model template includes a Tool Tip reader aid that provides suggestions for which tools to use to create that model.

Companion Content

You are welcome to download the RML model templates to use as you create the models from this book on your projects. A full set of templates for the RML models is available at:

http://go.microsoft.com/FWLink/?Linkid=253518

Instructions in the compressed file explain how to use the templates. A brief overview is repeated here: Download the compressed file and extract its files to a convenient location. There is one template for each model. The models that are Microsoft Visio files include both a template and a stencils file, both of which are required to make the template work correctly. The rest of the templates are either Microsoft Excel or Microsoft Word formats. The quick lookup models grids are also in the compressed file.

Acknowledgments

From our team at Seilevel, to our requirements colleagues around the world, to our customers who inspired and helped us refine RML over the years, this book would not have been possible without the collaboration of all of you.

Many thanks to the employees at Seilevel who helped with research, reviews, writing, editing, drafting models, and asking really good and hard questions: Joyce Grapes, James Hulgan, Betsy Stockdale, Michael Liu, Candase Hokanson, Jeremy Gorr, Balaji Vijayan, Marc Talbot, Matt Offers, Ajay Badri, Jason Benfield, Geraldine Mongold, Kell Condon, Clint Graham, David Reinhardt, Weston Eidson, Abdel Mather, Kristin DiCenso, Rob Sparks, and Lori Witzel.

Our deepest gratitude goes to the many reviewers who took time to read the manuscript and give their thoughts and critiques to help improve the book: Joyce Statz, Kent McDonald, Sarah Gregory, Ljerka Beus-Dukic, Mary Gerush, Karl Wiegers, Ellen Gottesdiener, Scott Sehlhorst, Ivy Hooks, and Anne Hartley. We want to extend a special thank you to Karl Wiegers and Ian Alexander, both of whom offered authoring mentorship and acted as philosophical sounding boards on the models.

We are deeply appreciative of the hardworking and fun editorial team who made this book a reality. Thank you to our acquisitions and developmental editor, Devon Musgrave, and our project editor, Carol Dillingham, both at Microsoft Press. We also want to thank our project manager and copyeditor, Kathy Krause; desktop publisher, Jean Trenary; proofreader, Jaime Odell; graphic artist, Jeanne Craver; and indexer, Jan Bednarczuk.

Finally, we want to thank our families, who endured the long writing process with us. Joy is grateful to her husband, Tony Hamilton, who helped her keep her sense of humor throughout the process, and her daughter, Skye, who was born in the middle of writing this book and learned to sleep through the night just as we finished writing. As it turns out, writing this book was a lot like having a baby: months of incubation, preparation, and nurturing. Anthony is appreciative of his wife, Gloria, for her support, and of his daughter, Mason, for letting him work when playing sounded like more fun and for being very quiet during conference calls. Finally, Anthony wants to thank Joy. Without her to drive the writing of this book through her sheer force of will, it never would have happened.

Errata & Book Support

We've made every effort to ensure the accuracy of this book and its companion content. Any errors that have been reported since this book was published are listed on our Microsoft Press site at oreilly.com:

http://go.microsoft.com/FWLink/?Linkid=253517

If you find an error that is not already listed, you can report it to us through the same page.

If you need additional support, email Microsoft Press Book Support at *mspinput@microsoft.com*.

Please note that product support for Microsoft software is not offered through the addresses above.

We Want to Hear from You

At Microsoft Press, your satisfaction is our top priority, and your feedback our most valuable asset. Please tell us what you think of this book at:

http://www.microsoft.com/learning/booksurvey

The survey is short, and we read every one of your comments and ideas. Thanks in advance for your input!

Stay in Touch

Let's keep the conversation going! We're on Twitter: *http://twitter.com/MicrosoftPress*.

PART I

An Introduction to Models

CHAPTER 1

Introduction to RML

With nine months until the holiday season, a prominent online retailer had identified a critical set of new features to add to its website that would greatly enhance the customer experience, directly increase sales, and reduce customer support calls in multiple countries simultaneously. The features were estimated to be worth $14 million a year and to cost less than $2 million. The product manager identified the requirements and business rules for the features, and the development team and project management team created estimates that showed that the project team would easily be able to finish by the start of the holiday season. The team was driving hard to the end date, often working nights and weekends to get releases out the door.

After eight months, the team was in final testing and feeling pretty good. They had completed a very long list of enhancements required to achieve the very hefty return. Then one of the testers noticed that the tax calculations were not right. Unfortunately, those calculations were just the tip of the iceberg. It turned out that the team had neglected to talk to the tax team. In fact, they hadn't even realized that it would be necessary to do so. If they had, they would have discovered that the tax rules required to operate in several of the countries were extremely complex, requiring integrations to third-party software that managed the rules. The project was delayed, and the $14 million return was lost for that season. The project manager was fired, and the product manager was reassigned to a different, less prominent project.

Software projects are often plagued by missed, incomplete, or unclear requirements (The Standish Group 2009). As a result of faulty requirements practices, most projects are doomed to fail (Ellis 2008). Poor requirements are at the root of many project failures, so it is disappointing to see that the success of the software requirements industry has not dramatically improved over the last 20 years. Although academia has been steadily identifying approaches for improving requirements techniques and engineering methods, commercial practices have remained largely the same. Software programming practices have matured considerably with the creation of a variety of new techniques and a plethora of tools, but software requirements are often still developed by using long lists of "shall" statements maintained in spreadsheets. Projects that use an agile approach are rarely better, often still maintaining their product backlogs and user stories in long lists in spreadsheets or tools.

RML Defined

RML (Requirements Modeling Language) is a language designed specifically to visually model requirements for easy consumption by executive, business, and technical stakeholders. RML is not a theoretical modeling language. In developing RML, we modified existing models for ease of use and created new models to address gaps. The result is a full set of models that, at its core, is specifically designed to model software requirements and is easily adopted by business stakeholders who are often challenged by complex models. We have successfully used the requirements models on many large-scale software development projects.

Challenges with Traditional Software Requirements Practices

Traditional practices unfortunately support the use of thousands of "system shall" requirements similar to the unwieldy list shown in Figure 1-1. These requirements are typically generated via interviews and working sessions with business stakeholders. Because the average person is limited by Miller's Magic Number (see the next section, "Limitations of the Human Brain"), it is nearly impossible to read the thousands of requirements and emerge confident that the requirements are complete. Moreover, one of the more significant problems is scope creep. When you have thousands of requirements, it is difficult to determine which requirements should be cut without some way to link those requirements to values that can be compared across the solution. Teams will often organize the requirements into logical groupings, but those groupings are still usually too large to be processed effectively.

Agile approaches such as Scrum have product backlogs, user stories, and acceptance criteria. Many Scrum evangelists say that the product backlog should be an unnested list of stories, which is no better than a long list of requirements. The acceptance criteria are also supposed to be listed out, sometimes on one side of a notecard. Those who work with large systems know that this lack of information organization simply isn't feasible on a project with potentially hundreds of stakeholders.

Limitations of the Human Brain

Analysts who use traditional practices to create software requirements experience common problems during analysis, organization, and consumption of the requirements. Traditional practices use long lists of text requirements in the form of shall statements, use cases, or, more recently, user stories and product backlogs. The challenge of working with long lists of items results from a fundamental limitation of human cognition. In the 1950s, cognitive psychologist George A. Miller found that humans can only remember and process seven plus or minus two items simultaneously (Miller 1956). This is often referred to as Miller's Magic Number.

More recent evidence has suggested that the number is possibly even as few as three or four (Cowen 2001). This number represents the capacity of the brain's "scratchpad" used to hold the information to solve problems. Regardless of the actual number, if a typical person is asked to think about 15 things at the same time, up to 9 (and probably fewer) of the 15 might actually be retained and processed. If more items are being processed, they are being processed a few at a time and are quickly switched in and out of memory. Think about going to a grocery store to purchase 15 items. If you don't have a written list, it's likely that you'll return home with items missing, or with incorrect items. In the same vein, if you have a list of requirements or a product backlog that is hundreds or thousands of items long, there is simply no way your brain can make sense of the complexity unless it is broken into smaller organizational groups.

Requirements Document

REQ001	System shall have fields for firstname, middle initial and last name.
REQ002	System shall display a name if there is one in the stored profile.
REQ003	System shall require name is completed.
REQ004	System shall have a field for position or title.
REQ005	System shall require title is completed.
REQ006	System shall display a position or title if there is one in the stored profile.
REQ007	System shall have a field for email address.
REQ008	System shall have a field for alternate email address.
REQ009	System shall display an email address if there is one in the stored profile.
REQ010	System shall display an alternate email address if there is one in the stored profile.
REQ011	System shall require email address is completed.
REQ012	System shall require alternated email address is completed.
REQ013	System shall have a field for daytime phone number.
REQ014	System shall display a phone number if there is one in the stored profile.
REQ015	System shall require phone number is completed.
REQ016	System shall validate all characters in the phone number field are digits when user exits the field.
REQ017	System shall display an error message if not all characters in the phone number field were digits.
REQ018	System shall have a field for a fax number.
REQ019	System shall require fax is completed.
REQ020	System shall display a fax number if there is one in the stored profile.
REQ021	System shall validate all characters in the fax number field are digits when user exits the field.
REQ022	System shall display an error message if not all characters in the fax number field were digits.
REQ023	System shall have two fields for a street address.
REQ024	System shall require the first street address field is completed.
REQ025	System shall display an address if there is one in the stored profile.
REQ026	System shall have a field for city.
REQ027	System shall require the city field is completed.
REQ028	System shall display a city if there is one in the stored profile.
REQ029	System shall have a field for state.
REQ030	System shall display a state if there is one in the stored profile.
REQ031	System shall require the state field is completed.
REQ032	System shall have a field for zip code.
REQ033	System shall display a zip code if there is one in the stored profile.
REQ034	System shall require the zip code field is completed.

FIGURE 1-1 An example of a long list of requirements.

Pictures Are Easy, Words Are Hard

What is the solution to this fundamental limitation of our primitive mammalian brains? The adage that a picture is worth a thousand words seems appropriate. *Models* are visual representations (pictures) of information related to the processes, data, and interactions within and surrounding the solution being developed. You probably use visual models every day without realizing it.

During a recent trip to a conference in a casino, after I checked in and got my room key, the woman at the desk told me how to get to my room. She said something along the lines of "From here you are going to go out to the right, then follow the path to the left, pass the bar, pass the slots, at the fountain go right, you'll go past a restaurant, and another, then you will reach a hall where you can turn left by some shops, and at the end of that you'll find elevators near the pool entrance."

I stared at her blankly. All I could think of at that moment was the sea of slot machines and tables I had walked through just to get to the registration desk from the taxi. I assumed that I would pass many more of them on my way to my room, which would further add to the confusion of what she had just said. Then she gave me hope: "And here is a map that shows you how to get there." She had drawn the path I needed to take from registration to my elevators, much like the map in Figure 1-2. I felt relieved, because I had absolutely no capability to retain all of her directions beyond the first few, but now I at least had a model to refer back to when I got confused. A map! Simply put, when human beings interpret information, pictures are easy, words are hard.

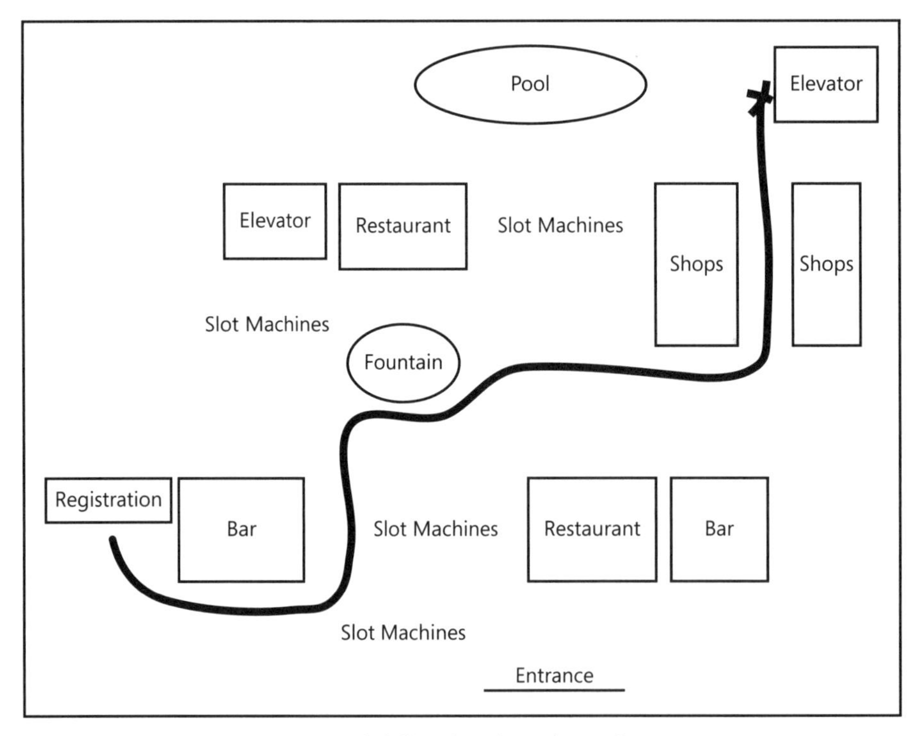

FIGURE 1-2 A map to accompany verbal directions through a casino.

Requirements Models

Requirements models organize and present large quantities of information, help you identify missing information, and give context to details (Gottesdiener 2002). Most importantly, models provide visual groupings that enable you to quickly analyze large amounts of disparate information by using limited short-term memory. It is difficult to read, interpret, and identify gaps in a requirements document of thousands of "system shall" statements, but models can help.

Imagine that you have a jumble of letters as in Figure 1-3 in front of you, and you have to find out which letters of the alphabet are missing.

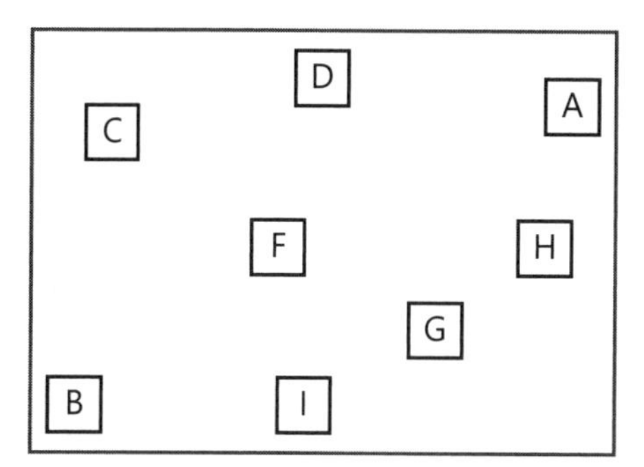

FIGURE 1-3 Jumbled letters—which one is missing?

If you just stare at the jumble or even line the letters up in a row with no order, it is going to be difficult to find the missing letters (in fact, you probably just tried to order them sequentially). If you order the letters alphabetically, as in Figure 1-4, all of a sudden the missing letter jumps right out.

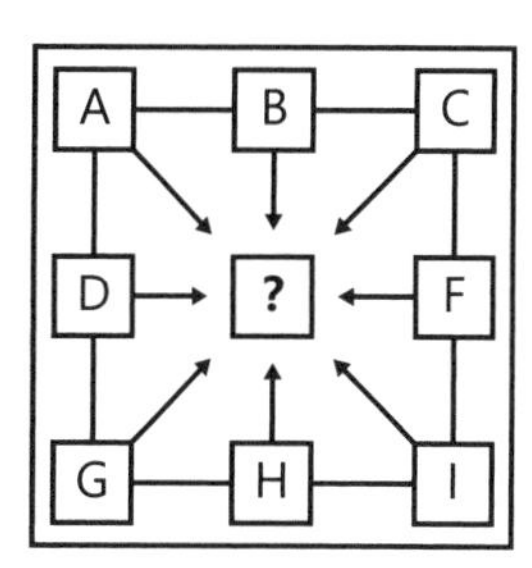

FIGURE 1-4 Organizing letters to identify the missing one.

The key to finding missing requirements is to take advantage of the fact that each requirement is related to other requirements in some way. It is extraordinarily difficult to ensure completeness when you are given a long list of "system shall" statements, but adding structure to the requirements takes advantage of their relationship and greatly simplifies the task by allowing you to analyze smaller groups of information at one time.

Requirements models are used throughout a project's life cycle. They are helpful for analyzing requirements, eliciting requirements in sessions with stakeholders, validating requirements with stakeholders, and communicating requirements to developers and testers.

Why Not UML?

The obvious question arises: Why not use the Unified Modeling Language (UML)? UML is a language used to visually specify the design of software systems (Object Management Group 2007). UML is a reasonable foundation for requirements modeling, but it is incomplete for modeling requirements because it lacks models that tie requirements to business value and models that present the system from an end user's point of view. In addition, its technical roots make it simply too complex for business stakeholders to adopt because its models are geared towards modeling the structure of the software architecture. Finally, UML is intended to be used to describe the technical design and architecture of a system and is at best retrofitted to model requirements, which are focused on business benefit, user actions, and business rules.

Models are most useful when they focus on only one or two aspects of a solution. If there are too many types of information in a model or if the syntax is too complex and difficult to understand, business stakeholders simply will not use it. In fact, our experience has shown that model complexity is one of the main reasons that some existing modeling languages are not adopted in large organizations.

RML models are designed with the simplest syntax possible that still allows the model to convey the information needed. The intent of RML is to provide a consistent syntax and semantic structures to be used by business stakeholders to analyze and understand the models on projects. The language is designed to be easy to learn and use for the entire team, including but not limited to business stakeholders, developers, and testers. The models are simplified to the most basic symbols and formats necessary to achieve the intended results within the requirements space. RML is not specific to a software development approach and can be easily adapted to work with any development approach or tool set.

Requirements vs. Design

Many of the RML models step into the realm that analysts traditionally consider to be design. For example, the Display-Action-Response model uses wireframes or screen mockups to document how a user will interact with screen elements, and the User Interface Flow shows how a user will navigate through various user interfaces.

There is a common saying related to requirements: "Requirements are what needs to be built, and design is how it will work." This distinction between requirements and design is important, because many people argue that anything that is design should not be grouped with requirements and should not be documented by business analysts. Unfortunately, there is an issue with this strict definition: "One level's requirement is another level's design."

One Level's Requirement Is Another Level's Design

At any conceptual level of a top-down solution, if you consider one level to be the "what," the next level down will be the "how." Therefore, using the what versus how definition, one level is a requirement and the next level down is design.

For example, a stakeholder might have a requirement to reduce the shopping cart abandonment rate of the company's site. At the next level of detail, a product manager might propose a few different solutions for reducing the shopping cart abandonment rate. For example, the team could reduce the number of steps in the checkout process, they could provide the capability to save the shopping cart to make purchases later, or they could provide free shipping. Each of the proposed solutions is a "how" or "design" answer to the "what" or "requirement" to reduce the shopping cart abandonment rate. In addition, the original "what" of modifying the system to reduce the shopping cart abandonment rate might also be the "how" to the "what" of trying to improve sitewide conversion rates.

What versus how is a poor way to distinguish between requirements and design.

Determining Actual Business Need

Another common definition says that anything that defines the actual solution, such as the algorithms used, the look and feel, or the user interface elements, is design and does not belong with requirements. However, there are circumstances in which a particular request could sometimes be a requirement, and at other times be design. For example, in certain industries, a product must use a specific cryptographic algorithm to be competitive; therefore, it is a requirement. For a different application, the specific cryptographic algorithm might be completely irrelevant, and it is only important that the application encrypt credit card numbers using any algorithm.

The key difference between something that is a requirement and something that is not is whether the business stakeholders actually need it. You know that stakeholders don't actually need everything that they say they need, so your role is to determine whether a specific request actually is a requirement—whether they really need it or not.

Requirements Defined

A *requirement* is anything that the business needs to have implemented in the solution. Requirements, therefore, can include functional requirements, non-functional requirements, business rules, and even what many people traditionally call design. Instead of telling the business stakeholders what types of things they are allowed to specify, you can focus on serving them by helping them truly understand what they need—by using models.

This section provides some definitions of requirement terms that we will use throughout this book. A *functional requirement* is a behavior or capability that the solution can provide irrespective of any qualifiers. A *business rule* is a requirement that represents a conditional statement that modifies a functional requirement, including, but not limited to, when the function is available and who is allowed to execute the function. A business rule contains words such as "if," "when," and "then." A *non-functional requirement* is any requirement that is not a functional requirement (including business rules). A *feature* is a short-form description of an area of functionality that the solution will ultimately include to meet the business objectives. Features are collections of requirements that are used to articulate and organize the requirements. Table 1-1 shows a few examples.

TABLE 1-1 Requirements Examples

Requirement	Type
The system shall be able to automatically approve or deny credit.	Functional requirement
When the credit score is above 750, the system shall automatically approve credit.	Business rule
The system shall use the following algorithm when automatically determining credit approvals for scores less than 750: [*algorithm would be included here*]	Business rule
Approvals shall be returned to the user within 30 seconds.	Non-functional requirement

An *assumption* is a statement taken as truth, upon which decisions are made. Assumptions include any predictions or forecasts of the future. Assumptions are a topic critical to requirements because they are constantly made but rarely understood or articulated. In fact, when analysts are asked to write down their assumptions, they typically write down trivial ones that are not impactful, missing the important ones. These example assumptions might result in failure to achieve the business objectives if they prove to be incorrect:

- Many people are willing to search online to resolve their technical issues.
- Fifty percent of people who are experiencing technical issues will be willing to wait for follow up.
- Ninety percent of the business's customers are online.
- The problems to be resolved can be solved by customers on their own.

Requirements Models Are Not the End Game

Using requirements models does not eliminate the need to write requirement statements. The models provide context and create a full picture of the requirements, but they do not represent the final requirements that will be used by the system developers and testers, so you will need to take additional steps to derive requirements from the models. Like a grocery list that is organized by aisle, the requirements form the checklist for the team to develop the solution. The value of models is in helping organize the requirements in a way that makes it easy to see when requirements are missing, extraneous, or incorrect.

You should include all the models you create as part of the complete set of requirements artifacts on a project. However, only the combination of textual and visual requirements can paint a full picture of the solution to be built (Wiegers 2003).

Using RML on Projects

You can think of the RML models described in this book as a toolbox of models and templates for use on software projects. Multiple models should generally be used together, and there are common approaches that define when to use specific models in the overall development life cycle. The approaches for applying requirements models on projects work with many development methods, such as agile, iterative, and waterfall methods (see Chapter 25, "Selecting Models for a Project").

Additional Resources

- "RML Quick Reference for Business Analysts" is a two-page summary of the models: *http://www.seilevel.com/wp-content/uploads/RML-Language-for-Modeling-Software-Requirements.pdf.*
- Karl Wiegers provides a solid introduction to the value of models in Chapter 11 of *Software Requirements, Second Edition* (Wiegers 2003).

References

- Chen, Anthony. 2010. "What vs. How – BRD vs. User Requirements vs. Functional Requirements": *http://requirements.seilevel.com/blog/2010/04/what-vs-how-brd-vs-user-requirements-vs-functional-requirements.html.*
- Cowan, Nelson. 2001. "The Magical Number 4 in Short-Term Memory: A Reconsideration of Mental Storage Capacity." *Behavioral and Brain Sciences* 24, 87-114.
- Ellis, Keith. 2008. "Business Analysis Benchmark Report." IAG Consulting. *http://www.iag.biz/images/resources/iag%20business%20analysis%20benchmark%20-%20executive%20summary.pdf.*
- Gottesdiener, Ellen. 2002. *Requirements by Collaboration: Workshops for Defining Needs.* Boston, MA: Addison-Wesley Professional.
- Miller, George A. 1956. "The Magical Number Seven, Plus or Minus Two: Some Limits on Our Capacity for Processing Information." *Psychological Review* 63, 81-97.
- Object Management Group. 2007. "OMG Unified Modeling Language Specification." *http://www.uml.org/#UML2.0.*
- The Standish Group. 2009. "CHAOS Summary 2009." West Yarmouth, MA: The Standish Group International, Inc.
- Wiegers, Karl E. 2003. *Software Requirements, Second Edition.* Redmond, WA: Microsoft Press.

CHAPTER 2

Model Categorization

Imagine that you need to cut a round hole in a sheet of plywood. You have a shelf full of tools that you could use. You would very quickly narrow your search to those tools that can cut. For example, you would immediately pass over the hammer, the file, and the screwdriver. But you would zero in on all the different types of cutting tools such as scissors, tin snips, drills, routers, ripsaws, jigsaws, and handsaws. From there, you would focus on selecting the one that could make the circular cuts you need in the easiest way possible. Some of the tools might require more setup because they use an air compressor instead of a battery or electrical outlet. The point is that you have "categorized" your tools by type and purpose.

You can apply the same concept of categorization to requirements models to help you select models for specific types of analysis. RML models are organized into categories of objectives models, people models, systems models, and data models, known collectively as OPSD. The RML classification, represented by the diagram in Figure 2-1, offers a complete toolbox of models for analyzing the solution to be built. The RML models together allow you to look at the objectives of the solution, the people who are using the solution, the systems themselves, and the data that is being processed. These models bound the analysis to provide you with the best possible chance to ensure that you don't miss key requirements and that you avoid including unnecessary requirements.

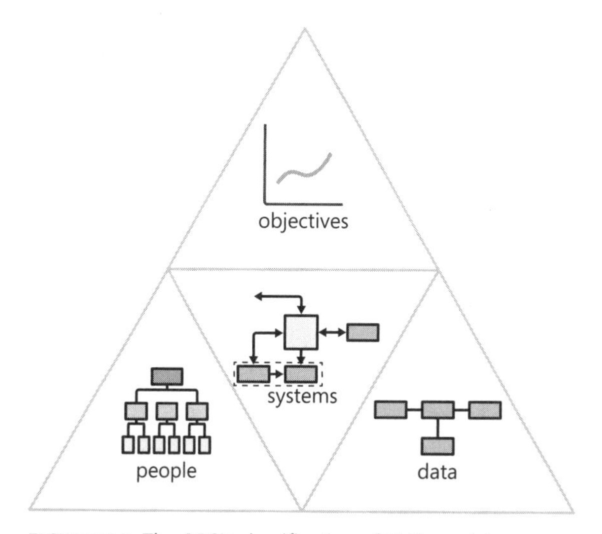

FIGURE 2-1 The OPSD classification of RML models.

Objectives, People, Systems, and Data Models

Software has a single purpose: to process data. Simply put, data enters the system, is processed, and then exits the system. The earliest models for software development, such as flow charts and structured design, took this design-centric view (DeMarco 1978). This view also considered how various systems in a multisystem environment transferred data to each other. Over the past 25 years, solution teams have discovered that another view is vitally important—that of the end user. Out of that discovery rose Use Cases, business process modeling, and other forms of user-centric modeling. Finally and most recently, executive stakeholders have been trying to determine how to align software development with end-user and organizational business objectives.

RML's organizational structure is based on these traditional model areas and groups models by objectives, people, systems, and data (OPSD). These areas represent four categories of information that you need to consider to thoroughly analyze your solution. RML models help you create boundaries around your solution by helping you start with information that you can easily ensure is complete.

Table 2-1 shows the RML models organized by OPSD.

TABLE 2-1 RML Model Categorization

	Description	Models	Bounding Model
Objectives	Describe the business value of the system and help you prioritize features and requirements based on their value	Business Objectives Model Objective Chain Key Performance Indicator Model Feature Tree Requirements Mapping Matrix	A Business Objectives Model bounds the objectives space
People	Describe who is using the system, along with their business processes and goals	Org Chart Process Flow Use Case Roles and Permissions Matrix	An Org Chart bounds the people space
Systems	Describe what systems exist, what the user interface looks like, how the systems interact, and how they behave	Ecosystem Map System Flow User Interface Flow Display-Action-Response Decision Table Decision Tree System Interface Table	An Ecosystem Map bounds the systems space
Data	Describe the relationships between business data objects from an end-user perspective, the life cycle of the data, and how that data is used in reports to make decisions	Business Data Diagram Data Flow Diagram Data Dictionary State Table State Diagram Report Table	A Business Data Diagram bounds the data space

Bounding Models

Each category of RML has a *bounding model* that can be created with a high probability of capturing all the information for that model. When you have strong confidence that a model is complete, you have fully bounded your analysis. For example, for some IT systems, all possible stakeholders can be identified from a corporate organizational chart, which can be used to create a solution Org Chart. Therefore, a complete list of relevant stakeholders to be interviewed is identified. By creating an Org Chart that contains all the possible groups of stakeholders, you have bounded your analysis and can be sure that you have not excluded stakeholders. The bounding models for each category of RML are the Business Objectives Model (objectives), Org Chart (people), Ecosystem Map (systems), and Business Data Diagram (data).

Using the appropriate bounding model from each category bounds the analysis scope by creating a foundation of comprehensive information. As the analysis proceeds to more detailed models within RML, it can become increasingly difficult to determine whether the model is complete. For example, as you dig deeper to understand individual users' Process Flows, it is more difficult to ensure that all tasks accomplished by the user are identified. Using models together can help you fill in the gaps (see Chapter 26, "Using Models Together").

All Four Categories Are Needed

Analysis of most solutions typically requires models from all four categories. The key value of analyzing a solution from different points of view is that it helps ensure that the solution is examined from all angles. Consider the four views of an object shown in Figure 2-2. If you were given only one, two, or three of the views, it is unlikely that you could draw the three-dimensional object correctly. All four views together help you correctly visualize the whole object shown in Figure 2-3.

In relation to software, some organizations tried to exclusively use Use Cases to analyze a system, but this would often leave out critical information regarding data and its flow through a system. In the early days of software, when flow charts, Data Flow Diagrams, and context diagrams were the main mechanisms for analyzing software, the resulting systems often were difficult to use. In present-day software development, a common issue is that features are not analyzed for overall value, and money is wasted creating features that very few users need—the benefit does not justify the cost. Development of models in each of the RML categories ensures that you have a bounded understanding of the solution and can maximize the chances that the team will build the right software. Chapter 25, "Selecting Models for a Project," further discusses how to select the appropriate models from each category based on project characteristics, project phase, audience, and development approach.

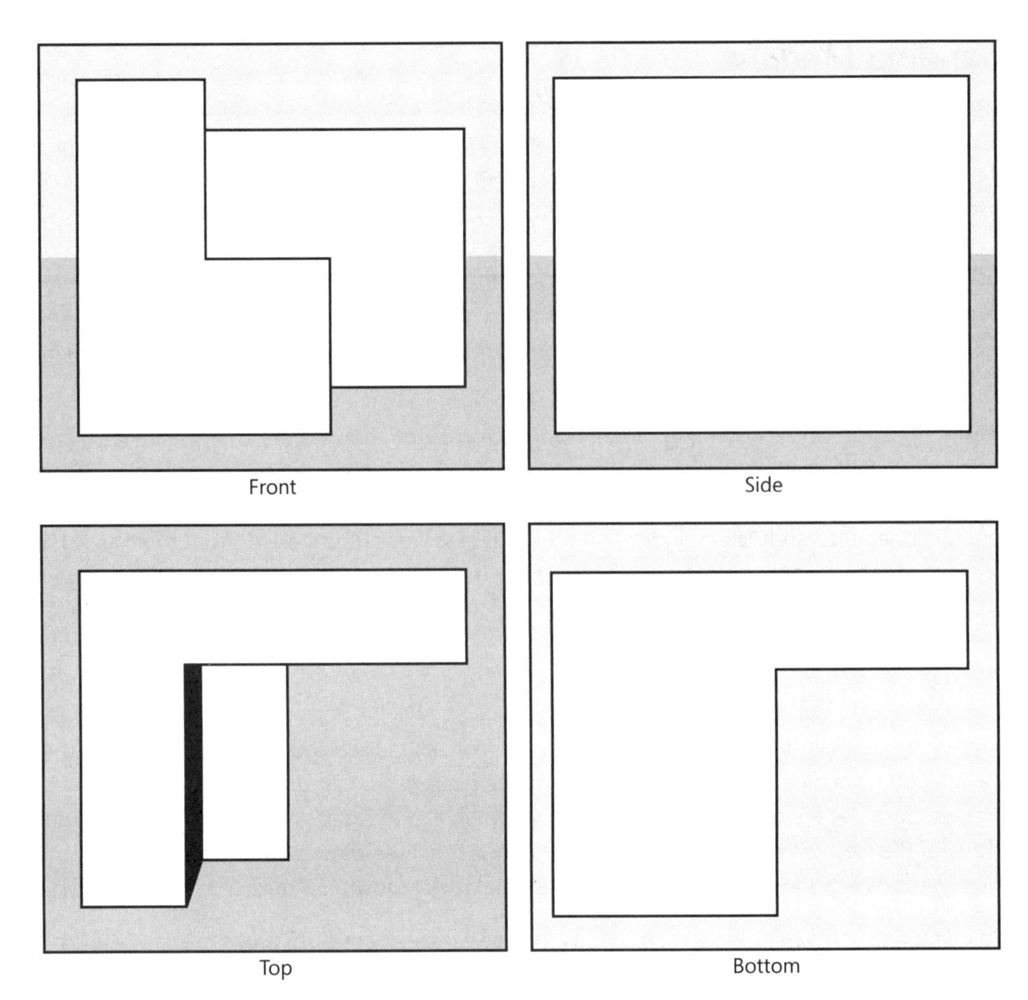

FIGURE 2-2 Four views of an object.

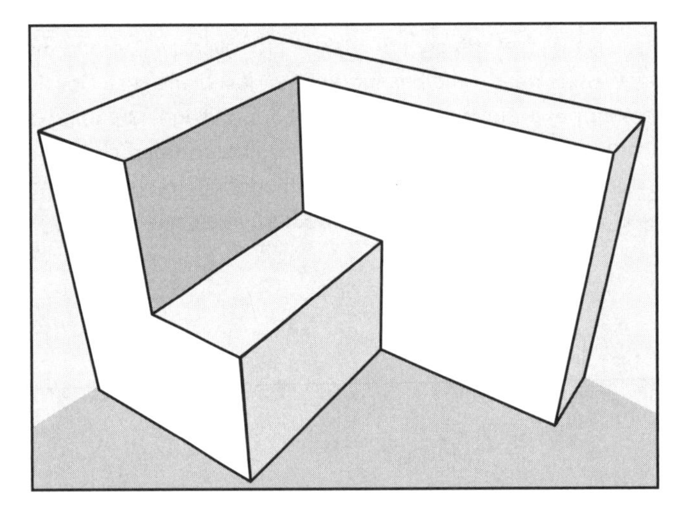

FIGURE 2-3 The complete three-dimensional object.

Objectives Models

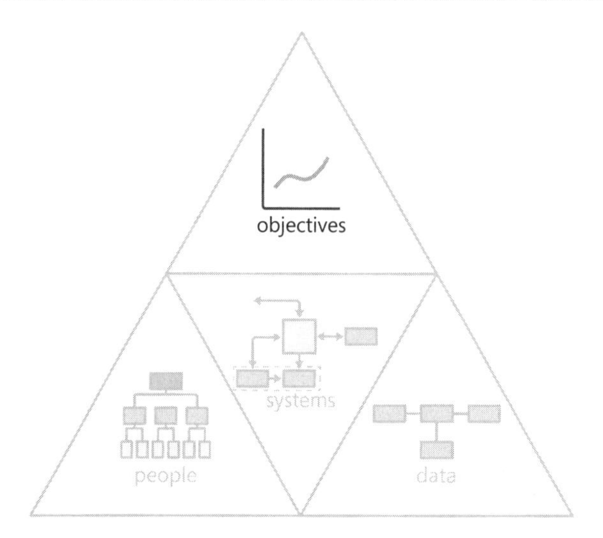

Objectives models describe the business value of the system and help you prioritize features and requirements based on their value. One of the most significant areas of project waste is the incorporation of features that contribute little value to the end user or organization. About 65 percent of features are rarely or never used (The Standish Group 2009). If you can cut those features before they are implemented, this leads to a direct reduction in your project's scope, risk, and budget. You save the most money from features that you never build.

The Business Objectives Model is the bounding model for the RML objectives models category. It enables you to map features to business objectives to help stakeholders to prioritize the features based on value, and cut the ones that provide the least value. In addition, the Business Objectives Model identifies the problems that need to be solved so that, during implementation, the development team can ensure that they not only implement the features but also solve the key problems.

Objectives models are useful early in the project to help project stakeholders agree on the business value of the project. During the project, they help you to elicit requirements by identifying which business objectives are not being satisfied by the requirements, and they help you to cut scope by identifying requirements that do not create significant value. When you use the Business Objectives Model, many requested features or requirements easily fall out of scope, and you can focus only on the requirements that contribute to achieving the business value.

After you have developed a Business Objectives Model, you have created a boundary around the scope of your system. The additional objectives models will help you to further refine the scope by creating more granular links between requirements and the value that they create.

People Models

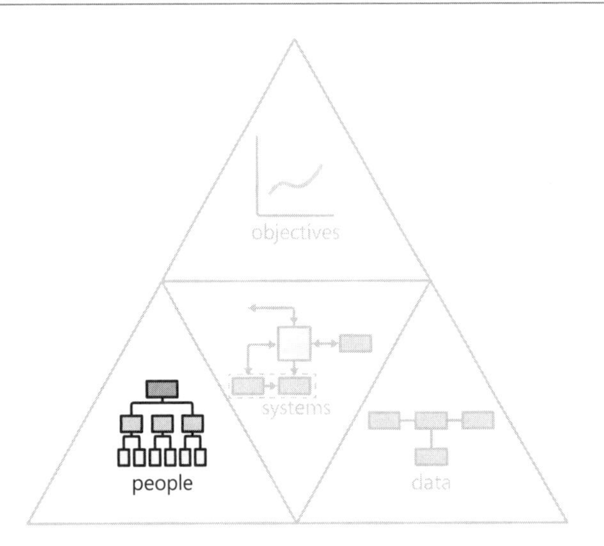

People models describe the stakeholders of the system, their business processes, and their goals. The Org Chart is the bounding model for the RML people models category. It is used to bound the people space by helping you ensure that you have considered all possible stakeholders. It is generally a straightforward task to identify all of the stakeholders in a business organization because people are used to thinking about the people they work with; however, there might be other business groups that are not so obvious. Org Charts include not only those who use the system, but also those who operate the system and those who build or maintain the system. You can identify a representative lead from each group who can act as a single decision maker to represent the user population and who can help to identify those with special knowledge of a facet of the system. In addition, you need to ensure that any subgroups are identified. For example, if there are two types of sales representatives who use the system in different ways, they should be identified as distinct users. Finally, if end customers (who obviously don't exist in your Org Chart) are using the system, you can use the Org Chart to identify the stakeholders internal to the organization who directly interact with those end customers and so might have the best information about their needs.

Other ways to bound the population of users include looking at the database of all users who have access to the system and the functionality of the system that they regularly use, identifying all developers who have checked code into the change control system, and all operations team members who maintain the system.

After you have identified the stakeholder population, there is a firm boundary that limits the unknowns. You might identify additional user classes, but, over time, the model will stabilize. The next step is to begin meeting with the various users and determine how they interact with the system. These interviews will result in the generation of additional people models to describe how the users expect to use the system and their desired outcomes.

Systems Models

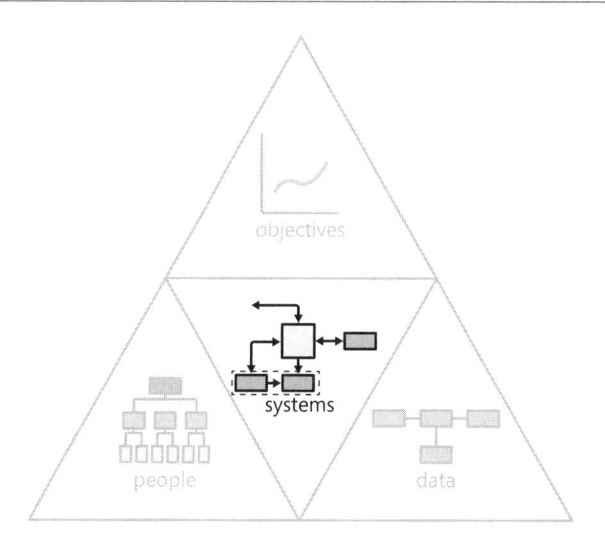

Systems models describe what systems exist, what the user interface looks like, how the systems interact, and how they behave. They identify all of the major applications that participate in a multisystem environment ("the ecosystem") and describe specific aspects of the system, such as the user interface, the interfaces between systems, and the automated processes executed by the system. The Ecosystem Map is the bounding model for the RML systems models category. Most IT, software as a service (SaaS), cloud, and even mobile software projects exist in the context of an application ecosystem. That ecosystem is composed of the myriad other systems and processes that interact with the system being changed. When you are looking at an existing application ecosystem for the first time, whether for a new development project, an upgrade to a preexisting system, or for a complete system migration, it is sometimes difficult to know where to begin the analysis process. To add to the problem, the existing application ecosystem is often not documented at all.

It is typically straightforward for users, operators, and maintainers to list the systems; however, it is much harder for them to detail all of the interactions between systems without some organized structure. An Ecosystem Map provides a visual framework that focuses on the relationship between any two systems, so that only the relationship between those two systems has to be considered at one time. This makes it much easier to capture all of the information about that relationship. The Ecosystem Map simultaneously shows all systems and, at a high level, the nature of the interactions. This list of all systems provides another boundary that is reasonably easy to achieve.

After you have identified a relatively complete Ecosystem Map, you have bounded the scope of all systems that can influence your development effort. You can use the additional systems models to document how the systems should look, how they should behave, and the details of how they should interact with each other.

Data Models

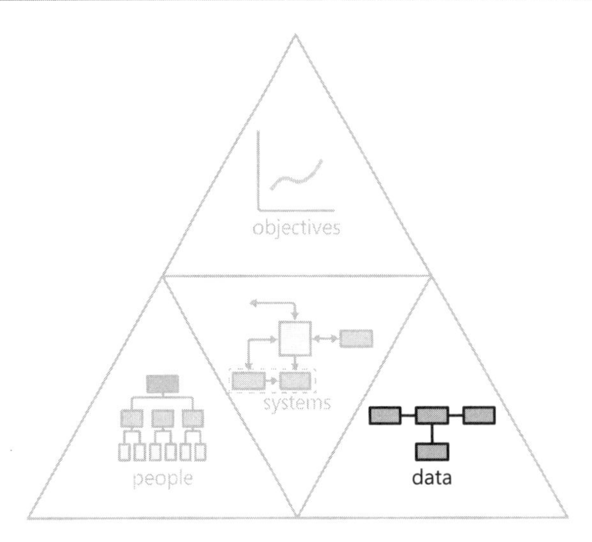

Data models describe the relationships of business data objects from an end-user perspective, the life cycle of the data, and how that data is used in reports to make decisions. The Business Data Diagram is the bounding model for the RML data models category. Business Data Diagrams document the full set of business data objects and their hierarchy. You can use existing data entry screens and reports to fully identify business data objects. Even if there is no existing screen, existing forms and paper reports can serve the same purpose. Because the number of these screens and reports is finite, you can be certain that they form a complete boundary around the data in the proposed solution.

After you have a reasonable Business Data Diagram, you can begin to create additional data models that describe more detail about how data is processed, the exact form of the data, and how users will use the data to make decisions. Data can only be created, updated, used, moved, copied, or destroyed. Therefore, when an object has been identified, these actions can be applied to the business data objects to identify requirements in a systematic way to help identify the specific ways users can interact with the data.

References

- DeMarco, Tom. 1978. *Structured Analysis and System Specification.* New York, NY: Yourdon Inc.
- The Standish Group. 2009. "CHAOS Summary 2009." West Yarmouth, MA: The Standish Group International, Inc.

PART II

Objectives Models

CHAPTER 3

Business Objectives Model

A major distributor gives away nearly $300 million in credits to its customers each year. The process of calculating the credits is fully manual, performed by an offshore team. The finance team has estimated that approximately $15 million annually is erroneously paid out but was not able to pin down exactly how much. A few high-profile errors of more than $1.5 million convinced management to charter a project to reduce the errors. The errors were primarily caused by sales contracts that specified credits that allowed customers to claim multiple credits on the same purchase. These overlaps were sometimes simply mistakes in date ranges, but sometimes they were deliberate on the part of the sales teams. To rectify this problem, executives chartered a project to automate the process and validate that the credits in sales contracts followed corporate policy.

During the six-month pilot of the new system with a few of the company's customers, the system caught approximately $4 million in accounting errors, indicating that the full yearly return might be higher than $15 million. The project cost approximately $1 million. Unfortunately, the project did not fully automate the process of transferring the contracts from the sales system to the finance system; the contracts had to be manually transferred, requiring three full-time resources, each costing $25,000 a year. As a result, the business team rejected full deployment until the process was completely automated, delaying achievement of more than $15 million a year!

The heart of every project is its value to the end users or the company. Yet too many times, teams lose sight of the essence of the value that a project is supposed to create. Without a focus on the business objectives to drive scope, projects can become loaded down with extraneous features that fail to contribute to the core objectives of the projects. The Business Objectives Model allows the stakeholders to identify the value of a project and then to use that value every day to make requirements decisions.

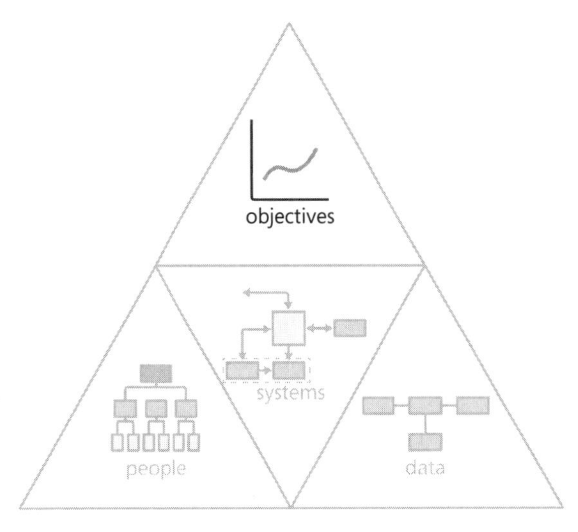

The Business Objectives Model is an RML objectives model. It defines the business problems, business objectives, product concept, and success metrics, as defined in Table 3-1.

TABLE 3-1 Business Objectives Model Elements

Element	Definition
Business problem	Issue preventing the business from achieving its goals.
Business objective	Measureable target that specifies when the business problem is solved.
Product concept	Vision of the actual solution that the business chooses to implement in order to meet the business objective. It is typically described by a list of high-level features.
Success metric	A business objective that will actually be measured to determine whether the project is successful, or additional measures that are related to the solution.

The Business Objectives Model elements are captured visually in a diagram that links them to one another, as shown in Figure 3-1.

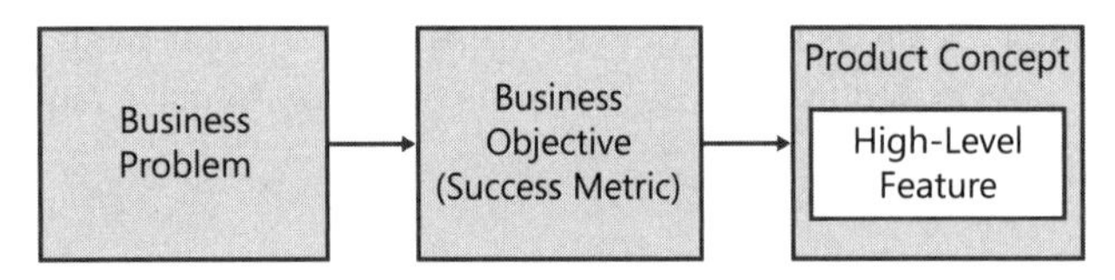

FIGURE 3-1 Business Objectives Model elements.

The business stakeholders might think in terms of the goals they are trying to achieve. Though goals are not part of the Business Objectives Model, it can be helpful to understand and talk about them with the business. Goals are similar to business objectives, but they are qualitative statements instead of measurable statements.

Business Objectives Model Template

The Business Objectives Model template consists of boxes that contain a business problem, business objective, or product concept with features, and arrows between the boxes to show how they are linked. Success metrics are captured in the same boxes as business objectives or as separate callouts. Each project can have only one product concept box, but there can be more than one of each of the other Business Objectives Model elements. You should use multiple element boxes in these situations so that each box only contains one instance of the element, and add a number that is unique across elements of the same type. For example, if there are multiple business objectives for one business problem, the template would look like the one shown in Figure 3-2.

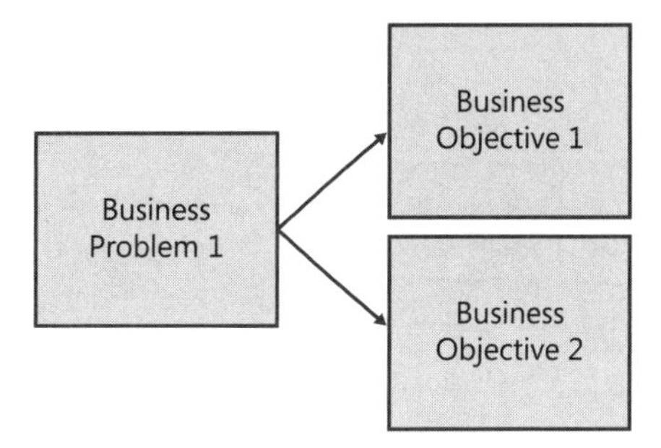

FIGURE 3-2 An example of multiple business objectives for one business problem.

Business problems and business objectives form a hierarchy of repeating problem/objective pairs. A Business Objectives Model always starts with a business problem, then has at least one business objective. Each business objective can lead to another business problem or to the product concept.

The success metrics can be any of the business objectives that can be measured to represent the success of the project. They are marked with an "(SM)" in the business objective box. Ideally, all business objectives would also be success metrics. Unfortunately, that is not always the case, because often the impact the solution has in achieving the business objectives is too difficult to measure directly, so those business objectives cannot be used as success metrics for the project. In addition, there might be success metrics that are not business objectives, but instead serve as measurable proxies for the business objectives. The success metrics that are not business objectives are captured as callouts on the business objectives for which they are proxies.

When you complete a Business Objectives Model, the model can be more complex than one level and might look like the variation shown in Figure 3-3. In this scenario, there are two business problems that map to three different business objectives, and those business objectives are mapped to four business problems that are mapped to four business objectives. Based on these business objectives, there is a product concept. Typically, the model is laid out from left to right for readability.

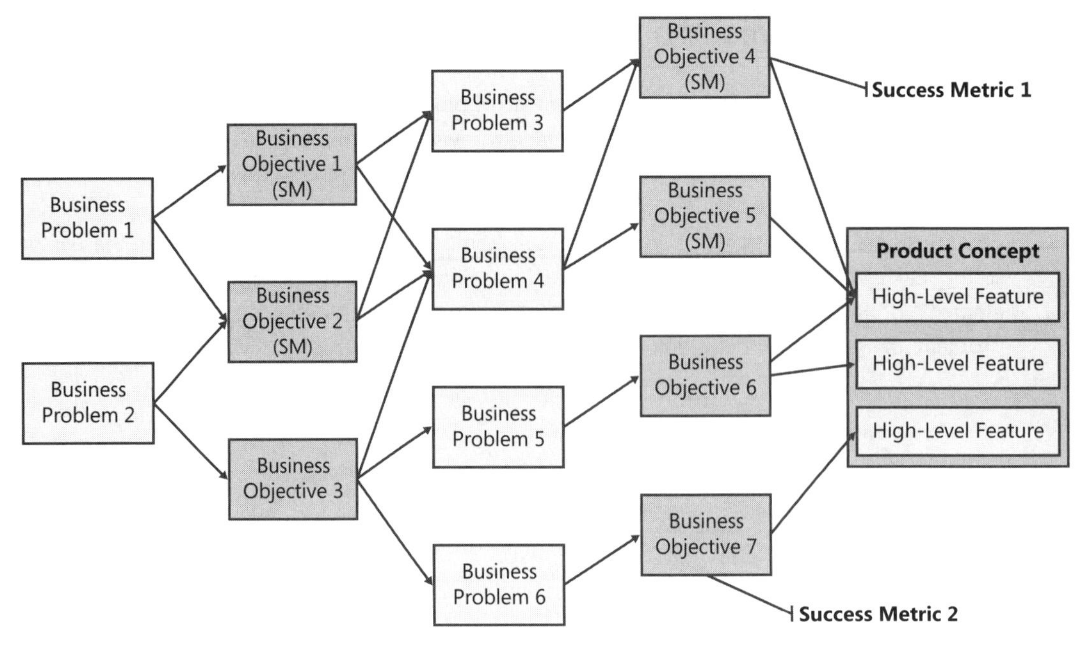

FIGURE 3-3 An example of a Business Objectives Model template.

Note that a product concept can span multiple solution components, such as multiple pieces of software, hardware, or processes. If you think you need to describe multiple product concepts, you most likely need multiple Business Objectives Models to describe the business value of different projects to implement them.

Tool Tip Business Objectives Models are typically created in Microsoft Visio or Microsoft PowerPoint. While you are creating them, you might find mind mapping tools to be useful. For large projects, it might be helpful to put the model in a requirements management tool to trace between the elements.

Example

Executives at a printer company are evaluating their financial issues. They realize that the profit on a few of their product lines has dropped. After further research, the analyst helps them realize that the reason for the profit issues in those lines is that the company has increased staff in the call center to support an abundance of incoming calls. The analyst works with the business leaders to establish that the business problem is as shown in Figure 3-4.

After further discussion, the executives determine that in order to cut expenses in the call center, 180 staff members must be moved out of the call center and into revenue-producing roles. However, if the staff members are moved, the call center will be able to support 3,000 fewer calls per day. Given this new target, they create a series of business problems and business objectives as depicted in Figure 3-5.

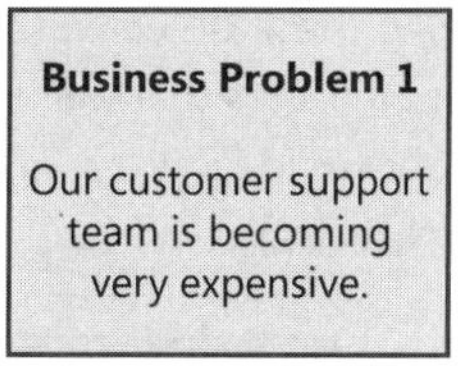

Business Problem 1

Our customer support team is becoming very expensive.

FIGURE 3-4 An example business problem.

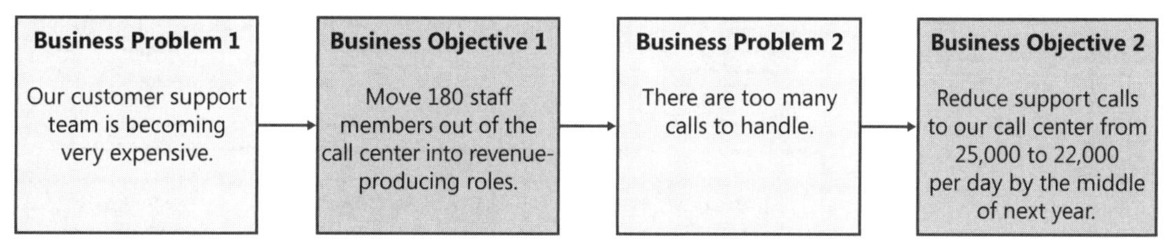
Business Problem 1
Our customer support team is becoming very expensive.
Business Objective 1
Move 180 staff members out of the call center into revenue-producing roles.
Business Problem 2
There are too many calls to handle.
Business Objective 2
Reduce support calls to our call center from 25,000 to 22,000 per day by the middle of next year.

FIGURE 3-5 An example of associated business problems and business objectives.

The analyst asks the question, "What is stopping us from achieving our objective today?" After evaluating data from the call center, the executives identify the two key reasons people call in:

- Fifty percent of callers want to find a solution to their new problem.
- Thirty percent of callers previously called with their problem, and because it could not be solved in real time during the call, they are calling back to check the status of it.

These two pieces of information form the next level of business problem. The analyst helps the executives identify two business objectives that, if met, will solve the business problems, as shown in Figure 3-6.

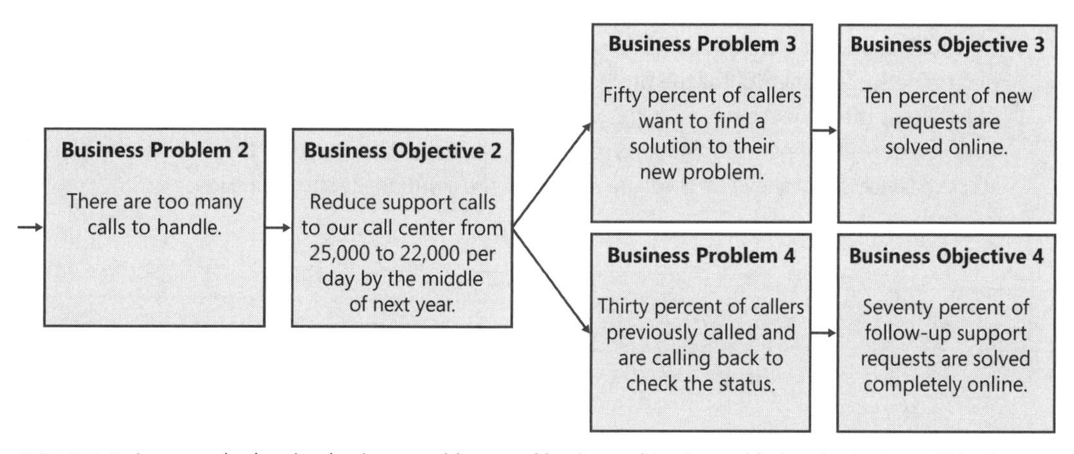
Business Problem 2
There are too many calls to handle.
Business Objective 2
Reduce support calls to our call center from 25,000 to 22,000 per day by the middle of next year.
Business Problem 3
Fifty percent of callers want to find a solution to their new problem.
Business Objective 3
Ten percent of new requests are solved online.
Business Problem 4
Thirty percent of callers previously called and are calling back to check the status.
Business Objective 4
Seventy percent of follow-up support requests are solved completely online.

FIGURE 3-6 An example showing business problems and business objectives added to the Business Objectives Model.

The analyst can then ask the question, "What is stopping us from achieving these objectives?" The answer is that there is no online support system. The team agrees on a set of features that make up a product concept that they think will reduce the calls in the call center, as shown in Figure 3-7. They identify four high-level features that will be key to meeting the business objectives.

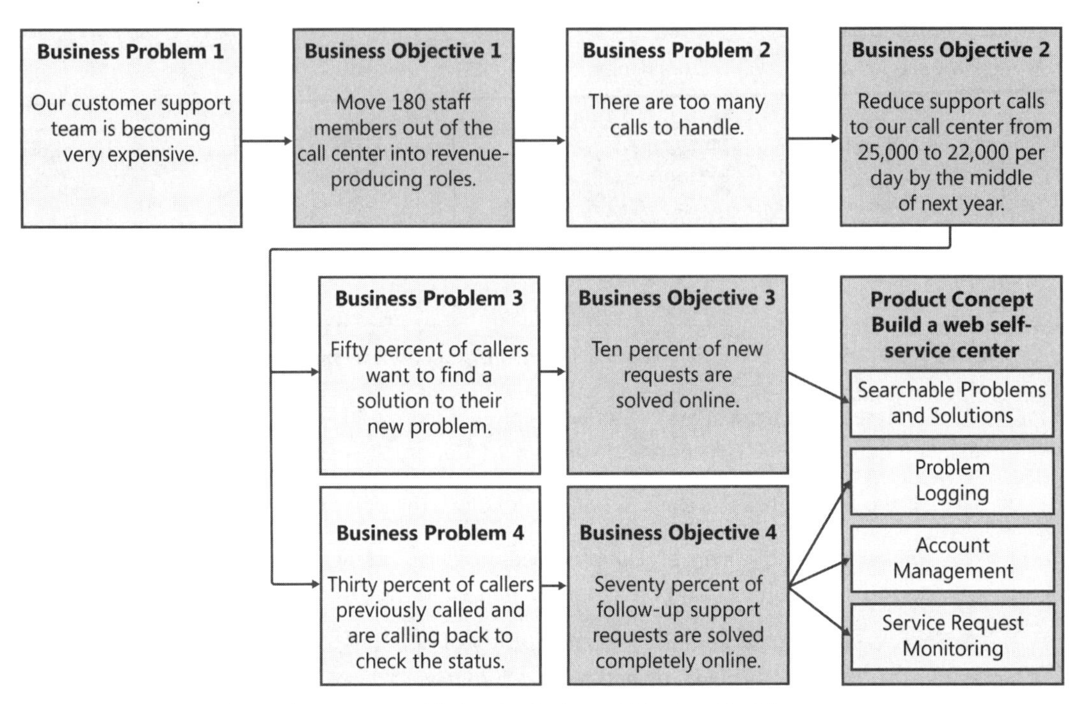

Business Problem 1
Our customer support team is becoming very expensive.
Business Objective 1
Move 180 staff members out of the call center into revenue-producing roles.
Business Problem 2
There are too many calls to handle.
Business Objective 2
Reduce support calls to our call center from 25,000 to 22,000 per day by the middle of next year.
Business Problem 3
Fifty percent of callers want to find a solution to their new problem.
Business Objective 3
Ten percent of new requests are solved online.
Business Problem 4
Thirty percent of callers previously called and are calling back to check the status.
Business Objective 4
Seventy percent of follow-up support requests are solved completely online.
Product Concept
Build a web self-service center
Searchable Problems and Solutions
Problem Logging
Account Management
Service Request Monitoring

FIGURE 3-7 An example product concept added to the Business Objectives Model.

Finally, the team identifies which business objectives can actually be measured and uses those to determine success metrics for the project, to confirm that they are on track to meeting the business objective as the project evolves. In this particular case, they decide that none of the business objectives can easily be measured and linked to the project's success. Instead, they create two proxy measures of success that they can measure as part of the solution, as shown in Figure 3-8.

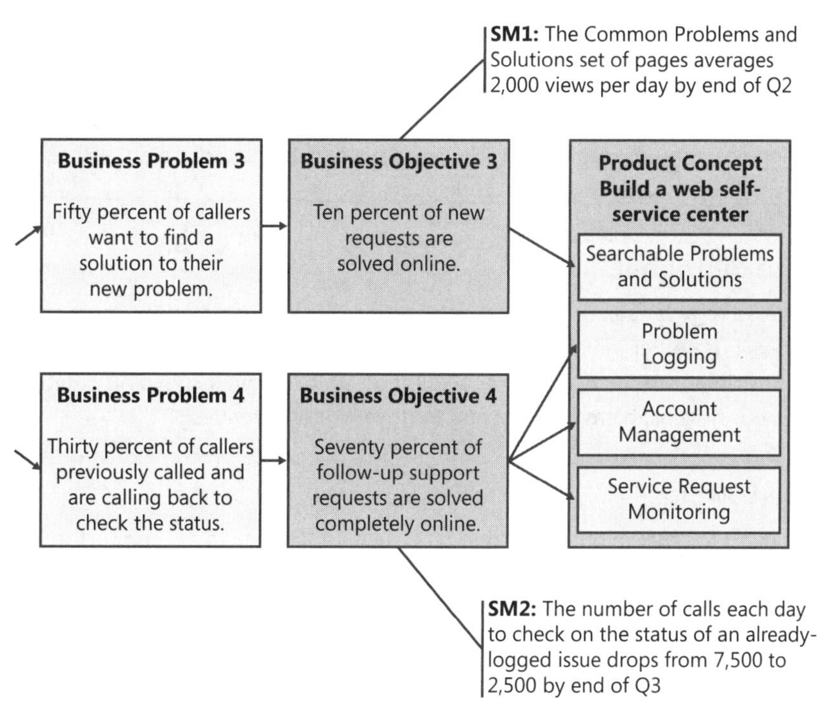
SM1: The Common Problems and Solutions set of pages averages 2,000 views per day by end of Q2
Business Problem 3
Fifty percent of callers want to find a solution to their new problem.
Business Objective 3
Ten percent of new requests are solved online.
Product Concept Build a web self-service center
Searchable Problems and Solutions
Problem Logging
Account Management
Service Request Monitoring
Business Problem 4
Thirty percent of callers previously called and are calling back to check the status.
Business Objective 4
Seventy percent of follow-up support requests are solved completely online.
SM2: The number of calls each day to check on the status of an already-logged issue drops from 7,500 to 2,500 by end of Q3

FIGURE 3-8 Example success metrics added to the Business Objectives Model.

Creating Business Objectives Models

Business Objectives Models have a natural order in which the elements are typically created, as shown in Figure 3-9. Business problems and business objectives are created iteratively until a product concept can be defined. Later in this chapter, in the section, "Understanding Projects That Are Underway," we discuss creating and using the model when the order is not followed.

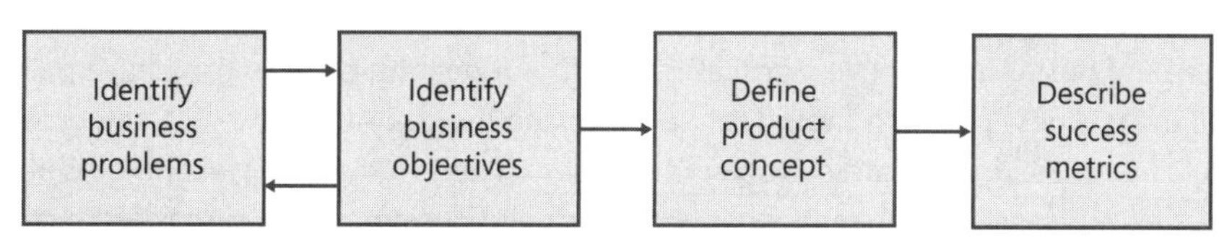
Identify business problems
Identify business objectives
Define product concept
Describe success metrics

FIGURE 3-9 The process for creating a Business Objectives Model.

Identify Business Problems

Organizations generally fund projects in order to solve a particular business problem, even if the problem has not been explicitly articulated. However, in many cases, project stakeholders do not have a shared understanding of the business problem. The good news is that you can map almost every business problem to either increasing revenue or reducing costs.

Revenue Needs to Be Higher

Business problems related to revenue are rarely stated directly as, "We need to make more money." Typically, the business will use other indicators that relate to making more money. For example, problems associated with customer retention, customer acquisition, and customer spending habits are all ultimately related to a business problem that is trying to drive higher revenues.

Costs Need to Be Lower

Business problems relating to costs might be more direct, such as, "Our customer support department costs too much," or they might be based on cost indicators. Cost indicators might be related, for example, to the number of people required to perform a task, costs of licensing a third-party system, cost of product returns, costs of failing regulatory compliance, or the amount of time required to perform a particular task.

Many people argue that compliance and regulatory issues are a third category of business objective. However, you should not call these out separately from increasing revenue or reducing costs, because regulatory and compliance issues are directly related to revenue or cost. For example, some types of compliance relate to revenue—the company simply cannot sell the product without certain compliance in place. Other types might relate to cost—the company might incur fines if compliance is not achieved. Although compliance does specifically map to revenue or cost, the cost impacts might not be measurable (or might be catastrophic), so stakeholders often assume that regulatory issues trump all other problems, when this might not be the case.

Eliciting Business Problems

Business problems and business objectives form a hierarchy of repeating problem/objective pairs. At the highest level, the business problem should relate directly to money. At lower levels, the problems relate to the level above. Eliciting business problems requires talking to the lead stakeholders and often the business executives to understand what is stopping the business from increasing revenue or reducing costs. Your starting point for identifying business problems is often an objective or possibly a product concept, if someone has already decided that they know what the product concept needs to be without having analyzed the business needs. You will need to then work your way up the hierarchy to a business problem that relates directly to money or down the hierarchy to problems that relate directly to business objectives that can help define the product concept.

For example, if the software project underway is to implement a web self-service center for customers, the analyst and an executive might have a conversation like the one outlined in Figure 3-10 to identify the business problem that initiated the project.

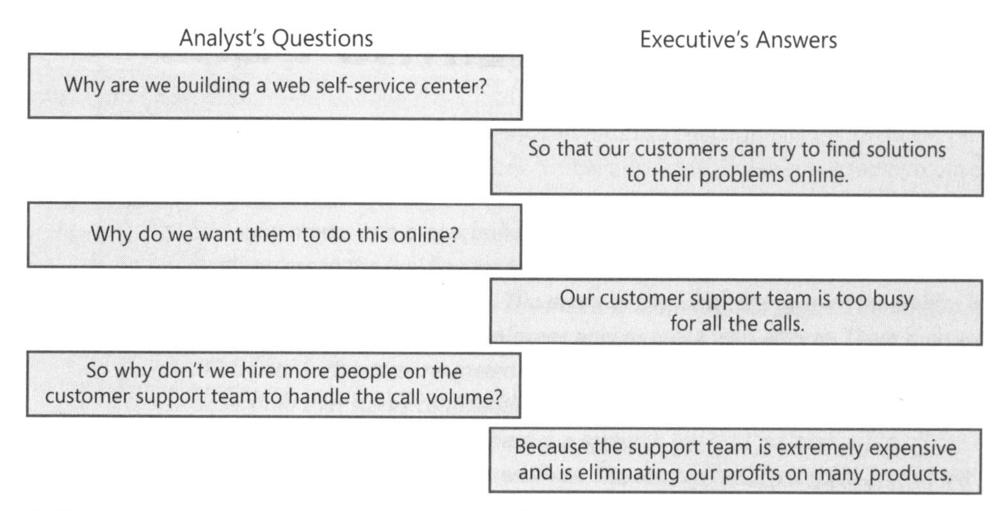

Analyst's Questions
Executive's Answers
Why are we building a web self-service center?
So that our customers can try to find solutions to their problems online.
Why do we want them to do this online?
Our customer support team is too busy for all the calls.
So why don't we hire more people on the customer support team to handle the call volume?
Because the support team is extremely expensive and is eliminating our profits on many products.

FIGURE 3-10 An example executive conversation for identifying the business problem.

In the third answer, the analyst identifies a business problem about cost. The real reason the company is building a self-service center for their customers is to reduce the costs of the support team. This means that in addition to building an online support system, the stakeholders can make sure that they focus on features that will reduce call volume. It might seem obvious that a self-service center is intended to reduce cost; however, it is easy to become so focused on the features when executing the project that the stakeholders forget that the goal is to reduce cost by reducing the volume of incoming calls, not the self-service center features themselves. When they don't maintain a focus on the business problem, stakeholders often implement the agreed-upon features while still failing to solve the business problem.

You might encounter objections to identifying business problems when the project is already underway, such as suggestions that it is a waste of time. However, a deep understanding of the business problem to be solved by the entire team will help everyone on the team to make better decisions during the project. This is more likely to result in a solution that actually solves the business problem versus just a solution that simply implements the requirements. It is also possible that understanding the business problems might drive an organization to completely redefine a project or even shut it down before resources are wasted on the wrong thing.

Identify Business Objectives

To identify the business objective associated with a particular problem, ask yourself, "How can I tell that this is a problem today? And if this problem were solved, what would the business look like?" Business objectives must be measureable and often have a time frame within which it would be appropriate to measure them.

To continue with the example from the previous section, after it is determined that the business problem is that the support team costs are too high, you can establish a target cost or profit number. If that is not possible, then stating a target number of staff members to move out of the call center into revenue-producing roles is appropriate as a proxy for the reduction in costs, because the number of staff members directly correlates to the cost of operating the call center.

Business objectives specify a change in value from a current number to a target number. Also, you should avoid using percent changes in business objectives, because people tend to forget the original baseline number that the percent is applied to, and it's harder for people to really understand the target number. Percent changes require the reader to know, look up, or assume the actual numbers, which results in a lack of shared understanding by stakeholders. Instead, use specific numbers that indicate the current level and the target level. In the following two objective statements, the second objective is much easier to remember than the first, making it less likely that people would unknowingly try to alter the target mid-project.

Statement 1: Reduce incoming support call volume by 12%

Statement 2: Reduce incoming support call volume from 25,000 to 22,000 calls per day by the middle of next year

One of the challenges analysts face when identifying business objectives is that people are often hesitant to commit to defined business objectives. Rarely is there a legitimate need to keep the revenue or cost targets private. In most cases, the hesitancy stems from fear of being held accountable for the results. In cases for which the business objectives simply cannot be obtained, do the best you can to generate agreement with the next level of measureable results—the success metrics. However, without measurable business objectives, the project is very much at risk of not providing sufficient value to the company because requirements will likely be implemented that stray from delivering that value.

Define Additional Problems and Objectives

After an initial business problem and business objective are defined at the top of the hierarchy, additional problem/objective pairs might need to be identified to help identify a clear product concept. Each problem/objective pair below the top level relates to solving the problems above it.

To identify the additional problems, the analyst should ask, "What is the primary reason that the business objective is not being achieved today?" This sounds simple, but it is typically very challenging because it requires data that might not be available. For example, there might be no data for why customers are making frequent support calls.

In the previous example, the reason 180 staff members cannot be moved immediately to other roles is that there are too many calls coming into the call center for the remaining staff members to handle. This newly identified business problem is added to the hierarchy. A new objective is created to represent what success for solving the new problem (too many calls) would look like: reduce the number of support calls to the call center from 25,000 to 22,000 per day by next year.

At any point, several potential problems might be keeping you from meeting a business objective. For example, there might be many possible reasons why the number of support calls cannot be reduced. In the example, the company's products themselves might have issues, the website might make it too easy for customers to call in, or the manuals might be too difficult to use.

You continue iterating between defining problems and objectives until the business objectives directly suggest features that would be implemented. Those features form the product concept. Generally, you will not need more than a few levels of problem/objective pairs; more than that will be too much information to understand and use effectively.

Define the Product Concept

Although the business objectives do not discuss a specific implementation, the product concept does. The product concept is the vision of the solution that the business chooses to implement in order to meet the business objectives.

The product concept includes the envisioned high-level features. The product concept could describe many aspects of a solution, including software, hardware, and business processes. A feature is a short-form description of an area of functionality that the solution will ultimately include to meet the business objectives. Features are collections of requirements that are used to articulate and organize the requirements. They typically can be communicated as a list that helps people unfamiliar with the project to understand the essence of the functionality that the project is delivering.

Eliciting the features that define the product concept is further discussed in Chapter 6, "Feature Tree."

Guiding Principles

Sometimes, the business makes general statements about things they care about in the solution, and although those things are not individual requirements, they are still important in creating the solution. These are guiding principles, and they provide the stakeholders with themes to consider as they begin to develop possible solutions to the business problem.

The guiding principles can be statements of market desires or stakeholder goals that apply across the solution. For example, the following are all guiding principles:

Develop all user-facing features with a focus on ease of use for new customers.

Apply generally accepted accounting practices (GAAP) to all finance calculations.

Maintain existing business workflows.

Change business process instead of implementing customizations.

If you do have guiding principles, you can capture them as part of the product concept.

Describe Success Metrics

The improvement in some business objectives can be directly measured and attributed to the success of the project. These business objectives should be labeled as success metrics. However, many business objectives measure large, long-term business goals that might often be influenced by factors outside of the solution being developed. Success metrics, like business objectives, are measureable in a specific time frame, but they apply to the product concept being developed. In some cases, success metrics are the business objectives themselves. In most cases, success metrics are intermediate measures that you can use as a proxy for the core business value when the business objective is difficult to measure directly or is influenced by so many other factors that you cannot directly measure the impact of the solution. If you are using success metrics as a proxy, you need to track any assumptions you are making about those being valid proxies.

To identify success metrics, consider those aspects of the solution being implemented that contribute to meeting the business objectives and that can be measured. For example, the product concept for the self-service support system is tied to the business objective of reducing the support call volume from 25,000 to 22,000 by the assumption that if the information is on the Internet, customers will use it. Therefore, a reasonable success metric for the project is to generate a certain number of views within a specified time frame and a certain number of clicks of the "Was this helpful?" button for a certain number of products. There might be other factors influencing the total number of inbound calls, such as a new product launch. So measuring the volume of people who are using the online help system could act as a more accurate measure of success than measuring the total inbound calls directly.

Merely creating the features to provide online support will not necessarily be sufficient for success, so it is vital to keep the stakeholders focused on the success metrics of the solution, not just implementation of the product concept. In the case of the online help system, the success metrics might drive other changes, such as marketing changes, website text changes, and email campaigns to highlight the new online system.

Developing success metrics before articulating requirements is helpful because some requirements will be derived directly from those success metrics. You can add more success metrics later, after you identify more detailed features and map them to Objective Chains (see Chapter 4, "Objective Chain"). The objective factors within the Objective Chains offer good project-specific metrics that might be easier to measure than the business objectives.

Questions to Ask to Complete the Business Objectives Model

Table 3-2 suggests a set of questions to ask to complete each portion of the Business Objectives Model. You should typically ask these questions of the executive sponsors or the stakeholder leads who represent them, because they are generally the stakeholders who are most connected to the underlying business problems.

TABLE 3-2 Questions to Help Identify Business Objectives Model Elements

Term	Questions to Ask
Business problem	What is the key issue preventing the organization from increasing revenue or decreasing cost? Keep asking the question, "Why is that a problem?" until you reach "money" in the answer. What is preventing the objective from being met today?
Business objectives	What measure will you use to determine that the problem has been solved? In what time frame do you expect to see the results? What is the baseline level that the change will be measured from? What other things influence the business objectives outside this project? What metrics can be used as a proxy to determine that the business problem has been solved?
Product concept	What products or processes must be built or changed to meet the business objectives? What stops the company from achieving the objective today, and what is the solution to resolve that? What are the approaches that could be followed to meet the business objectives, thereby solving the business problem? What problems or aspects of problems are being solved, and in what way? What are the key requirements (features) that will contribute to achieving the business objectives? What are the guiding principles that will restrict the possible set of solutions or features?
Success metrics	Can the impact of the solution on the business objectives be measured directly? If not, what metrics can be used as proxies to determine whether the product is a success? How will the stakeholders know whether the solution fully enables its intended contribution to the business objectives?

Using Business Objectives Models

A Business Objectives Model should be created early in the project, typically as the first model created. It should be used throughout the entire life cycle of the project to keep the stakeholders focused on the value of the solution.

Providing a Common Understanding of a Project's Value

The Business Objectives Model provides a framework for stakeholders to have a shared understanding of the purpose and value of the project. The structure of the model allows the project value to be viewed in one page for easy consumption. When the stakeholders focus on the Business Objectives Model first, the requirements that are described from the other models will be the right ones to support the specific business objectives. Executives can use this model to validate the investment they are making.

Bounding the Solution Space

Articulation of the business problem is one of the first things you should do on any project. A clearly written Business Objectives Model helps all stakeholders understand and bound the solution space to solutions that are specifically targeted to solve the problems and achieve the objectives. Completing the Business Objectives Model is a way to ensure that the entire group of stakeholders is in agreement about the business problem that the project is trying to solve. In conjunction with other models, a Business Objectives Model can ensure that only the most valuable features get developed. This will be discussed further in Chapter 4.

Understanding Projects That Are Underway

The Business Objectives Model is fundamental to every project. Most projects do not actively use business objectives to define the project up front, let alone for daily decision making. Therefore, we designed the model to work well for projects that are already underway.

A Typical Approach That Doesn't Work

Most projects start with the equivalent of a product concept already defined. The project team might define some success metrics; however, they typically jump immediately into defining requirements and designs. The problem with this approach, which is shown in Figure 3-11, is that without agreed-upon business objectives to guide the project scope, the team is liable to stray from the intended goals of the business.

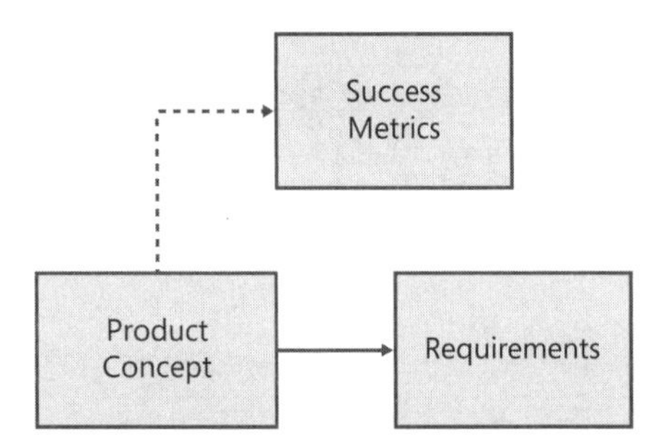

FIGURE 3-11 The typical approach to identifying requirements.

This is a problematic situation. If analysts push forward with gathering requirements for each of the features, several problems can arise:

- Unnecessary requirements are developed. If a requirement cannot be mapped back to a particular measurable business objective, then why should it be implemented? Why should time be spent developing those requirements?
- After the requirements are defined, the development team might come back and indicate that they cannot implement all of the requirements with their current staff and budget. They will want to know which requirements to cut, and if the requirements are not mapped to value, it becomes very difficult to have a dispassionate discussion about which ones need to be

removed to bring the project in on budget. People will fight for their favorite features, often regardless of the quantitative value to the business.

- Even if a requirement is written that aligns with the business objectives, the solution might be built in such a way that the business objective is still not achieved. For example, at an insurance company, the team thought that the business objective was to combine seven IT systems into a single system. However, the actual business objective was to merge seven business teams into a single team; instead of seven small groups with completely different skills, there would be one large team with overlapping skillsets so that management could minimize the people needed to handle periodic extra processing. You can imagine how easy it would be to merge seven systems into a single system, yet not achieve the real business objective.

An Ideal Approach That Starts with Problems and Objectives

An ideal approach, as shown in Figure 3-12, is to start with the business problem and define business objectives and additional problems iteratively until you reached a point where features of software could achieve the business objectives. You would then define the product concept with high-level features and success metrics that you would use to drive the process to eventually identify requirements. This approach is ideal because it ensures that the requirements that are developed are always driven by the solution to the business problem.

The drawback to this approach is that it does not reflect the reality of how organizations operate. Most organizations are less top-down in their thinking about projects. Furthermore, this approach often does not work because analysts are typically engaged in projects well after the work to define business value has occurred.

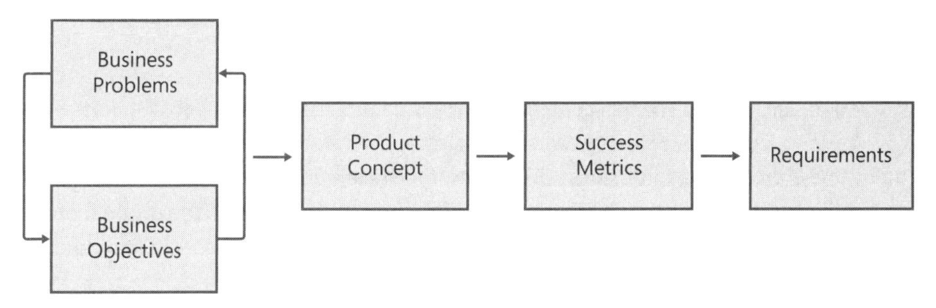

FIGURE 3-12 Ideal approach to identifying requirements.

A Realistic Approach

Many projects start with a product concept simply because of when the analysts are engaged. Therefore, the ideal approach described previously, starting at the business problems, is not realistic; however, the elements can still be created to achieve success, as shown in Figure 3-13.

When projects start with a product concept, a set of preliminary requirements is often already defined. However, working backwards from the product concept, you can still understand the business problems that need to be solved. In fact, the business problems and objectives might be known, just not documented. When the analyst asks, "Why is that a problem?" eventually a business problem will emerge that relates to either generating revenue or cutting costs. With clearly defined business problems and business objectives, you can be sure that the product concept will meet the business objectives and solve the problems.

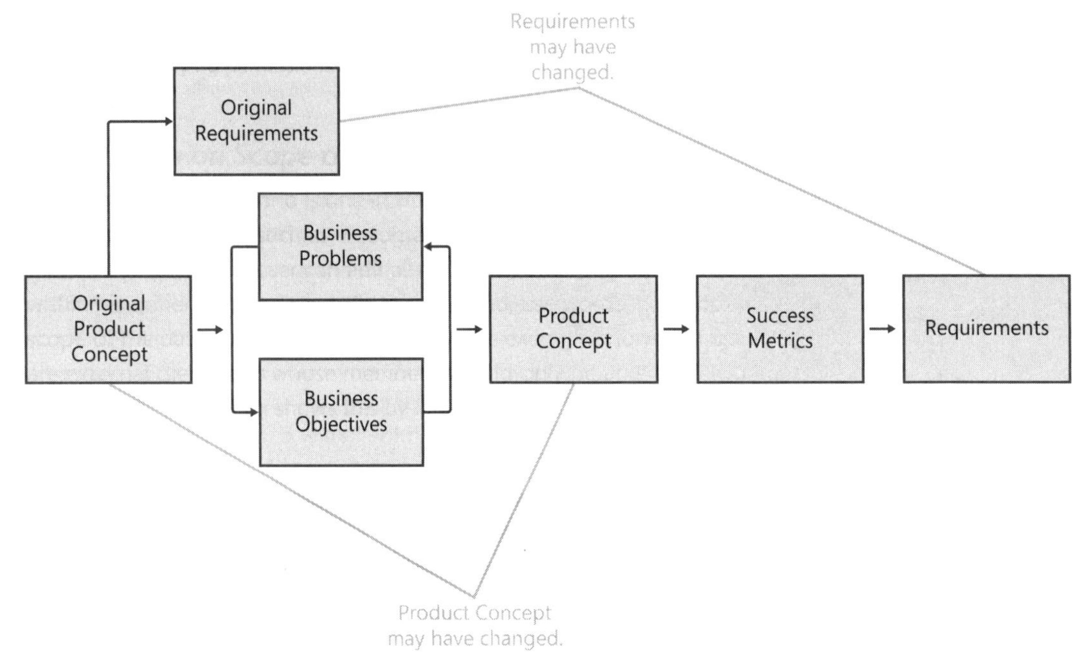

FIGURE 3-13 A realistic approach to identifying requirements.

Using the business problem and business objectives, the stakeholders can define a clear product concept with high-level features, which might or might not be the same as the original product concept because of an improved understanding of the business problems. Then you should develop success metrics for the solution. Finally, you can use the Business Objectives Model elements to identify a first draft of requirements. Note that the requirements might have changed from the original suggestions.

An analyst who starts on a project can immediately identify or define the business problems and business objectives, even if the product concept has already been defined. A careful examination of the business objectives often causes some changes in the product concept. If this is likely to be the case, it is best to discover the need and make the changes earlier in the project rather than later.

Deriving Requirements

Because the Business Objectives Model articulates very high-level business goals, it is difficult to derive requirements from it. However, the Business Objectives Model does document features, which are equivalent to high-level requirements. Based on the business problems and business objectives, you will identify high-level features that you can then use to organize detailed requirements in a Requirements Mapping Matrix (see Chapter 7, "Requirements Mapping Matrix").

When to Use

A Business Objectives Model should be used on any project that has new functionality that can be mapped to business value. This includes enhancements, new custom development projects, and even Commercial Off the Shelf (COTS) deployments that have significant customizations.

When Not to Use

For projects such as legacy conversions in which the stakeholders are implementing a new system to replace an old one, rather than mapping new features to business value, the stakeholders are simply trying to maintain existing key performance indicators (KPIs) with existing business processes. In these cases, a Key Performance Indicator Model (KPIM) (see Chapter 5, "Key Performance Indicator Model") is more useful. The KPIM helps to assign value to existing Process Flows, allowing the stakeholders to assign priority to existing functionality.

Common Mistakes

The following represent the most common mistakes that we have seen with Business Objectives Models.

Not Understanding the Business Problem

If the analyst does not understand the real business problem underlying a project, the business objectives and ultimately the derived solution have a high chance of not solving the problem. A more common issue is that without a clear understanding of the business problems and business objectives, the stakeholders have no objective standard for determining when features should be cut from scope. Scope creep is one of the most common reasons that projects go over budget or experience delays.

Defining Business Objectives That Are Not Measurable

Business objectives might be captured but not measurable. This is often a mistake on the part of executives who have a fear about the metrics, as discussed earlier in this chapter. Poorly written business objectives are better than none, but the analyst should still strive to define measurable business objectives.

Articulating the Wrong Type of Information in Business Objectives

Business objectives should tie very closely to money. Often the product concept is incorrectly listed as the business objective. For example, in the insurance example introduced earlier, the business objective was documented as "combine seven systems into one." However, that is the product concept. The real business problem was that there were seven business teams that could not do each other's jobs. One suggested cause of that problem was that each team was trained on a different system. The product concept was a new system that combined seven systems into a single system.

Related Models

The Business Objectives Model captures business problems and objectives, similar to other modeling languages; however the RML model is very simple to understand. There is a rationale model that adds information beyond what is in the Business Objectives Model, tracking the "rationale" for scope decisions. It tracks why decisions were made, which is helpful to ensure that decisions are not revisited unnecessarily (Alexander and Beus-Dukic 2009).

There is a concept very similar to Objective Chains called minimum marketable features that can be used to help analysts decide project scope by comparing values of features.

The following list briefly describes the most important models that influence or are enhanced by Business Objectives Models. Chapter 26, "Using Models Together," contains a more thorough discussion about all related models.

- **Objective Chains** These directly use business objectives, allowing the value of individual features to be compared.
- **Feature Trees** These further develop the high-level features originally defined as part of the product concept in the Business Objectives Model.
- **Key Performance Indicator Models (KPIMs)** These are used instead of Business Objectives Models to prioritize projects that are only replacing existing functionality and maintaining KPIs.
- **Requirements Mapping Matrices** These are used to organize requirements by business objectives and features from a Business Objectives Model.

Exercise

The following exercise is intended to help you to gain a better understanding of how to use this model. The exercise is open ended, and therefore the answer you come up with could be substantially different than the answer that we have provided. There are potentially many correct solutions. The answer provides an explanation of how we arrived at our solution. You will gain the most out of the exercise by attempting to do it yourself before looking at the solution. The answers for the exercises can be found in Appendix C.

Instructions

Prepare a Business Objectives Model for the following scenario. Capture any questions you would ask to create the model and the made-up answers you expect from the executives. Also list any assumptions that you made.

Scenario

Your company sells lawn flamingos and related accessories. You have approximately 100,000 customers, and your annual revenue is $10 million. There is already a project underway to create an eStore, but you are asking the business executives to identify the issues that drove them to want to build this new system so that you can help them prioritize the requirements.

Additional Resources

- *Discovering Requirements* has a discussion on identifying business needs, which are similar to business objectives (Alexander and Beus-Dukic 2009). This resource also has a summary of the rationale model and the value it adds to a project.
- Wiegers discusses business objectives as part of Business Requirements in Chapter 21 of *More About Software Requirements* (Wiegers 2006).
- "The Single Most Important Failure with Requirements" describes common reasons projects fail as they relate to not having or having poor business objectives: *http://requirements.seilevel.com/blog/2010/09/the-single-most-important-failure-with-requirements.html.*
- The Enterprise Analysis Knowledge Area of the BABOK has a task for defining a business need (IIBA 2009).
- The Enterprise Business Motivation Model (EBMM) has a purpose much like that of the Business Objectives Model; the two even share common terms (Malik 2009).

References

- Alexander, Ian, and Ljerka Beus-Dukic. 2009. *Discovering Requirements: How to Specify Products and Services.* West Sussex, England: John Wiley & Sons Ltd.
- Malik, A. Nicklas. 2009. Enterprise Business Motivation Model. *http://motivationmodel.com/wp/*
- Wiegers, Karl E., 2006. *More About Software Requirements: Thorny Issues and Practical Advice.* Redmond, WA: Microsoft Press.
- International Institute of Business Analysis (IIBA). 2009. *A Guide to the Business Analysis Body of Knowledge (BABOK Guide).* Toronto, Ontario, Canada.

CHAPTER 4

Objective Chain

Suppose I am in the market to buy a new car and my main objective is to spend the least amount on a car that meets my basic needs. I care about gas mileage, long-term repair costs, frequency of repairs, cargo space, and safety. To decide which of these are most important to me, I think about how much each one contributes to the overall value of the car.

- *I can get great gas mileage with a hybrid vehicle, but that feature will cost me $10,000 and save me only $700 a year based on the miles I drive. Given the likely life of the vehicle, the feature does not have enough value to justify buying a hybrid car. Yet if I drive more miles each year or if I assume that gas prices will triple, then it could be worthwhile.*
- *Research indicates that certain brands require less maintenance than others and therefore also have lower long-term repair costs, but those brands are about $5,000 more for a comparable car.*
- *I know that if I buy a sports utility vehicle (SUV), I will have a lot of cargo space and off-road capability, which I need because of my outdoor lifestyle. Plus I will have plenty of passenger room to drive my children and their friends around. However, those features are expensive because an SUV costs about $8,000 more than a car within the same brand that is not an SUV.*

Based on these considerations, I deprioritize the gas mileage and decide to buy an SUV in a brand that has a good rating, but not the best. In doing this, I have linked my wishes to my objective with a statement about how each wish meets the objective, and I have placed a value on the wish. I now know which aspects of a car are most important and which can be eliminated.

All too often, analysts see projects whose scope is too large to be accomplished with the resources that are currently available, including time, money, and people. The most effective way to control the scope of any project is to limit the project to only those features that provide the most value to the users or the business. One study found that 65 percent of the features developed are rarely or never used in a typical piece of software (Standish Group 2009). If you eliminate the features that provide little value, you can achieve a majority of the project's value while dramatically cutting costs and improving time to market. This philosophy holds true for consumer-oriented software as well.

The Objective Chain is an RML objectives model that measurably links features to business objectives (see Chapter 3, "Business Objectives Model"). Because multiple features typically map to each business objective, and each feature might address multiple business objectives, it is useful to have a model to help determine the relative value of each feature.

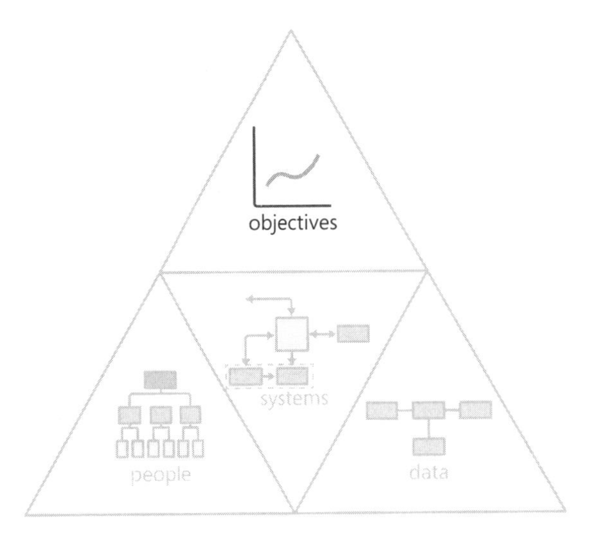

An Objective Chain is a hierarchy that contains business objectives at the top of the hierarchy and features at the bottom of the hierarchy. Each level of the hierarchy between a business objective and a feature is a qualitative statement about how that level contributes to the level above it in the chain. For example, my objective in the story at the beginning of this chapter is to spend the least amount on a car that meets my basic needs, and one of the features I am considering is a hybrid engine. Qualitatively, a hybrid engine increases the number of miles I can drive per gallon of gas. Increasing the miles per gallon decreases the cost per mile.

Each level in the chain can also contain an estimated calculation that quantitatively explains how a feature contributes to the business objective. For example, suppose that for the car-purchase story, the manufacturer has indicated that a hybrid engine will get 50 miles per gallon as compared to 25 miles per gallon for a non-hybrid version. Assume that gas costs $4.00 per gallon and that I drive about 1,000 miles per month. The hybrid costs eight cents per mile, and the non-hybrid costs sixteen cents per mile; therefore, the hybrid costs $80 per month and the non-hybrid costs $160 per month.

An Objective Chain provides a way to include an approximate calculation of the value of any feature, even if that feature is far removed from an objective. If you create Objective Chains for all features, you can compare their relative values to determine which features to cut from scope. The model allows teams to debate how the value of the features is calculated, rather than with emotions associated with the features.

Objective Chain Template

Objective Chains are described in a hierarchy of boxes by using a tree structure, as shown in Figure 4-1. The box in the upper left is a business objective, and the boxes placed in the lower right—the "leaves" of the tree—are features. The branches in between the two include a series of boxes containing objective factors and objective equations.

Objective factors are qualitative statements about how one level in the hierarchy contributes to the level above it in the hierarchy. *Objective equations* capture the quantitative values of the relationship between objective factors. Objective equations are captured in boxes within their associated objective factors boxes. The features are shown in a different color or are shaded to help differentiate them from the objective factors.

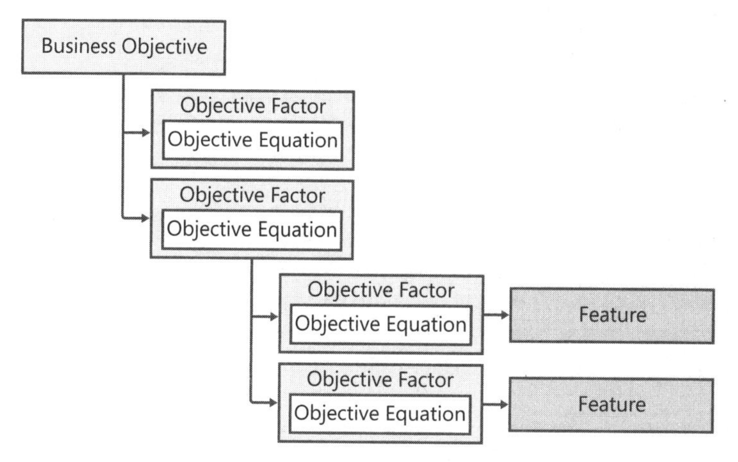

FIGURE 4-1 The Objective Chain template.

Tool Tip You might use sticky notes and a whiteboard to create the hierarchy initially, but the best tools for creating Objective Chains are software tools such as Microsoft PowerPoint or Microsoft Visio. Ideally, Objective Chains should be stored in a requirements management tool, so that any traceability functionality can be used to help maintain the links in the hierarchy.

Example

A sales organization has learned that sales representatives who receive regular product training and pass tests on the training sell significantly more products than their peers who do not receive the training. The organization's business objective is to increase revenue by increasing the amount each sales representative sells. It is logical to conclude that training is important because it helps sales representatives learn about new products. When they know more about these new products, the sales team is better able to sell them.

Sales representatives' test scores measure how well they learn the material in the training sessions. The more tests sales representatives pass, the more products they learn about, and the more they tend to sell.

As an example, suppose that the average revenue per sales representative who has not passed the test for a particular product is $1,000 per day. If, however, the sales representative takes the training and passes the associated test, his average revenue increases to $1,200. This is a metric that would clearly communicate to the business that having a sales force that has passed the test is valuable and that the business should look for opportunities to help more sales representative pass the training tests.

The objective factor in this example can be stated as, "Increasing the number of sales representatives who have passed tests increases sales," as shown in Figure 4-2.

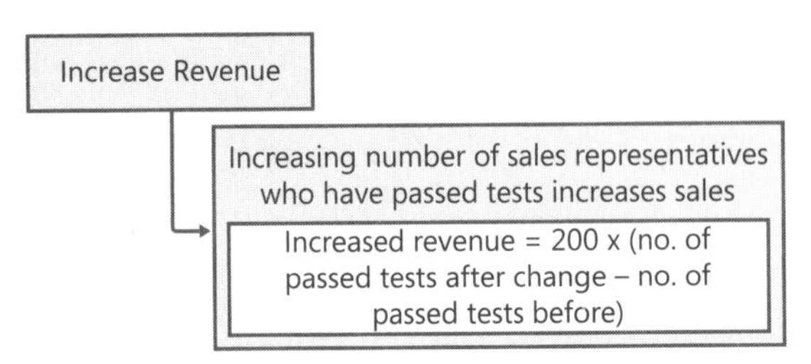

FIGURE 4-2 Objective factor for increasing the number of passed tests.

There are several features that could conceivably increase the number of sales representatives who pass the training tests. Analysis of the potential features reveals which of them would provide the most value.

One possible feature is to provide online training. This allows the sales representative to take the training at their convenience, rather than a few times a quarter, which is when the training is currently scheduled. Further research has revealed that due to the schedule of the sales team, about 40 percent of the staff misses these in-person training events. If there are 1,000 sales representatives, typically about 600 of them would attend the training. With the additional online training, forecasts indicate that the number could be increased to as much as 900, an additional 30 percent of sales representatives. Historical data has also revealed that completing the training prior to taking the test increases the pass rate from 25 percent to 90 percent. This would increase the number of sales representatives who pass the test from 640 to 835. (Ninety percent of the 900 sales representatives who take training plus 25 percent of the 100 who do not results in 835 total sales representatives passing the tests.) Moreover, because people who pass the test average 20 percent more in revenue, revenue would be increased by $39,000 a day. (Each of 195 additional sales representatives passing the test creates an additional $200 in revenue per day.) Figure 4-3 shows this example.

Note that the first two objective factors each have an objective equation with existing data applied. These equations help assess how much an online training feature adds to the business objective. The equations might also have assumptions that significantly affect the analysis. For example, the analysis assumes that if online training is available, the number of sales representatives taking training will increase from 60 percent to 90 percent. If a debate arises about feature priorities, the debate can be focused on the validity of the assumption that online training will increase the number of sales representatives taking training by that amount, instead of on subjective arguments about whether online training should be implemented. In addition, as the subfeatures of online training are considered, the team can stay focused on the idea that features that will increase the number of sales representatives who take training are the most important. These might include features such as email messages and automated reminders for sales representatives to take the training. Finally, the analyst can perform a breakeven analysis to determine what increase in participation would be required for the project to generate revenues just equal to the cost of implementing online training. Even if the team is not sure exactly what participation rate can be achieved, the team might be able to agree that a small increase in participation is very likely. If that small increase is still profitable, then the project to implement online training potentially has much less risk.

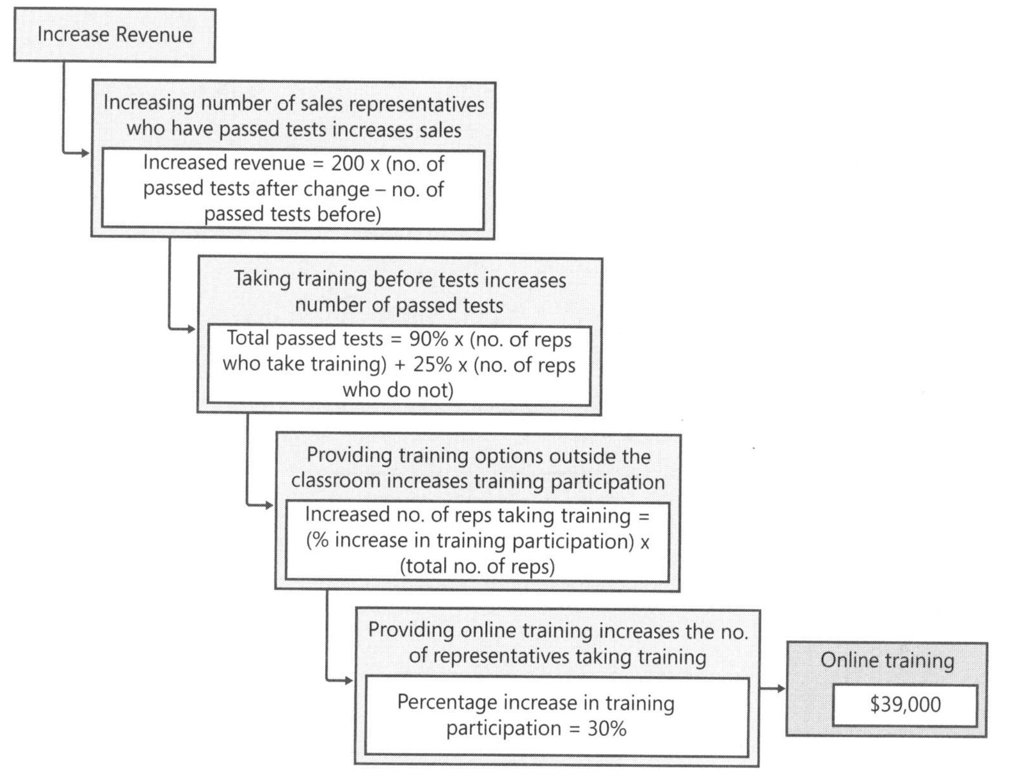

FIGURE 4-3 Objective factor and objective equation data on taking training before tests.

The next feature to analyze is downloadable training, which can be completed while the participant is offline. This feature sounds reasonable and would help increase the overall passing rate of the sales team because the training is even more convenient. In talking to the sales team, the analyst might discover that most of the sales team has near-constant online connectivity. There are some members of the sales force who drive to appointments, but this is time that could not be spent training anyway. There are others who often fly to clients and could use an offline training option, but overall only about 2 percent of sales representatives would benefit from being able to take the training offline. In applying the objective equation to this objective factor, it can be determined that by providing downloadable training, only 20 additional sales representatives would receive training, and only an additional 18 sales representatives would be passing tests (90 percent of 20 possible sales representatives). This feature increases revenue by $3,600 a day (18 sales representatives earning $200 additional revenue each day). Figure 4-4 shows the full Objective Chain.

Instead of debating the usefulness of the feature with stubborn stakeholders ("The feature for sales representatives on planes to be able to take training is a must-have!"), you can focus the debate on analyzing the return. Depending on the cost of adding offline training, the team can make an unemotional, strictly business decision to keep or cut the feature. In this example, the analyst applied the objective equation to the objective factor, and found that although downloadable training does add value, the value added is not as large as the cost to implement. Using objective factors and objective equations with estimated data values helps limit the scope of a project to those features that will most benefit the project and ensure that it meets the business objectives.

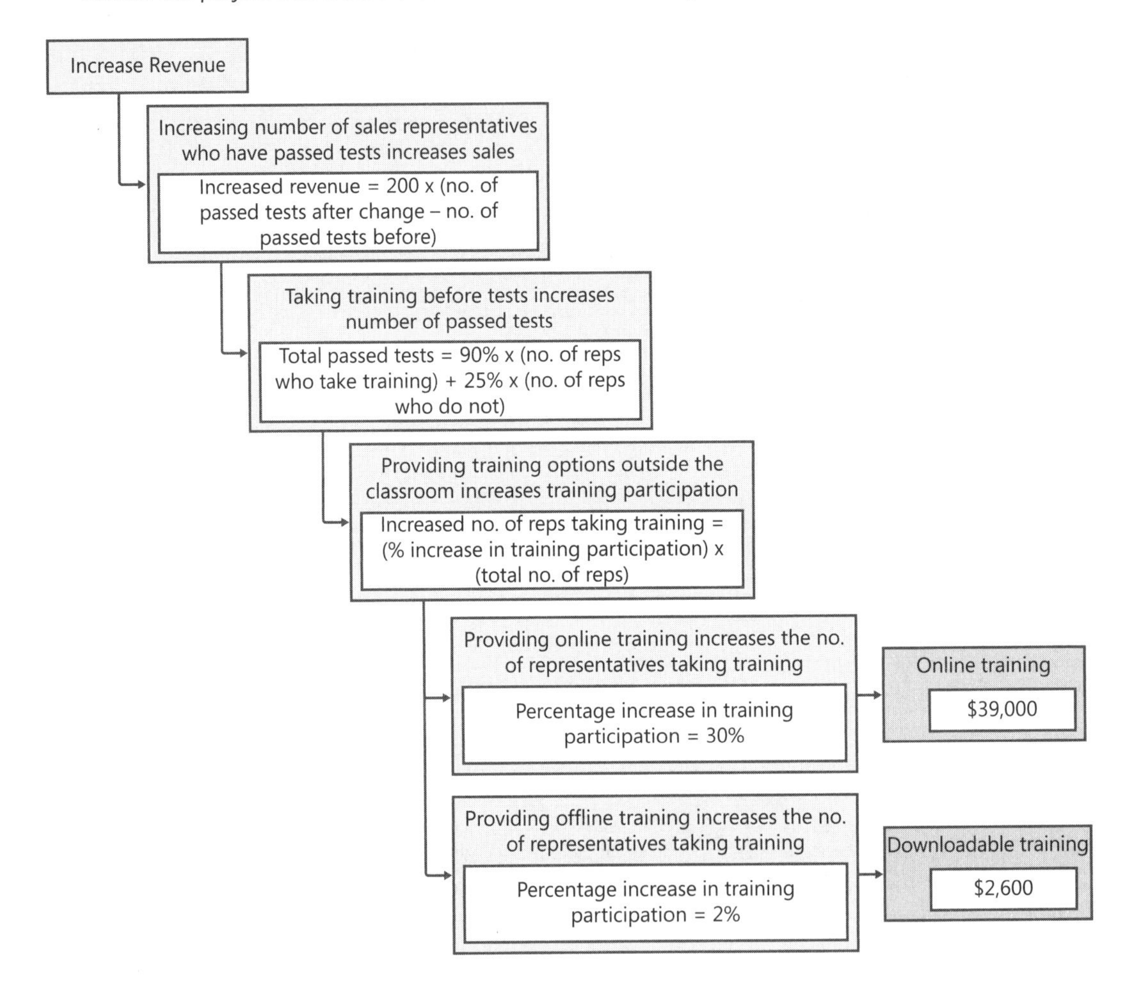

FIGURE 4-4 Objective factor and data for downloadable training.

Creating Objective Chains

The process for creating an Objective Chain, outlined in Figure 4-5, builds upon the results of other models created early in the project. Objective Chains are typically created primarily by the analyst; however, the rest of the team will have to provide input to explain how features contribute to achieving the business objectives.

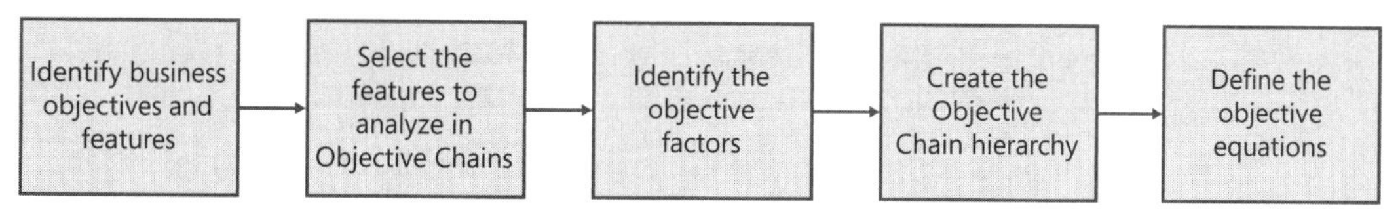

FIGURE 4-5 The process for creating an Objective Chain.

Identify Business Objectives and Features

Here are a couple of definitions as reminders:

- Business objectives are the measureable targets that specify when the business problem is solved.
- A feature is a short-form description of an area of functionality that the solution will ultimately include to meet the business objectives. Features are collections of requirements that are used to articulate and organize the requirements.

In Chapter 3, we discussed the process for identifying business objectives as part of the Business Objectives Model. In Chapter 6, "Feature Tree," we discuss the process for identifying features by using Feature Trees. Together, these two models should give you sufficiently complete business objectives and features for use in the Objective Chains. If you have not yet created a Feature Tree, the features you identify in the Business Objectives Model represent a good starting point.

Select the Features to Analyze in Objective Chains

Objective Chains do not need to be created for every feature. You should create Objective Chains for the highest-level features while still getting the granularity necessary to make scope decisions. We describe the different levels of features (L1, L2, and L3) in more detail in Chapter 6. The following guidelines can be applied when you are selecting the appropriate level of features to analyze:

- Select the level of features at which each feature is relatively independent. Often, you can use L1 features in the Objective Chain, only bringing in L2 features when necessary. For example, consider an L1 feature for "claims management" that has the L2 subfeatures "submissions," "adjustments," and "approvals." "Submissions" typically is of limited value without "adjustments," and neither "approvals" nor "adjustments" makes any sense without "submissions." It probably makes sense to develop the Objective Chain on the "claims management" L1 feature as a whole instead of on these individual L2 features. If the priority of the L2 features comes into question, the Objective Chain can be extended to those subfeatures at that time.

- Select features at a level where the cost of developing each feature represents at least 1 percent of the value. Because you only care about the order of magnitude of the value of the features, drilling too deeply to analyze features that contribute too little to the overall value or cost has diminishing returns.
- If you cannot cut any features at the L1 or L2 level, then you can look for opportunities to cut L3 features across all of the L1 features. Cutting 20 percent of the L3 features from 10 different L1 features is similar to completely cutting 2 out of 10 L1 features, assuming that the effort to implement each L3 feature is similar. If you need to cut in this manner, you will have to do significantly more Objective Chains modeling to analyze the L3 features.
- Focus Objective Chains modeling on the features that comprise the primary value of the product concept in the Business Objectives Model, rather than on housekeeping features that support other features. For example, many solutions include user administration features. In most cases, managing users is not the goal of the software, but it supports a real goal of the software, such as controlling access to information. Therefore, in most projects, you might not bother to evaluate the user administration features in an Objective Chain.

Identify the Objective Factors

To identify objective factors, consider the mappings from business objectives to features one by one. Start with the first business objective and feature pair and answer the question, "How will the feature contribute to the business objective?" as shown in Figure 4-6. The answer should be of the form "increasing or decreasing X increases or decreases Y" (or something synonymous such as, "providing functionality increases Y").

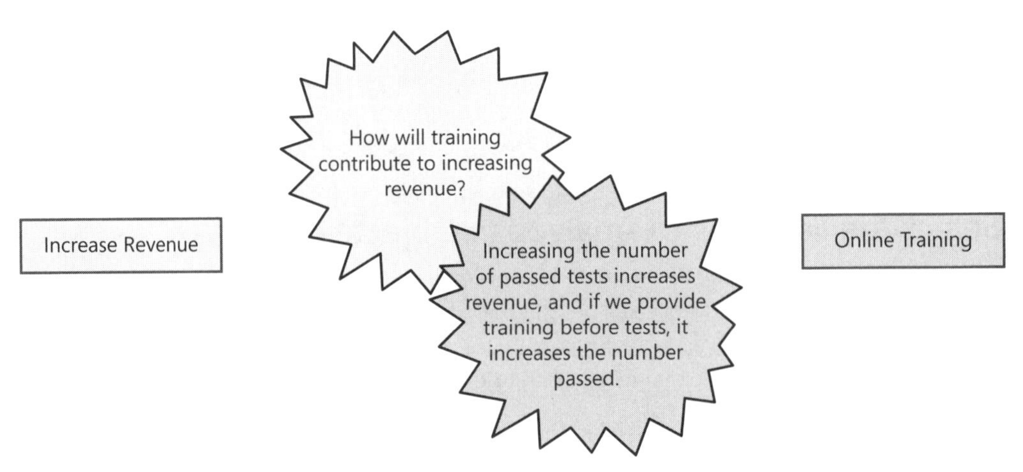

FIGURE 4-6 The thought process linking the "online training" feature to the "increase revenue" business objective.

Use the Business Objectives Model

The Business Objectives Model maps problems to business objectives to features, but it doesn't indicate how the features contribute to achieving the business objectives. The Objective Chain is meant to show a more granular view that communicates how each feature is related to each business objective. However, you can use the hierarchy of problems and objectives in the Business Objectives Model to help you identify the answer to the question of how a feature contributes to the business objective.

For example, for the objective to increase revenue and the feature for online training, you might have the hierarchy shown in Figure 4-7.

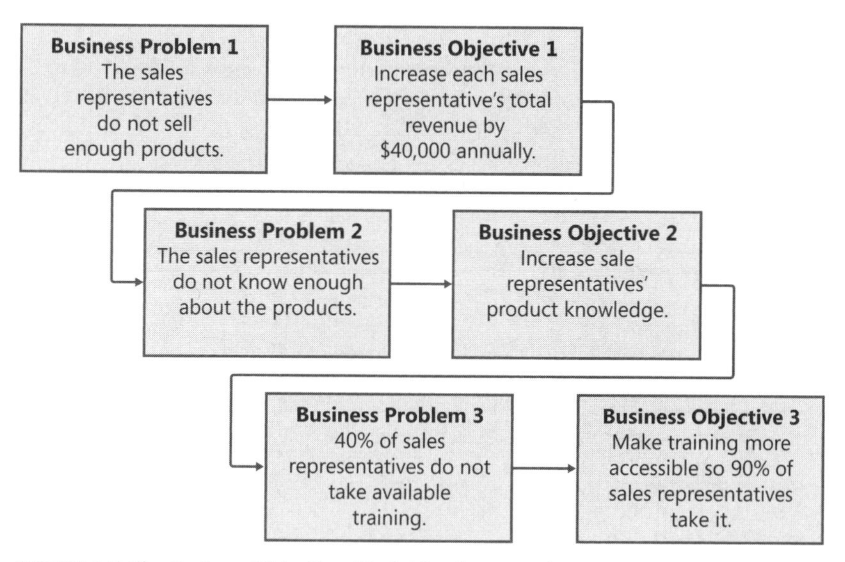

FIGURE 4-7 The Business Objectives Model for the example.

These objectives help you see how the online training feature helps increase revenue. To write the actual objective factors for this feature, start at the bottom and work up the chain, as in Figure 4-8.

You won't always have a one to one mapping of objective to objective factor. In the Business Objectives Model, you might have made leaps in your objective hierarchy (because they were obvious) that you cannot make when defining the relationships in Objective Chains hierarchy.

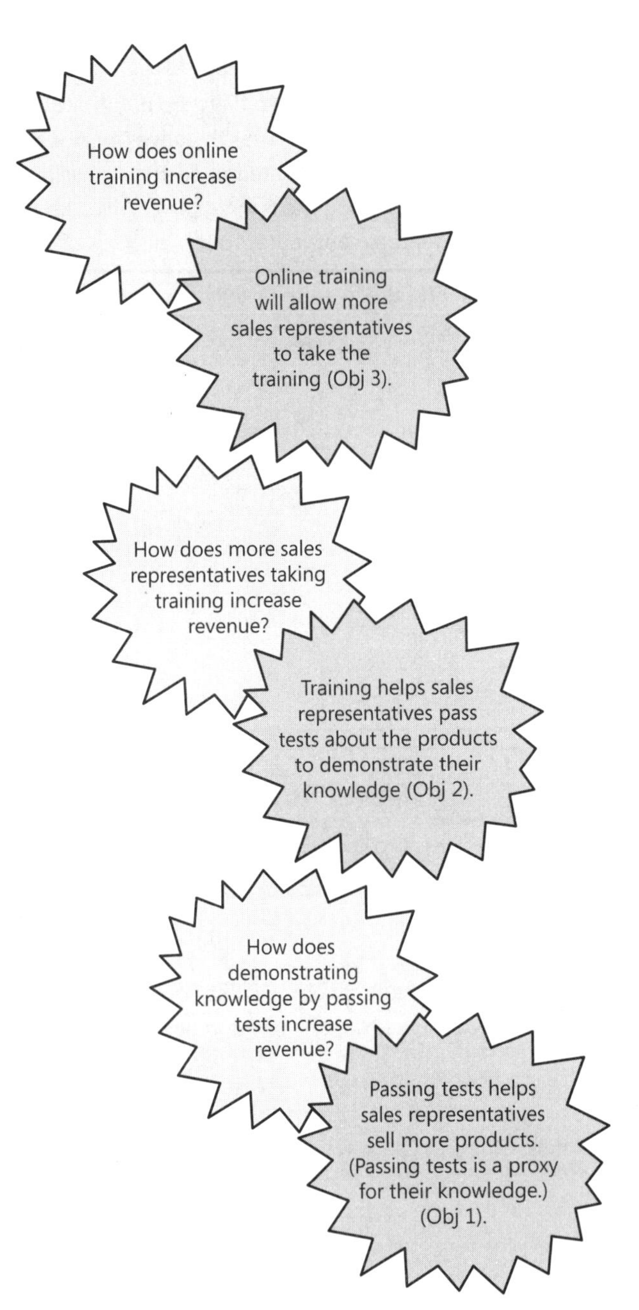

FIGURE 4-8 The thought process using the Business Objectives Model to help define the Objective Chain hierarchy.

Simplify Objective Factor Statements

If the answer to how a feature contributes to the business objective is a compound sentence or a paragraph, with words like "and," "so," and "therefore," there are probably multiple levels of objective factors that you should separate into discrete objective factors. In this example, there are four objective factors that should be written, as shown in Figure 4-9.

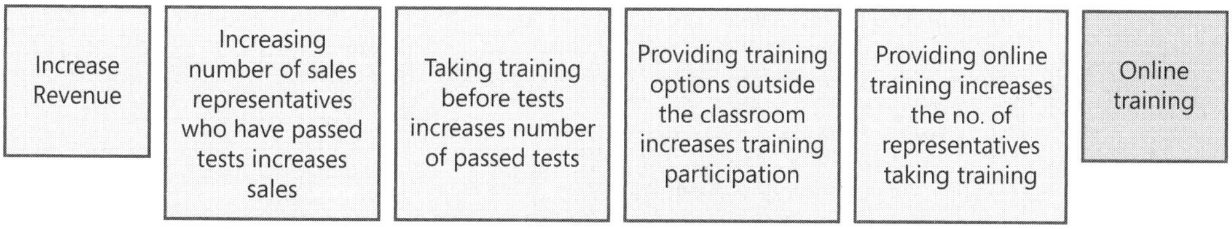

Increase Revenue
Increasing number of sales representatives who have passed tests increases sales
Taking training before tests increases number of passed tests
Providing training options outside the classroom increases training participation
Providing online training increases the no. of representatives taking training
Online training

FIGURE 4-9 Objective factors linking the "online training" feature to the "increase revenue" business objective.

An objective factor might influence multiple parent objective factors up the chain. For simplicity, organize each objective factor so that it maps to a single parent by selecting the parent that is most affected.

Create the Objective Chain Hierarchy

At this point, each feature has objective factors that link it to a business objective. Creating an organized tree of this information removes redundancies that might occur, as shown in Figure 4-10, and makes the information easier to read and understand.

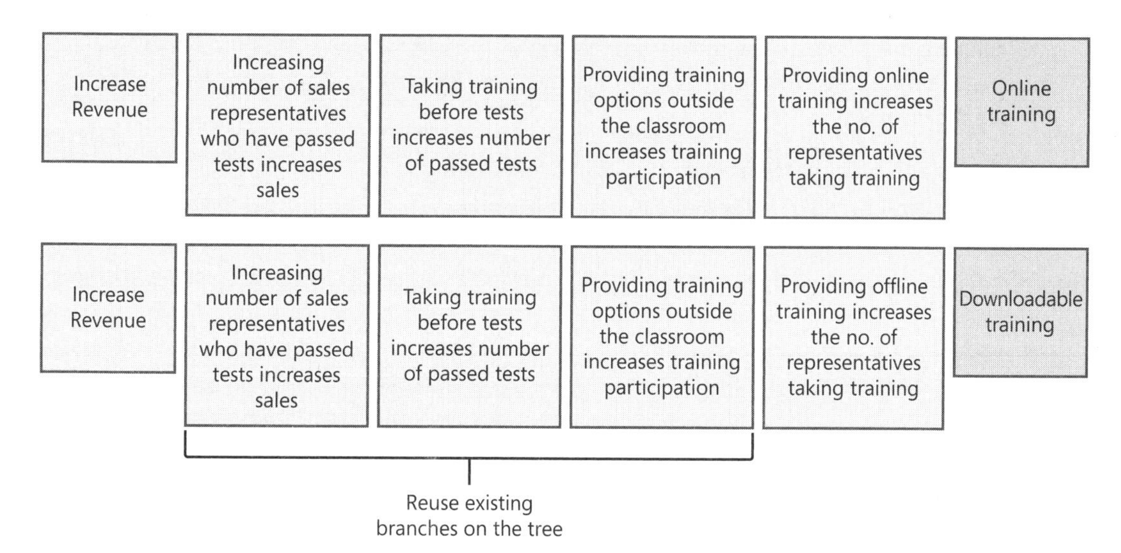

FIGURE 4-10 Objective factors for the "online training" and "downloadable training" features.

To begin creating the Objective Chain hierarchy, put the first business objective at the top of a tree. Next, chain the objective factors off the business objective, linking the business objective to its first feature. Add the feature to the end of the chain to produce a tree hierarchy, as shown in Figure 4-11.

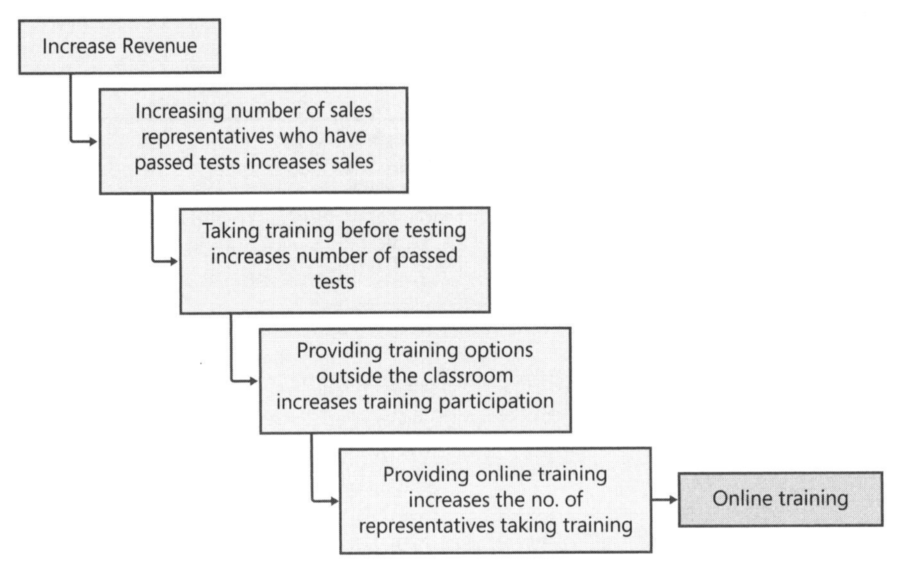

FIGURE 4-11 The Objective Chain for the "online training" feature.

Now examine the second feature and the objective factors that link it to the business objective. Create a chain from the business objective to all of the objective factors that link it to the second feature, adding them to the same tree hierarchy as the first feature. If any of the objective factors are already on the tree, reuse them; do not repeat them. The resulting Objective Chain will look like the one shown in Figure 4-12.

Continue adding the objective factors and features to the hierarchy for the first business objective until all of the selected features are in the model. Repeat the entire process to create a new hierarchy for the remaining business objectives.

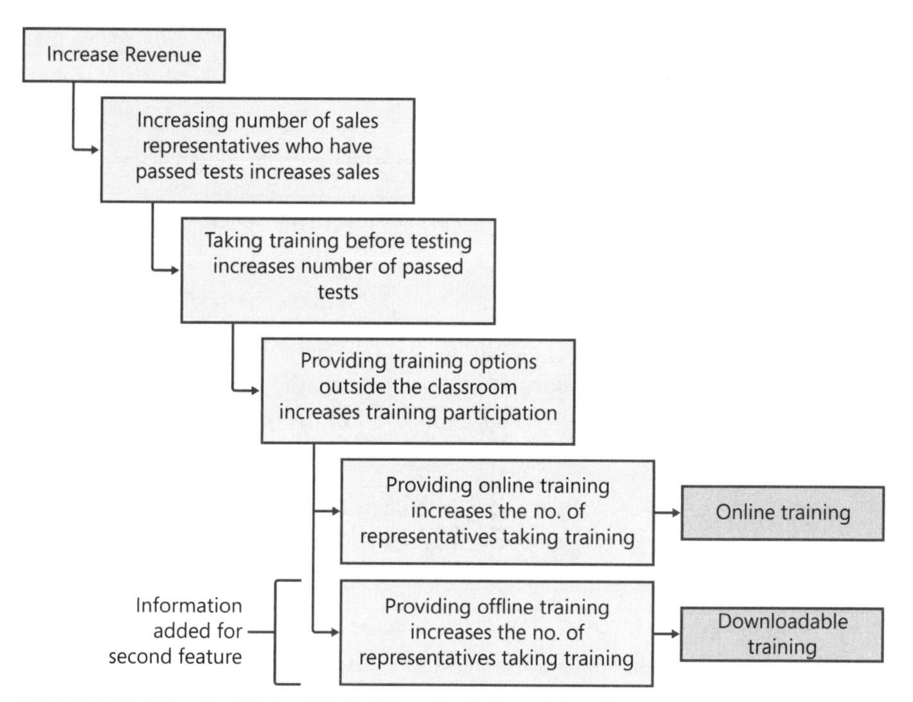

FIGURE 4-12 Objective Chain with the "downloadable training" feature added.

Define the Objective Equations

After you have identified the objective factors, review each objective factor to determine the contribution of the feature to the business objective. Objective equations provide a mechanism to quantitatively support the statements made in the objective factors. This enables the analyst to calculate the dollar contribution for any given feature. Objective equations are not meant to be precise calculations; rather, they are meant to provide relative value for comparison.

Format the Equation

When you write objective equations, they should use relative values and be in equation form. For example, "Increased revenue = 200 x (number of passed tests after change – number of passed tests before)" is based on using the number of passed tests from before training relative to the number after training. The example objective equation is shown with its corresponding objective factor in Figure 4-13.

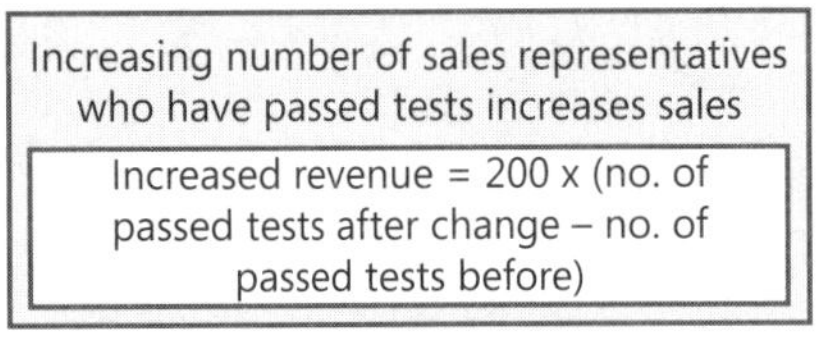

Increasing number of sales representatives who have passed tests increases sales

Increased revenue = 200 x (no. of passed tests after change – no. of passed tests before)

FIGURE 4-13 Objective equation for increasing number of passed tests to show increase in revenue.

Identify Data Values

Objective equations are based on either obtainable data, data with reasonable proxies, or approximations. You can obtain the data from any reasonable source, such as existing systems, similar projects, industry standards, and informed estimates. The business stakeholders' intuition about these metrics is usually a good place to start.

Creating objective equations can seem daunting, especially with a lack of data. However, the goal is only to determine an order of magnitude estimate of the value of each feature that allows an apples-to-apples comparison between features.

In the example objective equations, each of the values—$200 additional revenue per day for a trained salesperson, 600 sales representatives attending training today, 900 sales representatives would take training online, the pass rate goes from 25 to 90 percent if the person has training first—represent data in the objective equations. In some cases, the data values are known, in others they are not known but can be approximated. In the case of the 900 sales representatives who will take training if it is online, the analyst is predicting the future. This is a key assumption that can be used to calculate the actual return after the project is deployed.

Debate Data Values

Note that if you document the objective equations, others can review the model and provide feedback if they have better numbers or other ideas. Moreover, the debate around feature prioritization shifts to the plausible value of each feature and away from emotional arguments around each stakeholder's favorite feature. Instead of debating whether a feature should be in scope, the team is debating assumptions such as whether 900 sales representatives will take online training. Often, the outcome of the debate is that the sponsor for the feature comes to realize that he needs to be responsible for the forecast. As a result, unneeded features are removed from scope because people are unwilling to be held accountable for impossible assumptions.

Measure Assumptions

Finally, when you use assumptions instead of actual data, requirements should be added that allow the assumptions to be measured, so that the team can determine whether the assumptions were valid. Over time, teams can improve their ability to develop accurate assumptions. For the example earlier in this chapter, the analyst assumed a 90 percent participation rate in online training. The analyst should add a requirement to measure the actual participation rate of the sales team. In addition, the project plan should include an activity to validate all assumptions after the solution has been deployed.

Using Objective Chains

When you complete the Objective Chains, you can use them to evaluate each feature's contribution to the business objectives in a measurable manner. The goal is to cut features from scope:

> *A project's biggest savings are realized from the features that are never developed.*

You should use Objective Chains early in a project to avoid working on requirements that will ultimately be cut.

Comparing the Relative Values of Features to Cut Scope

You can compare the individual contribution of each feature to others and cut features from scope beginning with those that provide the least value. When this approach is used, the debate about which features to cut centers around the calculated value of each feature instead of the emotions tied to each feature. In the example used earlier, the model demonstrates that downloadable training does not add considerable value to the overall business objective, and in fact, downloadable training can be cut completely.

This approach works from the top down and provides a systematic way to find out what groups of features add business value. Many L1 features really do not contribute that much value, so you can cut whole branches if you work from the top down. After you have made your initial round of cuts, you might want to use the technique again when looking at the next level of detail for the remaining features. In the previous example, if online training was being compared to other unrelated features and it was ultimately cut from the scope, there would be no value in analyzing the subfeatures of online training.

The tree structure of an Objective Chain is helpful for this analysis because it shows the feature values next to one another for easy comparison.

Determining the Value of a Feature Mapped to Multiple Business Objectives

When a feature maps to multiple business objectives, and therefore to multiple objective factors and objective equations, the value of the feature is the sum of the values for each applicable objective equation.

For example, a feature to provide online training might be linked to a business objective to reduce trainer staff costs, in addition to the business objective to increase revenue. Reducing the number of trainers reduces costs, and providing online training reduces the need for any trainers, creating the Objective Chain shown in Figure 4-14. Continuing the example, it can be determined that the cost of a trainer is $6,000 for 600 students. All of those students can take online training in the future, eliminating the need for a trainer, so the total value of the feature as it relates to reducing cost is $6,000. The value of the online training feature overall is $45,000 = $6,000 + $39,000 (calculated in the example).

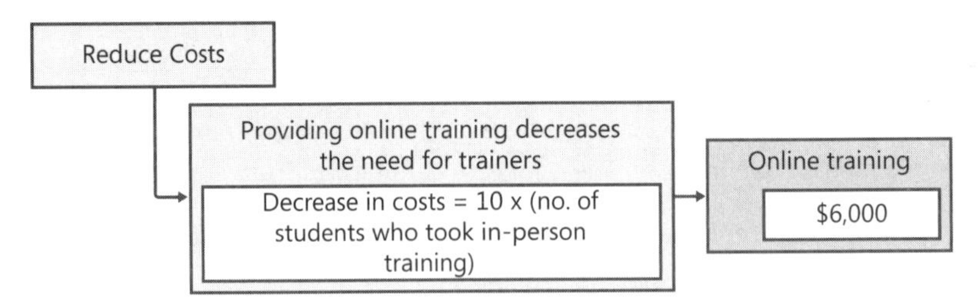

FIGURE 4-14 The Objective Chain with "online training" linked to reduce costs.

Determining the Value of Multiple Features Mapped to the Same Objective Chain

If multiple features are mapped to the same Objective Chain, spread the result of the objective equation across the features. Spreading the result is a little tricky when the features cannibalize each other.

Let's say a company has a system for which they provide telephone support and they want to reduce the support costs. Based on industry standards, stakeholders learned that they can reduce their support costs by 4 percent for every 10 percent of their support interactions that they convert to online support. Therefore, they would like to consider adding features for both chat and email support. Again, based on industry averages, they estimate that adding email support alone would convert 35 percent of their support to online support, for a 14 percent cost reduction. Similarly, adding only chat support would convert 40 percent of their support to online support, for a 16 percent cost reduction. However, if they add chat support and email support, they will convert 50 percent of their support to online support (not 75 percent), given that there is an overlap in the customers converted by email alone or chat alone. Implementing email and chat together gives them a total cost reduction of 20 percent. This data is summarized in Table 4-1.

TABLE 4-1 Online Support Options Analysis

Feature	Conversion to Online Support	Percent Cost Reduction	Savings on $10,000 Support/Day
Email support only	35%	14%	$1,400
Chat support only	40%	16%	$1,600
Chat and email support	50%	20%	$2,000

If they assume that email is worth $1,400/day and chat is worth $1,600/day, they overstate the value of the features if they add them together to get $3,000/day, given the conversion rate that tells them that it only provides a 20 percent cost reduction of $2,000/day. On the other hand, if they split the $2,000 cost reduction evenly between email and chat, each feature is only worth $1,000/day, and they might cut both from scope as having insufficient value.

In this situation, pick the feature you believe to have the most value, considering development and maintenance costs, and allocate its full value to it. Then allocate the remainder of the combined value to the other feature. In this example, the company has determined that email support has the most value; even though they will receive a slightly higher number of conversions with chat support than with email support, the cost to develop and maintain chat is roughly three times that of email support. Given this decision, they allocate the full value to email support, $1,400/day, and the remainder of the combined value to chat, $600/day ($2,000–$1,400). If more than two features mapped to the same Objective Chain, successively apply this logic.

Determining the Value of Features Attached to Emotional Objectives

On occasion, there might be features that map to emotional objectives that have intangible benefits. They legitimately do not map to concrete value. For example, these could be features that help the environment, help a very small user population, or help prevent executives from going to jail. In these cases, you can still assign a value that you are choosing to "donate." These features still might get cut based on the limit of resources the organization is willing to spend on these intangible benefits. Alternatively, you can assign value to the features based on the public relations or marketing value of being environmentally conscious and of executives not going to jail.

Determining Project Success

After the solution is deployed, you can use the Objective Chain to determine the project's achieved value. Because there might be many other factors outside the project that can influence revenue, it might be difficult to see the impact of the solution directly in the revenue or cost numbers. If, for the previous example, product revenue had gone down after online training was implemented but the participation rate exceeded the 90 percent assumption, the project should still be considered a success. Even though you might not be able to measure the project's direct revenue impact, if the participation rate turned out to be 90 percent, then based on the Objective Chain, you most likely achieved the revenue goal of the project and some other factor caused revenue to decline. If the participation rate of sales representatives ended up only being 80 percent and all other assumptions were correct, you can recalculate the theoretical improvement in revenue based on the actual value of the assumption.

Deriving Requirements

Objective Chains are not used to directly derive requirements. They are used to prioritize features. Further, they help you narrow the set of requirements you do have to derive. If features are cut from scope using Objective Chains, then you can avoid wasting time deriving requirements related to those features.

When to Use

You should use Objective Chains on any project for which you use a Business Objectives Model, so that you can prioritize features against the business objectives in a systematic way.

When Not to Use

If you have a system for which you are primarily replacing existing functionality, Objective Chains are not as helpful because they are used to prioritize features against one another. In those cases, use a Key Performance Indicator Model (see Chapter 5, "Key Performance Indicator Model") instead to help you to understand which of your Process Flows are the most important and prioritize those.

Common Mistakes

The following represent the most common mistakes that we have seen with Objective Chains.

Not Creating Objective Chains Because Data Doesn't Exist

Teams opt to not use Objective Chains if they do not have specific data for the objective equations. As discussed earlier, Objective Chains are still valuable in this situation if reasonable assumptions and educated guesses are used.

Skipping Levels in the Hierarchy

In the Business Objectives Model, you can often make a leap in the hierarchy because it's obvious how objectives are related to one another. In Objective Chains, that leap in the hierarchy typically does not work because you have to show how one level affects the next level up in the hierarchy. If you oversimplify this hierarchy, the relationships will not make sense and it will be hard to assess a concrete value for the features.

Related Models

There is a concept very similar to Objective Chains called minimum marketable features that compares values of features to help analysts decide which to include in scope and when to develop them. *Software by Numbers* describes in detail how to calculate the return on investment to do this evaluation (Denne and Cleland-Huang 2004).

The following list briefly describes the most important models that influence or are enhanced by Objective Chains. Chapter 26, "Using Models Together," contains a more thorough discussion about all related models.

- **Business Objectives Models** These provide the business objectives and L1 features for Objective Chains.
- **Feature Trees** These provide the features for Objective Chains and additional information about those features.

Exercise

The following exercise is intended to help you to gain a better understanding of how to use this model. The exercise is open ended, and therefore the answer you come up with could be substantially different than the answer that we have provided. There are potentially many correct solutions. The answer provides an explanation of how we arrived at our solution. You will gain the most out of the exercise by attempting to do it yourself before looking at the solution. The answers for the exercises can be found in Appendix C.

Instructions

Prepare an Objective Chain for the following scenario and list any assumptions you made to complete the Objective Chain.

Scenario

Your company sells lawn flamingos and other lawn decorations in a variety of colors and poses. Your team has already identified a business objective to "Increase revenue from $10 million to $12.5 million by the end of next year." There are currently 100,000 customers annually, without a lot of repeat business. The team has agreed to implement an eStore to achieve this business objective, by offering a full online product catalog and online order placement. Currently, the average order size is $100, and no business is done online.

From your prior experiences, simply by offering the online purchase path, you expect to attract 20,000 new visitors to the site because of the ability to market and sell in a variety of new channels, and industry data indicates that 90 percent of those visitors can be converted to customers within the first year. By having the products in an online catalog, your company expects that each customer will purchase one additional product per online order, and you estimate that the product will typically be sold for $10.

There are additional features being debated among the team, including cross-sell recommendations and ratings and reviews. Industry data has shown that cross-selling increases the average order by 3 percent. Ratings and reviews have been shown to increase the average order by 10 percent.

Additional Resources

- "What Do You Do When the Client Isn't Focused on the Business Outcome?" highlights an example in which Objective Chains are applied but the business does not want to use the results to make decisions about scope: *http://requirements.seilevel.com/blog/2009/06/what-do-you-do-when-the-client-isnt-focused-on-the-business-outcome.html.*
- There is a video that further describes Objective Chains in "What's Killing Your Software Projects?": *http://requirements.seilevel.com/blog/2011/03/whats-killing-your-projects.html.*
- *Software by Numbers* describes valuing minimum marketable features for scoping projects (Denne and Cleland-Huang 2004).

References

- Denne, Mark, and Jane Cleland-Huang. 2004. *Software by Numbers: Low-Risk, High-Return Development.* Santa Clara, CA: Sun Microsystems Press, Inc.
- The Standish Group, 2009. "CHAOS Summary 2009." West Yarmouth, MA: The Standish Group International, Inc.

CHAPTER 5

Key Performance Indicator Model

Texas is famous for barbecue, particularly beef brisket that is cooked at low temperatures for a long time. The typical cooking time is 1.5 hours per pound of brisket. Because a typical brisket might be 12 pounds, we usually start a brisket the night before and let it cook overnight. When I first got my barbecue smoker, I decided to barbeque a brisket for a football party the next day. It was my first brisket, and I knew how long briskets could take. I still mistimed it. Because of the long cooking time, the brisket was literally not done until every last person had gone home. When it was done, it really was the best brisket I had ever eaten.

During the process, I measured the temperature of the grill and the temperature of the meat. The target grill temperature was 250 degrees Fahrenheit, and the target internal temperature of the meat was 190 degrees Fahrenheit. I monitored the internal temperature of the brisket and calculated the change in temperature per hour. Based on the change in temperature per hour, I could forecast whether the brisket would be done in time for the party. With this level of monitoring, if it was not on target to finish on time, I could stoke the fire to increase the heat to speed the cooking. The issue I had was that the fire went out overnight. I knew from the previous night's data when I got up the next morning that there wasn't enough time to finish cooking.

The *Key Performance Indicator Model (KPIM)* is an RML objectives model. A *key performance indicator (KPI)* is a metric used to measure the success of an activity. As applied to requirements, the KPIM uses KPIs as measures associated with business processes that help teams prioritize the requirements that map to those business processes. Monitoring the temperature to forecast when a barbecued brisket will be done is an example of using a KPIM.

KPIMs are particularly useful for ensuring that business outcomes stay consistent when a significant part of a new system replicates existing functionality in an older system. Because it is primarily used to prioritize requirements, the KPIM is an RML objectives model.

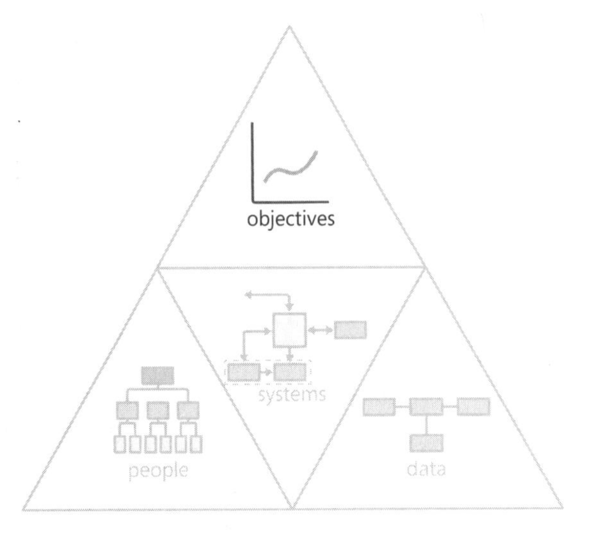

KPIs are used in business to help ensure that software projects achieve their value. Up to this point, we have discussed business objectives (in Chapter 3, "Business Objectives Model") and Objective Chains (in Chapter 4, "Objective Chain") as mechanisms to ensure that a project achieves the value that the business desires. These two models are designed for measuring the success of systems and processes that are functionally changing, but they are not good for measuring whether performance is at least as good as it was before the change.

When an existing system is being replaced, there will always be a mismatch of the new system to existing business processes. In most cases, you can reduce risks produced by that gap by simply adopting a new business process as defined by the new system. In some cases, you might decide that a customization to the software is required. But as you convert from the old system to the new system, how can you prioritize your existing business rules, requirements, and business processes to determine what processes change and what functionality gets developed? Many stakeholders attempt to hold the line by stating, "I need to have everything that I have today," as if someone understands what that is. But this is unclear. Does it mean that every single business process needs to be identical? Every screen looks the same? The new system looks and works exactly like the old system? Stakeholders should stay focused on ensuring that their business outcomes are the same, and KPIMs help them do that.

KPIM Template

A KPIM is depicted by overlaying KPIs on a Process Flow. (See Chapter 9, "Process Flow," for information about Process Flows.) An individual KPI is shown as text with a bracket symbol, as in Figure 5-1.

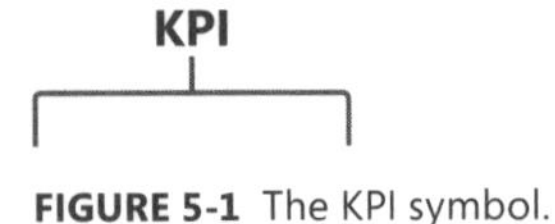

FIGURE 5-1 The KPI symbol.

The bracket encapsulates the Process Flow step or steps to which the KPI applies. The full KPIM template is similar to the one shown in Figure 5-2.

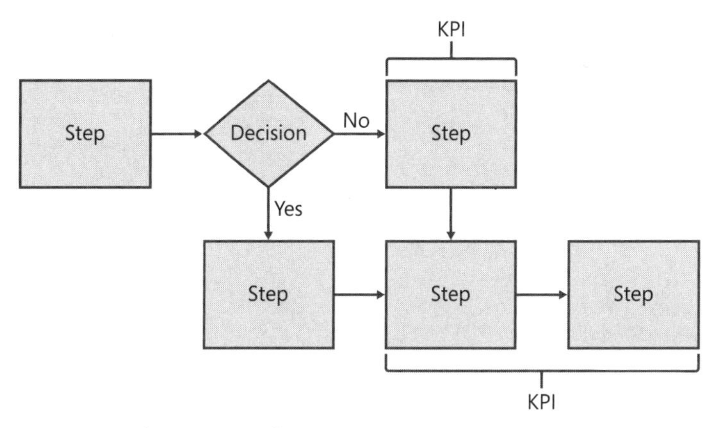

FIGURE 5-2 The KPIM template.

Tool Tip KPIMs are created in a process modeling tool such as Microsoft Visio.

Example

A mortgage company would like to implement a new loan origination system. The software vendor's salespeople estimate that the mortgage company will save approximately $100 million a year by switching. This makes the $50-million licensing price tag for the new system seem inexpensive. The system provides many new features that are improvements over the old green-screen system, and the sales team has done a thorough gap analysis to show that the new loan system has all of the features of the existing system and more. This should be an easy project, yet this story rarely ends well.

The analyst begins investigating exactly how to configure the software to meet the needs of the business. He looks at the process that a loan processor uses to manage all the documentation that is collected for a mortgage application, such as house inspections, personal financial statements, and appraisals. All of this information needs to be ordered in a particular way, sent to underwriting for approval, either printed or organized into a PDF, and sent to a bank in the appropriate format for that specific bank. Processors send a significant number of documents back and forth as information is collected, and often there is missing information that will need to be collected later.

In the current system, each loan processor can handle 60 loans per day. To meet the organization's defined quality level, a loan file must be complete so that the underwriting team and the bank do not require any additional information to make an approval decision. The timespan from the point at which the information is collected for a mortgage application to the point at which it is sent to the bank is an average of five business days. Concrete examples of KPIs for this process are the following: the number of claims a processor can organize per day, the number of errors found after auditing, and the total time to complete an application. The KPIM that reflects this process is shown in Figure 5-3.

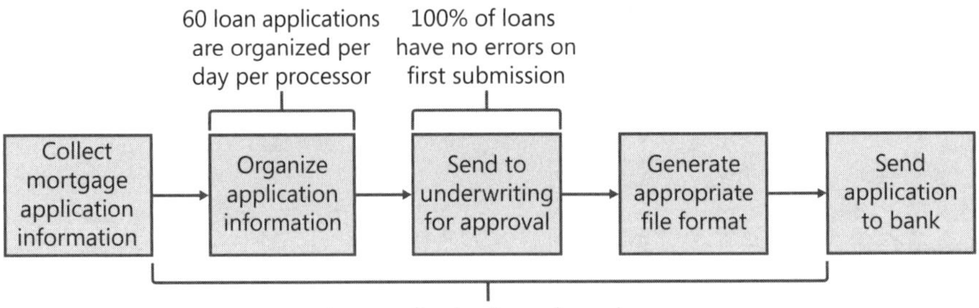

FIGURE 5-3 A loan origination KPIM.

The old system has a feature that allows many PDFs to be imported, split up electronically, reorganized, merged back into a single PDF, and printed out in a particular order. Unfortunately, the new system does not let a loan processor reorder the PDFs, so each document needs to be scanned into a stand-alone file in the correct order. However, the new system prints large separator sheets with tables of contents so that information can quickly be found, whereas the old system requires separator sheets to be manually inserted. The new system also keeps track of which types of information still need to be collected for the file to be complete. The old system has keyboard shortcuts and macros that are quite fast; the new system requires the use of the mouse. These two systems have the same "features," yet they accomplish them in very different ways. The loan processors really like the way they do things today because it is very convenient to scan a whole stack of documents and then manually assign the pages to the correct document type.

Two questions that arise in this situation are, "Do we need to add the ability for the new system to scan in a stack of documents as a PDF and reorder them electronically?" and, "Do we need to add keyboard shortcuts?" The loan processors insist that this functionality is critical for them to do their job. They indicate that scanning in one document at a time would be a nightmare and would slow them down significantly.

KPIMs can help to manage this roadblock in several different ways. A new system often creates more costs in one area while streamlining another area. The overall net effect might be zero, or even negative. In this case, the analyst can use the overarching goal of 60 applications per day with 100 percent of the applications complete to help determine whether the new system needs to be customized. This could be as simple as discussing how the new system makes some things faster, such as the automatic insertion of separator sheets and tables of contents. However, it could also require a pilot program in which time-motion studies are done to determine the actual speed to accomplish the task and to calculate the error rate in a mockup of the new system. It might turn out that executing tasks in the new system really is slower and the loan processors can really handle only 45 loans per day using the new system. In that case, either the system must be customized or loan processers must be added to meet the KPI goal. Or, if the loan processing team actually has excess capacity that can be utilized, a drop in processing efficiency might be okay because it does not decrease the total number of loans that can be processed by the company and might not cause increased costs.

If any KPI targets cannot be met, other KPIs should be analyzed to understand the overall net effect. If the benefits of other aspects of the system to other departments (such as the sales team or the funding team) are large enough, even if one department suffers, another might benefit disproportionately such that there is overall benefit to the company. To continue the example, if improvements to the sales process increase revenue significantly, an increase in the cost of loan processing might be acceptable. For instance, the sales team might currently lack the capability to forecast which previous clients will be likely to upgrade their houses. In the new system, there is a set of features that use data mining to forecast when prior clients are likely to upgrade their houses, and these features trigger the sales and marketing team to start targeting those clients. The vendor says that this feature will also increase the average loan size and hence increase the average fee KPI by 25 percent. If the processing team takes a 10-percent hit, the total revenue increase will more than balance the loss in efficiency.

Each department or group tends to optimize for its job. KPIs enable an apples-to-apples comparison of requirements across the entire system to ensure that there is overall benefit while minimizing scope creep.

Creating KPIMs

The process for creating KPIMs, outlined in Figure 5-4, builds upon the results of other models created early in the project.

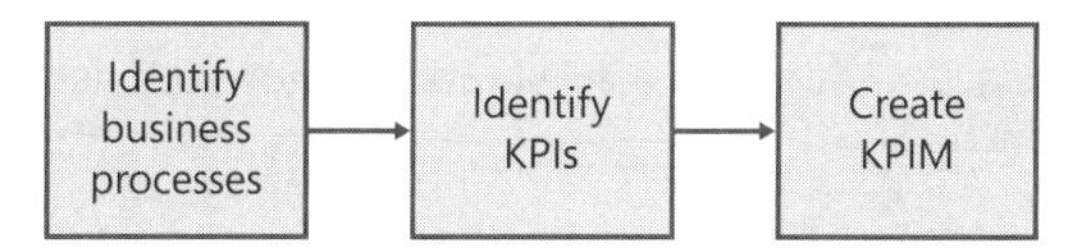

FIGURE 5-4 The process to create a KPIM.

Identify Business Processes

The process for identifying and creating Process Flows to describe business processes is discussed in Chapter 9. Identifying the business processes for KPIMs involves selecting both the specific business processes to model and the level of Process Flow (L1, L2, or L3) to use in the KPIM.

Selecting the Right Level

KPIMs are typically created by using L2 Process Flows. L1 Process Flows are often too high level to describe the steps that have measurements, and L3 flows are more detailed than necessary.

To decide which level to use, consider a few guidelines:

- Select the level at which the business process maps to a consolidated business outcome. For example, consider an L2 Process Flow step to "process loan" that has many L3 process steps such as "ensure appraisal is complete" and "check credit." It probably makes sense to develop the KPIM on the L2 step instead of on these individual L3 process steps. If the priority of requirements mapped to the L3 processes comes into question, the KPIMs can be extended to the L3 Process Flows at that time.

- Select a process level where a requirement has been identified that represents at least 1 percent of the software value. The reasoning behind this guideline is to keep the total number of KPIs down to a manageable number. The estimated impact of requirements is what is used in priority decisions, and grouping requirements together (using Process Flows) will save you from having KPIs for every requirement. Most departments have just a few KPIs that really matter, and you should stay focused on those KPIs.

Selecting the Right Processes

One of the most challenging steps in creating KPIMs is to decide which processes warrant having a KPIM. Here are some guidelines to help you select the right ones:

- Start KPIM modeling on the processes that comprise the bulk of the cost of the process (in other words, those that take the longest time, require the most resources, or are the most vital to get correct).
- Ask the different departments how they are measured or what performance targets they have, and use that as a basis to determine which processes are associated with those measures.
- Consider every Process Flow. You can run through a list of processes with the stakeholders to determine which ones are critical to maintain or measure performance of.

In reality, the decision about the level of Process Flow might be made in conjunction with deciding on the specific KPIs.

Identify KPIs

To identify KPIs, look at every step of every identified Process Flow. For each step, ask the following questions:

- What is the outcome of this step? Is it a critical business deliverable?
- Is the department measured against the results of this step?

It typically is not necessary to create KPIs for every process step. However, if the answers to those questions indicate that a particular step is critical for measurement, then probe further to identify one or more KPIs for that step. Each step could have more than one KPI, such as a time to complete, a typical volume, a maximum volume, and a quality level KPI. Other interesting KPIs might include the number of resources required to complete a task, or financial measures. The following questions help to identify the actual KPI for the step:

- How much volume will go through this step?
- How do we determine the quality of the step?
  - How many errors are acceptable?
  - How often is manual intervention required?
  - How large of an error is acceptable?

- How long does it take to complete the step?
- How many people does it take to complete the step?
- How many people in the company execute this step?

Create the KPIM

Create the KPIM by overlaying the KPIs on the process step or steps in the Process Flow as callouts so that they are easily identifiable. If there are many KPIs for a particular step, log the KPIs in a list and reference them from the Process Flow.

Using KPIMs

KPIMs should be used early in a project to help prioritize the development effort so that the most important features are worked on first. In addition, KPIMs can help cut features by helping the team compare features against each other in an apples-to-apples way. After the KPIMs are completed, you use them to evaluate each requirement's contribution to the business value of the system in a measurable manner. The goal is to cut requirements from scope, because the biggest project savings are gained from the requirements that are never developed.

Prioritizing KPIMs When Business Objectives Don't Help

The following is an example to contrast KPIMs to business objectives: A recent project had a goal to reduce costs by switching to a system with lower licensing fees. The company would save around $5 million per year in licensing fees by converting to a new system. The business objective was quite simple for this project: "Save $5 million each year." Yet there were no specific features being developed that could map to saving $5 million each year. This is because in many projects, especially those that replace existing systems, there is an unstated goal of maintaining all existing business outcomes at their current levels. In many cases, no one has written down the current business outcomes, or if they have, those outcomes are scattered throughout every department. The KPIM is a mechanism to identify, organize, and document the business outcomes across an entire business process to ensure that any changes to the system maintain the existing business outcomes at or above the current level.

Prioritizing When Replacing Existing Functionality

You cannot realistically prioritize by using both KPIMs for all process steps and Objective Chains for all features; instead, select the model that is best, based on the type of project. Generally use KPIMs for upgrading existing systems and automating business processes, and use Objective Chains for new features or new systems. More specifically, use KPIMs when there are existing measurement targets to maintain or improve, and use Objective Chains to estimate the value of proposed features.

The reason for this distinction is that if you are adding new features representing new business processes to a system, you do not have KPIs for those features but you might have business objectives that you are trying to achieve. But if you are replacing a manual process with an automated one in the system, you are probably going to want to ensure that the overall performance of the process is not degraded, or if it is, that you understand the tradeoffs.

In some projects, the company is trying to improve a process. For example, suppose you have reduced a process from 90 minutes to 15 minutes, which is below your target of 20 minutes. You could make additional changes to automate the process and decrease the time further to 10 minutes. But because you have achieved the target, is it worth investing resources to go from 15 minutes to 10 minutes in the grand scope of the project? Maybe the development time would be better spent improving another process to its target level. Because of the way development teams are structured, it is easy for teams to do too much local optimization while not considering whether the time could be better spent optimizing something that creates more value for the company. Sometimes keeping things just as they are is good enough. Each department or group tends to optimize for its job, so using KPIMs can enable you to optimize across departmental boundaries.

Comparing the Relative Values of Requirements to Cut Scope

For large projects, there can be hundreds of KPIs that have to be maintained as a system conversion occurs. By using the same techniques explained for Objective Chains, you can calculate the relative monetary value for each KPI. Because KPIs are attached to process steps, and process steps map to requirements (see Chapter 7, "Requirements Mapping Matrix"), the individual value contribution of each requirement can be compared to the others. You can cut requirements from scope according to those KPIs that provide the least value. When teams use this approach, the debate about which features to cut centers around the contribution of the requirement to accomplishing the business process instead of the emotions tied to each requirement.

Essentially, use the KPIMs to decide which process steps have the highest priority, and then examine the requirements to ensure that the KPIs for the highest value areas are met first.

In the loan origination example discussed earlier in this chapter, the loan processors were insistent about being able to reorder the PDFs in the system. However, in comparing the KPIMs of the overall system without additional information, it is unclear that electronic reordering of PDFs provides enough value to include it regardless of the cost to develop.

Deriving Requirements

KPIMs are not used to derive functional requirements directly. They are used to prioritize Process Flows and ensure that business throughput can be maintained where needed. They can be used to derive non-functional requirements.

When to Use

You should use KPIMs on any project in which you have existing systems or processes that you need to maintain.

When Not to Use

KPIMs are not helpful on projects that are implementing all-new functionality; for these, Business Objectives Models should be used instead. However, most projects have some existing functionality or processes that will be maintained or converted, so KPIMs can be used for those. For software that has no business processes at all (such as some packaged software), KPIMs are not helpful.

Common Mistakes

The following represent the most common mistakes that we have seen with KPIMs.

Not Using KPIMs Because KPIs Don't Exist

Many organizations do not use operational metrics to monitor business processes, and teams opt to not use KPIMs if they do not have the data for the KPIs. However, in most cases, KPIMs can be created during the project, and the measurements can be taken to evaluate the current state and a new target state. In addition, KPIMs can be gathered in a just-in-time fashion based on features that might be in question.

Not Using KPIMs Due to Fears of Being Held Accountable

Not surprisingly, there is often resistance from business organizations for creating KPIs, because measurement means that the business is now accountable for KPIs they might never have had to meet before. The analyst can help the business stakeholders see how KPIs can be used internally to help improve their operations and make better implementation choices in the new system.

A Lack of Ongoing Monitoring

When teams do choose to use KPIMs, they often neglect to provide a mechanism to monitor the KPIs on an ongoing basis.

Related Models

KPIs exist in many organizations as a list. KPIMs map those KPIs to Process Flows to put the KPIs in context.

The following list briefly describes the most important models that influence or are enhanced by KPIMs. Chapter 26, "Using Models Together," contains a more thorough discussion about all related models.

- **Process Flows** These provide the business flows for KPIMs.
- **Requirements Mapping Matrices** These provide the mapping from process steps to requirements so that requirements can be cut when Process Flows are cut.

Exercise

The following exercise is intended to help you to gain a better understanding of how to use this model. The exercise is open ended, and therefore the answer you come up with could be substantially different than the answer that we have provided. There are potentially many correct solutions. The answer provides an explanation of how we arrived at our solution. You will gain the most out of the exercise by attempting to do it yourself before looking at the solution. The answers for the exercises can be found in Appendix C.

Instructions

Prepare a KPIM for the following scenario and provided Process Flow.

Scenario

Your company sells lawn flamingos and other lawn decorations in a variety of colors and poses. The sales team that sells the flamingo products uses a Microsoft Excel template and email to create orders that are sent to customers for review. The sales reps then enter the approved orders manually into the order fulfillment system. With the implementation of a new eStore system, a comprehensive order management solution will be integrated into the eStore.

Sales managers find that with the manual process currently in use, their sales representatives can submit 30 orders per hour, and the sales managers do not want their productivity to drop in the new system. Because the current system uses a manual process to review the orders with the customer, the orders are usually correct by the time they are submitted to the order processing center, and the only errors that occur at the time of submission are due to keying mistakes. Right now, only about 2 percent of orders are entered incorrectly. The managers do not expect the total order processing time to be any slower with the new system; currently it takes no more than three days from the point of receiving the order to its shipping. The Process Flow for this scenario is in Figure 5-5.

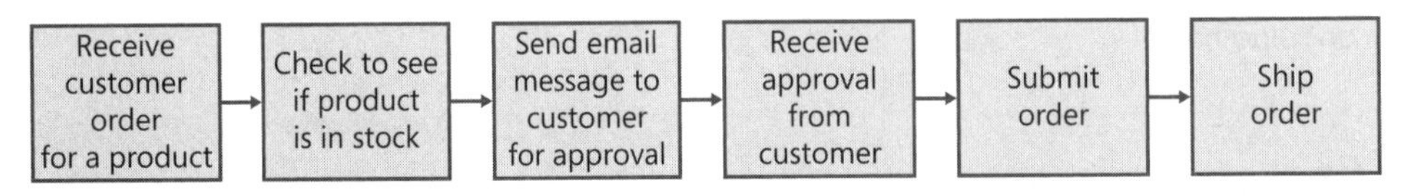

FIGURE 5-5 Exercise Process Flow.

Additional Resources

- There is a wealth of information and example KPIs at: *http://kpilibrary.com.*
- Business Objectives, KPIs, and Legacy Conversions: *http://requirements.seilevel.com/blog/2011/10/business-objectives-kpis-and-legacy-conversions.html.*

CHAPTER 6

Feature Tree

If you have ever bought a new car, you probably thought about what things you cared about in a car, including number of doors, exterior color, whether it was convertible or not, engine size, seat covering type, interior color, whether it was a hybrid or not, and the quality of the sound system. These are basically "features" of a car.

If you were to list these features and start to put them into groups such as exterior features, engine features, internal features, and audio features, you would probably identify new features you cared about. In fact, if you started to look at audio features and saw that you had only identified a "sound system," you probably would think more about whether that meant a CD player, a DVD player, or an MP3 connection, and what type of speakers came with the system.

Effectively, you would brainstorm your features and organize them to find any missing features. When you go to the dealer to look at cars, you might even take your organized features with you to stay focused on cars that meet your needs. Later you might take your list one step further and prioritize your features to actually choose your car.

The Feature Tree is an RML objectives model that shows the organization of the features in logical groups, displaying the full scope of a solution in a single page.

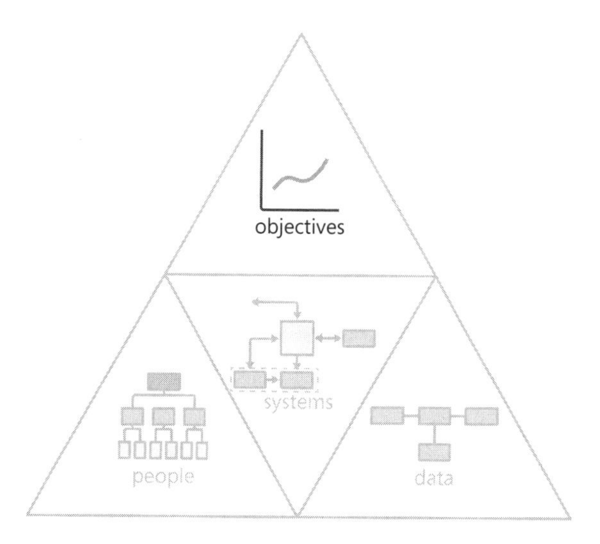

The structure of Feature Trees is based on fishbone diagrams or Ishikawa diagrams, which are commonly used to organize information into logical groupings based on relationships. Fishbone diagrams are typically used to model cause-and-effect relationships (Ishikawa 1990), but Feature Trees specifically organize the features of a solution.

A *feature* is a short-form description of an area of functionality that the solution will ultimately include to meet the business objectives. Features are collections of requirements that are used to articulate and organize the requirements. There are three possible levels of features that might be useful for organizing the requirements: level 1 (L1), level 2 (L2), and level 3 (L3). Below L3 are individual requirements themselves. You do not have to have all three levels; if the solution is simple, there might be just L1 features and requirements.

Feature Trees show all of the features at once, giving a quick view of the solution's breadth of functionality. Further, organizing the features in this model makes it is easier to identify missing features and redundant features. Finally, the Feature Tree provides a functional decomposition of the solution for use throughout all phases of the project, including organization of the requirements, organization of work around the requirements (planning), and bounding of the scope of work on requirements. Feature Trees provide a much denser view of features than a simple list could show.

Feature Tree Template

Feature Trees are models that visually show the relationships between features. The features are simply words on the tree, and the lines link related features together.

The basic building block of the model is a feature with a single line, as shown in Figure 6-1. The name of the feature should be a noun phrase and should be brief, typically two or three words. Also, the most important words in the feature name should be first. For example "content management" is better than "managing content" because the word "content" is the interesting and useful word. (Also, "managing content" is a verb phrase.)

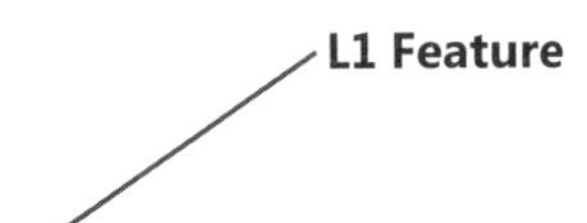

FIGURE 6-1 A feature in a Feature Tree.

At any feature level, each feature has its own unique line. Each subfeature also has its own line, but these are strung off the main feature's line, as shown in Figure 6-2. In this example, the L1 feature has four subfeatures at the L2 level. The order in which the subfeatures are attached to the line is not important, as long as common subfeatures are grouped off the same parent feature line.

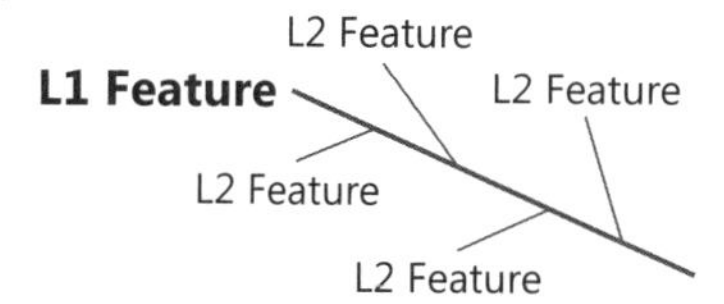

FIGURE 6-2 Grouping of features in a Feature Tree.

At the highest level, the L1 features can be shown in a box, as in Figure 6-3, to highlight those features on the tree as the main features under which subfeatures fall. This enables anyone who skims the model to understand the big picture of the scope of the solution.

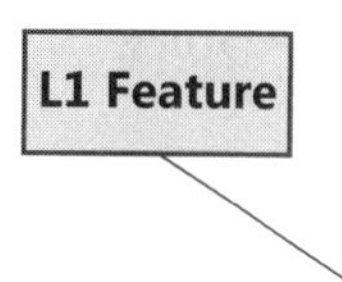

FIGURE 6-3 The L1 feature of a Feature Tree.

The lines of features are strung together recursively in the same fashion, from top to bottom, as shown in Figure 6-4.

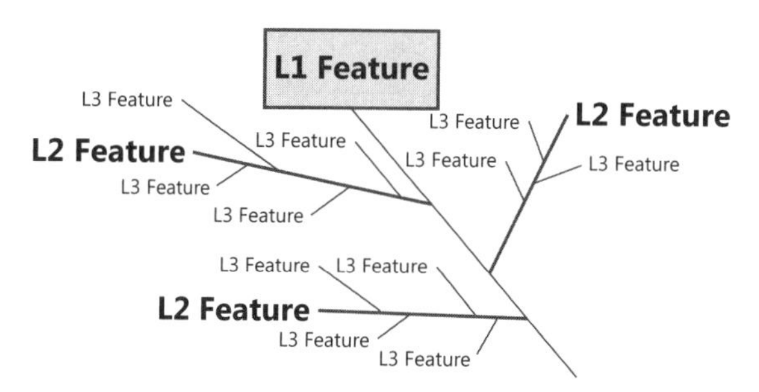

FIGURE 6-4 One branch of a Feature Tree.

The main horizontal line down the middle of the model is the "spine" of the fishbone diagram, with a box at the end that is the product concept being developed, as shown in Figure 6-5.

FIGURE 6-5 The product concept in a Feature Tree.

When all of the L1 features are strung off the product concept line, as in Figure 6-6, the tree looks like the bones of a fish, thus the name "fishbone"!

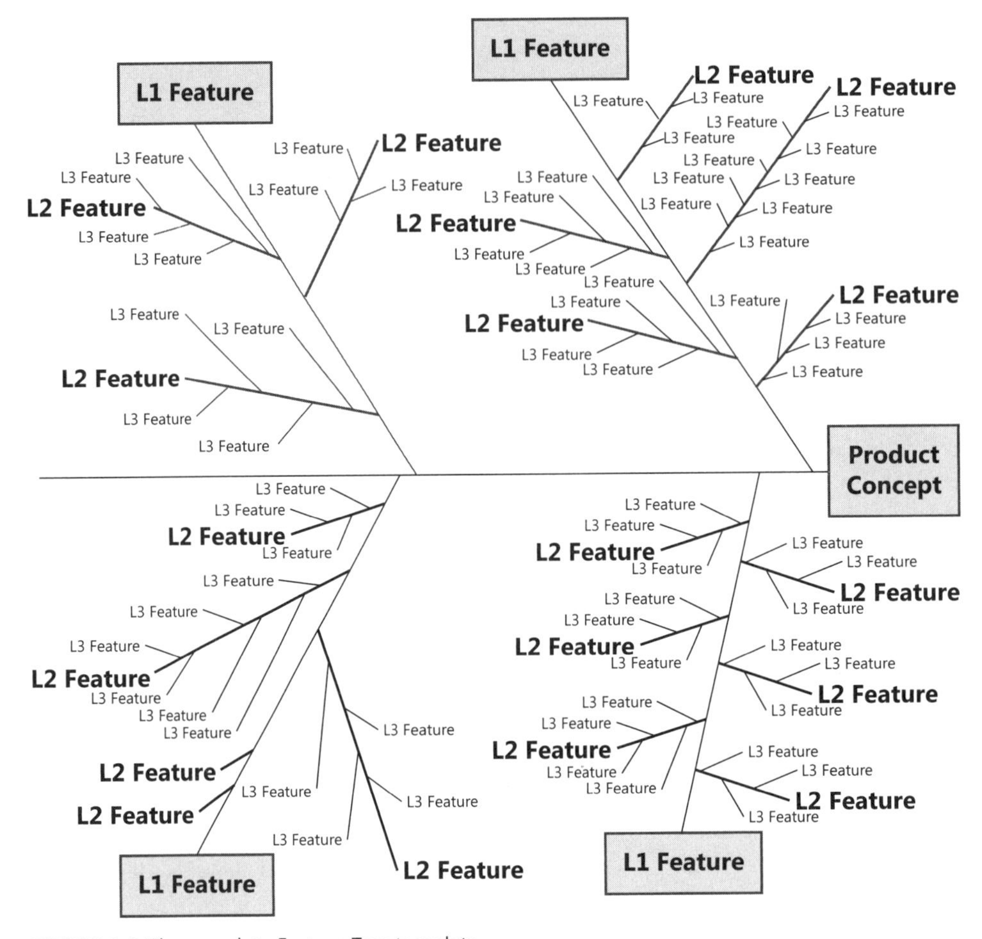

FIGURE 6-6 The complete Feature Tree template.

Tool Tip Feature Trees can initially be created by using sticky notes or a mind-mapping tool, to facilitate the dynamic nature of organizing them. Mind-mapping tools or Microsoft Visio tend to work best for creating Feature Trees in their final form.

Example

A training organization is building a customer portal that provides customers with access to training collateral. Because some of the content is not public, the portal must restrict access to some of it. Users must authenticate and have the proper authorization to view content. Figure 6-7 shows the Feature Tree for the example solution.

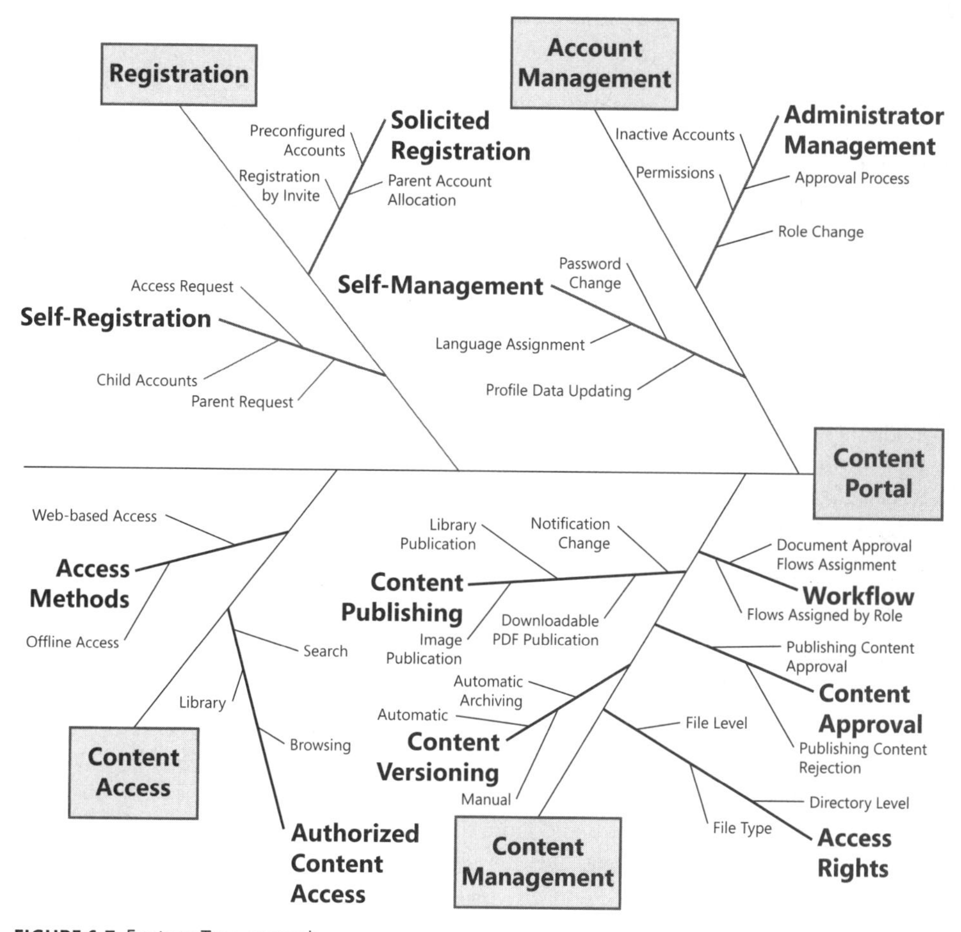

FIGURE 6-7 Feature Tree example.

In this example, there are four L1 features: Registration, Account Management, Content Access, and Content Management; the subfeatures are grouped accordingly underneath each of those. When the features are organized in this model, it is possible to start looking for gaps. For example, in looking at Content Access, you can see that there are only two L2 features, so it is worth considering whether there might be other features necessary. If the business wants to allow users to see a list of content they cannot access with their current permissions, for instance, they might want to add a sub-feature called "Content Access Request."

Creating Feature Trees

The process for creating Feature Trees is shown in Figure 6-8.

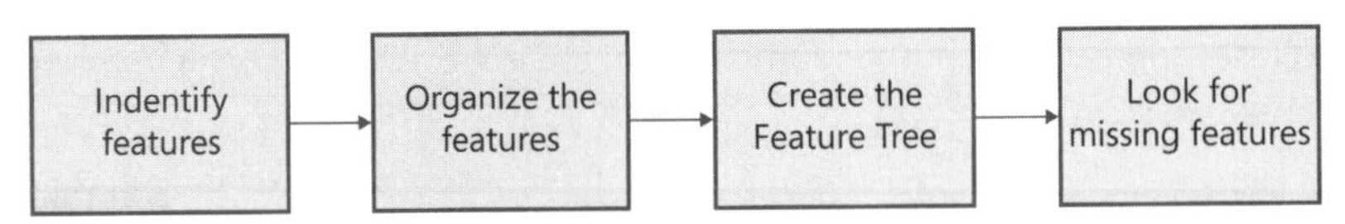

FIGURE 6-8 The process for creating a Feature Tree.

Identify Features

When you create a Business Objectives Model, some of the high-level features might be identified when you define the product concept (see Chapter 3, "Business Objectives Model," for more information). However, that set of features is probably very high level, so the process of identifying features begins by thinking about features that are at the same level as those high-level features, or that are subfeatures to those. It can be useful to use these high-level features as your L1 features so that the Feature Tree directly traces to your Business Objectives Model.

When identifying features, be sure to consider end-user functionality, administrative needs, and system-to-system interactions. Additionally, as will be discussed further in Chapter 10, "Use Case," data can be created, updated, destroyed, used, moved, and copied. Many features map to these actions, so consider them when you are identifying the features that can manipulate data. All or some of these actions can be combined into one feature, depending on the granularity you want to have for the features.

It can be difficult to know how granular to make the features, and there is no specific rule for this. The goal of the Feature Tree is to clearly communicate the scope of the project. Features will usually be more granular for smaller solutions and less granular for larger solutions. As a rule of thumb, be consistent in the level of granularity used within a Feature Tree. One approach for dealing with large systems is to break them out into subsystems and then create a Feature Tree for each subsystem. Another guideline is that there should be no more than three layers of features: L1, L2, and L3. Very small systems might only contain L1 and L2 features. The list of L1 and L2 features can rapidly communicate the core functionality of the product concept to someone new to the project.

Organize the Features

After the initial pass of feature identification is complete, you should organize the features, grouping similar features together. As you organize the features, you might see that new L1 features might be needed or that some of the original L1 features could be combined into a single feature.

Organize the features into L1, L2, and L3 features. There might be some features that are subfeatures of the same feature—organize them together.

Subfeatures of More Than One Feature

When a subfeature is a child of more than one feature, it might be difficult to decide which group to add it to. Pick the group in which it best fits or with which it most closely aligns, based on criteria such as where you forecast that it will most often be accessed. If it is not obvious which is the best choice, then just pick one, but don't duplicate features in the tree.

Parentless Subfeatures

Be aware that there might be several features that are really children of a feature not yet identified. For these, simply create a new parent feature at the L1 or L2 level as appropriate, and group these subfeatures under it.

Create the Feature Tree

When the feature organization begins to take shape, move the features into a Feature Tree format to finalize it. You don't want to do this too soon, because you'll find that it can be harder to move things around within the tree; early in the process, you'll want to move them around a lot.

A Feature Tree should be easy to review and understand, so that each feature ideally has no more than 7 +/- 2 subfeatures directly below it. If necessary, you can put more than nine features under a parent, but at least consider whether the parent should be split into two separate parent features and the subfeatures divided between them, or whether some of the subfeatures are really another level lower. Similarly, there should be no more than 7 +/- 2 top-level features. Group similar features together and create subfeatures as needed to keep the groupings this size. You should never have more than three levels of features. For communicating functionality, three levels (approximately 1,000 features) should be sufficient.

The order of the features in the tree is not important. However, it will help readability if there is a logical flow to them from left to right, then top to bottom. There are several reasonable ways to lay out the features. For example, you could put the features that a user would encounter first in the upper left, you could put the highest-value features in the upper left, or you could put customer features in the upper left.

Look for Missing Features

After the Feature Tree is assembled, review it to look for missing features. The Feature Tree organization provides the review team with a logical, methodical way to walk through the feature sets and make sure each grouping is complete. If a specific feature has only one to three subfeatures, consider whether additional subfeatures at that level might be missing. You should engage other reviewers to help with this, including the initial brainstorming team or another team with knowledge about the desired features.

Using the previous training collateral example, by asking if whether the four L1 features identified will meet all the needs of end users, other systems, or administrators, you might uncover a need for system administrators to monitor the system and review usage data. Or asking whether there are really only two ways to create accounts might lead to a feature that allows administrators to create accounts.

As additional features are identified, add them to the Feature Tree and move other features around accordingly.

Affinity Diagrams for Brainstorming and Organizing

The activities described for creating Feature Trees are very similar to the techniques common to affinity diagrams. Affinity diagrams are used to organize any type of information. They are typically used for brainstorming information and organizing it to find more information. Figure 6-9 shows a partially completed affinity diagram used to organize the training features from the previous example.

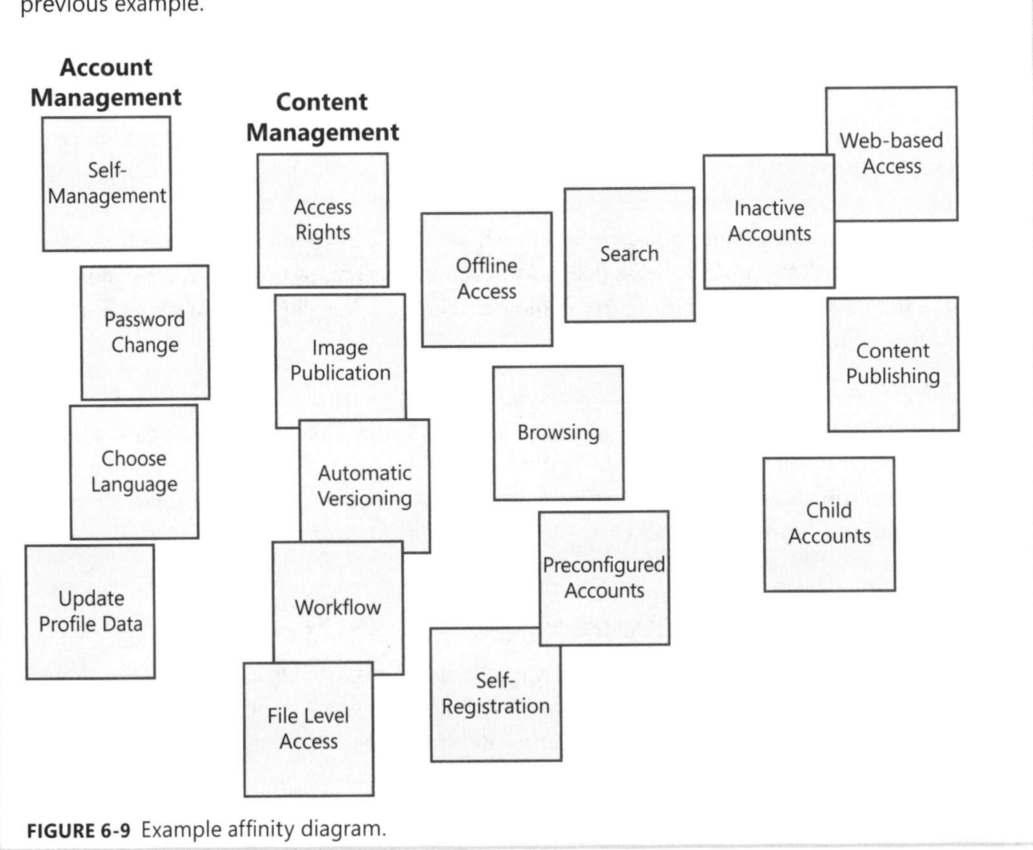

FIGURE 6-9 Example affinity diagram.

Using Feature Trees

You should create a Feature Tree early in a project to define the breadth of work that will be completed, but it is used throughout the project to communicate scope and help the team organize their work.

In the previous example, the analysts had to define requirements for the training portal, but they did not know anything about the features required to manage training collateral. They gathered existing documentation and did high-level interviews with stakeholders to gain an initial broad understanding of the functionality required. One of the first models the team created was a Feature Tree. They used this to brainstorm and review the major components of the functionality with the team of subject matter experts. Because they modeled this information in a Feature Tree, it was much easier to review the features with the stakeholders than if they had used a list of the same information. When the tree was finalized, the team used the organization within the Feature Tree throughout the project to organize the requirements efforts and specifications as well as to communicate the scope of the project to executives.

Depicting Project Scope

The Feature Tree should be used to set and communicate the scope of the project. It is a useful model to circulate among executives and lead stakeholders to quickly communicate the scope of the solution. Because 100 features can literally fit on one page, the Feature Tree is a good choice when you need a diagram that anyone can look at quickly to understand the gist of the solution. If the same content were created in a list of text, it would not fit easily on one page and would be difficult to understand. For packaged software, a Feature Tree provides the features that go in a short list or description of the product's functionality.

Because there is no way to guarantee that a Feature Tree is complete, you should review it with the stakeholders and make sure it reflects their expectations. The earlier that gaps are identified, the better, because finding them late in a project can derail the project. Update the tree after scope is cut to reflect the final set of features.

When you join a project midstream, it is always a challenge to get a high-level picture of what an existing system does or what a new system is supposed to do. Feature Trees allow all team members to understand and agree about the capabilities of the solution at a high level. They show the breadth of the solution scope at a consistent level of depth.

Organizing the Requirements

The divisions in a Feature Tree are an essential way to organize requirements in deliverables so that the information is grouped by feature. In a requirement deliverable, all of the requirements for an L1 feature and its subfeatures can be grouped together, and the same is true for the next L1 feature, and so on. For the example discussed earlier, there could be a full set of models and requirements for Account Management and another for Access Management.

Further, features defined in Feature Trees can be used in Requirements Mapping Matrices (see Chapter 7, "Requirements Mapping Matrix") to organize requirements. The features are also used in Objective Chains (see Chapter 4, "Objective Chain") to prioritize groups of requirements.

Organizing the Requirements Work

You can use Feature Trees to organize requirements gathering activities. The team can identify the requirements completely for an L1 branch before moving on to the next branch, or divide L1 features among team members if there are enough resources. In an agile project, the Feature Tree can be translated to a product backlog to help determine which features get worked on first.

The Feature Tree segments the solution, allowing the team to discuss pieces of the full solution and organize work around those pieces. Feature Trees are useful for most solutions and critical for large solutions, in which complexity can derail a team's productivity; imagine leading a team of 10 analysts and trying to determine who will or is working on what without a Feature Tree. A Feature Tree naturally lends itself to subdividing the work among the team.

Deriving Requirements

Initially, Feature Trees are helpful to ensure a complete set of features. After a draft Feature Tree is created, it also should be used to identify any major missing features. Each feature can be considered for additional subfeatures that might not have been discovered in the initial brainstorm. The top-level features should be reviewed again for missing features, and redundant features can be removed.

Feature Trees are also useful for identifying gaps in other RML models. Feature Trees can be reviewed against Process Flows, System Flows, and Use Cases to determine whether those models fully span all of the features. If any features are not covered, a Process Flow, System Flow, or Use Case is probably missing. Further, Process Flows and Use Cases should be reviewed to make sure they map to features in the Feature Tree. If one does not map to a feature, either an external process was identified or a feature is missing from the Feature Tree.

Check the Feature Tree against the Ecosystem Map (see Chapter 12, "Ecosystem Map") to identify any features that could be needed to exchange data with other systems. Similarly, any features in the Feature Tree that indicate that data must be exchanged with another system might identify missing interactions in the Ecosystem Map.

After the features have been identified and the requirements are organized by feature, you can derive additional requirements by noticing which features do not have many individual requirements. If you have 30 individual requirements, it is hard to know whether any are missing. However, if you group those 30 individual requirements into features, then you can look at one feature at a time to see what requirements might be missing.

When to Use

You should use Feature Trees on most projects to define features to organize the requirements and communicate the scope in one summary view. On Commercial Off the Shelf (COTS) projects, they are useful for summarizing the features that are most important during the selection phase.

When Not to Use

Feature Trees are not as useful in a COTS implementation phase, because the features being implemented are really those from the packaged software.

Common Mistakes

The following represent the most common mistakes that we have seen with Feature Trees.

Wrong Number of Features at Each Level

A common mistake is having the wrong number of features at any one level. The 7 +/- 2 number is critical to making Feature Trees consumable, so be sure that there are no more than 10 subfeatures under any feature. Further, if there are only one or two features at each level, either there are missing subfeatures at the L2 and L3 level or the existing ones at L3 might not be necessary.

Poor Feature Names

As odd as this sounds, it can be challenging to name features. The key is they should be named consistently across the whole tree so that all of the features are parallel to one another. If some are written as nouns and others as verbs, the Feature Tree will be hard to read. Features should be written as noun phrases using two or three words.

Related Models

Feature Trees use the same visual structure as fishbone diagrams. However, fishbone diagrams, or Ishikawa diagrams, are typically used to model cause-and-effect scenarios. Affinity diagrams are models used in brainstorming that help create Feature Trees.

The following list briefly describes the most important models that influence or are enhanced by Feature Trees. Chapter 26, "Using Models Together," contains a more thorough discussion about all related models.

- **Business Objectives Models** These identify the initial draft of L1 features in the product concept.
- **Objective Chains** These prioritize the features in the Feature Tree.

- **Requirements Mapping Matrices** These use the features in Feature Trees to organize requirements.
- **Process Flows, System Flows, and Use Cases** These are used to describe the features in detail. They are also used to identify missing features from the Feature Tree.
- **Ecosystem Maps** These show interactions between features.

Exercise

The following exercise is intended to help you to gain a better understanding of how to use this model. The exercise is open ended, and therefore the answer you come up with could be substantially different than the answer that we have provided. There are potentially many correct solutions. The answer provides an explanation of how we arrived at our solution. You will gain the most out of the exercise by attempting to do it yourself before looking at the solution. The answers for the exercises can be found in Appendix C.

Instructions

Prepare a draft Feature Tree for the scenario. Some features are suggested, so start with those and then brainstorm additional obvious features.

Scenario

In this project, you are helping to build an eStore to sell plastic flamingos and flamingo-related accessories. Customers should be able to browse for flamingos, purchase flamingos, create lists of flamingos they want, and be able to share those lists with other people. Customers should also have the ability to rate the flamingo products and submit reviews of products that they have previously purchased. While browsing, they will get to see other flamingos that might be of interest to them. Business managers should be able to update the online catalog of flamingos, link products for cross-sell opportunities, and review site usage data and order data to make decisions about marketing flamingos. System administrators need to be able to monitor the load on the system and access the system logs if there is a technical problem. Customers should be able to create accounts so that if they return, they don't have to re-enter shipping and billing information.

Additional Resources

- "Business Analyst Training on Using Sticky Notes to Create Affinity Diagrams" is a video explaining how to create affinity diagrams. This technique can be used in creating Feature Trees: *http://requirements.seilevel.com/blog/2011/06/business-analyst-training-on-using-sticky-notes-to-create-affinity-diagrams.html.*
- The PDF available at this URL provides in-depth information on creating affinity diagrams: *http://www.balancedscorecard.org/Portals/0/PDF/affinity.pdf.*
- Davis has a lengthy discussion about brainstorming using affinity diagrams (though he doesn't call them that) (Davis 2005).
- Gottesdiener has a discussion on visually organizing information that mentions both affinity groups (affinity diagrams) and mind maps (Gottesdiener 2002).
- Feature Diagramming Overview provides an overview of a feature diagraming technique that is a hierarchy model: *http://www.jarrettinteractiondesign.com/?p=32.*
- Feature Trees can be used to organize a team's efforts. The IIBA has a discussion on functional decomposition in the BABOK, applied to decomposing work for analysis purposes (IIBA 2009).

References

- Davis, Alan M. 2005. *Just Enough Requirements Management*. New York, NY: Dorset House.
- Gottesdiener, Ellen. 2002. *Requirements by Collaboration: Workshops for Defining Needs*. Boston, MA: Addison-Wesley.
- International Institute of Business Analysis (IIBA). 2009. *A Guide to the Business Analysis Body of Knowledge (BABOK Guide)*. Toronto, Ontario, Canada.
- Ishikawa, Kaoru. 1990. *Introduction to Quality Control*. New York, NY: Productivity Press.

CHAPTER 7

Requirements Mapping Matrix

Going on vacation is supposed to be fun, but planning a vacation can be very time consuming. Have you ever wondered whether you were forgetting something when you started packing for your trip? Or when your trip nears and it's been months since you booked it, have you ever wanted to recheck your hotel reservations, your ride to the airport, and your flight times?

I have a standard process I go through to plan my vacations. First and foremost, I decide where I want to go and check to see if I have enough vacation days for what I want to do. Most of my vacations are to Hawaii, but I still have to select which island to visit each trip. If I don't have enough vacation days, I check to see how far out I have to plan my trip to ensure that I will have enough vacation days. When I know when I can go, I decide which specific days that I want to travel on. I usually try to determine what the typical price of a plane ticket is to my destination and then proceed to check flights around the dates that I want to leave and come back. After my destination and flights are finalized, I tackle the arduous task of finding the right hotel. I am pretty cheap, so I always look for a good deal on the hotel. Then I look at the activities that I want to participate in while I am there. On every trip, I know I will surf, but I will need rest days between surfing days. When the time for my vacation is approaching, I start to pack, based on the activities that I planned. Every time I go, I have a standard pack list that includes my flip flops for the beach, a swimsuit, my rash guard, three dressy outfits for the evenings, five casual outfits, comfortable walking shoes, and a camera. Then I add to my packing based on any additional activities I've planned.

As I plan my vacation, not only do I have a process I follow, but I also have requirements for each of the process steps. For example, when I reserve my flights, I always consider when I can go and what the ticket prices are before finalizing them. For the hotel, I have to have an inexpensive option on the right island. When I get to the packing step in my process, I have a predetermined list of things I pack, but I also have to leave room for variety.

The Requirements Mapping Matrix (RMM) is an RML objectives model that maps information in models to requirements and business rules. An RMM can contain multiple levels of mappings. The most useful mappings are from Process Flow steps to requirements and requirements to business rules. Other useful mappings include business objectives to features, features to requirements, requirements to code, and requirements to test cases. RMMs are useful because they help you to prioritize requirements, identify missing requirements, and highlight unnecessary requirements.

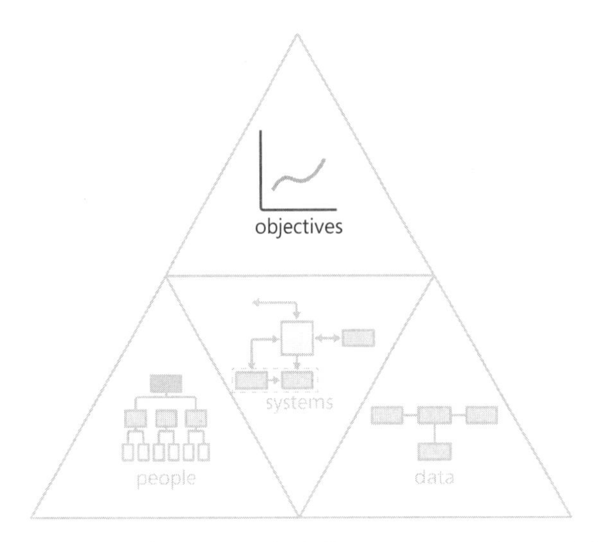

A *traceability matrix* is similar to an RMM. A traceability matrix is used to compare the relationships between all instances of only two types of objects (such as requirements and tests) to ensure full coverage of one by the other. An RMM shows the relationships between multiple types of objects. A traceability matrix is better when your information has mostly many-to-many relationships. For example, if each requirement has many tests, and each test maps to many requirements, then a traceability matrix might be appropriate. Each cell shows the relationship of a particular requirement with a particular test. However, the RMM is better when your information has mostly one-to-many relationships. For example, if each requirement has many tests but each test only tests a single requirement, then an RMM could be more useful, because you can incorporate more than two objects in your trace (such as business objective to feature to requirement to test).

RMM Template

RMMs are created in a matrix. There are typically at least five columns; the first three columns contain L1, L2, and L3 Process Flow steps, respectively, the fourth contains unique requirement identifiers, and the fifth contains the requirements. (See Chapter 9, "Process Flow," for a detailed explanation of L1, L2, and L3 Process Flows.) Each row of the matrix contains one mapping from a Process Flow step to a requirement.

Additional columns are added as needed to capture additional levels of mappings or relevant metadata such descriptions or notes. Columns are commonly added to organize the requirements by features from a Feature Tree and to map business rules to requirements. Further organizing requirements by features is useful when there are more than 7+/–2 requirements mapped to a single process step. If you have just a few business rules per requirement, then you should consider including each business rule in a column, keeping a single row for each requirement and all of its associated business rules. However, if you have many business rules per requirement (more than 5 to 10), you should keep the business rules in a separate matrix and reference the requirement from the business rule. One final option is to duplicate the requirements in the RMM and put each unique business rule in its own row.

The template for a standard RMM is shown in Figure 7-1. In this case, a feature column was added and two business rule columns were added.

L1 Process Step	L2 Process Step	L3 Process Step	Feature	REQID	Requirement	Business Rule 1	Business Rule 2

FIGURE 7-1 A Requirements Mapping Matrix template.

There are some simple solutions that do not have L3 Process Flows, and in those cases, you can leave the L3 column out of the template. Also, if the model is used to map something other than Process Flows and requirements, you can just substitute those models or model elements in the appropriate columns. For example, possible columns include business objectives from a Business Objectives Model, cells in a State Table, or even elements from a Display-Action-Response model.

In requirements management tools, it is common to see two objects from an RMM in a traceability matrix with high-level objects as either rows or columns and low-level objects in the other, as shown in Figure 7-2. Relationships between the two objects are denoted by a check, *X*, or directional arrow indicating a relationship between the two objects. The issue with this matrix is that it only shows the relationship between two objects at a time, so to see the relationship across more than two objects, you have to flip between multiple matrices. Ideally, you can configure the requirements management tool to more closely match the RMM template. However, if that is not an option, you might have to just use the traceability functionality within your requirements management tool as your RMM.

	Process Step 1	Process Step 2	Process Step 3	Process Step 4	Process Step 5	Process Step 6	Process Step 7	Process Step 8	Process Step 9	Process Step 10	Process Step 11	Process Step 12
Req1												
Req2												
Req3												
Req4												
Req5												
Req6												
Req7												
Req8												

FIGURE 7-2 An example traceability matrix template.

Tool Tip RMMs are best captured by using a requirements management tool that can automate the process of checking for missing links. They can also be created in Microsoft Excel or as tables in Microsoft Word, but checking for missing links is more time consuming with these tools. In addition, there can be a significant amount of redundancy with objects that have many-to-many relationships.

Example

An insurance company has a basic process that all insurance agents execute to create new policies, from receiving a request for a policy to generating the policy and billing the customer. The L1 Process Flow for this scenario is shown in Figure 7-3.

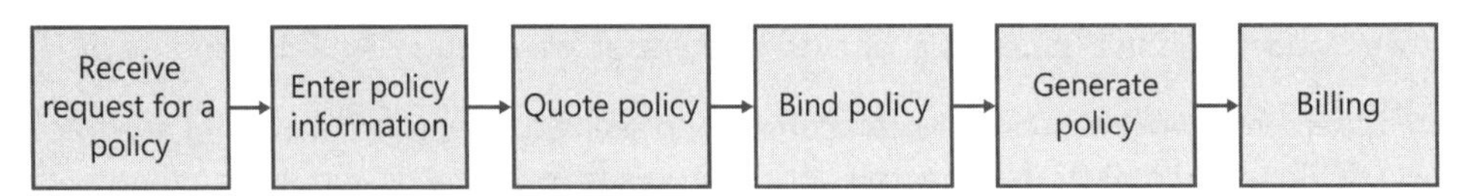

FIGURE 7-3 An example L1 Process Flow.

There are L2 Process Flows for each of the L1 process steps. One example of an L2 Process Flow for the "Enter policy information" step is to create the new policy request from an existing submission. Part of the L2 Process Flow is shown in Figure 7-4.

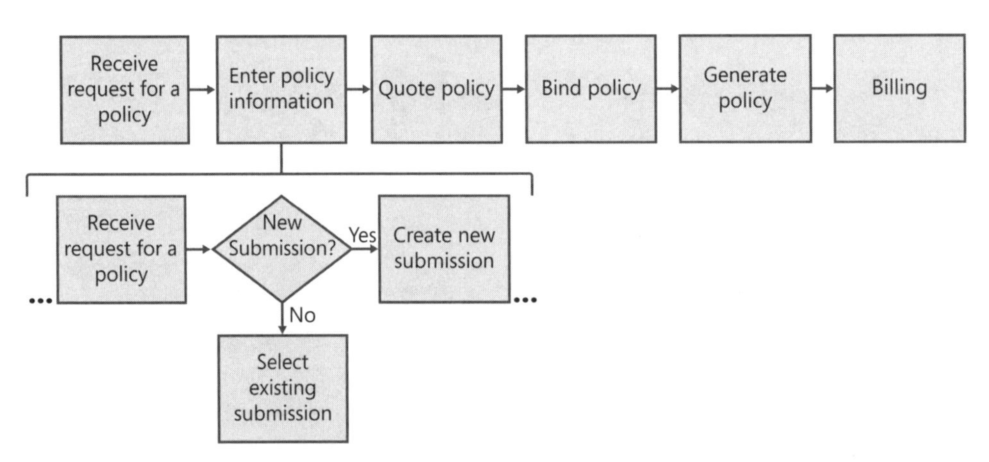

FIGURE 7-4 An example L2 Process Flow.

Finally, there is an L3 Process Flow for the "Select existing submission" L2 step that describes the process to search for and select an existing submission. Part of that L3 Process Flow is shown in Figure 7-5.

The requirements are mapped against the L3 Process Flow steps in the RMM. A small section of the RMM with these requirements is shown in Figure 7-6.

Further, because there are many business rules in this project, they are kept in a separate matrix and are mapped to the requirements in that matrix, as shown in Figure 7-7.

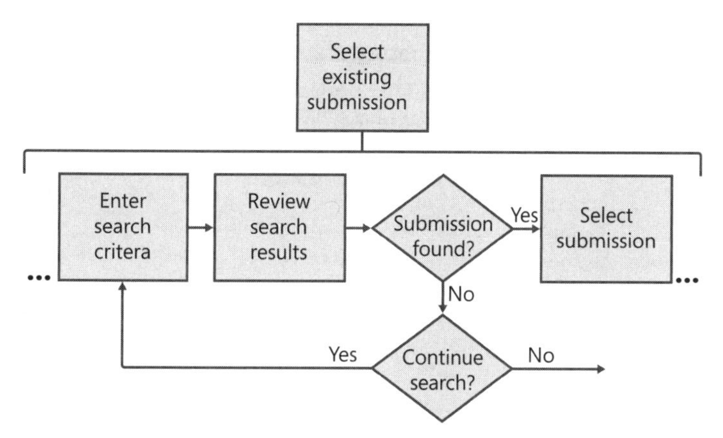

FIGURE 7-5 An example L3 Process Flow.

L1 Process Step	L2 Process Step	L3 Process Step	Feature	REQID	Requirement
Enter policy information	Select existing submission	Enter search criteria	Search	REQ001	Allow user to search for existing submissions
Enter policy information	Select existing submission	Review search results	Search	REQ002	Allow user to sort by one column
Enter policy information	Select existing submission	Review search results	Search	REQ003	Allow user to sort by multiple columns
Enter policy information	Select existing submission	Review search results	Search	REQ004	Allow user to sort ascending or descending for one or more columns
Enter policy information	Select existing submission	Review search results	Search	REQ005	Allow user to further filter out search results using initial criteria options

FIGURE 7-6 An example RMM.

REQ ID	Requirement	Business Rule ID	Business Rule
REQ001	Allow user to search for existing submissions	BR_001	The exact capitalization or lack thereof used in spelling any and all search terms by the user will be ignored for the purpose of finding a match in the system.
REQ001	Allow user to search for existing submissions	BR_002	The user can enter search terms using any combination of uppercase and lowercase characters.
REQ002	Allow user to sort by one column	BR_003	Sort submission by priority, status, submission number, submission date, Primary Name Insured, Broker Name, Primary State, and Product
REQ003	Allow user to sort by multiple columns	BR_004	Sorting by multiple columns can be in any order that the user specifies for the columns selected
REQ004	Allow user to sort ascending or descending for one or more columns	BR_005	Sorting will first be ascending (a-z, 1-10), except for date which will be descending
REQ004	Allow user to sort ascending or descending for one or more columns	BR_006	Default search results to be ordered by creation date in descending order as the first ordered column

FIGURE 7-7 An example matrix of business rules mapped to requirements.

Creating RMMs

It is important to remember that RMMs are not restricted to mapping Process Flows and requirements. RMMs are often useful to map other models such as State Tables, State Diagrams, and Business Data Diagrams to derive missing requirements. The process to create RMMs is described in the context of mapping requirements to Process Flow steps, but the steps are the same for other models. The steps in the process are summarized in Figure 7-8.

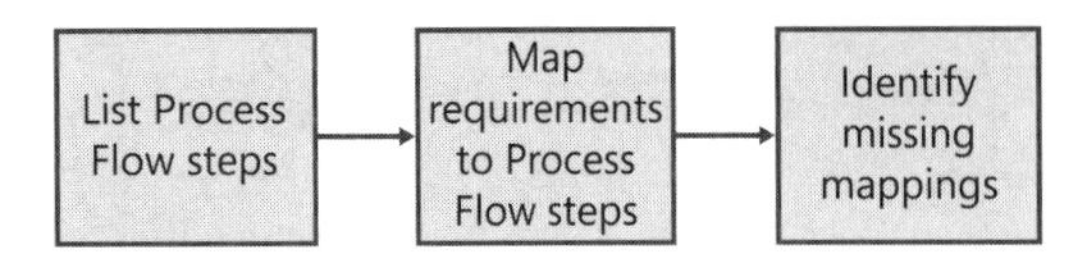

FIGURE 7-8 Process to create RMMs.

List Process Flow Steps

One assumption about creating RMMs is that the objects you are mapping are reasonably complete because it is time consuming to edit the matrix row by row when there are many changes after the RMM is initially created. For example, if you are mapping requirements to Process Flow steps, then the Process Flows should be complete, ideally including completed business reviews.

First, list the L1 Process Flow steps in the first column of the RMM. Next, for each L1 Process Flow step, list the L2 Process Flow steps that map back to the L1 step in the second column. Copy the name of the L1 Process Flow step for each of the rows that has an L2 step. Do the same thing for L3 Process Flow steps. Figure 7-9 depicts how this is done for the example in the previous section. Notice that Process Flow decision boxes are treated the same as Process Flow steps. There are multiple rows with the same L3 Process Flow step in this figure because there are multiple requirements for those steps. You might decide to duplicate the rows now if you know that, or you can do it in the next step when you map requirements to the Process Flow steps.

L1 Process Step	L2 Process Step	L3 Process Step
Enter policy information	Select existing submission	Enter search criteria
Enter policy information	Select existing submission	Review search results
Enter policy information	Select existing submission	Review search results
Enter policy information	Select existing submission	Review search results
Enter policy information	Select existing submission	Review search results

FIGURE 7-9 Listing L1, L2, and L3 steps in an RMM.

Also, if there is additional metadata that needs to be captured for the Process Flows, create an additional column for each piece of information and capture that data at the same time. For example, there might be a business area or categorization that is useful for filtering the matrix later.

Map Requirements to Process Flow Steps

The next step is to organize all of the requirements. List each requirement next to the Process Flow step it supports. If you are using this matrix to elicit requirements, just go through every step to identify the requirements and write them next to the appropriate steps as they are identified. If you are also going to map business rules to requirements, then repeat this step for those as well.

Many-to-Many Mappings

When a Process Flow step maps to more than one requirement, as is often the case, the Process Flow step is repeated and is entered in multiple rows in the matrix—a duplicate row for each requirement to which it maps.

A requirement can also map to multiple process steps (or a business rule to multiple requirements), though in practice this is not very common. However, when this is a valid scenario, it is challenging to model if you are using a spreadsheet such as Excel, because it requires the repetition of requirements. Similarly, most requirements management tools do not support a multi-parent hierarchy. In these instances, there will be multiple rows with the same requirement, each with a different Process Flow step.

Different Ways to Map Business Rules

The best solution for mapping business rules to requirements is to keep the business rules in a separate matrix and map the business rules to the appropriate requirement, as shown in Figure 7-10. One problem with this method is that it is difficult to quickly see which business rules apply to a particular step in a Process Flow because those are in the RMM.

REQ ID	Requirement	Business Rule ID	Business Rule
REQ001	Allow user to search for existing submissions	BR_001	The exact capitalization or lack thereof used in spelling any and all search terms by the user will be ignored for the purpose of finding a match in the system.
REQ001	Allow user to search for existing submissions	BR_002	The user can enter search terms using any combination of uppercase and lowercase characters.
REQ002	Allow user to sort by one column	BR_003	Sort submission by priority, status, submission number, submission date, Primary Name Insured, Broker Name, Primary State, and Product
REQ003	Allow user to sort by multiple columns	BR_004	Sorting by multiple columns can be in any order that the user specifies for the columns selected
REQ004	Allow user to sort ascending or descending for one or more columns	BR_005	Sorting will first be ascending (a-z, 1-10), except for date which will be descending
REQ004	Allow user to sort ascending or descending for one or more columns	BR_006	Default search results to be ordered by creation date in descending order as the first ordered column

FIGURE 7-10 An example of mapping requirements to business rules in a separate matrix.

Another option is to put all of the business rules in one cell with identifiers before each one, such as BR1, BR2, and BR3, as shown in Figure 7-11. The difficulty with this method is that the business rules don't exist as individual elements, which makes it impossible to sort or query on the business rule.

As mentioned previously, if you have a lot of business rules per requirement or need to manipulate the matrix based on the business rules, you will need to put each business rule in its own row. In this case, you duplicate the requirements in each row when multiple business rules map to a particular requirement, as shown in Figure 7-12. This actually can work quite well when you need to view the business rules tightly linked to the requirements in the context of the Process Flow Steps, instead of in a separate matrix.

Finally, if there are only a few business rules that map to each requirement, it is easier to create multiple columns to map them in the same row, as shown in Figure 7-13. This allows all business rules to be seen right next to their parent requirements.

L1 Process Step	L2 Process Step	L3 Process Step	Feature	REQID	Requirement	Business Rule
Enter policy information	Select existing submission	Enter search criteria	Search	REQ001	Allow user to search for existing submissions	BR1: The exact capitalization or lack thereof used in spelling any and all search terms by the user will be ignored for the purpose of finding a match in the system. BR2: The user can enter search terms using any combination of uppercase and lowercase characters.
Enter policy information	Select existing submission	Review search results	Search	REQ002	Allow user to sort by one column	BR1: Sort submission by priority, status, submission number, submission date, Primary Name Insured, Broker Name, Primary State, and Product
Enter policy information	Select existing submission	Review search results	Search	REQ003	Allow user to sort by multiple columns	BR1: Sorting by multiple columns can be in any order that the user specifes for the columns selected
Enter policy information	Select existing submission	Review search results	Search	REQ004	Allow user to sort ascending or descending for one or more columns	BR1: Sorting will first be ascending (a-z, 1-10), except for date which will be descending BR2: Default search results to be ordered by creation date in descending order as the first ordered column

FIGURE 7-11 An example RMM with business rules in one cell in the same row as the requirement.

L1 Process Step	L2 Process Step	L3 Process Step	Feature	REQID	Requirement	Business Rule
Enter policy information	Select existing submission	Enter search criteria	Search	REQ001	Allow user to search for existing submissions	The exact capitalization or lack thereof used in spelling any and all search terms by the user will be ignored for the purpose of finding a match in the system.
Enter policy information	Select existing submission	Enter search criteria	Search	REQ001	Allow user to search for existing submissions	The user can enter search terms using any combination of uppercase and lowercase characters.
Enter policy information	Select existing submission	Review search results	Search	REQ002	Allow user to sort by one column	Sort submission by priority, status, submission number, submission date, Primary Name Insured, Broker Name, Primary State, and Product
Enter policy information	Select existing submission	Review search results	Search	REQ002	Allow user to sort by multiple columns	Sorting by multiple columns can be in any order that the user specifes for the columns selected
Enter policy information	Select existing submission	Review search results	Search	REQ003	Allow user to sort ascending or descending for one or more columns	Sorting will first be ascending (a-z, 1-10), except for date which will be descending
Enter policy information	Select existing submission	Review search results	Search	REQ004	Allow user to sort ascending or descending for one or more columns	Default search results to be ordered by creation date in descending order as the first ordered column

FIGURE 7-12 An example RMM with business rules in multiple rows, duplicating the mapped requirement.

L1 Process Step	L2 Process Step	L3 Process Step	Feature	REQID	Requirement	Business Rule 1	Business Rule 2
Enter policy information	Select existing submission	Enter search criteria	Search	REQ001	Allow user to search for existing submissions	The exact capitalization or lack thereof used in spelling any and all search terms by the user will be ignored for the purpose of finding a match in the system.	The user can enter search terms using any combination of uppercase and lowercase characters.
Enter policy information	Select existing submission	Review search results	Search	REQ002	Allow user to sort by one column	Sort submission by priority, status, submission number, submission date, Primary Name Insured, Broker Name, Primary State, and Product	
Enter policy information	Select existing submission	Review search results	Search	REQ003	Allow user to sort by multiple columns	Sorting by multiple columns can be in any order that the user specifes for the columns selected	
Enter policy information	Select existing submission	Review search results	Search	REQ004	Allow user to sort ascending or descending for one or more columns	Sorting will first be ascending (a-z, 1-10), except for date which will be descending	Default search results to be ordered by creation date in descending order as the first ordered column

FIGURE 7-13 An example RMM with business rules in multiple columns in the same row as the requirement.

Using a Tool to Create Mappings

If you are using a requirements management tool, the same creation steps described in this section apply conceptually, but the implementation is different. The first step is to populate the tool with all of the Process Flow steps. Then populate the tool with all of the requirements and business rules. Finally, create the mappings, typically via a linking feature. Every tool is different in the method it uses to generate the RMM; some might require you to explicitly go to a requirement to create a mapping, whereas others might require you to go to a specific mapping screen to create the mappings. Some requirements management tools actually enforce a system of mappings as defined by the requirements architecture.

Identify Missing Mappings

Review the full matrix to identify any missing mappings. If a requirement does not have a corresponding process step, then it should be flagged to determine whether it is out of scope or whether there is a missing process step. If a process step is missing requirements, then it should be flagged to determine whether there actually are requirements needed to support that process step.

Using RMMs

RMMs can naturally follow the way you think about building solutions from beginning to end. For example, you start with a business objective, create a Process Flow that further defines the business objective, derive requirements from the Process Flow, write business rules, and then write code and test cases to implement and test the requirements and business rules. This is oversimplifying the software life cycle; however, the point is that there is a hierarchical relationship in the artifacts you create, and you can map that hierarchy in RMMs with each level being represented by a column in the matrix, as shown in Figure 7-14.

Business Objective	L3 Process Step	Requirement	Business Rule	Code	Test
Reduce policy production time to 1 day	Enter search criteria	Allow user to search for existing submissions	The user can enter search terms using any combination of uppercase and lowercase characters.	search.existing()	search.1 search.2 search.3
Reduce policy production time to 1 day	Enter search criteria	Allow user to search for existing submissions	The exact capitalization or lack thereof used in spelling any and all search terms by the user will be ignored for the purpose of finding a match in the system.	search.existing()	search.4
Reduce policy production time to 1 day	Review search results	Allow user to sort by one column	Sort submission by priority, status, submission number, submission date, Primary Name Insured, Broker Name, Primary State, and Product	search.sort()	search.5 search.6
Reduce policy production time to 1 day	Review search results	Allow user to sort by multiple columns	Sorting by multiple columns can be in any order that the user specifes for the columns selected	search.sort()	search.7
Reduce policy production time to 1 day	Review search results	Allow user to sort ascending or descending for one or more columns	Sorting will first be ascending (a-z, 1-10), except for date which will be descending	search.sort()	search.8 search.9 search.10
Reduce policy production time to 1 day	Review search results	Allow user to sort ascending or descending for one or more columns	Default search results to be ordered by creation date in descending order as the first ordered column	search.sort()	search.11 search.12

FIGURE 7-14 An example RMM with code and tests mapped to requirements.

RMMs are used to perform several validation and verification checks on requirements. *Validation* is the act of checking requirements to ensure that they are needed to fulfill the business objectives of the project. *Verification* is the act of checking requirements to ensure that they will result in a functional solution.

Reviewing in an Easy-to-Read Structure

When requirements and business rules are organized by Process Flow step, business stakeholders have a much easier time reviewing the requirements. They can look at a corresponding Process Flow diagram for visual context of the full flow, then flip to the RMM to analyze the requirements and business rules that are necessary for each step in that Process Flow. A large volume of requirements can be reviewed relatively quickly in context. The RMM is one of the single most powerful review tools.

Identifying Missing Requirements

Mapping Process Flow steps to requirements is a forward mapping and is used to perform verification in RMMs. Each Process Flow step in the RMM without a requirement is a step that might not have sufficient detail to be properly implemented in the solution, as shown in Figure 7-15. This means that there are additional requirements that need to be created in order for the Process Flow to function properly.

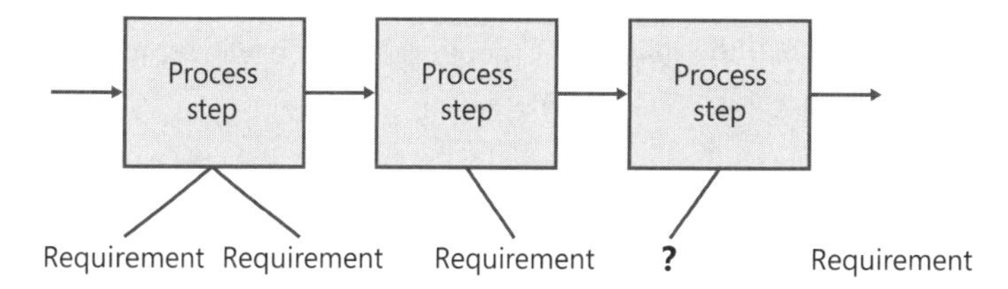

FIGURE 7-15 A missing requirement.

Keep in mind that there are valid scenarios in which there are no requirements for a particular step. For example, if there is a user process step or a decision that a user has to make in the Process Flow, then there might not be any requirements to support that step.

Identifying Extraneous Requirements or Missing Steps

Mapping a requirement to a Process Flow step is backward mapping and is used to perform validation in RMMs. Each requirement in the RMM without a Process Flow step might indicate scope creep or potentially missing process steps, as shown in Figure 7-16. Requirements that are not mapped to any step do not need to be implemented.

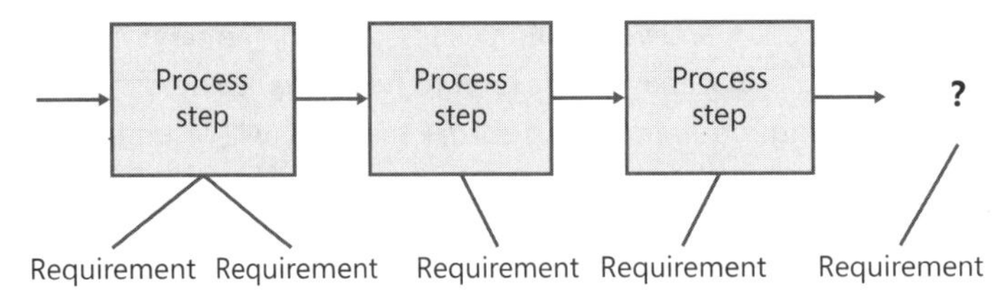

FIGURE 7-16 Identifying an unnecessary requirement.

Because unneeded requirements can be introduced anytime during the life cycle of a project, you should keep the RMM updated to ensure that new requirements are always mapped and tested against Process Flows and business objectives.

Backward mapping is also used for impact analysis, because it will show the ramifications of failing to implement a specific requirement. That analysis is especially useful when there are technology constraints involved in a project that can create disproportionate costs for certain requirements.

Prioritizing Scope

An RMM lends itself to rapid production and is better suited than an Objective Chain to mapping high volumes of information. When RMMs are used together with KPIMs or Objective Chains, you can use them to cut specific steps or entire Process Flows from scope. The RMM helps determine what additional requirements will not need to be implemented. When this is done, we have experienced that projects can easily end up with half the number of requirements as originally intended, while still netting 80 percent of the original return on investment.

Advantages of Using a Requirements Management Tool

A requirements management tool can automate several of these tasks. Many tools will automatically check for missing mappings between two types of objects as defined by the requirements architecture. Some will go even further and review the existing links to ensure that they are not circular. Requirements management tools also often show the RMM from the top-level object all the way down to the lowest-level object in a tree view. This is much harder to do manually in tools such as Excel or Word. The tree view provides an excellent setting for performing impact analysis, because all of the ramifications of a single change can be viewed in one place.

Deriving Requirements

Much like they are used to identify missing requirements, RMMs can be used to derive new requirements. In fact, you can list the Process Flow steps and draft your initial requirements right in the matrix, working through the Process Flow step by step.

When to Use

You should use RMMs on most projects to help manage scope. They are particularly useful when you have a project like converting existing system functionality, in which scope creep is common.

When Not to Use

You might not use an RMM when there are not obvious models or model elements to map to one another. However, in most cases, you should at least map back requirements to business objectives or KPIs by using this model. If you are creating a traceability matrix to map many-to-many relationships, you probably do not also need an RMM for those objects.

Common Mistakes

The following represent the most common mistakes that we have seen with RMMs.

Not Mapping to Process Flows

Teams often create long lists of requirements in a spreadsheet, and then only organize them by feature areas. This is a weak method of mapping requirements because it is very difficult to ensure completeness in a feature list. The reason it is so difficult is because there is no simple heuristic to use a single requirement to identify other requirements. Instead, use Process Flow steps to organize the requirements, because a Process Flow is a very good model to ensure completeness. This is because, for each step in the Process Flow, stakeholders have to remember only what comes before and what comes next. Moreover, using a Process Flow to structure a review session around the requirements associated with each process step keeps stakeholders interested and engaged.

Not Using or Updating RMMs

Teams often create RMMs and never use them or update them again because they are too busy. In these scenarios, they typically create them because a methodology says they have to, but they do not prioritize using them beyond that because they do not see value in using them.

Related Models

RMMs are similar to traceability matrices. The major way in which they differ from traceability matrices is that a traceability matrix attempts to diagram the relationship of every instance of exactly two object types, whereas an RMM maps multiple object types.

The following list briefly describes the most important models that influence or are enhanced by RMMs. Chapter 26, "Using Models Together," contains a more thorough discussion about all related models.

Although most models can be used in an RMM, the most common one is a Process Flow.

- **Process Flows** These are the models that requirements are mapped to most commonly.
- **KPIMs and Objective Chains** These can be used in conjunction with RMMs to cut scope.

Exercise

The following exercise is intended to help you to gain a better understanding of how to use this model. The exercise is open ended, and therefore the answer you come up with could be substantially different than the answer that we have provided. There are potentially many correct solutions. The answer provides an explanation of how we arrived at our solution. You will gain the most out of the exercise by attempting to do it yourself before looking at the solution. The answers for the exercises can be found in Appendix C.

Instructions

Use the provided Process Flows (Figures 7-17, 7-18, and 7-19) and requirements (Figure 7-20) to create an RMM to map the steps to the requirements. You can also add additional requirements and business rules to the RMM based on the data in the scenario.

Scenario

You are on a project to launch a new flamingo eStore that will allow your customers to browse and purchase decorative flamingos and other lawn accessories online. Whenever the stock of a product goes below 20 (at which point it becomes known as an "under-stock item"), the eStore will flag the item. At the end of each day (5:00 P.M. Flamingo Standard Time), a report is run and a list of under-stock items is sent to a supply chain analyst. The supply chain analyst determines whether or not these under-stock items should be re-ordered from the Adventure Works vendor. When the supply chain analyst has placed a minimum order of 20 for any specific product, the eStore will pull the associated order data into the catalog and update the catalog inventory with the number of flamingos available. This last step will remove the flag on the item.

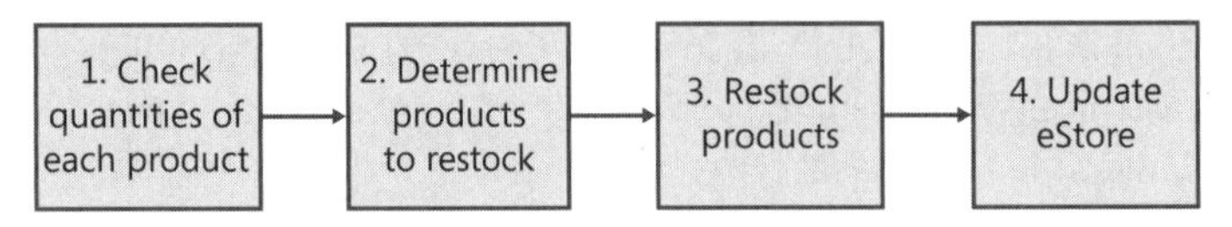

FIGURE 7-17 L1 Process Flow for "Managing product inventory."

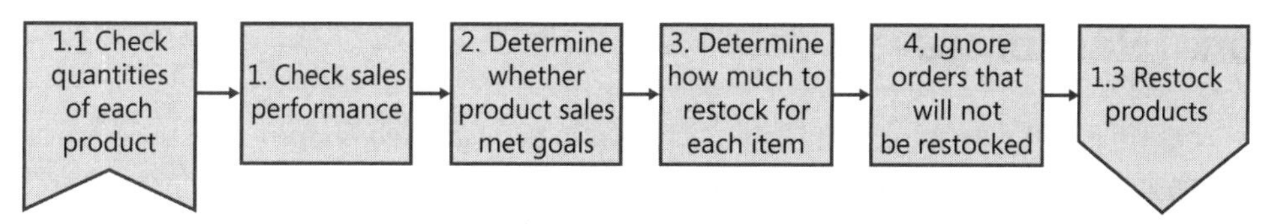

FIGURE 7-18 L2 Process Flow for "Determine products to restock."

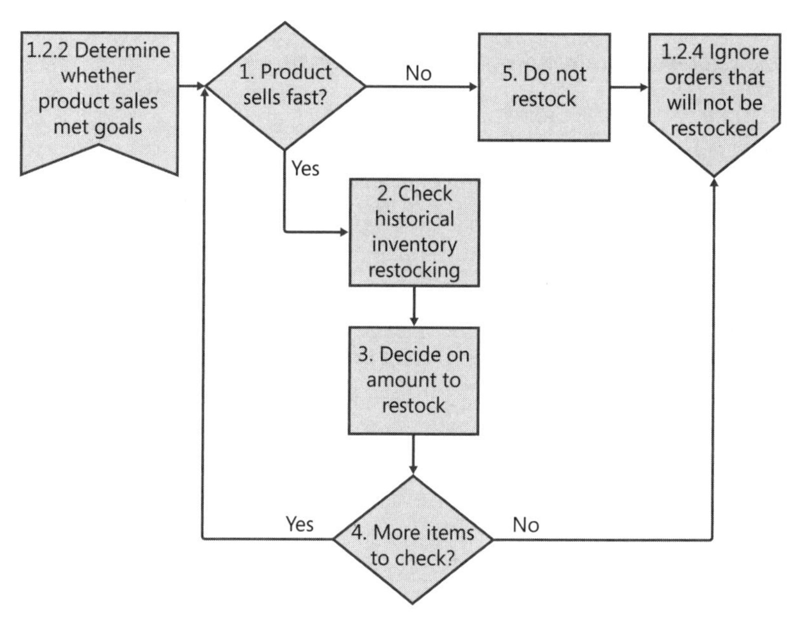

FIGURE 7-19 L3 Process Flow for "Determine how much to restock for each item."

REQID	Requirement
REQ001	Automatically compare historical sales rate against a predefined threshold
REQ002	Sales rate thresholds can be based on margin, units, or revenue
REQ003	Sales rate thresholds can be compared over an arbitrary period
REQ004	System automatically restocks items below a threshold
REQ005	System requests manual restocking when calculated automated restock exceeds the threshold
REQ006	System shall be able to automatically determine which items need to be examined for restocking

FIGURE 7-20 Requirements for the exercise.

Additional Resources

- The "Links in the Requirements Chain," chapter in *Software Requirements* describes trace relationships in detail, including the types of things you might trace, the types of traces, and the reasons for tracing (Wiegers 2003).
- The following URL provides a training video on traceability matrices: *http://requirements.seilevel.com/blog/2011/06 /a-traceability-matrix-in-software-requirements-gathering.html*
- Is Traceability Possible Without a Requirements Tool?: *http://requirements.seilevel.com/blog/2010/12 /is-traceability-possible-without-a-requirements-tool.html*

References

- Wiegers, Karl E. 2003. *Software Requirements, Second Edition*. Redmond, WA: Microsoft Press.

PART III

People Models

CHAPTER 8

Org Chart

In high school, I was in a marching band of 200 students, divided into 11 sections, each with a section leader. There were three drum majors who each oversaw the organization of three or four sections of band, and our director was ultimately responsible for the whole band.

We practiced four days a week to learn and perfect our performance. Once a week, the drum majors gave the section leaders music and marching skills to work on with the people in their individual sections. After a few hours of sectional practices, the band would get back together and practice again as a full unit.

For competitions, coordinating 200 high school students required significant planning and organization. The director relied on the drum majors, who relied on the section leaders to ensure that everyone was where they were supposed to be on time. Each section leader was responsible for going through a checklist of the people in his or her section after the students loaded onto the buses to leave for the show. The drum majors went through their checklist of sections to make sure that no full sections of the band were missing. And the three drum majors reported back to the director when everyone was present, or with a specific list of individuals who were missing and an action plan around those individuals. They repeated this process when they were at the competition site and were ready to perform. They also used the checklists again when it was time to depart from the competition site for home.

There is no possible way the band director could have organized his practices or competition trips without a full list of the people in the band. And he made it much more manageable by dividing the band across drum majors and into sections. In essence, he was using an Org Chart to run his marching band.

The Org Chart, short for the more formal name Organization Chart, is an RML people model that shows the structure within which the people or roles in an organization work. It is used to identify all users and *stakeholders* who might be using or have input to the solution. When used properly, Org Charts help ensure that you identify all stakeholders.

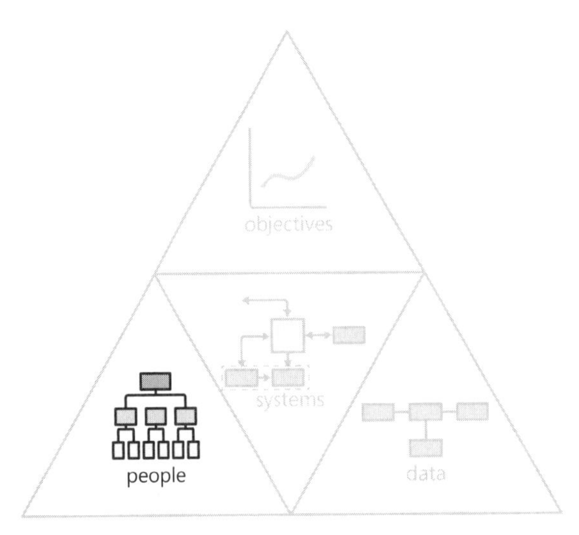

Org Charts are used by many organizations, so most people are probably already familiar with them. Many people might not think that an Org Chart could be used as a requirements model. However, for many types of projects, it should be one of the first models you use on your project. (See Chapter 25, "Selecting Models for a Project"). The most significant value provided by Org Charts is in helping to ensure that you talk to any groups of people who can have influence over the requirements.

There are three levels of Org Charts that can be helpful on a project: departmental, role, and individual. Departmental Org Charts show only the hierarchical relationship of group entities, such as departments, of an organization. Role Org Charts show the hierarchical relationship of the roles within the department. Individual Org Charts show the hierarchical relationship of the actual people in the department. For example, a role could be "Financial Analyst" with four people who have that role. All four would show up as individual boxes in the individual Org Chart. In progressing from departmental to role to individual, it is also likely that only parts of the prior level's Org Chart will need to be represented in the lower level. For example, a departmental Org Chart might show the entire company, whereas the role Org Chart might show the roles for only the relevant departments. Typically, it is important to start with a departmental Org Chart and possibly do a role Org Chart. The individual Org Chart, with names, is less important than an Org Chart that identifies the correct groups of people, because determining whether a group of stakeholders is missing is much easier from these higher-level Org Charts.

Org Chart Template

An Org Chart is a collection of boxes connected by lines with a hierarchical structure. Each box contains the name of an organizational department, role, or individual person, and the lines between the boxes show the hierarchical reporting relationships within the organization, as shown in Figure 8-1. Typically, each box in an Org Chart contains the same level of information. For example, if the Org Chart includes individuals' names and titles, then each box will include one person's name and one title, and none of the boxes will include a department or role name. Higher levels in the structure are placed at the top of the chart, with subordinate levels in the hierarchy placed below.

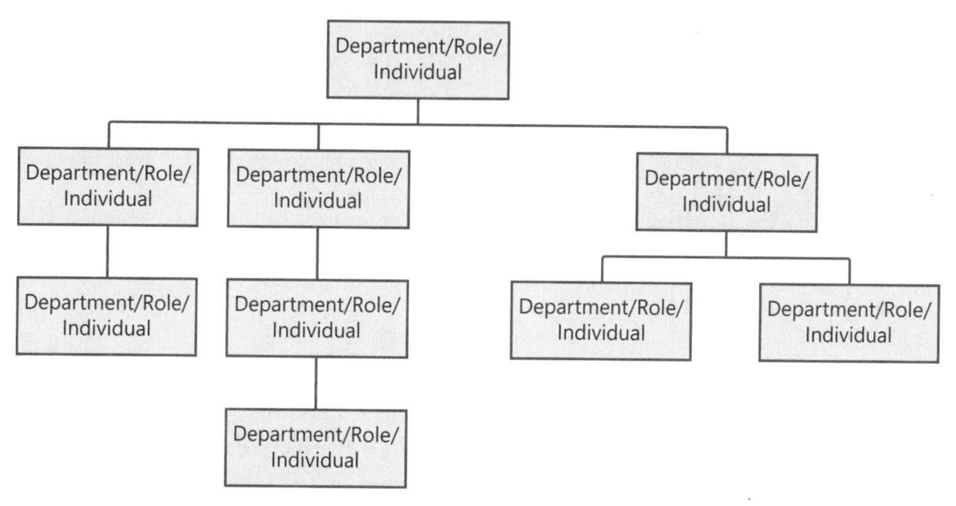

FIGURE 8-1 The Org Chart template.

You can use color to accentuate Org Charts in order to provide additional information. Color can be used to distinguish between different groups of people who have specific types of influence on the project. For example, one color could represent IT stakeholders, whereas another might represent finance stakeholders, and yet another could represent marketing stakeholders. If you use color, it is important to include a legend to explain the colors in order to make the color coding meaningful to the reader of the Org Chart. It's also recommended that you use a visual variance such as different shades, patterns, or borders for any readers who cannot see colors or for when the chart is printed in black and white. Avoid using dark colors if you plan to print in black and white; dark colors and shading tend to obscure the text within a box. Figure 8-2 shows the template with both colors and patterned borders on the boxes, although the print copy of this book will only show the patterns and shading differences.

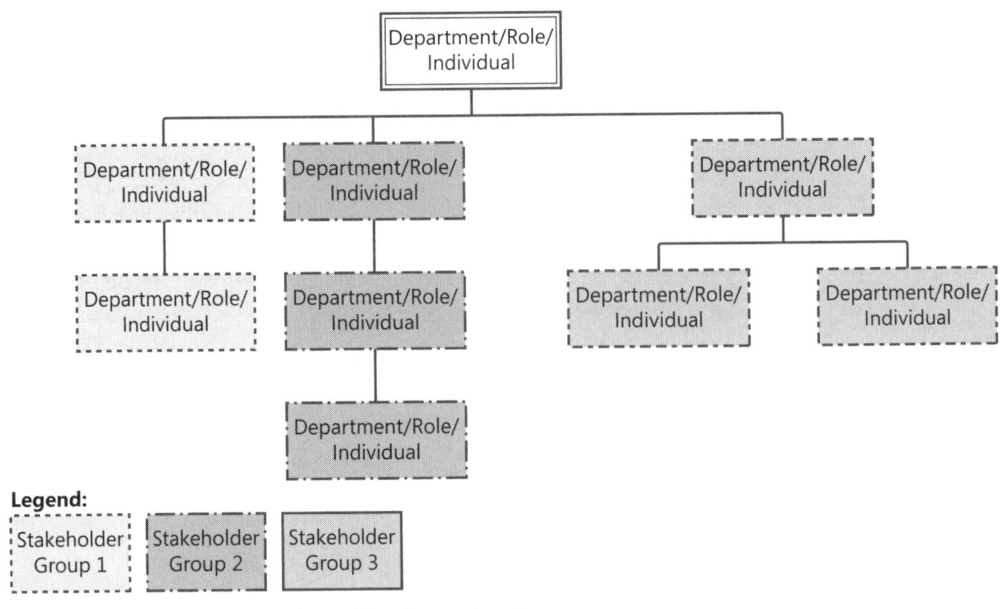

FIGURE 8-2 An Org Chart template with colors and patterns.

Tool Tip Typically, an Org Chart is created as a project artifact in Microsoft Visio, Microsoft PowerPoint, or a modeling tool. Org Charts can be sketched on paper, whiteboards, or with sticky notes, drawing lines between the boxes. However, if you start with a temporary version, such as on a piece of paper, it is important to eventually put it in a tool so that it can be easily maintained and referenced throughout the project.

Example

Figure 8-3 shows a departmental Org Chart for an automobile manufacturing organization. This Org Chart might be applicable to a project to build an online auto sales purchase system. By reviewing an Org Chart at this level of detail, the team can determine whether they need to elicit or review requirements with each of the different departments. In this example, the business analyst team determines it is likely that all of Sales and IT Systems will be engaged in the project, as well as the Product Marketing and Graphic Design departments (within Marketing) and the Supply Chain department (within Manufacturing). They believe that the Design department (within Manufacturing), Operations, Outbound Communications (within Marketing), Research, and Finance departments will not be included, but they will leave them on the departmental Org Chart without any details under them, just to be sure.

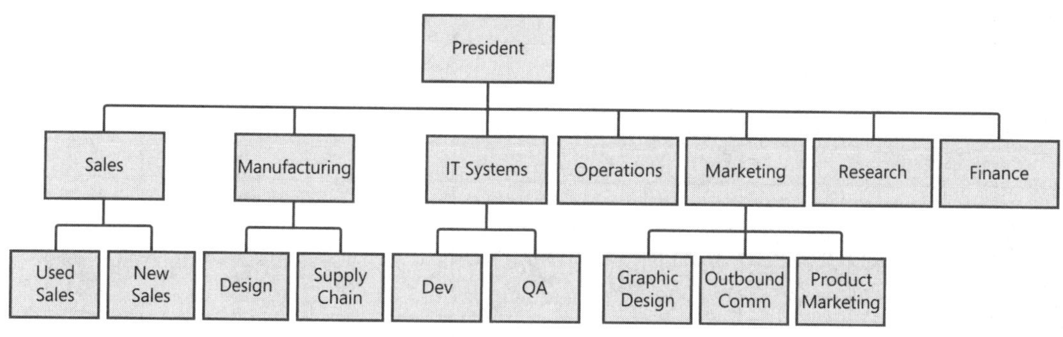

FIGURE 8-3 An example departmental Org Chart.

Because this Org Chart includes only department names, additional information is required in order to identify specific stakeholders within each department. It is possible that the business analysts can interview managers in each department to identify the contacts for the project. Alternatively, and particularly if the departments are large, the requirements team should complete a role Org Chart for the relevant bottom-level boxes, capturing the roles within each department. Notice in Figure 8-4 that the roles were defined for only the parts of the organization that the team deemed relevant, not the entire company. In fact, after they determined that used cars would not be sold online, they cut the Used Sales section of the Org Chart.

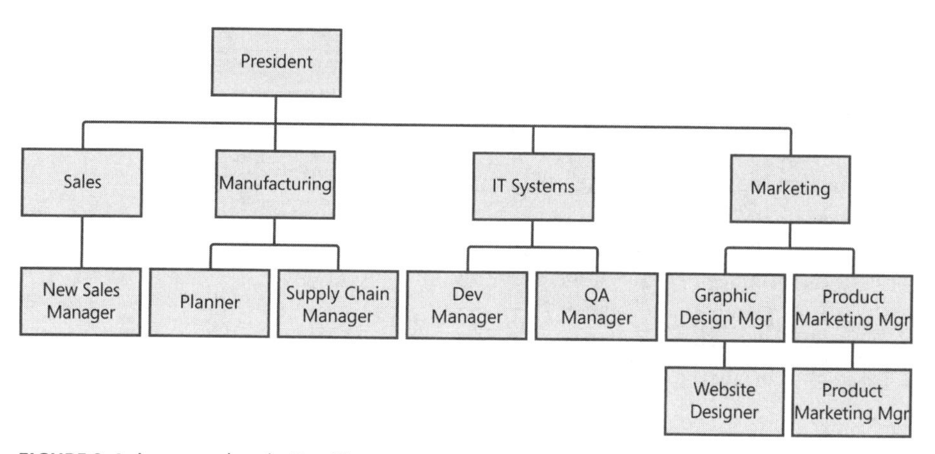

FIGURE 8-4 An example role Org Chart.

It can also be helpful to take this one level deeper and define an individual Org Chart, to capture actual peoples' names. An example individual Org Chart is shown in Figure 8-5.

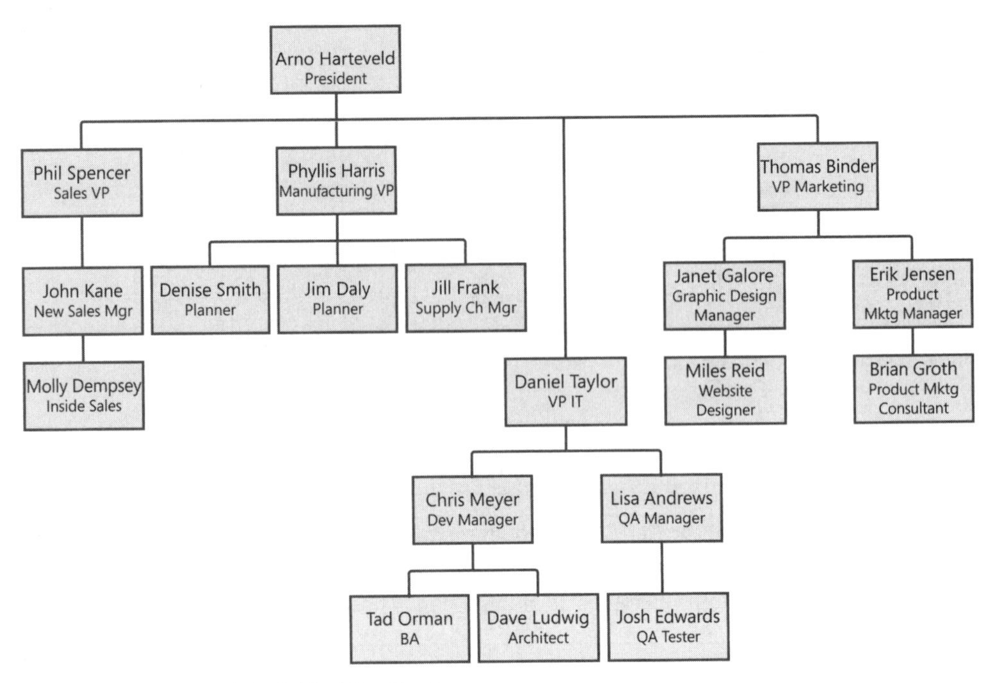

FIGURE 8-5 An example individual Org Chart.

Creating Org Charts

The typical process to create Org Charts is shown in Figure 8-6.

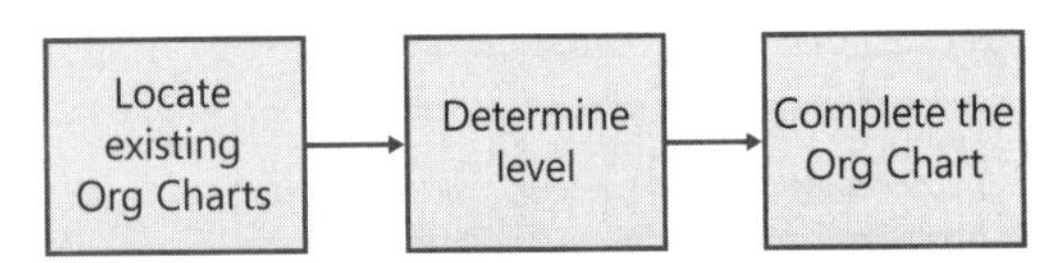

FIGURE 8-6 The process for creating Org Charts.

Locate Existing Org Charts

In many cases, organizations already have Org Charts for the entire organization, in which case, creating the Org Chart is simplified. Even if an existing Org Chart is out of date or incomplete, it can provide a good starting point for creating a project-specific Org Chart. Additionally, it might be possible to derive an Org Chart from an email system or online directory. If the organization has configured its email system to define who reports to whom, the organizational hierarchy can be teased out of those reporting relationships. However, some organizations do not have Org Charts, in which case you will have to create one yourself.

Determine the Right Level of Org Chart

In cases where an Org Chart does not exist or needs to be supplemented, the first decision to make is the level at which to start. The Org Chart must capture all of the parts of the organization that have users of the solution, managers of users, or anyone who makes decisions about the scope. It is almost always useful to start with a departmental Org Chart at a minimum, and then create role and individual Org Charts if needed.

Another important decision to make when creating an Org Chart is what information to include in each box. For departmental Org Charts, you include the department or group names, role Org Charts should add role names, and individual Org Charts should add individual peoples' names. If there are few people per role, you can combine the information from an individual Org Chart into a role Org Chart, listing both the role and individual names in each box. If there are a significant number of people, it can be helpful to use a grouping box to group stakeholders who belong to the same department.

Complete the Org Chart

Completing the Org Chart will require diligently interviewing your way through the Org Chart, asking each manager to provide his or her department makeup (roles and actual direct reports) as well as who each manager thinks his or her peer groups are. As each level of the Org Chart is created, if any boxes are left blank, those should be noted as action items to follow up on and complete. A missing box might represent an entire stakeholder group that should be involved.

You can also use other RML models to ensure your Org Charts are complete. This concept will be discussed later in the chapter.

Departmental Org Charts

Organizations typically have many people within each department. Starting with a departmental Org Chart will simplify your role and individual Org Charts, minimizing the number of boxes you must include. Particularly if you are creating an Org Chart for a large company, you should start with a departmental Org Chart, and build the Org Chart based on groups or departments, rather than individuals or specific roles. We recommend that for a departmental Org Chart you include the entire organization, even if it is large. Start with the uppermost level of the organization, typically a president or CEO. From there, you can trace your way down from the top level to each of the subordinate levels by identifying each person or group who reports to the president or CEO. At the second level, you might not have very many boxes.

After the second level of the departmental organizational hierarchy is documented, you can repeat the process for each second-level box that either is or might be relevant to your project. If you do not know, keep the box in the Org Chart until you feel confident about cutting it. For the example in the previous section, if you determine that the Research department will not affect or be impacted by the project, there is no need to continue to include more depth for this group in the Org Chart. This helps to quickly pare down the Org Chart to the boxes that are useful and to provide detail for and maintain those.

Continue completing the remaining levels in the same manner, until you have all of the relevant departments or groups in the Org Chart.

Role Org Charts

Each group of the departmental Org Chart that is within scope of your project needs to have a role Org Chart that shows the specific roles within the groups. Ideally, the full role Org Chart will still fit in one chart, but if the organization is large and many departments are involved, it will be necessary to create role Org Charts for each department. In these cases, show each department in a separate diagram.

Each organization typically has multiple people within each role, but the role Org Chart really is capturing the groups of people by role name. Keep in mind that the roles might not be formal job descriptions. They might be based on the variations of work each person does. After you prune out roles that are not needed, you can remove them to simplify the Org Chart.

If you don't need to document each individual within a part of the organization, you can stop at a role Org Chart. For example, if you are using the Org Charts to ensure that you are meeting with all of the groups and are finding individuals to represent every group, that is often sufficient.

Individual Org Charts

Finally, you can create an individual Org Chart that shows peoples' names in the reporting hierarchy. This is very helpful to determine exactly whom the team should be interacting with throughout the project.

If you do decide to document each person's name in an individual Org Chart, keep in mind that the Org Chart will be a snapshot of the organization's makeup at the time the chart is completed. As individuals join and leave the organization, the Org Chart must be updated to be accurate. For even short-term projects, changes at the individual level can be important, so keeping an Org Chart up to date can be an equally important task.

Though it might be sufficient to ensure only that you interview several people from each role, you need to be very careful. Often, regional or locational differences in a job are significant enough that two people in the same role in different locations should really be considered to be in different roles. Alternately, people within roles might service different types of customers, data, or systems, requiring you to create additional role names that do not map to job descriptions. Finally, for each role, the managers of the teams involved can identify the specific representatives whom they feel will be the best subject matter experts. They can then authorize them to speak for the entire team.

Using Org Charts

As stated previously, although Org Charts are fairly common, many people would not think to use them for requirements activities, even though they are absolutely critical to identifying stakeholders.

Identifying the People Who Have Requirements

At the very beginning of a project, Org Charts are used to identify who has an interest in the solution and who will be using the solution. This tells you who will have requirements for the solution, and who will be the key people to include in requirements elicitation and review sessions. In addition, an Org Chart can be reviewed to see which people or groups are related to already-identified stakeholders. The visual structure of an Org Chart makes these connections obvious as compared to just a list of stakeholders, which helps to reduce the chances of missing any constituents. For example, if you already knew that you had to meet with Jim the Planner, by looking at who he works with in his department, you can identify that you might also need to meet with Denise the Planner.

After you have an Org Chart for the project, you can look at each block on the chart to decide whether it represents a stakeholder. This will help you to ensure that you identify all stakeholders. At the most basic level, you can review each box in an Org Chart and ask:

- Is this person or role a user of this system?
- Does this group, role, or person have any requirements for the system?
- Is this group, role, or person influenced by something we are doing in the system?
- Which part of the process are they involved with?
- Are there any processes that don't have a group to execute the process?

These questions are important to ask on every box of the Org Chart. It is much better to take the time to do this, rather than assuming that a box has no users, requirements, or interest in the requirements discussions and being wrong.

In one particular organization we worked with, a project was clearly going to affect many parts of the organization, so an Org Chart was the basis for identifying all the possible stakeholder groups. We printed out the entire company's Org Chart on many pieces of paper and plastered the walls with all of the sections, each including 6 to 10 boxes of the full Org Chart. The project sponsor came into the room, and we gave him a marker so that, for each section of the Org Chart, he could easily either put an "X" through any stakeholders who were not relevant to the project, or circle stakeholders so that the team would know who did need to be included in elicitation. If he was unsure, he put a question mark on the section, and that prompted us to talk to those people directly to find out. From that 30-minute effort, we could quickly focus our conversations with each part of the organization and determine whether they indeed were users of the project or had some stakeholder interest in it.

Identifying Internal Users

If the solution is an internal IT system, the Org Chart is useful because almost all of the possible users are somewhere on that Org Chart. Therefore, when the chart is reviewed with diligence, you are virtually guaranteed that all of the possible users of an internal system are identified in an Org Chart, ensuring that no users are missed during analysis.

You will have to use judgment as to how many of the individual users in the Org Chart you actually need to meet with. For example, if there are 3,000 sales representatives, you can assume that you do need to meet with more than one of them but not all 3,000 of them. You can send a survey to 3,000 sales representatives to get some basic information, and then just meet with some fraction of them in person, as long as the sampled population represents the breadth of the organization in terms of geographic location, experience, and training levels. However, you might need to meet with significantly more to have full coverage, especially if you identify groups of sales representatives who use different processes because of their customer base or possibly because of the particular products they sell.

Identifying External Users

If the system will have users external to the organization, there might still be stakeholders on the Org Chart who represent the external user populations internally, and identifying those representatives within the Org Chart will help find their counterparts outside the organization. For example, if you were developing a finance system for customers to check the status of their invoice payments, your Org Chart would include the customer managers who represent those customers. Seeing these internal individuals on the Org Chart will remind you to include them in your elicitation activities, providing you with a link to the system's intended, external users.

An Org Chart might not be useful for portions of the system that only the end customers will use. In these cases, you might need to use other stakeholder analysis techniques, such as persona analysis. A persona is an example of a user that contains the user's background information and motivations for using the system. Personas are not a visual model, because they do not provide a visual mechanism to ensure that you have captured all the information. Their purpose is to help the team imagine who they think will use the system (Cooper 2004).

Also, when you are looking for stakeholders outside your organization, an onion model might help identify them (Alexander 2005). An onion model is a template of circles to show stakeholders and their relationships to each other and the product being developed. An onion model can be used with internal stakeholders to trigger them to think of additional stakeholders.

Identifying People Used in Other Models

The groups or roles identified in departmental and role Org Charts are often the role names for the swim lanes of Process Flows, as discussed in Chapter 9, "Process Flow." Similarly, the roles identified by Org Charts are often the actors used in Use Cases, as discussed in Chapter 10, "Use Case." A word of caution in taking the step from the Org Chart roles to Use Case actors: there might not be a one-to-one mapping of user group to actor, because an actor can often cross various organizational roles, or groups can span multiple actors. Finally, the list of roles in the role Org Chart or people in the individual Org Chart is often useful for deriving the roles dimension of a Roles and Permissions Matrix, as described in Chapter 11, "Roles and Permissions Matrix."

Using Org Charts with Process Flows for Completeness

As fantastic as Org Charts are for identifying stakeholders up front, they can prove to be invaluable mid-project as well. The user performing a Process Flow step is represented in an Org Chart. Therefore, when reviewing the steps of a Process Flow, you should cross-check them against your Org Chart to make sure that the appropriate departments, groups, and roles are in your Org Chart and involved in your reviews. If you are using Org Charts along with swim lanes, this is even more obvious, because the swim lanes likely apply directly to one of the Org Chart levels. To ensure good coverage, at each step of the Process Flow, ask "Who performs this?" and "Am I meeting with them already?" to ensure that you do not miss any groups. Referring to your Org Chart when creating your Process Flow will ensure that you use consistent naming of groups. Using an Org Chart when creating a Requirements Mapping Matrix (described in Chapter 7, "Requirements Mapping Matrix") can help ensure that every step of the Process Flow has specific and identified owners.

For example, the project from earlier in this chapter involves configuration and pricing processes and rules for ordering cars online; naturally, the team created Process Flows. Figure 8-7 is a simple example of one of their Process Flows.

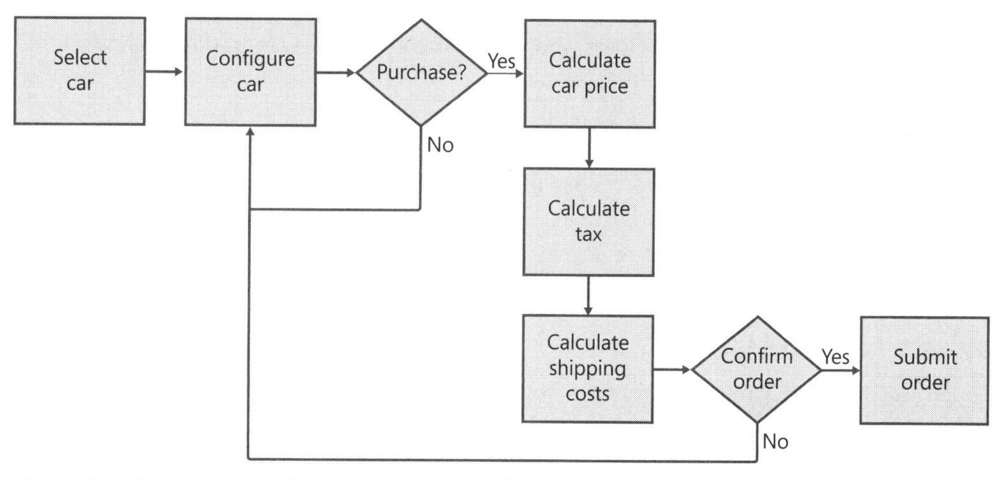

FIGURE 8-7 The Process Flow for purchasing a car online.

Suppose that, a few weeks into the project, stakeholders are reviewing the Process Flows for sign-off. One of the stakeholders notices a step in the Process Flow to "Calculate tax," and says, "I don't know how that works. That's not my department." This prompts the business analyst team to look at the role Org Chart and realize that they need to meet with the stakeholders in the tax department to review the requirements. Figure 8-8 shows the roles Org Chart they use.

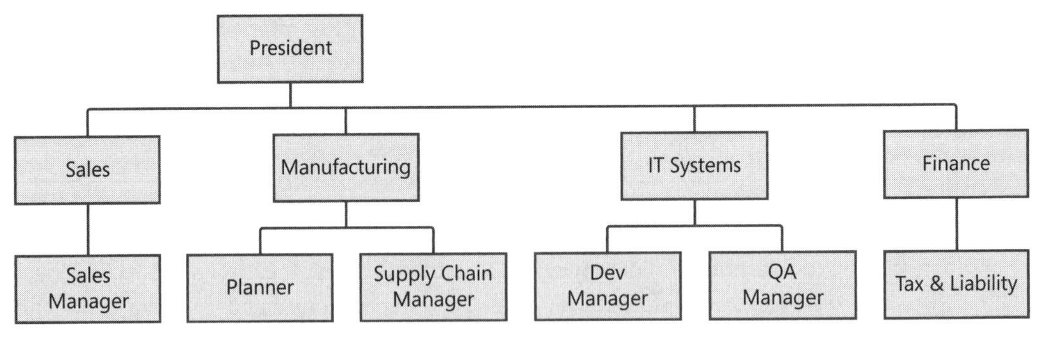

FIGURE 8-8 A roles Org Chart for an auto manufacturing organization.

If they had not caught this stakeholder group from the Org Chart, they would have had a major setback in the schedule. However, by catching the tax stakeholder group when they did, they have time to add tasks for reviews and updates to the requirements into their schedules prior to affecting development.

The concept of cross-checking Process Flows and Org Charts can be applied to other models, such as Ecosystem Maps, to see what groups of users interact with systems, or Business Data Diagrams, to identify the roles that manipulate data in the systems.

Deriving Requirements

Requirements are not usually derived directly from an Org Chart. Instead, Org Charts are used to ensure that you capture all stakeholders whom you need to interview for requirements.

When to Use

Use Org Charts whenever there are internal users that exist in an organizational hierarchy. Those users could exist within your own company, or in your customers' company. You might also be able to use them to identify stakeholders who represent external users.

When Not to Use

For projects that are purely consumer focused, an Org Chart might not be helpful. If your internal stakeholders rarely interact with or do not represent external users, an Org Chart will not be helpful. In those cases, use personas to identify the archetypes of the users that you imagine will use the software, and onion models to help identify external stakeholders.

Common Mistakes

The following represent the most common mistakes that we have seen with Org Charts.

Not Using Org Charts to Identify Stakeholders

Sometimes teams create Org Charts but never use them. They have them as a contact list for team members but do not use them to understand what additional groups of people they need to talk to.

Only Including Project Team Members

Another common mistake occurs when teams only document members of the project team, not stakeholders in the business who will eventually have to approve and use the software or who will benefit from it in some way.

Related Models

Org Charts are often used in organizational modeling, for understanding the organization's roles, relationships, and reporting structures (IIBA 2009). The Org Chart model in RML expands upon this by grouping the hierarchy by departments, roles, and individuals. It also is used specifically in conjunction with other models to ensure completeness in the elicitation process.

Stakeholder analysis is an approach that uses lists of stakeholders to identify and track the stakeholders and information about them. Although stakeholder analysis does not rely on the Org Chart model, the role Org Chart can support this analysis. It can help identify stakeholders for more detailed profiling. Also, as mentioned earlier in the chapter, personas and onion models can be useful in stakeholder analysis.

The following list briefly describes the most important models that influence or are enhanced by Org Charts. Chapter 26, "Using Models Together" contains a more thorough discussion about all related models.

- **Roles and Permissions Matrices** These are created by using an Org Chart to identify stakeholders who have a role with corresponding permissions in the system that is being developed.
- **Process Flows** These are cross-checked against Org Charts to ensure that no stakeholders are missed in the elicitation efforts for a process. Similarly, they can help drive Org Charts to completion by ensuring that roles identified in swim lanes are represented in the Org Chart.
- **Use Cases** These are often identified by using an Org Chart to first identify actors and then to analyze what system interactions those users need.
- **Ecosystem Maps and Business Data Diagrams (BDDs)** These might help identify groups of users to complete Org Charts.
- **Requirements Mapping Matrices** These are useful for mapping users from Org Charts to Process Flow steps, to ensure that all steps have a specific owner.

Exercise

The following exercise is intended to help you to gain a better understanding of how to use this model. The exercise is open ended, and therefore the answer you come up with could be substantially different than the answer that we have provided. There are potentially many correct solutions. The answer provides an explanation of how we arrived at our solution. You will gain the most out of the exercise by attempting to do it yourself before looking at the solution. The answers for the exercises can be found in Appendix B.

Instructions

Create a departmental, role, and individual Org Chart for the scenario.

Scenario

You are on a project to launch a new eStore to sell flamingos and other lawn accessories, and you have to document all of the requirements.

When you start the project, it's clear that there are a lot of stakeholders. In order to keep track of the relationships and identify different sources for requirements, you decide to create Org Charts to represent the people and their reporting relationships to ensure that you don't miss anyone.

Rob Young seems to run the place around here—you've heard many people refer to him as the president. Rob Young has five vice presidents who work under him—Debra Garcia, Dan Park, Robin Wood, Ben Miller, and Linda Timm. Debra is in charge of Consumer Sales, and she oversees the work of two managers—Ryan Danner (who runs the East Territory) and Anna Lidman (who runs the West Territory). Dan oversees Product Management, with Steve Luper managing Inventory and Kern Sutton managing Suppliers under him. Robin Wood has Finance, with April Stewart in charge of Accounting and Kevin Cook managing Payroll. Ben Miller is in charge of IT; however, you do not know how his department is organized. Linda Timm is in charge of Human Resources, but her department will not be engaged on the project.

Additional Resources

- Gottesdiener describes stakeholder analysis, including stakeholder categories, which list the types of people who have an interest in the project by using a customer/user/other classification to help identify them (Gottesdiener 2002 and 2005). She also describes stakeholder profiles, which capture detailed information about stakeholders, including interests, roles, and responsibilities (Gottesdiener 2005).
- Alexander and Beus-Dukic devote all of Chapter 2 to stakeholders in *Discovering Requirements*, including a variety of techniques to identify stakeholders internal and external to your organization (Alexander and Beus-Dukic 2009).

- Onion models are described in the previous resource; however, Alexander provides a detailed explanation of the onion model in the context of stakeholder analysis in his stakeholder taxonomy (Alexander 2005).
- *The Inmates are Running the Asylum* devotes a chapter to what personas are, why they are needed, and different types of personas (Cooper 2004).

References

- Alexander, Ian. 2005. "A Taxonomy of Stakeholders: Human Roles in System Development, "*International Journal of Technology and Human Interaction, http://easyweb.easynet.co.uk/~iany/consultancy/stakeholder_taxonomy/stakeholder_taxonomy.htm.*
- Alexander, Ian, and Ljerka Beus-Dukic. 2009. *Discovering Requirements: How to Specify Products and Services*. West Sussex, England: John Wiley & Sons Ltd.
- Cooper, Alan. 2004. *The Inmates Are Running the Asylum: Why High Tech Products Drive Us Crazy and How To Restore the Sanity.* Indianapolis, IN: Sams.
- Gottesdiener, Ellen. 2002. *Requirements by Collaboration: Workshops for Defining Needs.* Boston, MA: Addison-Wesley.
- Gottesdiener, Ellen. 2005. *The Software Requirements Memory Jogger.* Salem, NH: Goal/QPC.
- International Institute of Business Analysis (IIBA). 2009. *A Guide to the Business Analysis Body of Knowledge (BABOK Guide).* Toronto, Ontario, Canada.

CHAPTER 9

Process Flow

I have decided to prepare a fancy meal for my family at the holidays. I want to prepare my menu ahead of time so I can shop for groceries the day before. I have to make a decision whether to buy beef or fish for the main meal. If I want fish, I need to go to the fish market in addition to the grocery store. If I decide on beef, I can get it at the same store as the rest of the groceries. On the night of the meal, I will set up my formal dining room for dinner, prepare the food ahead of time, serve drinks before we eat, and serve three courses—salad, main meal, and dessert. If we finish earlier than 10 P.M., I will clean up after everyone goes home. Otherwise I will rinse the dishes and leave the rest of the cleaning for the next morning.

I realize I need to do a bit more planning around preparing the food ahead of time because of the complexity of the meal. For example, for the salad, I need to wash the lettuce, chop the vegetables, and mix the salad dressing. For the main meal, I need to put the meat into the oven for three hours and boil the potatoes, mash them, and mix them with cream and butter. I need to steam the green beans and put them in the warming drawer. I will prepare a cake for dessert first because it will also use the oven. As I get further into my planning, I realize that there are a lot of activities for me to perform for this meal, so I decide to break the tasks up into groups and assign them among my family members. The boys will help with setting up the dining room and preparing the meat. My daughter and niece will mix the cake ingredients, but I will help them with the oven. And my mother can help by chopping all of the ingredients for the meal, while I put them together.

In this story, I have outlined my process to get the meal ready for my family. I have a high-level picture of what I need to do, but then I find that I need to define more details for how I'll execute the tasks, because they are complex.

The Process Flow is an RML people model that describes a *business process* that will be executed by people. Process Flows show the activities to be performed, the sequence in which they are performed, and the different decisions that the users make to achieve a desired outcome. Process Flows help you to understand complex information by describing processes graphically so that you can quickly see how steps are related. They also simplify the analysis, allowing you to consider a single step and only the steps to which that single step is related. If a sequence has no decisions, a simple list of steps would be sufficient; however, when a process begins branching, a diagram is extremely helpful. Because Process Flows are visual, they are much better for engaging business stakeholders in reviewing a process than long lists of requirements .

Process Flows should not be confused with System Flows (see Chapter 13, "System Flow"). A Process Flow describes actions that users execute, whereas System Flows describe activities that systems execute.

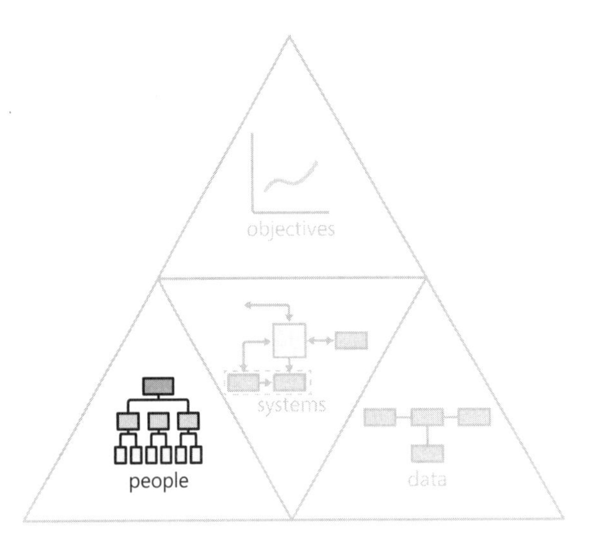

Most projects require the people involved to have a firm grasp of the business process being created, replicated, or improved. Without this understanding, there is little chance that users will adopt the new solution. Process Flows are among the most common and effective models to facilitate this understanding.

Multiple levels of Process Flows are often needed to describe a significant process with a sufficient amount of detail while still keeping each flow to a consumable size. To create multiple levels of a Process Flow, you decompose a process step or set of steps at one level into an entirely new Process Flow at the next level. For most projects, three levels of Process Flows are typically sufficient. These levels are called level 1 (L1), level 2 (L2), and level 3 (L3) Process Flows. L1 Process Flows show the full end-to-end process for your solution. L2 Process Flows show detail for one or several steps in the L1 Process Flow. L3 Process Flows show an additional level of detail for one or several steps in an L2 Process Flow.

When a new project is launched, an L1 Process Flow is typically one of the first models that should be created after an Org Chart (see Chapter 8, "Org Chart"). The Process Flow will provide a high-level overview of the entire process and is an excellent way to understand and communicate the scope of the project. Process Flows are among the easiest models for business and other non-technical users to comprehend, so they are a useful tool for most requirement elicitation and review meetings.

Process Flow Template

Process Flows always have process steps connected by directional arrows that indicate all of the possible paths the process follows. Each Process Flow has a clearly defined starting and ending point; in most cases, these are actually entry or exit points for other processes.

The elements of Process Flows in RML are shown in Table 9-1. They have some overlap with Business Process Model and Notation (BPMN) terminology and definitions (OMG 2011). Because the goal in RML is to define processes only to a level of detail that is sufficient for deriving requirements, the full BPMN framework is not needed. We have specified a minimum set of notational elements that is sufficient for most requirements modeling purposes.

TABLE 9-1 Process Flow Elements

Element	Meaning
Step	This is a basic process step that a user takes. It is named with a verb phrase.
→	The directional arrow connects process steps or other elements to one another. The direction of the arrow shows the order of the steps. If the line is coming out of a decision step, it is labeled with the decision choice it represents.
Decision	The decision step splits Process Flows in specific ways based on the choices from this step.
Outgoing	The outgoing reference is used to show that the flow is moving to another flow. This is typically used at the end of each lower-level Process Flow to indicate which flow comes next.
Incoming	The incoming reference is the complement to the outgoing element. It indicates that the flow is resuming from another flow. This is typically used at the beginning of each lower-level Process Flow to indicate which flow came before.
Other Process	The other process element references another process mid-flow and bounces back to this flow after that process ends.
	Swim lanes divide the Process Flow to show which roles are executing the steps. Swim lanes' names are names of users or groups of users.

Element	Meaning
	The fork and join symbols are identical; the first one in a Process Flow indicates a fork, and the one that follows is a join. A fork splits a process to show that although all steps must execute, they do not have to be done sequentially. The fork allows the Process Flow to avoid forcing sequencing where no sequencing exists. A fork will always be followed by a join at some point further down the flow. All steps before the join must be executed before the next step after the join can be processed. A join will always be preceded by a fork somewhere in the flow. Forks and joins can be rotated to any angle when it helps with the layout of the Process Flow.
Provide additional contextual information in a callout	A callout is used to provide additional contextual information about a specific activity or event.
Grouping	Groupings add additional information to a diagram for readability. Typically, a grouping surrounds a subprocess that is not split out into its own flow. The grouping is usually named after that subprocess.
Event	An event indicates that something external to the process happens during the process. An event is part of the normal flow. For example, an event can occur at specific times, after a length of time, or indefinitely until another event occurs.

The types of symbols and number of alternative paths vary with each process, but a template in its simplest form looks like the one shown in Figure 9-1.

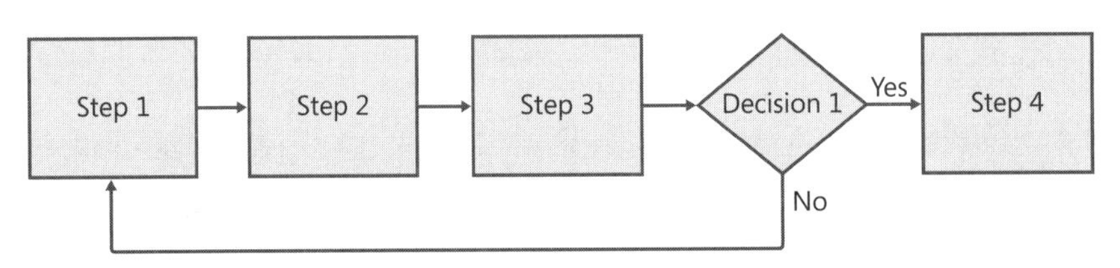

FIGURE 9-1 A Process Flow template.

It is often useful to divide the Process Flow by using swim lanes. Swim lanes divide the full flow into several sections to account for the different groups of users performing their specific process steps. These swim lanes should be horizontal across the entire page. All process steps performed by a user or group of users go in the swim lane assigned to them. Figure 9-2 shows a Process Flow template with swim lanes.

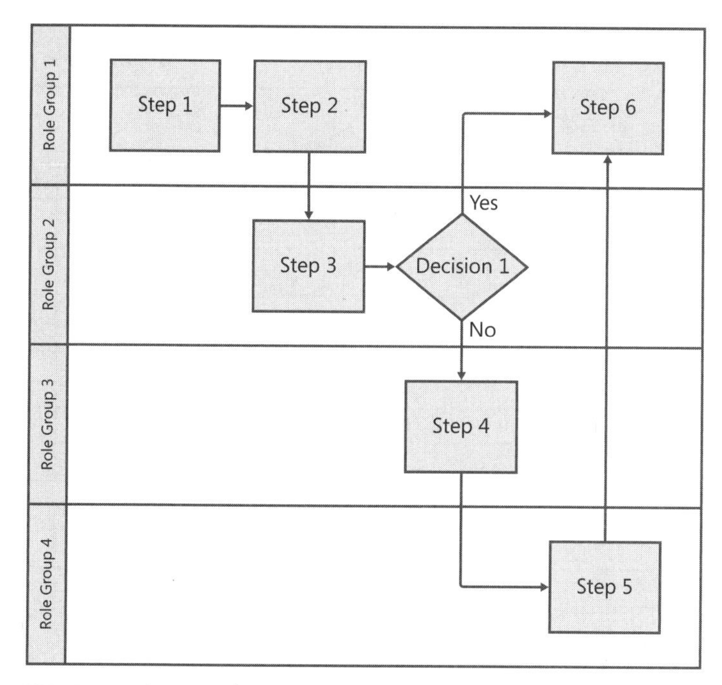

FIGURE 9-2 An example Process Flow with swim lanes.

The other symbols will be discussed later in this chapter, but Figure 9-3 shows an example of a Process Flow that uses more of the symbols.

The numbers on the steps in this flow let you talk about or reference each step. Notice that there is no start or end step in these flows. Either the first step is the start, or more commonly, the incoming reference represents the previous flow in the overall order of flows and is the start of the flow (1.2 in this diagram). The same is true for the end; typically, the flow goes to an outgoing reference (1.4 in this diagram). Between step 7 and the grouping of steps 8 and 9, the process forks and then rejoins before outgoing reference 1.4 to show that steps 8 and 9 must be completed before going to the next step. Also, step 6 has an event before it, indicating that step 6 cannot be taken until the event occurs.

You can also use color to provide additional context to your symbols, but if you do this, you must include a legend to explain the meaning of each color.

Tool Tip Process Flows should be created in a tool that allows easy manipulation of the shapes. The tool that is most common for process diagramming is Microsoft Visio, but many requirements management tools allow for easy Process Flow modeling directly in them as well. If you have access to a requirements tool that supports process modeling, use the tool because it will be easier later to map the process steps to individual requirements.

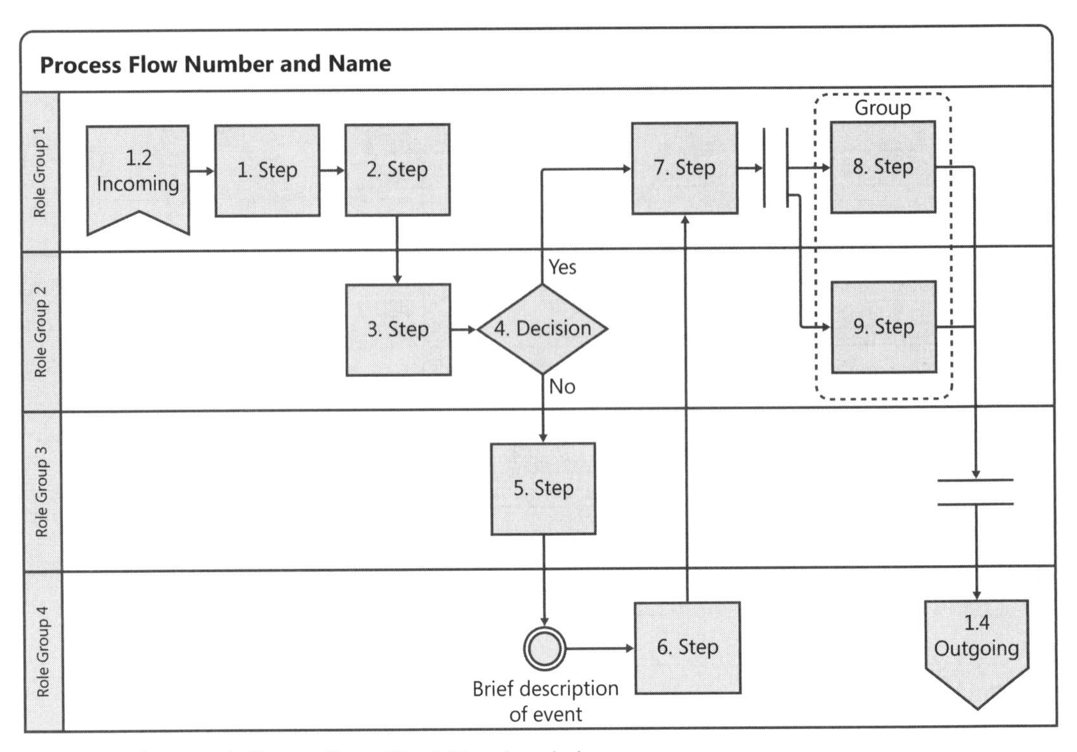

FIGURE 9-3 An example Process Flow with additional symbols.

Example

A printer company is implementing its entire product life cycle from sales through product shipment. The process includes configuring products, creating a quote for the customer, negotiating the deal with the customer, turning the quote into an order, setting up credit so that the customer can pay, manufacturing the order, shipping the order, and finally, collecting payment from the customer to pay off the credit. The L1 Process Flow in Figure 9-4 shows the full end-to-end process.

There would be multiple L2 Process Flows for this L1 flow. Figure 9-5 takes the "1.3 Configure products" step from the L1 Process Flow to the next level of detail in an L2. This Process Flow also has identifiers for the steps so that you can talk about them easily. This technique is useful in elicitation and review sessions as well. Further, note that the grouping symbol is used on step 3 and step 4 to show the reader which steps are related to determining and handling product eligibility issues. Step 1 indicates that this flow starts from an incoming Process Flow, "1.2 Find customer," and outgoing reference 1.4 indicates that after this flow ends, it goes to another Process Flow called "1.4 Create quote."

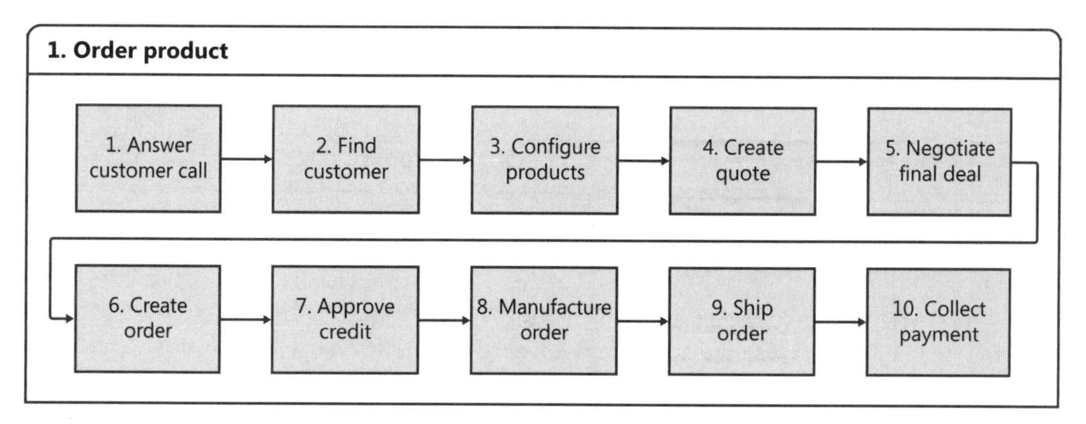

FIGURE 9-4 An example L1 Process Flow.

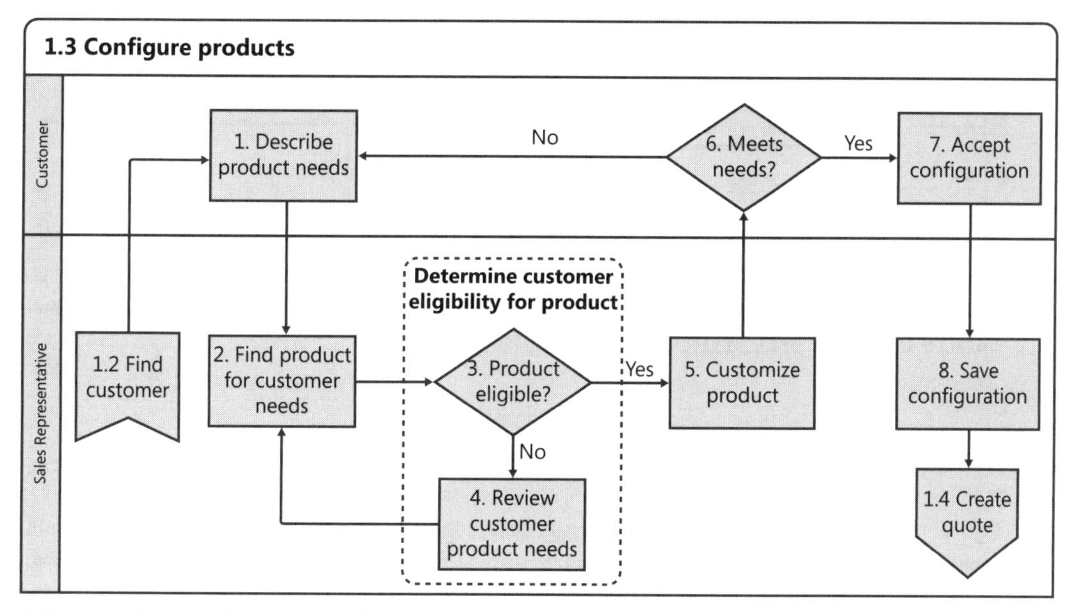

FIGURE 9-5 An example L2 Process Flow.

In Figure 9-6, the L3 diagram shows more detail on the portion of the flow within the grouping markers in the L2 flow, "Determine customer eligibility for product." In this example, notice that the callout symbol adds context for the reader about why a sales rep might not be able to sell a product. The L3 Process Flow also has an event on step 5 to indicate that the flow has to wait for the customer's cart information to transfer to a new sales representative.

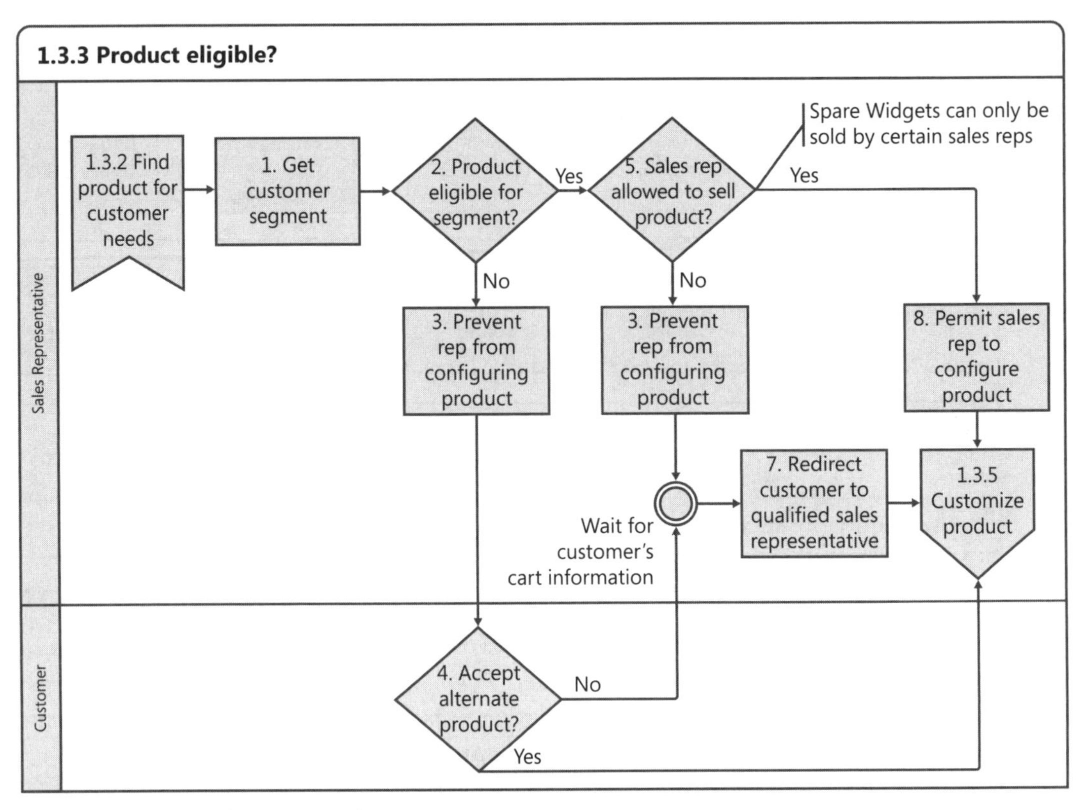

FIGURE 9-6 An example L3 Process Flow.

Creating Process Flows

Figure 9-7 depicts the process of creating a Process Flow. Discovering process steps is an iterative process. It is often helpful to use high-level Process Flows to elicit the intermediate process steps for the lower-level Process Flows. You start with the L1 Process Flow, and then you derive the L2 Process Flows from the L1, and the L3 from the L2 Process Flows.

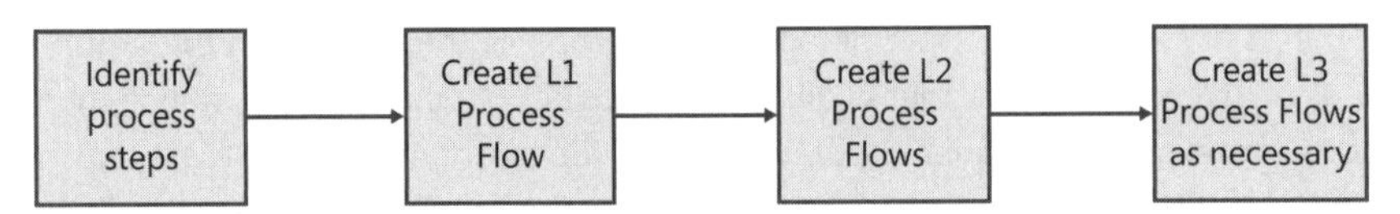

FIGURE 9-7 The process for creating a Process Flow.

Create an L1 Process Flow

You should create an L1 Process Flow early in the project to show the full scope of the process, to derive additional Process Flows, and to work with business stakeholders to sketch the very highest level of activities that define the full solution, end to end. You should keep L1 Process Flows to less than approximately 20 steps to keep them as simple as possible.

Creating the Diagram

After the high-level steps have been identified, put them in an L1 Process Flow as basic steps with directional arrows between them. The key to making the L1 Process Flow useful is to properly choose the level of detail that each step represents, and use that level of detail consistently throughout the entire flow. If you do not do this, your reader will have a hard time following the flow, because they will have to jump from high-level to low-level activities. L1 Process Flows typically do not have decisions, because the steps are too high-level to accurately show branching. Save the lower-level tasks and decisions for the more detailed L2 and L3 Process Flows. If done at the correct level, the L1 Process Flow should be 7+/–2 steps and should fit on one page while still covering the entire breadth of the solution end to end.

Each step should have the form <*verb*> + <*object*>. Each L1 step should have a number, and then each L2 Process Flow should restart the numbering. The combination of L1, L2, and L3 numbers creates a hierarchical numbering convention such that each step can be uniquely identified. The numbers do not imply an order to the steps. Some Process Flow tools automate numbering, which can save a considerable amount of effort.

We do not recommend putting the full hierarchy of step numbers in each step, because that takes up valuable space. Instead, use a combination of the level hierarchy in the title of the Process Flow and the number of the current step to get the full hierarchy. For example, if the title of the Process Flow is "1.3 Configure Products" and the step is step 5, then the hierarchical number is 1.3.5.

The title of the diagram should be prominently displayed at the top. For L1 processes, it should describe the entire set of flows. For L2 and L3 processes, the title should be the hierarchy number plus the name of the process step from the level above. You will quickly develop a hierarchy of Process Flow numbers. You do not have to number your L1 unless you have more than one L1 flow.

Scope of an L1

You should include the entire end-to-end process in your L1, even steps that are not within the scope of the project. This will allow you to show the context for the project, as well as clearly delineate what the project will and will not cover, in discussions with business stakeholders. It is important to include steps before and after the scope that the project is actually modifying to explicitly describe what is in and out of scope.

You might need to put steps in your L1 Process Flow that are detached from the main flow (there will be no arrows connecting them). This is a useful way to depict activities that are high level and that occur outside the normal flow. For example, reporting might be a box you want to capture in the L1 that has lower-level Process Flows associated with it, but that occurs asynchronously from the Process Flow. In addition, there might be processes that simply cannot be depicted as part of a linear sequence, and it might make sense to include those in a separate L1 flow. However, in most cases, if you abstract the process at a high enough level, you can find a linear order.

After the first draft of the L1 is complete, show it to the business stakeholders to review for completeness and correctness. Do not begin the L2 Process Flows until the L1 is stabilized, because the L1 defines the start and end point of each L2.

Create L2 Process Flows

After you have created and reviewed the L1 Process Flow, begin work on the L2 Process Flows. Typically, each step of the L1 Process Flow will have its own L2 Process Flow. The exceptions to this guideline are:

- If you have steps in the L1 Process Flow that are out of scope for the project, you do not need to create an L2.
- If you need to, you can group multiple steps in the L1 Process Flow into one L2 Process Flow, if the steps are simple enough and are related.

Figure 9-8 illustrates how an L2 Process Flow provides more detail for one step in an L1 Process Flow.

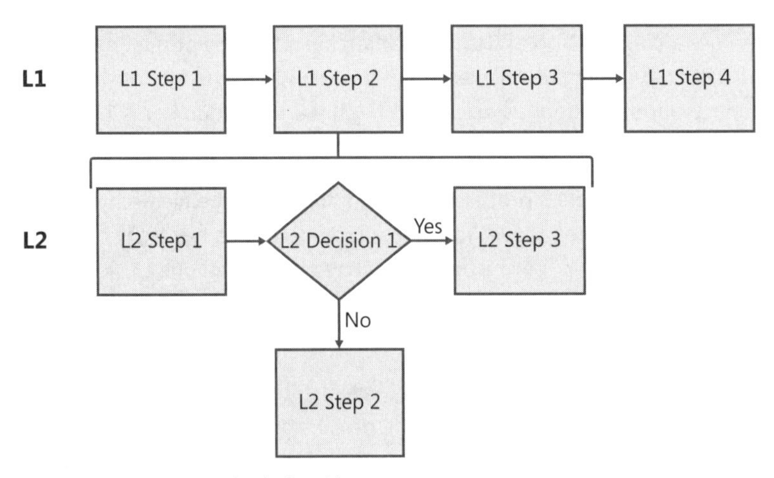

FIGURE 9-8 An L1 to L2 relationship.

Identifying Process Steps

There are many ways to identify process steps. Some of the most common are:

- **Conduct elicitation sessions** Meet with the subject matter experts and have them describe the process.
- **Observe** Watch users execute the process.
- **Perform a walk-through** Walk through existing applications to discover the process.
- **Review existing processes and Process Flows** Start with existing Process Flows when they are available, particularly if you are defining new business processes or adding new functionality to existing systems. If such Process Flows do not exist, you can also use process and procedure training documentation.

Writing Steps

Just as with the L1 Process Flow, make sure that the process steps are all at a similar level of detail, and save the lower-level details for the L3 flows. Because of the 7+/-2 rule, each level should have fewer than 10 steps. If a Process Flow exceeds 20 steps, consider splitting it into two Process Flows. If it does not make sense to split the Process Flow, then color code or group related steps into groups of fewer than 10. This will typically be sufficient for most solutions.

When you create the steps in a Process Flow, you need to include as much information as possible in a small box, so be selective in your word choice. Typically, L2 Process Flows are named by using the general format *[user]* + *<action>* + *<object>* + *[in system]*, as in "configure product." Specifying the user and system are optional, depending on your needs. If you are not using swim lanes and more than one user group performs different activities, you will need to include the user group name in the box to indicate who is performing the activity. If one user group is performing all of the activities, you can include that group's name in the title of the flow. For example, "accept configuration" would be "customer accepts configuration" if you are not using swim lanes. Further, if the name of the system that the activity takes place in is important, then that system name should go in the step name also.

Naming decision steps is a bit more difficult, because the diamond leaves little room for a name. Typically, these ask a question and are just a couple of words, as in "product eligible?" Additional context can be provided via a callout symbol, if needed.

Finally, add numbers to your steps as identifiers. Remember, the numbers do not have to be sequential, and in fact, won't be if you have branching.

Using Swim Lanes

Swim lanes are useful if there are many user groups (or users) interacting in the same Process Flow. If most of the flow is executed by a single user group, it is generally better to use a Process Flow without swim lanes, to keep the diagram simple. As mentioned previously, if there are multiple user groups interacting, you should use swim lanes to avoid having to include the user group name in each box to specify who is performing the activity.

Notice that in Process Flows, the swim lanes are only used to represent user roles or user groups from your Org Chart. They are not used to represent systems, because alternating between actual users and the system can create gaps in the Process Flow due to different types of information being mixed. Your result probably wouldn't have all of the system or people steps identified. The purpose of the Process Flow is to understand the steps users take to accomplish their task, which often is independent of a system. The focus is completely on the users and their needs. If you want to show activities between systems, use System Flows (see Chapter 13, "System Flow"). If you want to describe how the system responds to the user, you can use a Use Case (see Chapter 10, "Use Case").

Adding References to Other Flows

If the L2 Process Flow does not begin at the absolute beginning of the entire L1 process, then use an incoming reference to start the flow and indicate which flow precedes it. Similarly, if the flow does not end at the absolute end of the entire process shown on the L1, use an outgoing reference to end the flow and indicate which flow comes next. If, in the middle of the flow, you find it useful to reference another flow for a set of steps, use the other process reference symbol with the name of that process in the box. If the software you use to create Process Flows allows it, consider making the references to other Process Flows hyperlinks to allow the reader to easily navigate to the referenced Process Flows.

Using Additional Symbols

Add events to your Process Flow as needed. Events are triggered by outside needs (such as audits) that might happen periodically, tasks that are repeated at a regular interval, or customers or outside stakeholders that cause a process to start from the middle rather than the beginning.

A fork and join are used if you have steps that all must occur in parallel to one another (not sequentially) before the process can continue. The fork and join symbols bound those parallel steps in the flow, with the fork appearing before the first parallel step and the join after the last.

Finally, add groupings and callouts for clarity as needed. For example, the grouping symbol can be used to show which steps within a Process Flow are in scope for automation in the project. This is helpful in reviews, to ensure that everyone is in agreement about what will remain manual versus what is automated in a process.

Create L3 Process Flows As Necessary

L3 Process Flows are created by taking each process step in the L2 Process Flows and making a new Process Flow for it, following the same approach used for L2 Process Flows. Continue this process only on steps in the L2 flows that need additional detail. The next level of detail beyond L3s can be Use Cases.

How do you know whether you need an L3? This is determined by the complexity of the process and the level of detail needed for the developers and testers. If an L2 has 20 or more steps, it might need to be split it into two L2s, or it might be necessary to take some of the steps and group them into an L3. Another way to tell is by looking at how many requirements are mapped to a process step. If a step maps to no more than 7+/-2 requirements, then you generally don't need additional levels of process detail.

If your L3 Process Flow details a step that is performed by a single user or user group, you do not need swim lanes, but consider using swim lanes anyway if that helps make the process clear to readers.

Using Process Flows

Process Flows facilitate communication with project stakeholders in both business and IT organizations because the flows are aligned with the way most people think about their jobs. In addition, they provide a way for readers to quickly visualize and understand complex process branching. Finally, they provide one of the best ways to organize long lists of requirements into digestible chunks. With three levels of 10 steps in each Process Flow, an entire set of Process Flows can total about 1000 steps.

Targeting the Audience with Different Levels of Detail

The L1 Process Flow shows the full context of the business processes for the project, so the L1 can be used to communicate scope to all stakeholders.

Because most business processes are very complex, when you use multiple levels of Process Flows, you can target communication at the level that any specific audience requires. Too much detail would confuse some project stakeholders, whereas too little detail would not be very useful for those who execute the process, as well as the development and test teams who have to automate it.

Running Elicitation and Review Sessions

Process Flows are easy for most users to understand, so they should be used in elicitation sessions. Showing an incomplete Process Flow is a much better starting point for elicitation than using a blank page. It is more efficient for users to look at a flow and quickly identify missing or wrong process steps, missing roles, or incorrect paths than to start from scratch and catch these things.

You can ask many questions of business stakeholders while eliciting requirements by using Process Flows. Try asking the following questions during elicitation and review sessions about the full Process Flow:

- Are any user groups missing?
- Are the correct users performing the steps in the flow?
- Is there sequencing in steps where none exists?
- What steps are done manually?
- What steps are done by the system we are defining or by other systems?

And you can ask this next set of questions about each step as you walk through the Process Flow:

- At each step, have all of the steps that need to be completed before this step been accounted for?
- How does the step that immediately precedes this step trigger this step?
- Are there multiple outcomes possible as a result of executing this step? If so, how are these outcomes determined?
- What KPIs (Key Performance Indicators) are associated with this step? (See Chapter 5, "Key Performance Indicator Model," for more about KPIs.)

Driving Completeness

Process Flows help business stakeholders think about a very limited set of information. When they analyze a single step, they have to think about only the things that come before and the things that come after. This means they have a very good chance of getting that set of information completely correct. Ultimately, you can chain these small groups of correct information together to have a very good chance of correctly documenting the entire Process Flow. Even very complex Process Flows have a very good chance of being completely correct.

Deriving Requirements

A Process Flow is a great tool for deriving and organizing requirements. Features, requirements, and business rules can all be derived from Process Flows. Note that Process Flows are not as helpful in identifying data requirements, non-functional requirements, and business rules that are not encapsulated in steps. As the requirements and business rules are derived from the steps, they should be associated with that process step in a Requirements Mapping Matrix (see Chapter 7, "Requirements Mapping Matrix").

Before beginning, make sure that the lowest-level Process Flows are detailed enough for deriving requirements. If this is not the case, consider producing another level of Process Flows to learn even more detail about the process. If the Process Flows were done at the right level, as described previously, each step should have only 7+/-2 requirements associated with it.

You should derive requirements from the lowest-level Process Flows that you have created. Because the low-level Process Flows map back to the L1 Process Flow, all of the requirements will maintain that mapping as well. Functional requirements are derived directly from the process steps, and business rules are derived from the decision steps and requirements. Process Flows will generally not provide enough granularity to allow you to derive all of the business rules, but they will provide a start and then will point toward areas where additional business rules might be needed.

It is often tempting to write just a single requirement for each process step, but in most cases this is not sufficient to properly define the system. However, if a process step is mapped to more than 7+/-2 requirements, it probably needs to be split into two steps. Try asking some of these questions about each step to find more requirements and business rules:

- What needs to be done before this step takes place?
- What are the different possible outcomes from this step?
- What possible error conditions might come out of this step?
- When this step is complete, what is triggered to let others know that the step is complete?
- What parts of the step are initiated by the user, and which are triggered automatically by the system?
- What rules are evaluated at this decision step?
- What are the possible outcomes emerging from this decision step?
- What calculation is performed at this step?

When writing the requirements, include enough detail about the context of each requirement, in case someone is implementing or testing the system without looking at the Process Flows.

When to Use

Process Flows should be used on any project with extensive user interfaces. Even consumer-facing applications without business processes could benefit from Process Flows because the flows can help the team gain a shared understanding of how the users will accomplish their goals, rather than just activating features.

When Not to Use

Process Flows should not be used for systems in which the user interface is minimal or nonexistent, such as control systems and some types of embedded systems. In those cases, System Flows would be more appropriate. In your Process Flow, if more than a few consecutive decisions are required in the process, consider using a Decision Tree (see Chapter 17, "Decision Tree") instead of a Process Flow. Process Flows do not handle the high number of branches (more than 7+/-2 branches) that some business rules demand. A Decision Tree is a better model for handling this branching and can simply be referenced from within the Process Flow.

Common Mistakes

The following represent the most common mistakes that we have seen with Process Flows.

Level of Detail Is Inconsistent Within a Flow

Details that are better suited for an L3 are sometimes captured in an L2. This can be addressed by aiming for a consistent level of detail throughout each flow and moving additional detail down a level. One way to tell that you are mixing levels of detail is when a Process Flow has more than 20 steps.

Reviewers Do Not Understand the Level of Detail

Sometimes reviewers do not understand what level of detail each flow intends to show. If a flow is an L1, the reviewers might insist that details are missing, even though those details are covered in the L2 and L3 flows. To prevent this, make sure to describe the entire framework of Process Flows to the audience.

Reviewers Forget to Look at the Full Process Flow

Process Flows are very simple to create and review, yet sometimes analysts get so busy trying to create the individual steps that they forget to step back and look at the whole picture in the flow. When this happens, some of the steps might be placed out of sequence, or decisions might be incompletely described.

Process Flow Has Too Many Steps

Process Flows should have no more than 20 steps, otherwise they are too complex to understand. Also, if you find yourself with more than 10 steps in your Process Flow, you should start thinking about splitting the Process Flow, grouping, or color-coding individual steps.

System Responses Are Mixed with User Actions

The purpose of a Process Flow is to focus on what the users are trying to accomplish. It is very easy to expand the scope of the Process Flow to include how the system responds, but the point of the Process Flow is to be exclusively focused on the actions of the user. Having the system as an actor in your Process Flow increases the complexity of the diagram and actually makes it more likely that some user actions or system actions will be missed. It is better to focus on the system actions in a System Flow (see Chapter 13).

Processes Outside the Scope of the Project Are Not Included

By including process steps that are outside the scope of the current project, you can bound your system and ensure that you haven't missed any steps.

Related Models

Process Flows are very common, but the name, format, and symbols used within them vary greatly. Process Flows are often called flow charts, cross functional process flows, or swim lane diagrams.

BPMN defines about 50 symbols for process modeling, and the list keeps growing. Many of these symbols are seldom used. RML uses only symbols that are most relevant for defining requirements.

Some Process Flows capture system activities, whereas RML separates Process Flows into System Flows (for system activities) and Process Flows (for user activities). If you want to define the steps that a system itself takes to accomplish a goal, use a System Flow rather than the Process Flow described in this chapter.

The following list briefly describes the most important models that influence or are enhanced by Process Flows. Chapter 26, "Using Models Together," contains a more thorough discussion about all related models.

- **System Flows** These show automated flows executed by the system.
- **Use Cases** These are used to flesh out specific process steps in greater detail.
- **Decision Trees** These are used to define complex decision logic that is embedded inside a high-level process step or decision point in a Process Flow.
- **Org Charts** These are used to show the users or user groups (departments) depicted as roles in swim lanes.
- **Key Performance Indicator Models (KPIMs)** These capture KPIs for Process Flows.
- **Requirements Mapping Matrices (RMMs)** These often map Process Flow steps to requirements.

Exercise

The following exercise is intended to help you to gain a better understanding of how to use this model. The exercise is open ended, and therefore the answer you come up with could be substantially different than the answer that we have provided. There are potentially many correct solutions. The answer provides an explanation of how we arrived at our solution. You will gain the most out of the exercise by attempting to do it yourself before looking at the solution. The answers for the exercises can be found in Appendix C.

Instructions

Prepare an L1, L2, and L3 Process Flow for the scenario.

Scenario

In this project, you are helping to build an online eStore for customers to order flamingos and other lawn accessories from Wide World Importers. The process is currently initiated when customers call sales representatives directly; these representatives use Microsoft Excel to fill out order forms that are manually input into the system. You have met with stakeholders and elicited an overview of the new process they want, as follows, starting with the high-level description.

Product managers will build a product catalog including all of the available flamingos and lawn accessories. The marketing team will add pricing to the catalog. A customer will come to the eStore to buy products. The supply chain team will manage inventory in their own application.

You break down the step in which a customer buys products from the eStore. A customer browses the catalog, finds products of interest, and adds them to a cart. The customer submits the order, and a sales representative verifies that there is enough information to fully process it. If anything is missing, the sales representative sends an email message to the customer and waits for the customer to update the order; otherwise the sales representative processes payment for the order. The representative makes sure the product ships. The customer receives a confirmation email message, which also triggers the step in the process for updating inventory.

Finally, you can put more detail around how the sales representative verifies that there is enough information on the order. The sales representative submits the credit card payment information for approval and notifies the supply chain to ship the order if the payment is approved. If it is not approved, the customer gets an email message and submits new payment information to try again.

Additional Resources

- Section 4.2 of *The Software Requirements Memory Jogger* has an extensive description of what Gottesdiener calls Process Maps (Gottesdiener 2005).
- The IIBA describes flowcharts as part of process modeling in version 2.0 of the BABOK (IIBA 2009).

References

- Gottesdiener, Ellen. 2005. *The Software Requirements Memory Jogger.* Salem, New Hampshire: Goal/QPC.
- International Institute of Business Analysis (IIBA). 2009. *A Guide to the Business Analysis Body of Knowledge (BABOK Guide).* Toronto, Ontario, Canada.
- Object Management Group (OMG). 2011. *Business Process Model and Notation (BPMN) version 2.0. http://www.omg.org/spec/BPMN/2.0.*

CHAPTER 10

Use Case

I recently had a meeting with my architect, who is helping me build a new beach house. The conversation I had with the architect went like this:

Architect: *How do you see yourself using the beach house beyond the usual house uses?*

Me: *Well, after a day at the beach, I'm worried about tracking sand in the house.*

Architect: *Well, let's say you are at the beach carrying your beach umbrellas, coolers, towels, and bags. You call it a day, so you walk over the dunes carrying all your stuff. You walk around to the front of the house, open the garage with a keypad, and then drop all your stuff in the garage.*

Me: *Well…it would be nice if we didn't have to walk around to the front of the house.*

Architect: *OK, so we put a door in the back that opens to the garage. Then you go to the back door, put in the key, and open the door to the garage.*

Me: *I liked the idea of not needing a key to open the garage door; is it possible to have keyless entry on the back door?*

Architect: *Of course. When you get in the garage, you drop off your stuff and enter the house.*

Me: *It still seems like a lot of sand would get everywhere. Is it possible for us to wash off?*

Architect: *So how about an outside shower? You shower off, enter the key code, then open the door and drop off all your stuff. There shouldn't be much sand left.*

Me: *Keep in mind that we want to rinse off all our stuff before we go in the garage. We want to make sure the outside area isn't all sandy, and we really need a flexible spray nozzle. The garage should have a drain or something so the water dripping off the rinsed toys doesn't just pool up. Maybe some racks to hang drying towels? We'd also like a heater or fan to make the stuff dry off faster.*

Architect: *Great—I think we identified several features, such as a garage drain, keyless entry, back garage entrance, outdoor shower with flexible spray nozzle, garage fan, drying racks, and heater.*

As soon as the architect knew how I would use the house, he was able to identify features that would fulfill my needs. Walking through the steps helped me to identify features that I wouldn't have otherwise included.

The Use Case is an RML people model that describes the interactions between the users and a system. The value of a Use Case is that it helps users picture themselves executing a task, allowing them to identify the features that might be required to support each step. In addition, the user has to think about only what comes after a step, which makes it much easier for him to correctly identify all previous steps and all successive steps without missing any. Use Cases describe what the user needs to do, what he is trying to accomplish, and how the system responds when he is using the software. The Use Case is a very natural model because it helps users to think about how they will use a system before you build or buy it, just like they do with products they buy at home. If you can understand how users will use the software and how they expect the software to behave, you can make sure that the software has the appropriate functionality and qualities to support that. Further, Use Cases provide context to developers and testers for the users' intended use of the system.

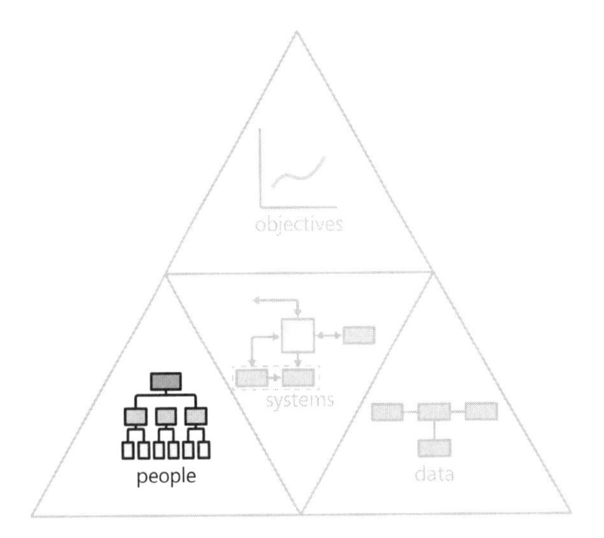

Use Case Template

Use Cases are structured text presented in a template table that has prespecified fields, as shown in Figure 10-1. The structure helps ensure that you don't forget any details when you are creating a Use Case and helps the Use Case reader jump to relevant information as needed. Note that a Use Case might have a different format when it is defined in a requirements tool.

It is useful to differentiate between header fields, which hold the metadata for the Use Case, and the fields that represent the user interactions with the system. The header fields are the name, ID, description, actors, organizational benefits, frequency of use, triggers, preconditions, and postconditions fields. The remaining sections are those that document the user's interaction with the system: main course, alternate courses, and exceptions. Each of these fields is defined within the template where the content of an actual Use Case would go.

There are several variations of Use Case templates. Regardless of the actual format, Use Cases should include the elements of the template shown here.

Name	The Use Case name. Typically the name is of the format <action> + <object>.
ID	An identifier that is unique to each Use Case.
Description	A brief sentence that states what the user wants to be able to do and what benefit they will derive.
Actors	The type of user who interacts with the system to accomplish the task. Actors are identified by role name.
Organizational Benefits	The value the organization expects to receive from having the functionality described. Ideally this is a link directly to a Business Objective.
Frequency of Use	How often the Use Case is executed.
Triggers	Concrete actions made by the user within the System to start the Use Case.
Pre-conditions	Any states that the system must be in or conditions that must be met before the Use Case is started.
Post-conditions	Any states that the system must be in or conditions that must be met after the Use Case is completed successfully. These will be met if the Main Course or any Alternate Courses are followed. Some Exceptions may result in failure to meet the Post-Conditions.
Main Course	The most common path of interactions between the user and the system. 1. Step 1 2. Step 2
Alternate Courses	Alternate paths through the system. AC1: <condition for the alternate to be called> 1. Step 1 2. Step 2 AC2: <condition for the alternate to be called> 1. Step 1
Exceptions	Exception handling by the system. EX1: <condition for the exception to be called> 1. Step 1 2. Step 2 EX2 <condition for the exception to be called> 1. Step 1

FIGURE 10-1 The Use Case template.

Tool Tip Use Cases are most commonly created in Microsoft Word, Microsoft Excel, or directly in a requirements management tool.

Example

A project for an online book seller includes adding a feature to save items for purchase later. In the Use Case in Figure 10-2, the customer has already found an item to purchase but is not ready to purchase right away, and therefore he wants to save the product for later action.

Name	Save item for purchase.
ID	UC_001
Description	While browsing items in the eStore, a user finds an item he is not ready to purchase yet, but he wants to save it to a list so that he can later find the item that he was previously interested in.
Actors	eStore customer.
Organizational Benefits	Increase sales by helping the customer remember products he was previously interested in.
Frequency of Use	20% of users save an item to be bought later each time they visit the site. 50% of saved items are purchased within one year of the saved date.
Triggers	The user selects an option to save an item.
Preconditions	User is viewing an item in the catalog.
Postconditions	The item selected to be saved is visible to the user when he views his saved items. The item selected to be saved is reflected as a saved item when the user views his eStore search and browse results.
Main Course	1. System prompts user to confirm saving selected item instead of purchasing it right away. 2. User confirms to save now (see EX1). 3. System determines user is not logged on and redirects user to log on (see AC1). 4. User logs on (see AC2, AC3). 5. System stores the saved item (see EX2). 6. System redirects the user to his saved items list to view the full list.
Alternate Courses	AC1 System determines user is already logged on. 1. Return to Main Course step 5. AC2 User logs off again. 1. Return user to Main Course step 3. AC3 User does not have an account already. 1. User creates an account. 2. System confirms account creation. 3. Return user to Main Course step 4.
Exceptions	EX1 User decides to purchase the item now. 1. See "Purchase item" Use Case. EX2 System fails on saving item to list. 1. System notifies user that an error has occurred. 2. Return user to Main Course step 1.

FIGURE 10-2 An example Use Case.

Creating Use Cases

You can create Use Cases throughout the requirements elicitation and documentation processes; however, they are not among the first models to be created. Typically, they are created after Process Flows (see Chapter 9, "Process Flow"), and only when it is determined that further details are needed around the interaction of the user with the system. You create a Use Case by following the steps shown in Figure 10-3.

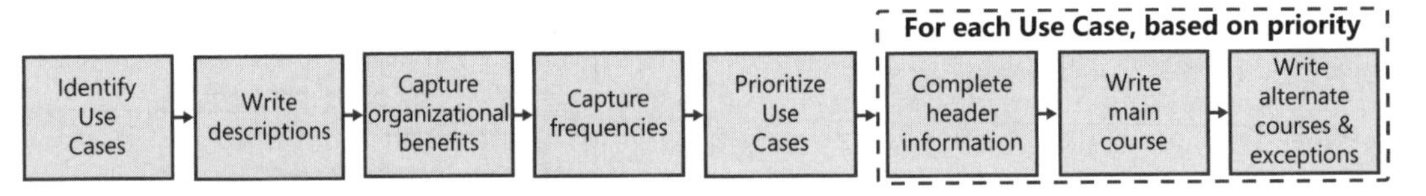

FIGURE 10-3 The process for creating a Use Case.

Identify Use Cases

It is useful to identify all of the Use Cases up front (or at least most of them, because some will be identified as you work). Brainstorm with the team about what Use Cases are useful to write, at this stage simply capturing drafts names of the Use Cases, knowing that the names might change when the Use Cases are written. As you identify Use Cases, you might want to create a matrix to store the list of Use Cases identified and some of their basic information, such as the description, frequency of use, and priority. Only after you start to flesh the details out would you put each Use Case in its template.

One way to brainstorm Use Cases is to first identify all the possible stakeholders by using an Org Chart (see Chapter 8, "Org Chart"). Then identify L1, L2, and L3 processes by using a Process Flow. Use Cases often are used to detail the process steps of L2 or L3 Process Flows. Another way to identify Use Cases is to look at the Feature Tree (see Chapter 6, "Feature Tree"). Typically, features are simply shorter names of Use Cases.

Use Cases should also focus on completing business tasks that are relevant to something the user wants to accomplish, and not to a functional context of the system. Many people struggle with how granular to make a Use Case. For the example in the previous section, the user wants to save an item for later. This is a good Use Case because it accomplishes a complete task for the user. However, a Use Case like "select item" does not accomplish a complete task for the user. Selecting an item is a precursor to or part of something the user really wants to accomplish (such as determining which item of several similar items is the right one, purchasing items, or adding items to a wish list). Similarly, "calculate shipping" is not a complete task, but "purchase item" is and makes a more complete Use Case. There might be cases where a task is too big, so you might want to decompose the Use Case into smaller, more easily understandable pieces.

Use Case names should use the format *<action> <object>*. Or, if the actor is not obvious based on the action and object, the name should include the actor, *<actor> <action> <object>*.

Table 10-1 shows the formats with examples.

TABLE 10-1 Use Case Name Formats

Name Format	Example Name
<action> <object>	Save Item for Purchase
<actor> <action> <object>	Small Business Shopper Saves Item for Purchase

From Process Flows

There are many ways to identify Use Cases. First, you can use Process Flows to identify them. In particular, L3 Process Flows are often better represented by Use Cases, which allow you to capture more detail than what fits in the small boxes of Process Flows. For example, Use Cases can have significantly longer descriptions of each step, describe how the system should respond, and include metadata about the process.

From Business Data Diagrams

Review each object in every Business Data Diagram (BDD) to identify Use Cases (see Chapter 19, "Business Data Diagram"). There are six verbs you can phrase into questions to ask about each object when you are looking for Use Cases that manipulate data:

- How is the object created?
- How is the object updated?
- How is the object used?
- How is the object deleted from the system?
- How is the object moved?
- How is the object copied?

As one example, consider an online bookstore that has a BDD with an "item" object in it. To identify Use Cases that manipulate "item," consider how items in the catalog are created, and you will find a Use Case called "Add Item to Catalog." By asking whether an item can be moved within or to another catalog, you can determine that there is no need for a Use Case called "Move Item to Another Catalog." On the other hand, if the software is a mobile phone music app, you could ask the question, "What does it mean to move music?" That would help you to identify a Use Case for when a user gets a new phone and wants to migrate her music catalog from her old phone to her new phone. If you ask, "What does it mean to copy a playlist object?" That could lead you to identify a Use Case describing the sharing of playlists with friends or with social networks.

From Org Charts or Lists of Actors

The roles in the Org Chart should be reviewed as well, to consider what activities those roles need to perform in the system. Also, look for additional actors who might trigger the identification of additional Use Cases. The following questions can be used to identify actors with Use Cases:

- Who uses the system?
- What is his or her job?
- Who installs the system?
- Who monitors the system?
- Who trains people to use the system?
- Who provides user support for the system?
- Who fixes the system?

- Who starts up the system and who shuts it down?
- Who maintains the system?
- Who creates, updates, and deletes information in the system?
- Who gets information from this system?
- Who provides information to the system?
- Which users in an Org Chart are going to use the system?

After a list of user types and actors is formed, then identify the Use Cases by asking, "What does this type of user need to do in the system?" The following questions help identify the list of Use Cases from this list:

- What functions will the user want to use in the system?
- Do the users need to create, update, or delete information?
- Does the system need to notify a user about changes in an internal state?
- What problems has the user had in the past?
- What steps are manual today that could be automated?

Write Descriptions

When you first identify a Use Case, capture a simple description for each to help distinguish the Use Cases from one another. The description should be a brief sentence that simply states the user's end goal for the Use Case. An example description is, "While browsing items in the eStore, users find items they are not ready to purchase yet, but they want to save them to a list so that they can later find the items." On the first pass, you can just capture what the user wants to do in the Use Case, and on a second pass, you can add the user's benefit to the description.

Capture Organizational Benefits

Be sure to capture organizational benefits for each Use Case because they help you to prioritize the Use Cases against one another. To understand each Use Case's organizational benefit, ask, "How does this Use Case contribute to the business objectives?" You might want to reference the business objectives from the Business Objectives Model directly in this field (see Chapter 3, "Business Objectives Model").

This step can be done in conjunction with writing the descriptions or after, but both should be done before prioritizing Use Cases.

Capture Frequency of Use

Identifying frequency of use helps the team appropriately prioritize the Use Case and ensure that it is implemented to support the volume of use expected. This field is typically documented in terms of something such as the following:

- Transactions per hour
- Number of times per day
- Number or percent of customers who execute it
- Volume of data flowing through the system

Prioritize Use Cases

Prior to fully documenting a set of Use Cases, it is helpful to prioritize them and continue the detailed work on them in order of importance to the business.

You can eliminate any Use Cases that map to features that were cut based on Objective Chains or Key Performance Indicator Models. Those models prioritize at a higher level of detail, allowing you to cut major areas of scope. For the remaining Use Cases still in scope, use the organizational benefit and frequency of use for each Use Case to help decide on a priority. Additionally, work with the development team to understand any development dependencies that would affect the prioritization order of Use Cases. One good way to prioritize the work is to order the Use Cases from 1 to *n* and work on them in that order.

Complete the Remaining Header Fields

When it is time to write an individual Use Case, complete the header fields. These fields might get updated when the main course is written, but at least draft them up front. The fields included in this section can be completed in any order.

Assign a Unique ID

Use a consistent format for unique IDs, such as UC_*xxx*, where *xxx* is a number. Do not worry about keeping the IDs in any order; you only need to ensure that they are unique and that each Use Case always keeps its same ID. If you are using a requirements management tool, it will assign these for you.

Identify Actors

If you identified the Use Case from users or roles in an Org Chart, or from a list of actors, then the actors field should come straight from the Org Chart. If not, use a role or individual Org Chart now to identify possible actors for the Use Case.

Avoid having system actors, because those interactions (system-to-system) should be represented visually in a System Flow (see Chapter 13, "System Flow"). If there is a human actor who is interacting with the system, and another system appears in the interaction, just call that system out on the appropriate steps of the Use Case. Actors are reserved for user types, because the purpose of the Use Case is to help the team understand what the user would like to accomplish. Systems don't have goals.

Identify Triggers

Because triggers are the system's cue to start the execution of a Use Case, they must be things that the system can actually detect, as compared to a user's intentions. For example, "The user selects an option to save an item" is a good trigger, whereas, "The user wants to save an item" is the intent behind the user's action, which is completely undetectable by the system. The user's intent is more appropriately captured in the Use Case description field. To understand the trigger for the Use Case, ask the question, "What event causes the Use Case to happen?" and then verify that it is actually an action that the system can detect.

Identify Preconditions

Preconditions are checks that the system must make before executing the Use Case. If the preconditions are not met, then the Use Case cannot proceed, and either another Use Case is executed or no system action is taken. If the preconditions are meant to be "one or the other," then an "or" statement can be used between them, but typically they are multiple conditions that all must be true.

The order of evaluation of triggers and preconditions is shown in Figure 10-4.

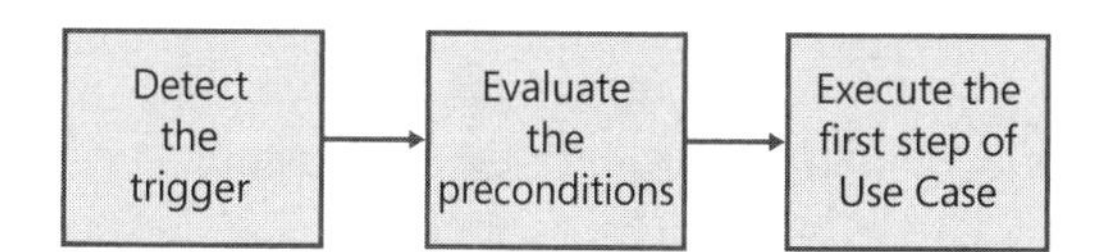

FIGURE 10-4 The order of evaluation of triggers, preconditions, and the main course.

To identify preconditions, you can just ask what conditions must be true, what states the system must be in, and what processes the user must execute outside the system before the Use Case can begin.

Identify Postconditions

Postconditions are aligned with the original goal of the Use Case found in the description. Postconditions should be something the user can observe, to verify that the Use Case met the user's goal. For example, a useless postcondition is "Item is saved," whereas a good postcondition is "The item selected to be saved is visible to the user when he selects an option to view his saved items." If an alternate course is followed in a Use Case, the postconditions should still be met. If they will not be met, then the alternate course is really an exception. The following questions can be used to identify postconditions:

- What conditions must be true when the Use Case ends?
- What state will the system be in at the end of the Use Case?

Write the Main Course

The main course of a Use Case is also sometimes called the "normal course" and describes the most common path of interactions between the users and the system. Note that it is not called the "happy path," because the most obvious and common path might not lead to a happy experience. The main course describes the steps that the user and system take in order for that user to accomplish a task in the system, ultimately achieving the goal outlined in the Use Case description.

When you are creating the Use Case's main course, it is best to limit the length to approximately 10 to 15 steps. If you have less than 10, it is quite possible that the Use Case is degenerate and did not need to be written at all, or that it is part of another Use Case. If you have more than 15 steps, the Use Case is probably too complex to be understood, and it should be split into two Use Cases, or an L3 Process Flow should be used instead. There are exceptions to this guideline, but it is a good one to follow for a rough sizing estimate.

The first step of a Use Case should always be a system step. It was mentioned in the previous section that the system needs to detect the trigger statement, evaluate the preconditions, and then start the Use Case. Therefore, the first step of the Use Case is really the system reacting to the trigger step.

The following questions can help you identify the steps of the Use Case:

- How does the actor interact with the system?
- What does the system do at this step (for example, present options, display data, execute a process)?
- What does the system do next?
- What does the actor do next?
- Is there part of this Use Case that is another Use Case?

The steps of the Use Case all represent either system actions or user actions and typically shift back and forth between the two. If there are a lot of system steps in a row without any user interactions, consider whether the steps are too granular and can be combined, or whether a Use Case is the right model. Perhaps a System Flow (see Chapter 13, "System Flow") would be better to depict that system interaction.

The steps themselves should be stated in very simple language. In fact, most steps will fit on one line in a Word document. If you have steps that are longer, you might be including too much detail, such as requirements or business rules, in the step.

Write the Alternate Courses

The alternate course section is one of the last sections to be written in Use Cases. However, it is helpful to note the obvious alternate courses by name while you are writing the main course. You should also re-evaluate the main course to look for additional alternate courses that you might have missed on the first pass. At each step of the main course, ask these questions:

- If something in the step doesn't or can't happen, what should happen instead?
- What other possible actions can the user take at each step?

Alternate courses have identifiers of the format AC*x*, where *x* is the next unique number, so that they are numbered AC1, AC2, and so on. Alternate courses are labeled on the main course steps in parentheses to show where they branch from. As an example, in Figure 10-5, on step 4, there is a reference to "see AC2, AC3." This is telling the reader that at step 4, the Use Case can branch to alternate course 2 (AC2) or alternate course 3 (AC3).

Main Course	1. System prompts user to confirm saving selected item instead of purchasing it right away. 2. User confirms to save now (see EX1). 3. System determines user is not logged on and redirects user to log on (see AC1). 4. User logs on (see AC2, AC3). 5. System stores the saved item (see EX2). 6. System redirects the user to his saved items list to view the full list.

FIGURE 10-5 Alternate courses as references from steps.

The alternate course will be written such that the top line identifies the condition for the alternate path to be executed, and the steps follow the name. The steps of the alternate course can refer to other Use Cases, and they must exit the Use Case or branch back into the main course with a step, as shown in the examples in Figure 10-6.

Alternate Courses	AC1 System determines user is already logged on. 1. Return to Main Course step 5. AC2 User logs off again. 1. Return user to Main Course step 3. AC3 User does not have an account already. 1. User creates an account. 2. System confirms account creation. 3. Return user to Main Course step 4.

FIGURE 10-6 Alternate courses.

Write the Exceptions

The exceptions can be written at the same time as alternate courses. As mentioned for alternate courses, it is helpful to note the obvious exceptions by name while you are writing the main course, and to re-evaluate the main course looking for additional exceptions. At each step of the main course, ask these questions:

- What might go wrong when the system executes the step?
- What possible error conditions exist at each step of the main course?
- What are the interrupts that can happen at any time?
- If the user cancels out at any step, what should happen?

Exceptions are labeled like alternate courses except that the abbreviation is "EX." Figure 10-7 shows an example.

Exceptions	EX1 User decides to purchase the item now. 1. See "Purchase item" Use Case. EX2 System fails on saving item to list. 1. System notifies user that an error has occurred. 2. Return user to Main Course step 1.

FIGURE 10-7 Exceptions.

Using Use Cases

Any time one or more users interact with a system, a Use Case can be helpful to describe those system interactions from the user's perspective.

Providing Context for Elicitation Through Implementation

Use Cases are easy to draft, and you can take straw-man versions into elicitation sessions to review them with business stakeholders. Use Cases help to frame the conversations and take less time to create than Process Flows. Because Use Cases describe interactions from the user's perspective, in a step-by-step fashion, they are easy for business stakeholders to review. Business stakeholders can easily envision themselves at each step in the Use Case, and they have to consider only what comes next, which minimizes mental juggling of information.

Prioritizing Work

Use Cases are often used to prioritize and organize development work. They represent units of work that a team can work on independently. If each Use Case is developed in full, this allows parts of the system to be released in phases, because full tasks will be executable.

Because they capture the organizational benefits of the actions to the user, Use Cases are very helpful in actually prioritizing the work for development. This can be particularly useful when adding functionality to an existing system, because Use Cases force the business to think about what benefits the user needs to receive but cannot achieve in the existing system.

Deriving Requirements

At one level, Use Cases help you identify features to support the story that you might not have otherwise identified. However, more commonly, Use Cases can be used to derive functional and non-functional requirements directly—the actions taken by the system based on user actions can be converted into traditional functional requirement statements about what functionality the system must support. To accomplish this, each step of a Use Case should be considered to see if there are any system functions necessary to support executing that step. If there are, those are requirements. "If" statements or statements that branch to alternate courses describe business rules.

A common reason that requirements are missed is because someone forgot to look at the exceptions or unique cases. Using alternate courses in Use Cases can help prevent missed requirements.

Reusing Use Cases

When writing Use Cases for a particular system, you might notice that various systems share similar user goals and steps to accomplish them, which is an indication that Use Cases and their associated requirements can be reused. For example, Use Cases for search operations are essentially the same across all systems. Reuse of Use Cases can help save you a lot of work when you are modeling requirements.

Using a Use Case as a Basis for a UAT Script

Furthermore, because Use Cases describe user and system interaction, they naturally lend themselves to the creation of user acceptance test (UAT) scripts. The Use Case model is one of the easiest models to use for this purpose. A business stakeholder simply follows the main and alternate courses, plugging in data values, to test the functionality described in the Use Case.

Using Models Similar to Use Cases

There are models that might be used in addition to or instead of Use Cases, based on specific scenarios. These models are Process Flows, user stories, and activity diagrams.

One key difference between Process Flows and Use Cases is that Process Flows do not show system responses to user actions, just the user actions. In addition, because Use Cases are text only, it is more difficult to use them to understand even relatively simple branching and looping decision flow. Use Cases complement L3 Process Flows by providing additional detail such as how the system responds and the specific interactions with the system, such as selecting from a list of options or entering specific information. The format of the Use Case allows you to include significantly more information about each step than is possible in a Process Flow. A Process Flow is good for visualizing how steps relate to each other. A Use Case is better for articulating detailed information about a step or about the series of steps. One other point: If multiple systems are interacting, a System Flow is a far better choice than a Use Case.

A user story is not an RML model but is similar to a Use Case. User stories are at the heart of agile development approaches. They are similar to Use Cases in that you capture the user's goal and activities from his perspective. However, user stories record much less of what the system is doing. One issue with user stories is that there is not a common standard for the level of detail that should be used. Because they are generally defined as being short, maybe only a paragraph, they don't necessarily hold very much information. In agile development, the expectation is that the user will work closely with development to communicate the requirements, with the user story acting as a discussion piece and as acceptance criteria used to document the business rules. The challenge with this approach is that people have short memories, and for very complex systems in which hundreds or thousands of decisions and choices are made over the life of the project, not documenting those decisions significantly increases risk.

Further, one of the challenges of this model is that after acceptance criteria pass the 7+/-2 number, it begins to be difficult to ensure that all are present. In many cases, there could be 30 to 40 confirmation statements. In addition, business rules are captured within the acceptance criteria, which makes it hard to track business rules at a global level. Finally, many proponents of agile approaches indicate that the user stories in a product backlog should never be nested. For large projects with hundreds or thousands of user stories and many project teams, it becomes very difficult to track and model the system with only user stories.

A user story consists of a name (in the same format as a Use Case name); a description or conversation in first person that describes what the user wants to do; and acceptance criteria for the story. Acceptance criteria are similar to the requirements, business rules, and test cases that are derived from Use Cases. Table 10-2 is an example of a user story.

TABLE 10-2 User Story

User Story: Save Item for Later Purchase	
Description	As an online retail customer, while browsing items in the eStore, I found an item I am not ready to purchase, and I want to save it for a later purchase so that I won't forget it and can easily purchase it later. I choose to save it, and I can revisit my list of saved items later to find all of the items I was previously interested in.
Acceptance Criteria	A few examples of acceptance criteria: Any selected item can be saved while browsing, for later purchase. Any selected item can be saved from the cart for later purchase. After an item has been saved for later purchase, the user can see it in the list of saved items.

Activity diagrams are visual representations of Use Cases with steps represented in boxes, linked by flow lines. Activity diagrams are useful for supplementing Use Cases when there is a lot of complex branching in the Use Case's main flow, but they contain less detail than Use Cases. Figure 10-8 shows an activity diagram for the example Use Case in this chapter.

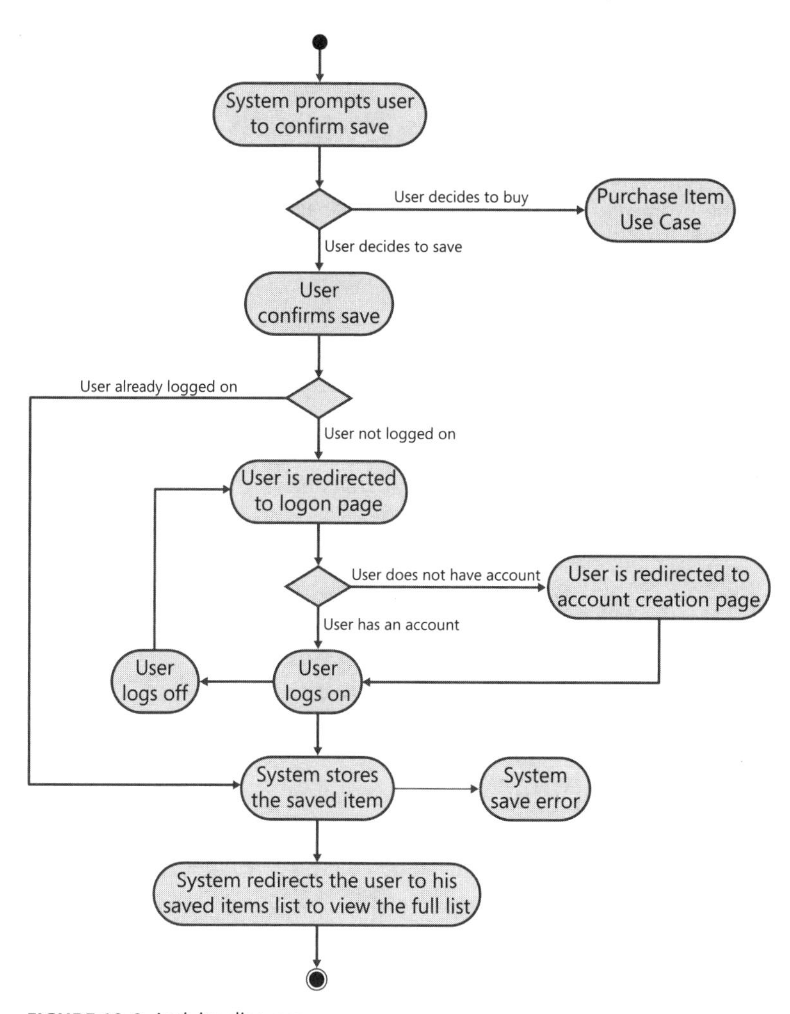

FIGURE 10-8 Activity diagram.

Further, Use Cases are most useful when the alternate and exception flows are straightforward and not deeply nested. For more complex branching scenarios, a Decision Tree (see Chapter 17, "Decision Tree") is a more appropriate model.

Use Cases Do Not Have to Be Perfect

One of the important caveats of Use Cases and all of the guidelines is that they don't have to be perfect to be effective. As with all models, this model alone will not be handed to developers and testers but will be supplemented by other models and detailed functional requirements. Use Cases are helpful to ensure that the team has a shared understanding of the goal of the user, and less-than-perfect Use Cases can still aid in that (Wiegers 2006).

When to Use

You should use Use Cases when you want to clearly define the back and forth of how the user interacts with the system. Use Cases can carry a lot of descriptive information about the process, so they are great when you want to communicate more than just the steps the user takes. You can often use them in lieu of L3 Process Flows.

When Not to Use

They should not be used to depict system-to-system interactions, because Ecosystem Maps (see Chapter 12, "Ecosystem Map") and System Flows provide a clearer view of this interaction. They also should not be used for complex decisions—Decision Trees should be used instead.

Common Mistakes

The following represent the most common mistakes we have seen with Use Cases.

Making Use Cases Too Granular

Making Use Cases too granular with too much detail hurts the readers' ability to understand the user's goal. Details such as requirements or business rules should not be included. A Use Case is a high-level representation of the user's actions and the expected behavior, intended to validate with the user that the interaction is appropriate to her need and to give the developer context. The requirements and business rules should be mapped to the Use Case, but not included in the Use Case.

Using Use Cases As the Only Documentation for Requirements

Some organizations try to use Use Cases as the only documentation for the requirements. This becomes exceedingly difficult to track, as the Use Case starts to incorporate a mixture of information types, such as functional requirements, business rules, and non-functional requirements. In this situation, there is no systematic way to ensure that the requirements are complete.

Allowing the System to Be an Actor

The purpose of Use Cases is to help the reader understand the motivations, actions, and expected results of an interaction with the system. The system is never an actor because it does not have motivations. In addition, one of the key values of the Use Case is to show what the user is trying to accomplish and how the system responds. If the system is the actor, the Use Case simply becomes a series of system steps. Use a System Flow to diagram system-only flows.

Related Models

There are many different formats for Use Cases. The format that deviates the most from the RML Use Case template is set up as two columns, one for user actions and one for system actions, as shown in Figure 10-9. The business stakeholder reads the Use Case by reading back and forth between the columns. In other formats, the same basic information is captured as in the RML Use Case template, but the display or field names are different.

Some Use Case approaches suggest that actors could be either human users or other systems that interact with the system being developed. We propose other RML models to handle system-to-system interactions, such as System Flows.

User stories are not included in RML because they provide no visual or textual representation to help identify missing requirements.

The following list briefly describes the most important models that influence or are enhanced by Use Cases. Chapter 26, "Using Models Together," contains a more thorough discussion about all related models.

- **Org Charts** These can be used to help identify actors for Use Cases.
- **Process Flows** These are used to identify Use Cases from L2 or L3 Process Flows.
- **System Flows** These document how the system responds automatically to various triggers. Use Cases can help to identify System Flows if there are many system response steps in a row.
- **Feature Trees** These are used to identify Use Cases.
- **Decision Trees** These are used to describe complex logic found in Use Cases.
- **Business Data Diagrams (BDDs)** These are used to help identify Use Cases when you consider the six verbs that occur on business data objects.
- **Business Objectives Models** These are mapped to Use Cases within the organizational benefit metadata.

Name	Save item for purchase.	
ID	UC_001	
Description	While browsing items in the eStore, a user finds an item he is not ready to purchase yet, but he wants to save it to a list so that he can later find the item that he was previously interested in.	
Actors	eStore customer.	
Organizational Benefits	Increase sales by helping the customer remember products he was previously interested in.	
Frequency of Use	20% of users save an item to be bought later each time they visit the site. 50% of saved items are purchased within one year of the saved date.	
Triggers	The user selects an option to save an item.	
Preconditions	User is viewing an item in the catalog.	
Postconditions	The item selected to be saved is visible to the user when he views his saved items. The item selected to be saved is reflected as a saved item when the user views his eStore search and browse results.	
Main Course	User	System
		1. System prompts user to confirm saving selected item instead of purchasing it right away.
	2. User confirms to save now (see EX1).	
		3. System determines the user is not logged on and redirects user to log on (see AC1).
	4. User logs on (see AC2, AC3).	
		5. System stores the saved item (see EX2). 6. System redirects the user to his saved items list to view the full list.
Alternate Courses		AC1 System determines user is already logged on. 1. Return to Main Course step 5.
	AC2 User logs off again.	1. Return user to Main Course step 3.
	AC3 User does not have an account already. 1. User creates an account.	2. System confirms account creation. 3. Return user to Main Course step 4.
Exceptions	EX1 User decides to purchase the item now. 1. See "Purchase item" Use Case.	
	EX2 System fails on saving item to list. 2. Return user to Main Course step 1.	1. System notifies user that an error has occurred.

FIGURE 10-9 Alternate Use Case format.

Exercise

The following exercise is intended to help you to gain a better understanding of how to use this model. The exercise is open ended, and therefore the answer you come up with could be substantially different than the answer that we have provided. There are potentially many correct solutions. The answer provides an explanation of how we arrived at our solution. You will gain the most out of the exercise by attempting to do it yourself before looking at the solution. The answers for the exercises can be found in Appendix C.

Instructions

Create a Use Case for the scenario described here, and provide several example requirements.

Scenario

You are working on a project to launch a new eStore to sell flamingos and other lawn decorations, and you are working with the flamingo product managers to document the requirements for adding a new flamingo or lawn decoration to the eStore. The new item already exists in the master product data set but is not yet sold in the eStore.

Additional Resources

There are entire books written on Use Cases and user stories, so you can refer to those for more detail. Here are some of our favorites:

- *Use Cases: Requirements in Context* is a thorough book on Use Cases, including a methodical analysis of each section of a Use Case, with many examples (Kulak and Guiney 2000).
- Section 4.7 of *The Software Requirements Memory Jogger* has an overview of Use Cases, including a discussion of how they relate to user stories (Gottesdiener 2005).
- Chapter 9 of *More About Software Requirements* is about Use Cases and has a good template. Use Cases, including their use as a basis for estimation, are discussed throughout the book, (Wiegers 2006).
- Chapter 2 of *Requirements by Collaboration* has a thorough discussion about how to use Use Cases (Gottesdiener 2002).
- *User Stories Applied: For Agile Software Development* is an entire book of practical suggestions for writing and using user stories (Cohn 2004).
- *Extreme Programming Explained, Embrace Change* has a detailed explanation of user stories (Beck and Andres 2004).

References

- Beck, Kent, and Cynthia Andres. 2004. *Extreme Programming Explained: Embrace Change, Second Edition.* Upper Saddle River, NJ: Addison-Wesley Professional.
- Cohn, Mike. 2004. *User Stories Applied: For Agile Software Development.* Upper Saddle River, NJ: Addison-Wesley Professional.
- Gottesdiener, Ellen. 2002. *Requirements by Collaboration: Workshops for Defining Needs.* Boston, MA: Addison-Wesley Professional.

- Gottesdiener, Ellen. 2005. *The Software Requirements Memory Jogger.* Salem, NH: Goal/QPC.
- Kulak, Daryl, and Eamonn Guiney. 2000. *Use Cases: Requirements in Context*. New York, NY: ACM Press.
- Wiegers, Karl E. 2006. *More About Software Requirements: Thorny Issues and Practical Advice.* Redmond, WA: Microsoft Press.
- Wiegers, Karl E. 2003. *Software Requirements, Second Edition.* Redmond, WA: Microsoft Press.

CHAPTER 11

Roles and Permissions Matrix

When a company moves into a new building space, the office managers have to work quickly to set up security access to the building for the employees. Imagine a building that is three stories tall, with 600 employees who need access. The doors to the lobby are open to the public, but access to the building beyond the lobby is for employees only or those with escorts. There is an executive suite on the third floor with access restricted to executives and their office managers. There is a human resources area that stores confidential employee files, and only certain people are allowed in that area without an escort from HR. There is a research lab that is closed off to all but a few specified researchers and, of course, the executives. The remainder of the third floor of the building is restricted to finance employees who have offices on that floor. All areas are accessible to anyone with an escort who has access, with the exception of the research lab, which requires special approval for any individual without access.

The Roles and Permissions Matrix is an RML people model that defines the types of roles and their associated permissions required to execute operations in the system.

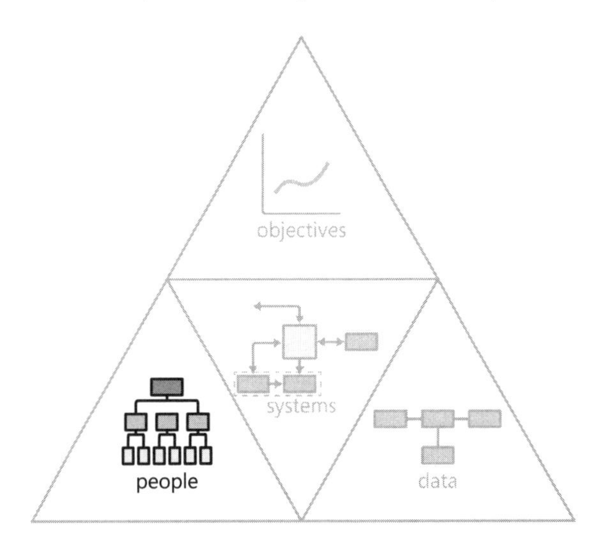

A *role* is a name for a collection of users who share common functions and access to a system. Typically, roles are grouped by type of role, such as Administrative, Customer, or Manager, or possibly by internal versus external users. An *operation* can be an individual function in the system or a group of functions, and it can be conceptual or an actual physical element in the user interface. Figure 11-1 shows the relationship between user, role, and operation. The "n" label in the diagram shows that there is a many-to-many relationship between operations and roles and between roles and users.

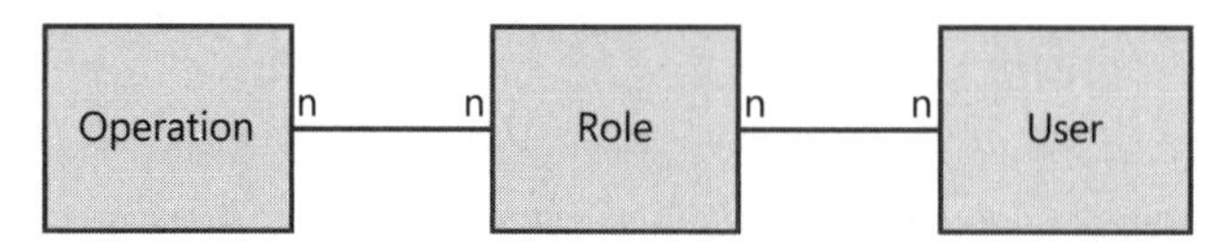

FIGURE 11-1 The relationships in a Roles and Permissions Matrix.

Many projects require you to define catalogs of users and their access to the system. The user list and corresponding permissions could be simple (for example, three users, all of whom are administrators). However, often the scenario is much more complex, with a user's access to system operations dependent on the role the user has in the system.

Roles and Permissions Matrix Template

Roles and Permissions Matrices are grids that define all of the possible user roles, system operations, and the specific permissions on those operations by role. Role names are represented in the columns, and system operations are in the rows. Both the roles and the operations can be grouped for ease of reading. Figure 11-2 shows the template for a Roles and Permissions Matrix.

Roles and Permissions Matrix	Role Group 1	Role 1	Role 2	…	Role Group 2	…	Role n
Operations Group 1							
Operation 1		X					
Operation 2		X					
Operation 3		X					
Operation 4		X					
....		X					
....							X
....							X
....		X					
....		X	X				
....		X	X				
....		X	X				
Operations Group 2							
....			X			X	X
....			X	X		X	X
....			X	X			
Operation n			X				

FIGURE 11-2 The Roles and Permissions Matrix template.

Each square in the grid indicates whether the intersecting role has permissions for the operation. The "X" indicates that the role for that column has permission to perform the operation for that row. For example, as shown in Figure 11-3, the first "X" in this template grid indicates that Role 1 can perform Operation 1. The "X" can be replaced with something that indicates the scope of the permission; this will be discussed later in the chapter. A blank cell indicates that there is no permission for that role and operation combination.

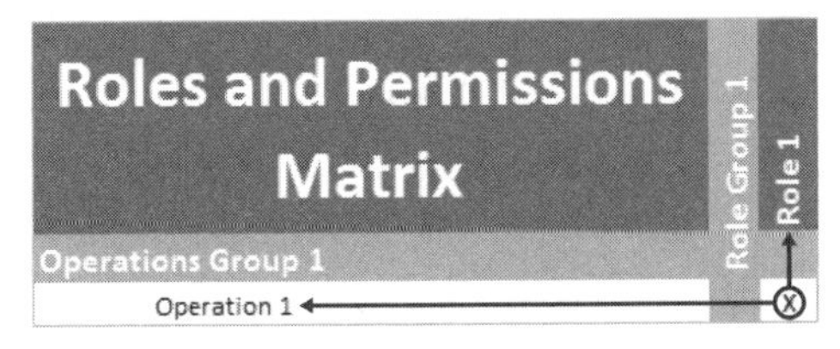

FIGURE 11-3 Example permission for Role 1 and Operation 1.

Tool Tip Roles and Permissions Matrices are created in a spreadsheet such as Microsoft Excel, a table in Microsoft Word or Microsoft PowerPoint, or in a requirements management tool.

Example

The Roles and Permissions Matrix in Figure 11-4 is for a financial portal and shows that there are five internal user roles, two external user roles, and approximately 20 operations in the system. In this example, all roles can perform the "Update profile information" and "Update profile password" operations. However, only users who have the role of Administrator can perform the "Create user account" or "Set access to portal" operations. If an internal user wants permission to view payment inquiries but doesn't already have it, this grid can be reviewed to see that the user must have an Administrator or Accountant role. It is up to an Administrator to determine whether the user should be assigned the new role, because it is the Administrator who has permission to perform the operation "Set client access to finance system."

Roles and Permissions Matrix	Internal Users	Administrator	Standard User	Accountant	Broker	Salesperson	External Client Users	Client Administrator	Client User
Accounts									
Create user account		X							
Set access to portal		X							
Set access to finance system		X							
Create client account		X							
Set up client account in portal		X							
Assign roles		X						X	
Set client access to finance system		X						X	
Update profile information		X	X	X	X	X		X	X
Update profile password		X	X	X	X	X		X	X
View access to client data		X	X					X	X
Write access to client data								X	X
Finance									
Create payment inquiries					X			X	X
Request payment deductions								X	X
Pay billing invoices								X	X
View payment inquiries		X		X				X	X
View payment deductions		X		X				X	X
View billing invoices		X		X	X	X		X	X
Reporting									
View schedule reports		X	X	X				X	X
Schedule reports		X							
Run ad-hoc reporting		X	X	X					
Communications									
Manage global announcements		X	X						

FIGURE 11-4 Example Roles and Permissions Matrix.

This example can be taken one step further if scope of data is applied to the matrix. Figure 11-5 shows a version of the Roles and Permissions Matrix that specifies what the users in each role can see: all data, their own company's data, or only their own profile's data.

Roles and Permissions Matrix	Internal Users	Administrator	Standard User	Accountant	Broker	Salesperson	External Client Users	Client Administrator	Client User
Accounts									
Create User Account		All							
Set Access to portal		All							
Set Access to finance system		All							
Create Client Account		All							
Setup Client Account in Portal		All							
Assign Roles		All						OC	
Set Client Access to finance system		All						OC	
Update Profile Information		All	OP	OP	OP	OP		OC	OP
Update Profile Password		All	OP	OP	OP	OP		OC	OP
View access to Client Data		All	All					OC	OP
Write access to Client Data								OC	OP
Finance									
Create Payment Inquiries					All			OC	OP
Request Payment Deductions								OC	OP
Pay Billing Invoices								OC	OP
View Payment Inquiries		All		All				OC	OP
View Payment Deductions		All		All				OC	OP
View Billing Invoices		All		All	All	All		OC	OP
Reporting									
View schedule reports		All	All	All				OC	OP
Schedule reports		All							
Ad-Hoc Reporting		All	All	All					
Communications									
Manage Global Announcements		All	OP						
**OP = Own Profile									
**OC = Own Company									

FIGURE 11-5 Example Roles and Permissions Matrix with scope of data defined.

Creating Roles and Permissions Matrices

Figure 11-6 illustrates the process of creating Roles and Permissions Matrices at a high level.

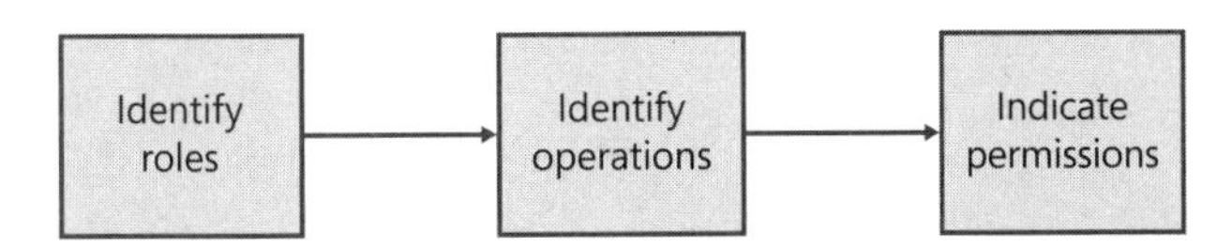

FIGURE 11-6 The process for creating Roles and Permissions Matrices.

Identify the Roles

First, identify the roles for the first row of the grid. Role Org Charts (see Chapter 8, "Org Chart") can be used to identify all types of roles in the organization, and then all of those should be reviewed to determine which ones need different permissions in the system.

For example, a role Org Chart for a sales department might contain a variety of parallel sales manager roles, each for a different segment of the organization. Upon further analysis, you might determine that one sales manager role is sufficient, because all sales managers need to have the same permissions in the system. Similarly, all of the sales managers' salespeople might also have the same permissions in the system, thereby requiring only one salesperson role. In this scenario, if each of these different roles was unnecessarily modeled separately in the matrix, it would require additional columns, making the matrix harder to use and drastically increasing the testing burden.

Use your judgment to determine which functional roles can be defined generically enough to represent a single role, using only one column of the matrix. Keep in mind that users with completely different job titles can still have the same role, and users with the same job title might actually have different roles.

One useful thing to know about a system implementation is whether multiple roles function in exactly the same way. If so, then in the Roles and Permissions Matrix, look for opportunities to create a composite role, allowing a wide variety of users to have access to the operation by giving them all the composite role name. For example, if some people in the organization have job titles such as Accountant, Mortgage Broker, and Sales Account Owner, all of whom can view financial information on a customer, but beyond that have very different permissions, then define a role called "Finance" and give that Finance role permissions on the financial operation. Then all of those people who have those job titles will have a Finance role, in addition to roles more specific to their jobs, such as Accountant, Broker, and Account Owner, respectively. Typically, it is assumed that if a user can be assigned more than one role, the permissions from the multiple roles are combined as a union of the permissions from each role. This is technically a business rule about the permissions and should be captured as such with the business rules.

This entire chapter focuses on assigning permissions by role, which is the most common use of the model. However, permissions could be assigned at an individual level as well. If there are not very many individual users to set up, particularly in initial deployments, the Roles and Permissions Matrix could be created with people names instead of role names. If there are more than approximately 20 to 30 users, however, this use of the matrix starts to get unwieldy, and roles should be used instead of individual user names.

Identify the Operations

Next you need to identify the operations of the system to which the permissions apply. Examples of operations are system functions, screens in the system, or menus within the system. For example, if a system is divided into pages with operations on them (such as an administrative page, a report page, and a collateral page) and within a specified page of the system, all operations should have the same level of access, then permissions can be defined at the page level. If the system is not subdivided in this way, it might be necessary to define permissions at the function level (for instance, for the update account, update account owner, view finance reports, and view sales reports functions).

To determine which operations to include in the matrix, use existing Business Data Diagrams (BDDs) to identify objects for which permissions are required to restrict access to that data (see Chapter 19, "Business Data Diagram"). The same is true for associated Data Dictionaries, in which specific attributes need different permissions (see Chapter 21, "Data Dictionary").

Further, as the operations are defined, consider what types of actions can occur within those operations. The possible actions are create, update, delete, use, move, and copy. For example, when you are thinking about an operation to "update profile," also consider the other five actions, to see whether they are valid system operations, and then define permissions on them by asking questions such as, "Who can delete a profile?"

You can also review menus and screens in the system for those that need to have security defined for them.

It's important to remember to have an operation to assign roles and permissions with permissions defined in the matrix. Otherwise, the system might require a developer to change code to add or change permissions as user roles are added or removed.

Indicate Permissions

After roles and operations are defined, the permissions are indicated in the grid, each with an "X." To complete the matrix, consider every role and operation combination by looking at every cell in the matrix, one at a time. If the role has access for the specific operation, put an "X" in the cell representing their intersection.

You will need to talk to the subject matter experts to determine which roles have access to each operation. Having the Roles and Permissions Matrix to facilitate this helps them think of permissions they might not have otherwise thought of. It is also worthwhile to consider any privacy statements or legal restrictions that might put restrictions on data access and therefore drive permissions. For example, most roles probably should not have access to users' Social Security numbers. If no users should have access to view a piece of data, then that field should be masked and specified as such in the Data Dictionary for that attribute, instead of being included in the Roles and Permissions Matrix.

Other specific scenarios that warrant further special handling in Roles and Permissions Matrices are described in the remainder of this section.

Permissions by Operation

Roles often have different permissions for a single operation. For example, a common situation is one in which one role can edit a piece of data whereas other roles can only view the same data. You can best handle this scenario in your matrix by creating different operations for each type of action that applies to the data, one for "edit" and one for "view," as shown in Figure 11-7.

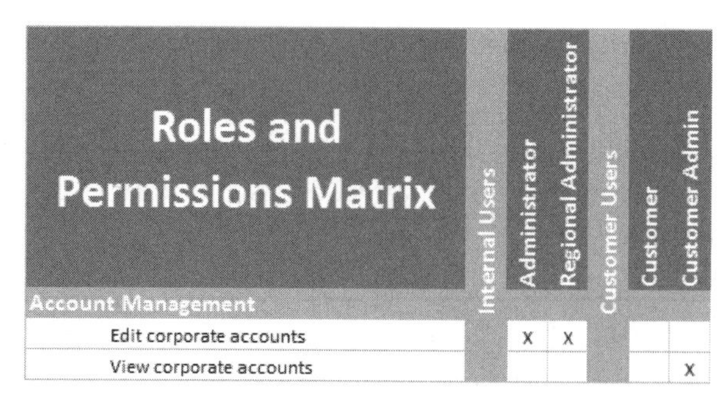

Roles and Permissions Matrix	Internal Users	Administrator	Regional Administrator	Customer Users	Customer	Customer Admin
Account Management						
Edit corporate accounts		X	X			
View corporate accounts						X

FIGURE 11-7 Varying permissions by types of operations.

Permissions on Scope of Data

Another common scenario is one in which users have permissions on only a certain scope of the business data objects, such as a geographic scope (local, regional, or global). For example, suppose that an administrative user can edit all accounts, but a regional account owner can edit accounts only within his or her region. To handle this scenario, use words in the box instead of an "X" to denote the scope of the data the role has access to. In the example shown in Figure 11-8, the roles to the far right are external client roles whose members should only be able to view data related to them, not that of all clients. The matrix shows this by labeling the box "client only" to show which data the external roles can see.

Roles and Permissions Matrix	Internal Users	Administrator	Standard User	Accountant	Broker	Salesperson	External Client	Client Administrator	Client User
Accounts									
Create user account		X							
Set access to portal		X							
Set access to finance system		X							
Create client account		X							
Set up client account in portal		X							
Assign roles		X						client only	
Set client access to finance system		X						client only	
Update profile information		X	X	X	X	X		client only	client only
Update profile password		X	X	X	X	X		client only	client only
View access to client data		X	X					client only	client only
Write access to client data								client only	client only

FIGURE 11-8 Varying permissions on scope of data.

If the scope of the data for a particular role is the same for every operation that it has permissions for, instead of labeling literally every cell in the column, use a shorthand notation and define it in a legend. For the prior example, if "client only" was the scope on all operations for the Client Administrator and Client User, all of the "X's" could be "C's," and a legend could explain that "C = client only" and "X = unrestricted access to the operation," as illustrated in Figure 11-9.

Roles and Permissions Matrix	Internal Users	Administrator	Standard User	Accountant	Broker	Salesperson	External Client	Client Administrator	Client User
Accounts									
Create user account		X							
Set access to portal		X							
Set access to finance system		X							
Create client account		X							
Set up client account in portal		X							
Assign roles		X						C	
Set client access to finance system		X						C	
Update profile information		X	X	X	X	X		C	C
Update profile password		X	X	X	X	X		C	C
View access to client data		X	X					C	C
Write access to client data								C	C
** C = Client only									
** X = Unrestricted access to the operation									

FIGURE 11-9 Varying permissions on scope of data for all operations for a role.

Common Permissions on Related Operations

Finally, another common scenario is one in which different but related operations, such as "Create report" and "Edit report" and "Delete report," have the same permissions. If they truly have the same permissions across all roles, then it is better to create one row for a combined operation, such as "Create, edit, and delete report" and use "X" to denote the permissions. Differentiate operations only if there is reason to do so. This is illustrated in Figure 11-10.

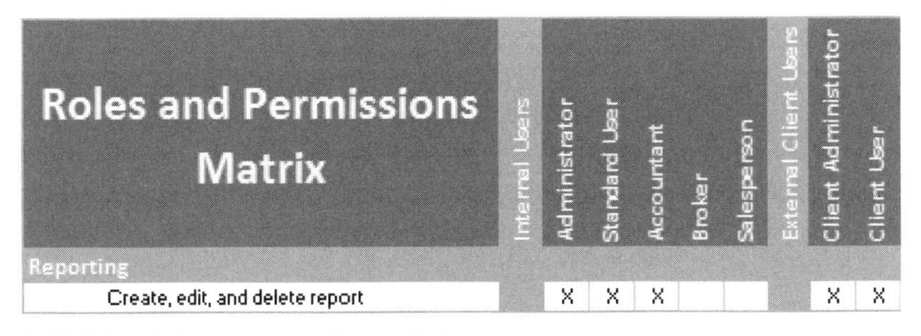

Roles and Permissions Matrix	Internal Users	Administrator	Standard User	Accountant	Broker	Salesperson	External Client Users	Client Administrator	Client User
Reporting									
Create, edit, and delete report		X	X	X				X	X

FIGURE 11-10 Common operations with the same permissions.

A Word About When to Create the Matrix

A Roles and Permissions Matrix should be created iteratively on a project. Specific sections of the matrix can be updated at the time the related operations with the system are analyzed. For example, as reports are analyzed, the reports permissions can be completed while the business experts are thinking about them.

Because the Roles and Permissions Matrix is created iteratively, you typically only need one on your project. However, if you have a large variance in systems, or parts of systems within the solution that have different types of roles and operations, you can create more than one matrix.

Using Roles and Permissions Matrices

The Roles and Permissions Matrix is most suitable for describing a role-based security model; if that is not the security model used, then this model might not be useful. Roles and Permissions Matrices are not meant to be used for projects in which users will be assigned permissions on an ad hoc basis in a live system, rather than by their roles. If ad hoc permission assignments at the user level should be allowed, you should include a requirement separate from the matrix for it.

Deriving Requirements

The Roles and Permissions Matrix itself contains business rules that support security requirements and is not typically used to derive requirements. For example, it might support an overarching requirement that states that "Users can only perform actions granted by their role." The matrix defines the business rules to support those requirements, but it does not help identify those overarching requirements. However, you can discover requirements when you are reviewing a Roles and Permissions Matrix with the business stakeholders. The permissions or operations might trigger them to remember additional needed functionality.

Driving Completeness

Roles and Permissions Matrices are simple in that they stand alone for development and testing purposes and do not require individual business rule statements to be written for them. In fact, trying to list out the roles and associated permissions as individual text statements without using the matrix would be challenging. It would be virtually impossible to ensure completeness of that list of business rules. In contrast, when you use the matrix format for analysis, if every cell in the matrix is considered, then it can be guaranteed that no role and permission pair has been overlooked. Business teams can also review the matrix easily, which is not the case with a long list of business rules.

Identifying Additional Functions

As mentioned previously, the Roles and Permissions Matrix should be defined on an iterative basis throughout the requirements effort on a project, rather than being left to the end. It is possible that asking about permissions on an operation will trigger a business stakeholder to remember other related functionality not yet identified. For example, a business expert might say something like, "We need a manager to be able to edit the account name," which prompts you to realize that you do not have a requirement in the system to support the account name being editable.

Configuring Systems

In custom-developed systems, the Roles and Permissions Matrix can be used directly to implement the rules for permissions and to grant access to the users in the finished system. For systems that are purchased and configured, Roles and Permissions Matrices are equally important for setting up the correct roles and users, and assigning permissions accordingly. In these instances, the operations are often predetermined by the software vendor.

Using a Roles and Permissions Matrix As a Basis for Setting Up User Data for Deployment

As just mentioned, one of the key values in using this matrix is to correctly configure a new system with roles for deployment. This matrix is very valuable if used together with user data to ensure that the actual users are set up correctly for deployment. When the list of users is developed for deployment, the Roles and Permissions Matrix should be used to ensure that consistent role names are given to each user so that the user can be assigned to that role in the system and receive the correct permissions. It is possible that users might need to belong to more than one role, so it is important to set up the user data to support users having multiple role assignments where appropriate.

Although the list of users for deployment does not belong in a requirements model, there are ways to take advantage of the Roles and Permissions Matrix model when creating one.

First, when you are creating the list of users for deployment, you can set up a table with the user attributes represented by columns. The attributes should be the same attributes that would be specified in the Data Dictionary for a user, such as first name, last name, role (or roles), job title, geographic region, department or segment, and email address. The most important attribute other than the user's name is the user's role, because in the context of defining permissions, that is almost always the primary discriminator. After the attributes are defined, the users can be added to the table, each user getting his or her own row. Figure 11-11 shows a typical format for user data.

Name	Role	Attribute 3	Attribute 4	...	...	Attribute n
User 1	Role for User 1	Attribute 3 value for User 1	Attribute 4 value for User 1	...	...	Attribute n value for User 1
User 2	Role for User 2	Attribute 3 value for User 2	Attribute 4 value for User 2	...	...	Attribute n value for User 2
User 3	Role for User 3	Attribute 3 value for User 3	Attribute 4 value for User 3	...	...	Attribute n value for User 3
...	...	...	...	...	...	...
...	...	...	...	...	...	...
...	...	...	...	...	...	...
...	...	...	...	...	...	...
...	...	...	...	...	...	...
User n	Role for User n	Attribute 3 value for User n	Attribute 4 value for User n	...	...	Attribute n value for User n

FIGURE 11-11 An example user data format.

The attribute values can be reused across users as appropriate. For example, User 1 and User 3 might have the same role. If users need multiple roles, those can be defined as separate columns or multiple values within the Role column. Figure 11-12 shows an example of a user data table with actual data in it. Note that each user in this table has only one role, but the roles are shared across users and are different from the job titles.

First Name	Last Name	Job Title	Role	Region	Languages	Company Name	Email
Luka	Abrus	IT Analyst	Standard User	West Coast	English	Contoso, Ltd	Luka.Abrus@contoso.com
Cynthia	Carey	Director of Procurement	Client Administrator	Texas	English, Spanish	Litware, Inc.	Cynthia_Carey@litwareinc.com
John	Evans	Intern	Standard User	East Coast	English	Contoso, Ltd	John.Evans@contoso.com
Ken	Ewert	Sales Manager	Standard User	East Coast	English	Contoso, Ltd	Ken.Ewert@contoso.com
Gabe	Frost	Chief Financial Officer	Administrator	West Coast	English	Contoso, Ltd	Gabe.Frost@contoso.com
David	Galvin	Marketing Manager	Standard User	East Coast	English	Contoso, Ltd	David.Galvin@contoso.com
Howard	Gonzalez	Executive Vice President	Client User	Texas	English, Spanish	Litware, Inc.	Howard_Gonzalez@litwareinc.com
Chris	Gray	Director of IT	Administrator	West Coast	English	Contoso, Ltd	Chris.Gray@contoso.com
Julia	Ilyina	Director of Sales	Administrator	East Coast	English	Contoso, Ltd	Julia.Ilyina@contoso.com
Sanjay	Jacob	Intern	Standard User	West Coast	English	Contoso, Ltd	Sanjay.Jacob@contoso.com
Katie	Jordan	Business Analyst	Standard User	West Coast	English	Contoso, Ltd	Katie.Jordan@contoso.com
Bob	Kelly	Procurement Analyst	Client User	Texas	English, Spanish	Litware, Inc.	Bob_Kelly@litwareinc.com

FIGURE 11-12 An example user data table.

As soon as a draft of the Roles and Permissions Matrix exists, it can be used to ensure completeness in the user data. All internal user roles in the Roles and Permissions Matrix should probably have some users defined in the user data; if this is not the case, some users might be missing or there could be unnecessary roles defined.

If your user data is set up correctly, you can use Excel pivot tables to look for any general trends in missing data. For example, a pivot table that shows the full list of roles and count of users in each role might trigger a business stakeholder to notice that there are too few users in a particular role. Further, the pivot table could actually group the users by role name to look for missing individuals in roles such as Administrator. Figure 11-13 shows a possible pivot table for the user data example.

Role	Count of Role
Standard User	10
Client Administrator	2
Administrator	6
Client User	2
Broker	1
Salesperson	3
Accountant	1
Grand Total	**25**

FIGURE 11-13 Pivot table showing number of users in each role.

This pivot table might prompt someone with knowledge about the system to question whether there should be additional Broker or Accountant users added to the system. Also, they should notice that only four total Client users are defined, which might be fine for an initial release but probably is not the final list for deployment.

When to Use

A Roles and Permissions Matrix should be used for any solution that has a role-based security model, including custom development or Commercial Off the Shelf (COTS) implementations. COTS implementations commonly have a role-based security model, and the Roles and Permissions Matrix can help the team configure the COTS software correctly.

When Not to Use

If permissions are not assigned by roles, a Roles and Permissions Matrix is typically not a helpful model.

Common Mistakes

The following represent the most common mistakes that we have seen with Roles and Permissions Matrices.

Missing Operations

Roles and Permissions Matrices are relatively simple to create, but a common mistake is to miss some of the operations.

Struggling to Organize the Roles

It is often a challenge to decide how to divide the roles to have the fewest number of roles and still achieve the required uniqueness. If you find that deciding on the number of roles is problematic, it is fine to have one or two extra roles if that makes the matrix easier to create and read.

Related Models

Some Roles and Permissions Matrices might have roles and operations, but instead of calling out unique operations on individual rows, the permissions are marked with some form of the acronym CRUD (Create, Read, Update, and Delete) to indicate the type of permission. For example, the operation might be "Report" and the role "Sales Manager," with the intersecting permission being labeled "R" because the sales manager can read reports, but not create, update, or delete them.

The following list briefly describes the most important models that influence or are enhanced by Roles and Permissions Matrices. Chapter 26, "Using Models Together," contains a more thorough discussion about all related models.

- **Org Charts** These are used to create Roles and Permissions Matrices because they identify types of roles or users who need corresponding permissions in the system.
- **Business Data Diagrams (BDDs)** These help identify business data objects that might require permissions so that access to those objects can be restricted.
- **Data Dictionaries** These can be used to capture the attributes of users mentioned in the user data.

Exercise

The following exercise is intended to help you to gain a better understanding of how to use this model. The exercise is open ended, and therefore the answer you come up with could be substantially different than the answer that we have provided. There are potentially many correct solutions. The answer provides an explanation of how we arrived at our solution. You will gain the most out of the exercise by attempting to do it yourself before looking at the solution. The answers for the exercises can be found in Appendix C.

Instructions

Create a Roles and Permissions Matrix for the scenario described here.

Scenario

You have been assigned to a project to launch a new eStore to sell flamingos and assorted lawn decorations. The eStore will have a basic catalog of products that internal Product Managers will set up. Each customer will be able to view all products, purchase any products, and view his or her own order history within the eStore. Customers can maintain their own account information, but there will be internal account representatives who can update information for them as well. Those account representatives can also view a customer's current shopping cart and order history. There are managers who will want to look at reports from the system to see what products are selling so that they can choose to feature or add additional products.

Additional Resources

- There is a high-level description of how to create Excel PivotTables (mentioned for using the Roles and Permissions Matrix with user data) at *http://office.microsoft.com/en-us/excel-help/pivottable-reports-101-HA001034632.aspx*.

PART IV

Systems Models

CHAPTER 12

Ecosystem Map

We recently moved into a new house and were trying to set up our home entertainment system so that it could be accessed from different rooms in the house. When we first moved in, we had the satellite company install an outlet for the receiver box for the master bedroom television. We also wanted to put a television in a home theater room without having to spend extra money to install and use an additional satellite receiver, but running extra cable to this location was not an option, so we needed a wireless solution.

We wanted to be able to stream music and movies from our home computer in a guest bedroom to the televisions in both the theater room and the bedroom. We had a streaming box that allowed us to transmit content from satellite receivers and other devices over a wireless Internet connection. The streaming box would solve the problem of putting the content from the satellite receiver onto the wireless network, but we needed a way to access the content on the television in the home theater room.

In addition, we needed to find a way to get the content from our computer to the streaming device and then find a way to access that content from the televisions in the bedroom and theater room. We already had a game station that could receive content from our home computer; however, it could not receive content from the streaming box. So we had to add a home theater application that could receive the streaming video over the wireless network and play it on a television.

To understand the proposed solution to our problem, I had to draw a diagram showing all of the systems and the information flowing among them (see Figure 12-1).

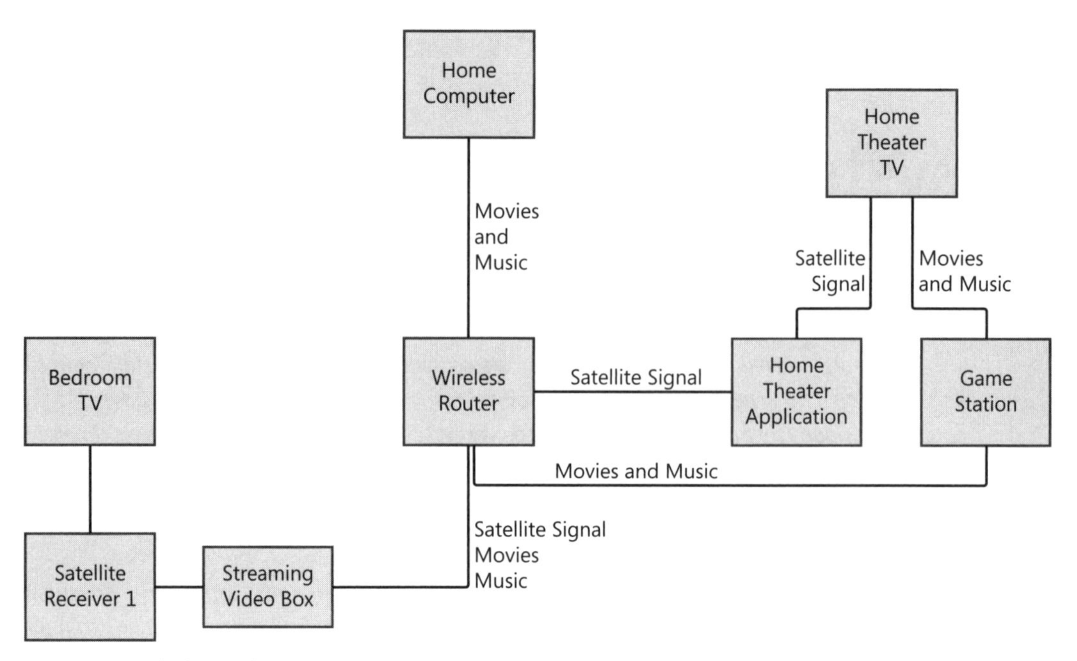

FIGURE 12-1 The home theatre Ecosystem Map example.

System models describe the systems themselves, what they look like, and how they interact with users and other systems. The Ecosystem Map is an RML systems model that shows which systems interact with each other and the nature of the relationship. The Ecosystem Map shows all of the systems in the solution ecosystem, which allows you to systematically ensure that you analyze all of the systems. In this model, it is a reasonably straightforward task to identify the systems and be confident that the diagram is complete. Note that each system is not necessarily a physical system but typically represents an application or logical system.

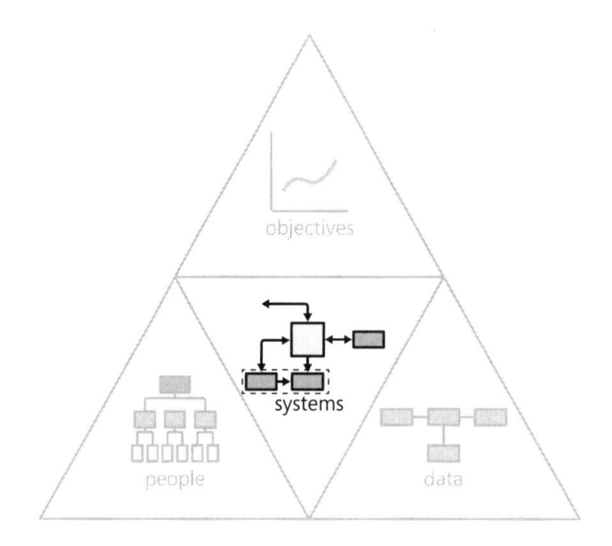

One of the primary advantages of an Ecosystem Map over a simple list of systems is that it is significantly easier to identify all the systems that a particular system links to, by looking at the possible combinations one at a time.

Ecosystem Map Template

An Ecosystem Map is a very simple diagram that requires the use of only two types of symbols: boxes, which represent systems, connected by lines that represent interfaces between the systems. There are also four optional symbols: arrows to indicate the direction that data flows between the systems, a label on a line to indicate a general description of the nature of the data passed between the systems, a faint line around a subset of the systems in the diagram to group any of the systems, and a callout with text to add supplemental information about the systems. The elements of an Ecosystem Map are summarized in Table 12-1.

TABLE 12-1 Ecosystem Map Elements

Symbol	Meaning
System	Any system in the ecosystem.
———	An interface between two systems.
Major Business Data Object	A label for any major business data object passed between systems. This optional label is added to the interface line, which typically has an arrow to indicate the direction in which the information flows.
System A — Callout to add supplemental information	The callout is used to define and explain a system in further detail. Typically, this is used to spell out the meaning of a system acronym or describe functions that a system has.
Grouping Grouping	A boundary to group systems together in a manner that facilitates readability. This can be represented as a dotted line around systems or as a colored box.

The symbols can be combined with as many systems and interfaces as necessary to depict the full ecosystem. When it is put together, the template looks like the one shown in Figure 12-2.

Labels can be added to the interfaces to show which major business data objects flow between systems. Typically, arrows are also added to the interface lines to indicate the direction in which data flows between the systems.

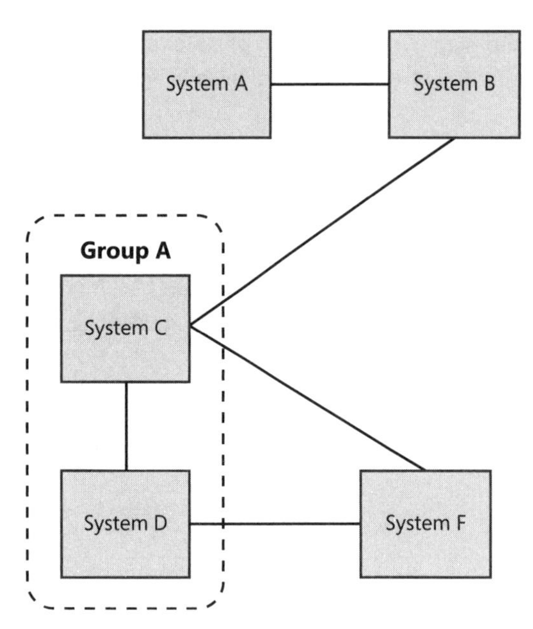

FIGURE 12-2 The Ecosystem Map template.

The example template shown in Figure 12-3 includes objects. Business Data Object 1 flows from System A to System B. Business Data Object 2 flows from System B to System A, as well as back and forth between Systems B and C. Notice that two interface lines are used to clearly show which direction Business Data Object 1 and Business Data Object 2 flow between System A and System B. Only one interface line is used to show the same business data object, Business Data Object 2, as it flows back and forth between Systems B and C.

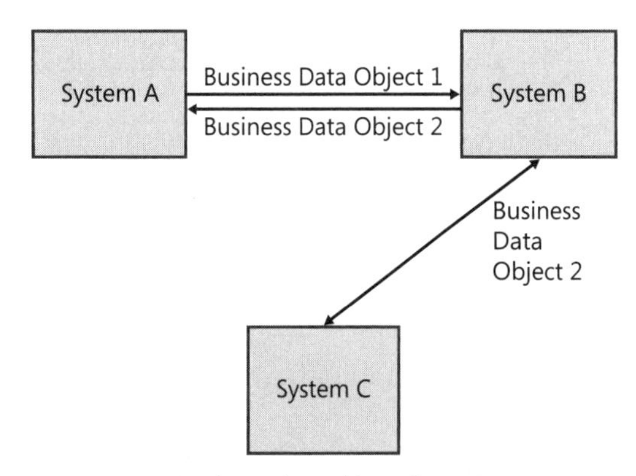

FIGURE 12-3 Business data objects in an Ecosystem Map template.

If it is important to describe the nature of the interface in more detail than that which fits on an Ecosystem Map, each interface can be documented by using a System Interface Table (see Chapter 18, "System Interface Table"). In this case, an identifier on the interface line is a reference to the relevant

System Interface Table. Figure 12-4 shows an example in which the interface between System A and System B would be described in the System Interface Table IT001 and the interface between Systems B and C is in IT002.

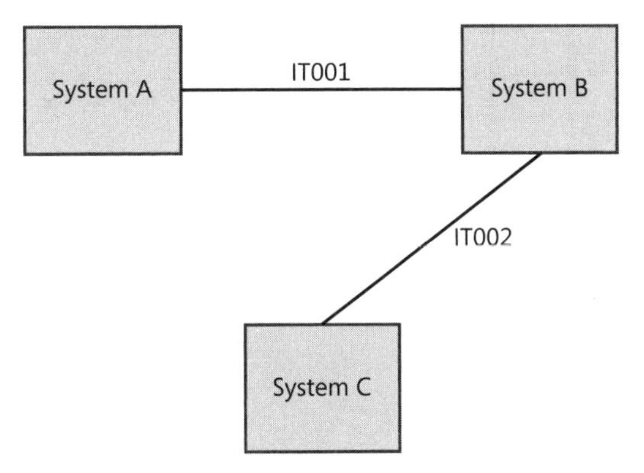

FIGURE 12-4 System Interface Tables referenced on an Ecosystem Map template.

Tool Tip Ecosystem Maps are most easily created in a tool such as Microsoft Visio, which allows you to easily maneuver the objects and lines. Often, it is easiest to initially create an Ecosystem Map by writing the names of systems on sticky notes on a whiteboard and drawing lines between them, because this allows the systems to be moved around quickly. This is a great visual way to draft Ecosystem Maps and get feedback before making a diagram in a tool.

Example

A retail company is building an order management system. When you review the Ecosystem Map in Figure 12-5, you can quickly see the following: The Order Routing and Tracking System (ORTS) interacts with the Order Entry, Fraud Services (FSS), Order Fulfillment, Accounts Receivable (ARS), and Data Warehouse (SDW) systems. The Data Warehouse system also interacts with the Accounts Receivable system. You can also infer that any order fulfillment, order entry, or fraud services information in the Data Warehouse is probably provided via the Order Routing and Tracking System. Finally, you can see that there are no other systems in the ecosystem relevant to the project..

You might have noticed that the diagram was hard to read because you didn't know all of the systems by their acronyms. Figure 12-6 shows an example of the same Ecosystem Map with some of the optional symbols in it for clarity. The callouts are helpful for people who read the diagram but are not familiar with the systems' common names. The grouping shows how the order systems are related as part of the full order delivery function. And the major business data objects are labeled to show what types of information pass between the systems.

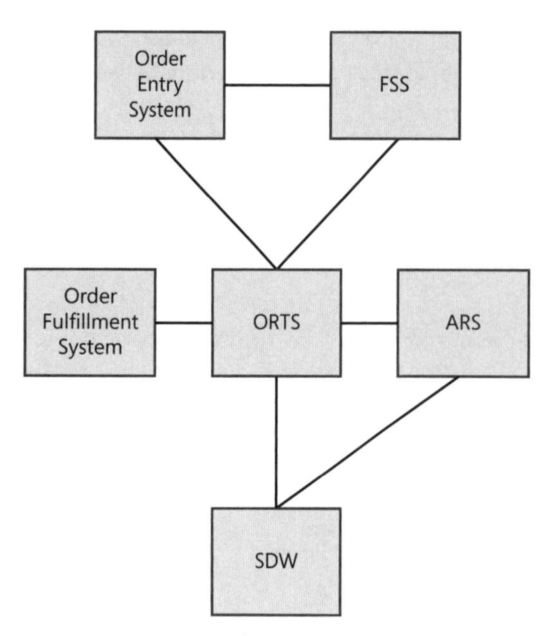

FIGURE 12-5 An example Ecosystem Map.

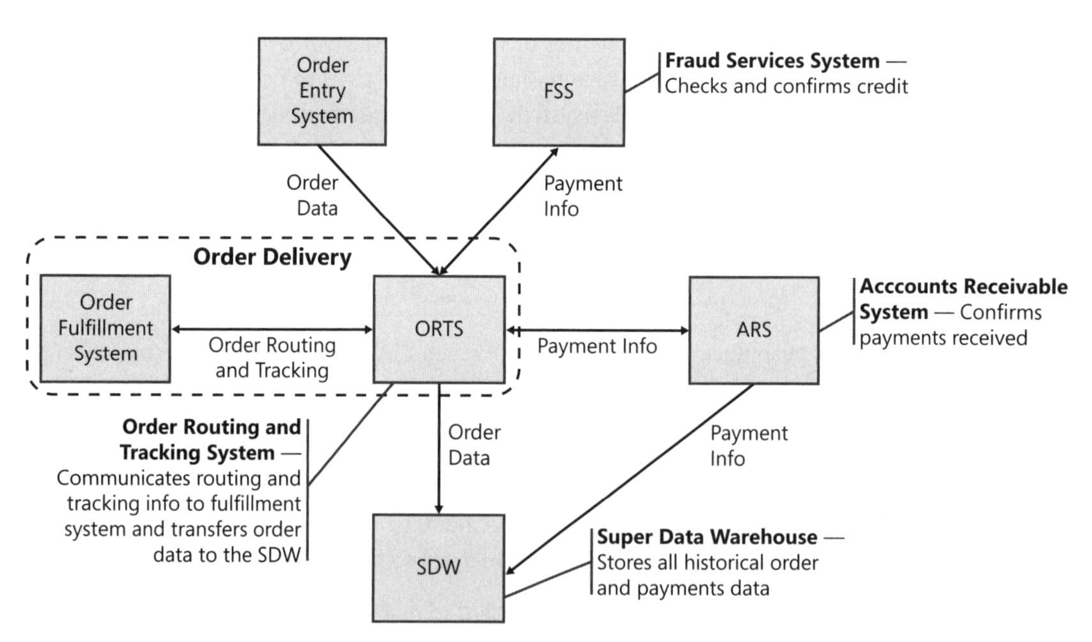

FIGURE 12-6 An example Ecosystem Map with optional symbols.

Creating Ecosystem Maps

Ecosystem Maps are created by considering all possible systems. With diligence, you can ensure that this model is complete. Figure 12-7 shows the process for creating an Ecosystem Map.

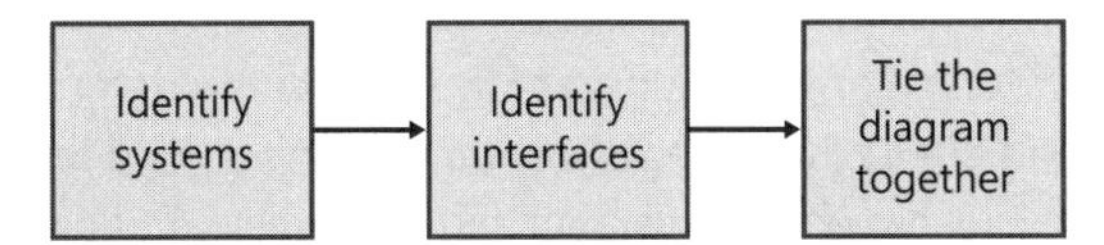

FIGURE 12-7 The process for creating an Ecosystem Map.

Identify Systems

What helps make the Ecosystem Map a robust model is that for each system, you only have to think about the systems that connect to it. Generally, stakeholders are readily able to completely identify connected systems for a single system. As you work your way through considering every system, the Ecosystem Map becomes a visual aid for identifying missing systems. This is much better than working with a list of systems, and it has the added benefit of allowing you to understand which systems interact with each other.

Start by identifying all the systems that you are aware of and how they connect. Create a first version of the diagram and begin using it without worrying whether you have every system documented. Over the course of time, stakeholders you interview will point out missing systems. You will find that you can very quickly get to a complete diagram.

You will probably need to talk with the more technical stakeholders and developers to get additional information. Technical teams often have diagrams that show applications mixed in with physical systems and databases, routers, and other network infrastructure components. These diagrams can be a good starting point for an Ecosystem Map.

If you're developing an Ecosystem Map for an existing system, you might be able to find information about the related systems from existing models that identify systems. You can use Process Flows, System Flows, Data Flow Diagrams, or Business Data Diagrams to look for missing systems, by answering the following questions:

- Which system or systems are used for each step of the Process Flow/System Flow? You can also look at the swim lanes in each System Flow to determine which systems are described in each lane.
- In a Data Flow Diagram, which systems run the processes that modify the data? In which systems does the data live?
- Which system or systems create, update, use, delete, move, or copy each business data object on the Business Data Diagram?

All of your systems should be listed in your project glossary. So while you're gathering information about the systems, be sure to capture a description of each.

When you are working with large enterprises, the Ecosystem Map can be very complicated. An ecosystem can have 25, 50, 100, or even more systems. With an Ecosystem Map, you are trying to provide the context relevant to your project. So the first thing you need to determine is whether or not you need to document the entire system landscape or just a subset of it. To make this determination, you need to understand what data is flowing out of the systems you are working on and into any related systems. Start with the systems that your project is impacting and trace the data flows into nearby systems. When you reach the point where your project is no longer affecting the data flowing out of a system, then the next system outwards is probably not important to your project and does not need to be on your Ecosystem Map. After you have completed this effort, you have found the subset of systems relevant to the project. You also have bounded the systems view to only the systems that the project will impact. This is typical of most analyses; you need to understand one step beyond what you are affecting, just to make sure your boundaries are correct. Talking to a technical architect can also help you determine which systems are relevant for a project.

When you need to document the entire ecosystem, one technique is to group related systems and refer to them as one super-system. You then create lower-level Ecosystem Maps that decompose the super-systems. If the example in this chapter was part of a bigger landscape, you could collectively refer to the Order Entry, Fraud Services, and Order Routing and Tracking systems as the "Order Management" super-system, which would interact with the Order Fulfillment, Accounts Receivable, and Data Warehouse systems. Don't group systems arbitrarily; group together only those systems that work together to perform a common function or set of functions.

Identify Interfaces

An Ecosystem Map models the direct system interfaces by showing you which systems are "talking" to each other. Systems have an interface only if they are exchanging information directly with each other. Using this chapter's example, the Data Warehouse might get information from the Order Fulfillment system, but it does not talk directly with it. The relationship is indirect, so there isn't an interface between them.

Optionally, you can also gather information about which actual business data objects flow between the systems, and in which direction. This information can take longer to get right. If chasing it down impedes your ability to obtain the basic information, leave it out; you don't want the pursuit of this information to delay a fundamental understanding of the systems and interfaces.

Generally the Ecosystem Map does not show people entering data into the system. However, on rare occasions, two systems are connected by a person who transfers data between the systems. In this case, include the person in the Ecosystem Map as a stick figure. The stick figure is not included in the Ecosystem Map elements table because it is rare that you need it.

If you have a large number of systems, it can be useful to create a system inventory matrix to allow you to thoroughly consider which interfaces exist. A system inventory matrix lists the systems as both rows and columns. You use this matrix to methodically look at each combination of systems and ask, "Is there an interface?" If the answer is yes, indicate it in the intersection of the systems on the matrix. Figure 12-8 shows a system inventory matrix for the example systems.

System Inventory Matrix	Order Entry	FSS	Order Fulfillment	ORTS	ARS	SDW
Systems						
Order Entry				x		
FSS				x		
Order Fulfillment				x		
ORTS	x	x	x		x	x
ARS				x		x
SDW				x	x	

FIGURE 12-8 A system inventory matrix used to identify interfaces.

If the Ecosystem Map does not contain business data objects or direction of flow, the system inventory matrix does not include them either. However, if you are planning to gather business data object flow information, you can use the table to indicate the business data objects and direction of flow for the interfaces if it will help in identifying these interfaces. Put the name of the business data object in the cell to indicate that there is an interface with data flowing from the system in the row to the system in the column. Figure 12-9 shows the table for the example Ecosystem Map that includes business data object flow.

System Inventory Matrix	Order Entry	FSS	Order Fulfillment	ORTS	ARS	SDW
Systems						
Order Entry				Order data		
FSS				Payment info		
Order Fulfillment				Order routing and tracking info		
ORTS		Payment info	Order routing and tracking info		Payment Info	Order data
ARS				Payment info		Payment Info
SDW						

FIGURE 12-9 The system inventory matrix with business data objects and flow.

You can also do a simple system inventory matrix with just Xs to identify the interfaces and then add the business data objects and flow only to the Ecosystem Map.

Tie the Diagram Together

Place your systems on a page and use lines to connect the systems that have interfaces. Arrange highly connected systems together, so that it is easy to see the connections and keep the diagram clean with the fewest crossed lines.

Ecosystem Maps follow the 7+/-2 rule. If a diagram gets very complex, use color coding or additional grouping boxes to segment the systems into logical groupings of no more than 10 items. You could use these boxes to group systems by function—for example, grouping the systems that are customer systems, sales systems, or order systems. If you use color coding, keep in mind that some readers will not be able to differentiate colors, and printouts might be in black and white, so using a patterned border on the grouping box will avoid this issue. Add callouts, if necessary, for clarity about the systems.

Using Ecosystem Maps

You should almost always use an Ecosystem Map, and it should be one of the first models you create for any project. The only exception is when the solution is a completely stand-alone system that does not interact with any other systems. Even if there are only a few systems that interact, it is still useful to create the Ecosystem Map to confirm that the picture is complete and convey that complete picture to anyone else working on the project.

Defining Scope with Ecosystem Maps

An Ecosystem Map assists the reader in understanding the big-picture view of the systems and interactions that are in scope for a project. If all systems in an organization are considered, the Ecosystem Map can guarantee that the scope is completely bounded. Ecosystem Maps are also used to indicate which integration points are in scope and which interfaces need to have requirements developed for them. In a sense, Ecosystem Maps provide a checklist for the interfaces between systems, allowing you to make sure that all possible interfaces are considered. Further, by looking at the systems, you can be reminded of user groups that you have not have talked to or missing Process Flows related to a particular system.

When you are changing a system, you need to consider whether the changes are isolated to that system, affect the interfaces with other systems, or, in fact, require changes to the other systems as well. Because you can create these diagrams fairly quickly up front, you can walk through them and ask these questions to make sure that the scope of your project is well defined.

Deriving Requirements

Because Ecosystem Maps identify system interactions, it's not surprising that they help you identify high-level interface requirements. Each line connecting systems represents an interface, so you possibly have requirements to create or modify the interface. However, these diagrams do not provide detailed information about the interactions between systems, the sequence of the interactions, or decisions. Other models, such as System Flows, Data Flow Diagrams, and System Interface Tables are more suited to convey that information.

Finally, create a matrix of the systems to use as a checklist to ensure that you are able to analyze each critical system, one at a time. It is difficult to use a diagram with many boxes as a checklist because of the two-dimensional nature of a diagram.

When to Use

Use an Ecosystem Map on any project where there is existing infrastructure with which the system you are working on will have to integrate.

When Not to Use

If the solution is a stand-alone system or packaged software, an Ecosystem Map is not necessary.

Common Mistakes

The following represent the most common mistakes that we have seen with Ecosystem Maps.

Showing Physical Systems

The Ecosystem Map is a simple diagram. One mistake analysts sometimes make is in showing physical systems, which clutters the diagram and shows information that business stakeholders generally are not concerned with. Occasionally, though, there might be a physical system such as a database that end users do access directly. Although it is a physical database, it also acts as an application and should be shown.

Too Much Documentation

Due to the simple nature of the Ecosystem Map, people sometimes try to show too much documentation about an interface, which makes the diagram confusing. Use a System Interface Table to document the details, and make a note on the interface line in the Ecosystem Map to reference the System Interface Table.

Lack of Organization

Finally, it is very easy to have 100 systems in an Ecosystem Map. The benefit of this is that you have a complete picture of the ecosystem in a single view. The challenge is that it is too complex to ensure completeness. To remedy this, group related systems together and label them as a higher-level entity. This approach can help you create an Ecosystem Map that has only the higher-level entities as well.

Related Models

Ecosystem Maps are relatively common, though their format can vary. One model related to Ecosystem Maps is called a context diagram. A *context diagram* has the system for which the project is focused at the center of the diagram in a circle, with external entities to that system arranged as the boxes around it. Only the interactions that occur directly between the system and the external entities are depicted. The Ecosystem Map also shows what other systems those systems interact with, showing the full ecosystem. Further, in context diagrams, the entities in boxes could be anything or anyone that interacts with the system, not just other systems.

Some modeling approaches consider the context diagram to be a high-level view of a Data Flow Diagram. In these cases, the context diagram also contains processes that transform the data. RML separates these two models.

The following list briefly describes the most important models that influence or are enhanced by Ecosystem Maps. Chapter 26, "Using Models Together," contains a more thorough discussion about all related models.

- **System Flows** These can represent the process of exchanging information between systems.
- **Process Flows** These show process steps executed by users, which might identify systems to support those steps.
- **Data Flow Diagrams (DFDs)** These provide information about how data is processed by various applications or processes.
- **System Interface Tables** These provide the details of the interface between two systems.
- **Business Data Diagrams (BDDs)** These identify which systems store or modify the business data objects.

Exercise

The following exercise is intended to help you to gain a better understanding of how to use this model. The exercise is open ended, and therefore the answer you come up with could be substantially different than the answer that we have provided. There are potentially many correct solutions. The answer provides an explanation of how we arrived at our solution. You will gain the most out of the exercise by attempting to do it yourself before looking at the solution. The answers for the exercises can be found in Appendix C.

Instructions

For the scenario, prepare an Ecosystem Map and a list of questions you would want to ask your technical subject matter experts so that you can create a more complete Ecosystem Map.

Scenario

In this project, you are helping to build an eStore to sell flamingos and other lawn decorations. Customers access the eStore directly. The eStore sends orders to the order processing system, which sends the final orders to the fulfillment system. The inventory system provides product inventory information to the order processing system and the storefront, and it is updated by the fulfillment system after an order is shipped. The credit system receives credit card information from the storefront and sends approval status back to the user in the storefront and to the order processing system.

The call center also allows sales representatives to see customer orders that are stored in the eStore so that they can discuss them with the customer. In addition, call center sales representatives can create orders for customers in the call center, and those orders flow through to the order processing system and the fulfillment system, just like eStore orders do. The call center also has the same interfaces to the inventory system and the credit system.

Finally, both the eStore and the call center use the same product catalog system to display product details to the customer.

Additional Resources

There are many resources that discuss models similar to Ecosystem Maps, though often they just call them context diagrams. Some of the most popular resources that discuss the alternative formats are listed here.

- *The Business Analyst's Handbook* describes this model as one level of Data Flow Diagram (Podeswa 2009).
- Section 4.3 of *The Software Requirements Memory Jogger* covers context diagrams with a focus on defining scope (Gottesdiener 2005).
- Chapter 17 of *More About Software Requirements* has a summary of context diagrams in the context of defining scope (Wiegers 2006).
- Version 2.0 of the BABOK Guide describes two different notations for context diagrams as part of scope modeling (IIBA 2009).
- Context diagrams are covered in depth in *Software Requirements & Specifications*, including a history of the model and a couple variations on it (Jackson 1998).

References

- Gottesdiener, Ellen. 2005. *The Software Requirements Memory Jogger.* Salem, NH: Goal/QPC.
- International Institute of Business Analysis (IIBA). 2009. *A Guide to the Business Analysis Body of Knowledge (BABOK Guide).* Toronto, Ontario, Canada.
- Jackson, Michael. 1998. *Software Requirements & Specifications: A Lexicon of Practice, Principles and Prejudices.* Reading, MA. Addison-Wesley Publishers.
- Podeswa, Howard. 2009. *The Business Analyst's Handbook.* Boston, MA: Course Technology, Cengage Learning.
- *Wiegers, Karl E. 2006. More About Software Requirements: Thorny Issues and Practical Advice.* Redmond, WA: Microsoft Press.

CHAPTER 13

System Flow

Day in and day out, when the temperature in your house gets too hot, the air conditioner comes on after a few minutes. When the house cools down, the temperature eventually reaches a preset value, but the air conditioner stays on for a bit longer. Then, after a specific amount of time, the air conditioner shuts off. The system doesn't require any action from you except for the initial setup of the target temperature. The air conditioner's thermostat functions by relying on timers and temperature sensors that trigger events.

The System Flow is an RML systems model that describes the activities that systems execute. They show system activities, their sequence, and system logic. System Flows help stakeholders understand complex system interactions in a visual manner so that they can easily see any back and forth interactions between systems, as well as complex branching within the systems. Note that, as in an Ecosystem Map, each system is not a physical system, but typically represents an application or logical system.

Process Flows describe the actions that a user executes, and System Flows describe automated system actions. They are very similar to Process Flows in terminology, template, and end results. However, they are very different in their content. Much of the activity described by a System Flow takes place without the user's knowledge. The user might have minimal interaction with the system, but behind the scenes, there are many actions and decisions taking place. Though users might indeed be involved in the overall process, a System Flow describes the actions of the system rather than those of the user.

We separate Process Flows and System Flows into two different models because Process Flows are focused on helping stakeholders understand how the business operates independent of systems. The System Flow describes autonomous actions of systems, so it uses some of the nomenclature in a different way to represent the most-often-used triggers, such as timers or events from physical devices. The purpose of a System Flow is to document automated processes that the business stakeholders care about, not to create a flowchart of how the entire system will operate. If there is a particular order of execution or algorithm that is important to the business stakeholders, then a System Flow would be appropriate. Remember, requirements are anything that the business stakeholders need. Usually, business stakeholders are not concerned with a majority of the automated operations in the system. However, there are cases in which they do care. For example, for a medical device that dispenses pharmaceuticals, there will be many business stakeholders (including lawyers) who want to know the exact sequence of logic that the device uses to dispense medication and how it behaves after various types of errors.

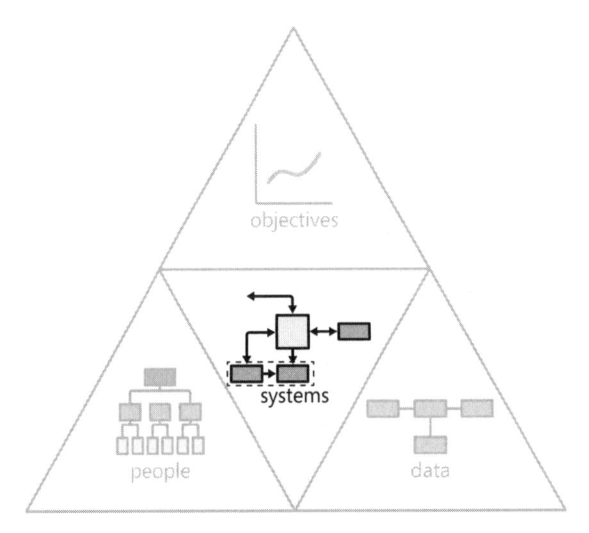

Multiple levels of System Flows are often needed to describe a flow with a sufficient level of detail, so the Process Flow hierarchy is still applicable. There are typically, at most, three levels of System Flows that might be helpful on a project: level 1 (L1), level 2 (L2), and level 3 (L3).

System Flow Template

The template for System Flows is almost exactly like the Process Flow template, so we encourage you to read Chapter 9, "Process Flow," before this one for a more detailed description. There are some slight variations in the elements' meanings, so we include Table 13-1 here to make them clear. The following list highlights the key differences of System Flow elements as compared to Process Flow elements:

- Steps and decisions are primarily actions that the system takes.
- Swim lanes are for systems instead of users.
- Incoming, outgoing, and other process references generally refer to other System Flows but might also refer to Process Flows.

The full template for System Flows looks like a Process Flow template, as you can see in Figure 13-1. It's important to notice that the swim lanes in a System Flow divide the full flow into several sections to account for the different systems that perform their specific system steps.

TABLE 13-1 System Flow Elements

Element	Meaning
Step	This is a basic system step.
→	The directional arrow connects system steps or other symbols to one another. The direction of the arrow shows the order of the steps. If the line is coming out of a decision step, it is labeled with the decision choice it represents.
Decision	The decision step splits system flows in specific ways based on the choices from this step.
Outgoing	The outgoing reference is used to show that the flow is moving to another flow. This is typically used at the end of each lower-level System Flow to indicate which flow comes next.
Incoming	The incoming reference is the complement to the outgoing symbol. It indicates that the flow is resuming from another flow. This is typically used at the beginning of each lower-level System Flow to indicate which flow came before.
Other Process	The other process symbol references another process in the middle of the flow and returns back to this flow after it ends.
	Swim lanes divide the System Flow to show which system is executing the steps. Swim lanes carry names of systems.
	The fork and join symbols are identical; the first one in a System Flow indicates a fork, and the one that follows is a join. A fork splits a flow to show that although all steps must execute, they do not have to be done sequentially. The fork allows the System Flow to avoid forcing sequencing where no sequencing exists. A fork will always be followed by a join at some point further down the flow. All steps before the join must be executed before the next step after the join can be processed. A join will always be preceded by a fork somewhere in the flow. Forks and joins can be rotated to any angle when it helps with the layout of the System Flow.

Element	Meaning
Provide additional contextual information in a callout	The callout is used to provide additional contextual information about a specific activity or event.
Grouping	Groupings add additional information to a diagram for readability. Typically, a grouping surrounds a subprocess that is not split out into its own flow. The grouping is named after that subprocess.
Event	An event indicates something external to the System Flow that happens during the process. An event is part of the normal flow. An event can be timed, which indicates that the process waits for a specific time before continuing. It could also be a trigger from a physical device such as a sensor, or it could be an event from a user.

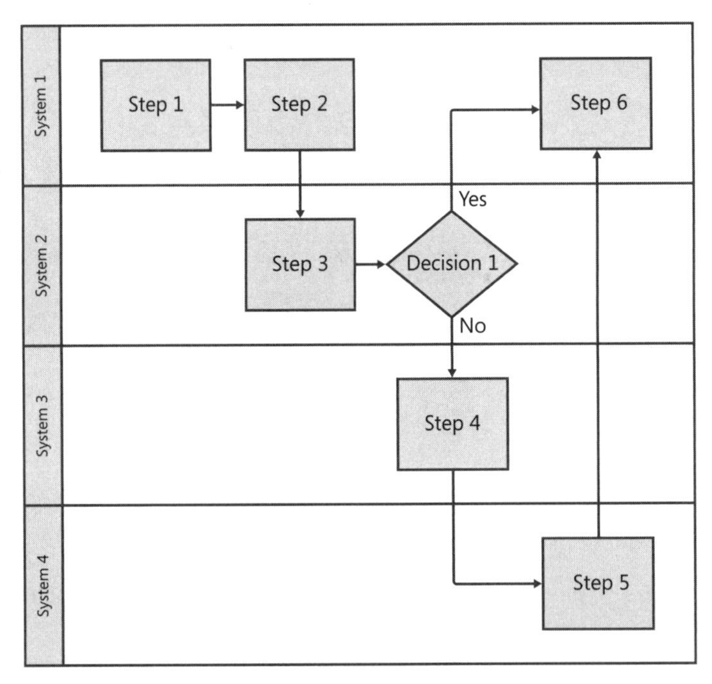

FIGURE 13-1 The System Flow template.

Tool Tip System Flows should be created in a tool that allows easy manipulation of the shapes. The tool that is most commonly used for process diagramming is Microsoft Visio, but many requirements management tools allow for easy System Flow modeling directly in them as well. If you have access to a requirements tool that supports process modeling, use the tool because it will be easier later to map the steps to individual requirements.

Example

This example describes a subway system, in which a customer buys a ticket, she enters the subway area, the subway takes the customer to her destination, and the customer leaves. The L1 System Flow in Figure 13-2 shows the full end-to-end System Flow.

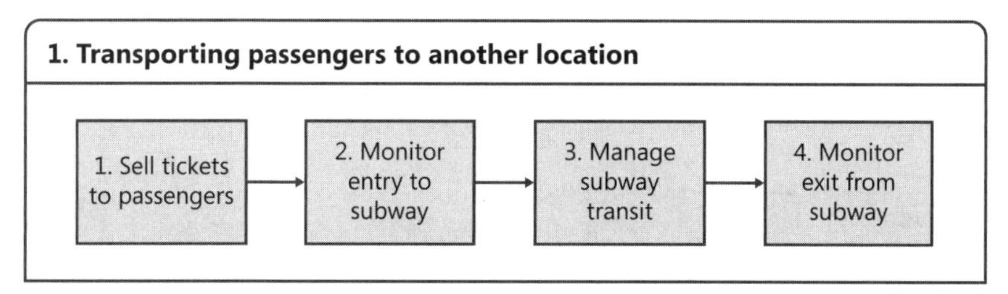

FIGURE 13-2 An example L1 System Flow.

There are multiple L2 System Flows for this L1 flow. Figure 13-3 uses an L2 System Flow to show the process for the "Manage subway transit" step from the L1 System Flow in more detail. Notice that this flow is a continuous loop that does not have to end. There is an event (the passenger exiting the system) that sends the customer to the "Monitor exit from subway" System Flow.

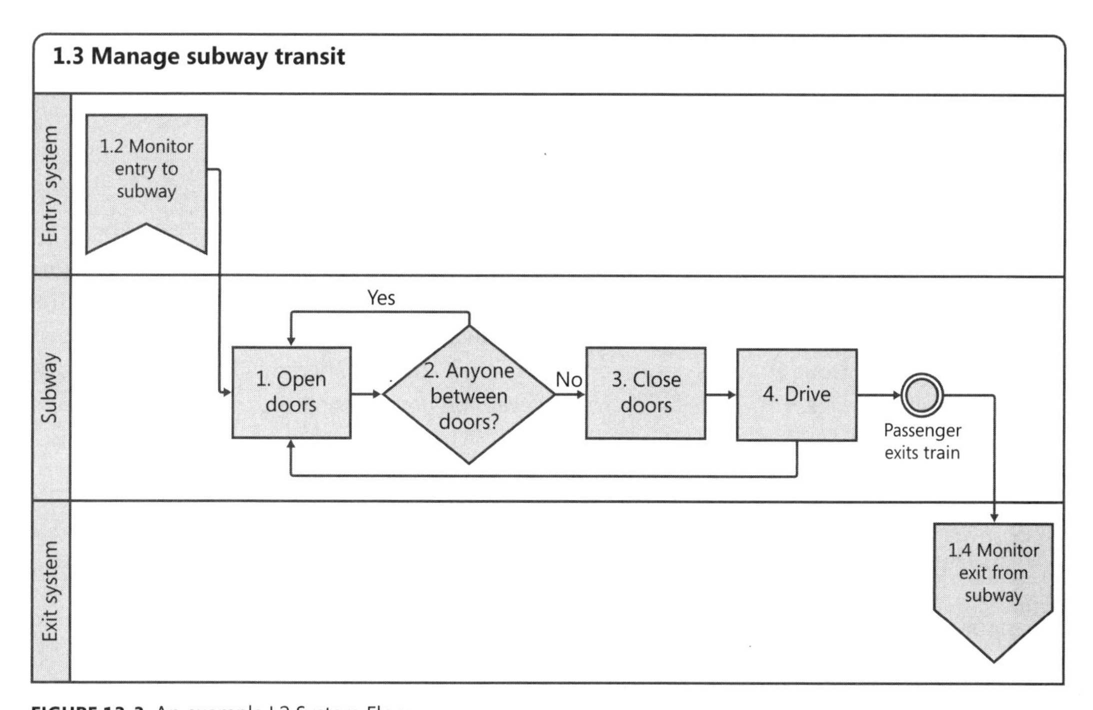

FIGURE 13-3 An example L2 System Flow.

Figure 13-4 goes into more detail on the "Drive" step in the L2 flow.

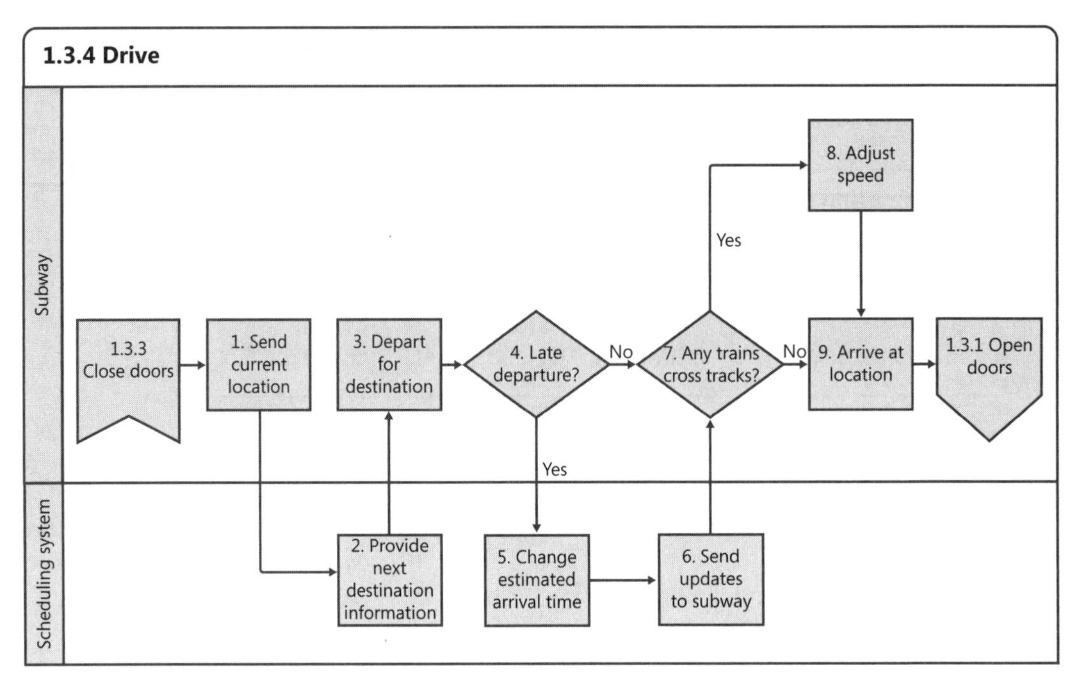

FIGURE 13-4 An example L3 System Flow.

Creating System Flows

For many automated flows, the business stakeholders will not care about the process that happens within the system. Leave the decisions to the development team. However, for the flows that the business stakeholders do want to specify, create System Flows. Figure 13-5 describes the process for creating System Flows. At a high level, you use the same steps as when creating Process Flows. We do not explain these steps again in this chapter; instead, we describe only the differences in executing the process.

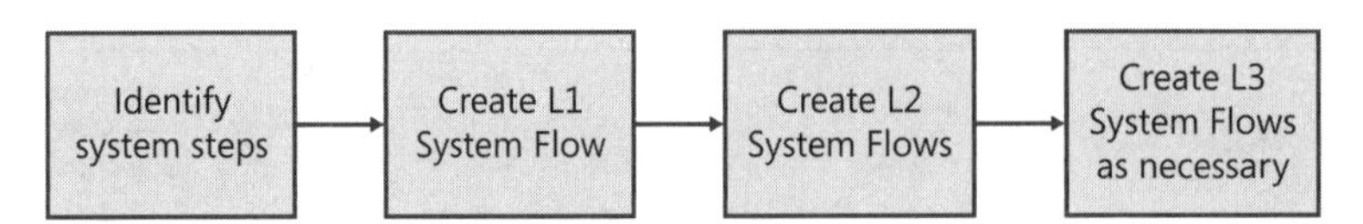

FIGURE 13-5 Process to create a System Flow.

As mentioned previously, the L1, L2, and L3 hierarchy applies for System Flows, as do the suggestions to name the System Flows according to that hierarchy. The intricacies of creating steps and recommendations for the number of steps in the diagrams are the same as for Process Flows. As with Process Flows, it is important to have System Flows reviewed early in the project because they build upon one another. However, with System Flows, you will want to involve more technical stakeholders in the review for accuracy, because they typically have a good understanding of what steps occur within the current systems.

System Flows often link to Process Flows when a user-initiated action in a Process Flow triggers a set of automated steps, and the result is delivered back to the user. For example, if a user submits a credit application for a loan, the system executes a significant amount of processing and decision logic to determine whether the applicant is approved. After the decision is made, the applicant is notified of the result automatically. It might be tempting to mix Process Flows and System Flows in the same diagram, but doing so will potentially lead to missed steps because of the switching of focus between users and systems. You can use the other process reference to call a Process Flow within the System Flow.

Although System Flows are similar to Process Flows, there are significant differences when it comes to identifying steps, and subtle differences in writing steps, using swim lanes, and using events.

Identify System Steps

The steps in System Flows are primarily system steps instead of user steps, though you might have some user steps in your System Flow for context. In systems with user interactions, users typically trigger complex system interactions, so you might model those user steps as events. The event would sit in the swim lane for the system that the user used to trigger the action, and you should note that the user, not the system, is triggering the action.

You might have external systems that interact with your system that are out of scope for changes. However, you can show these interactions to verify that nothing is changing in the other systems.

Feature Trees

If you have a Feature Tree (and if not, a list of features will do), identify all of the L1 features that need to be executed within your system. The execution of those features might correspond to the steps in the L1 System Flow. In the subway system example, the top-level features are ticketing, subway entry, transit, and subway exit. They are chained together in a reasonable order to represent the L1 System Flow.

Data Flow Diagrams

Data Flow Diagrams (DFDs) are useful for identifying the steps in L2 and L3 System Flows. Most of the activities that occur within systems generally involve reading or writing data to input/output devices, other systems, or data stores, all of which are described in DFDs. Therefore, looking at your DFD can help you to identify some steps within a System Flow, and by capturing these activities in a System Flow, you can better depict the exact order in which the steps occur (which is not obvious in a DFD).

Write Steps

System Flow steps are named in the format [*system*] + *<action>* + *<object>*. The system is optional in the step name, depending on whether you use swim lanes. If you are not using swim lanes and more than one system performs activities throughout the flow, you will need to include the system name in the step boxes to indicate which system is performing each activity. For example, "Add configuration" would become "CRM adds configuration." If one system group is performing all of the activities, you can just include that system's name in the title of the flow.

Typically, a user step would be in a Process Flow and would link to the System Flow as the first step of the System Flow. Users in System Flows should generally not be performing activities other than steps that initiate a process or events that interrupt a system process. When you do include user steps, name them like steps in a Process Flow.

Swim Lanes

The decision about whether to use swim lanes is the same as with Process Flows and depends on how many systems are interacting in the flow. However, swim lanes in System Flows only represent systems. The purpose of the System Flow is to understand the steps that systems take to accomplish their tasks, which are usually independent of a user. If you want to show activities primarily between users, you should use Process Flows (see Chapter 9).

When a system step is within a swim lane, it implies that the primary action in the step is being performed by the system named in the swim lane, even though that system might very well read or write data to other systems during that step. In this case, specify the target system as *<action>* + *<object>* + *<target system>*. Finally, all of the systems that are used in your swim lanes should be in your Ecosystem Map.

Events

Though most of the symbols in System Flows are the same as in Process Flows, note that you will probably use the event symbol more often in System Flows. Often, events are used to show user-triggered processes in the system. Further, many systems activities are triggered at a specific time, at specific intervals of time, or by external events generated by sources such as sensors or user interfaces.

System Flows are used to define real-time and embedded systems. One key characteristic of a real-time system is that it must respond to an event within a defined time period. It must also be able to handle a certain number of the same events. For example, a telephone switching system, which executes the same flow thousands or millions of times per day and responds to thousands of off-hook events, must be documented so that the engineers understand the performance needs of the real-time system. Label these events in the System Flow with a callout to describe any required response times on the events, such as a maximum time to wait before moving to the next step.

Using System Flows

System Flows provide a way for the business stakeholders to quickly visualize and understand automated processing that is otherwise hidden from them. In fact, System Flows are essential for describing interactions and activities that are not obvious to a user.

Running System Flows Parallel to Process Flows

A System Flow can run parallel to a Process Flow that describes a user's activities. By modeling the same scope of a scenario in both a System Flow and a Process Flow, you can quickly see the full solution from both perspectives. Figure 13-6 has an example to show each perspective.

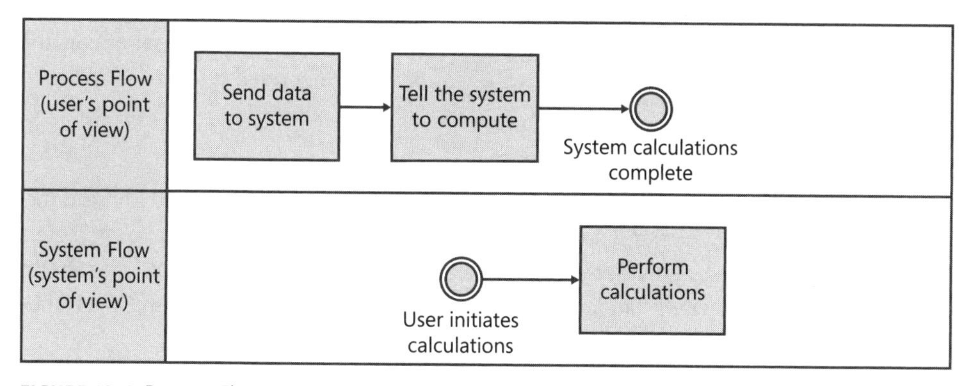

FIGURE 13-6 Process Flow vs. System Flow perspective.

Often, you really need only one of these perspectives to describe the solution sufficiently to derive requirements. However, if the user has to do a lot of manual work at the same time that the system is doing a lot of work by itself, you might want to model both types of flows, to ensure that you really understand the solution.

In a car, for example, the user cares about setting the gear shift, pushing the gas pedal, and getting and keeping the car moving. From a system perspective, the system maintains timing, reduces knocking, and monitors tire pressure. These two views are best kept separate, because most drivers care only about driving the car, but some more technical drivers and car designers care about how the car operates in addition to the context in which the user drives.

Deriving Requirements

System Flows are great tools for deriving and organizing requirements when a business stakeholder is very concerned about the internal operation of the system. System Flows are helpful in identifying data requirements, non-functional requirements, and business rules. Some of the more interesting questions to ask about steps in System Flows to identify requirements and business rules include:

- What events trigger the step?
- What possible error conditions might occur at this step, and how should they be handled?
- What calculation is performed?
- What data manipulation occurs?
- How fast does the system have to respond to events?
- How many events should be expected?
- What kind of failure rate is acceptable?

When to Use

System Flows are used to describe activities within the system that do not involve users performing the steps. Use them when the system is automating a process for which the business stakeholders care about the details of execution, when a complex set of steps happens after a user action, there is little or no user interaction, or when the system is a real-time or embedded system.

Describing Hidden Activities

The main difficulty with systems that require a lot of behind-the-scenes activity is that it is difficult to identify all the system activities and nearly impossible to know whether your list is complete. A system might require many system interfaces, business data objects, and customizations that nobody is aware of because the behavior is hidden from the users of the system. The System Flow is the main tool for fleshing out the behavior of the system.

Describing System Interactions

Identifying the systems in your Ecosystem Map that connect directly to each other will help you identify where you might need a System Flow to describe that interaction. Though System Interface Tables (see Chapter 18, "System Interface Table") capture the details of the actual interface, a System Flow will better show the sequence of steps that occur between these systems. This is useful when there is a lot of back-and-forth communication between systems or when a significant manipulation of data is passed between them.

Describing Exception Handling

Your System Interface Tables might also need System Flows to describe how exception handling occurs. In these cases, you will need to work with the business stakeholders to understand what they want the system to do when an error occurs in the interface.

When Not to Use

System Flows are not helpful if the business stakeholders aren't concerned about the nature of the automated system processes or the behind-the-scenes calculations. Also, they are not needed if there are calculations, but those calculations are equations rather than a series of steps or iterations. Consider using a Decision Tree (see Chapter 17, "Decision Tree") instead of a System Flow for complex logic.

Common Mistakes

The mistakes that were cited in Chapter 9 for Process Flows are also common to System Flows.

Related Models

Many people don't differentiate between System Flows and Process Flows. RML separates them into System Flows (for system activities) and Process Flows (for user activities).

The following list briefly describes the most important models that influence or are enhanced by System Flows. Chapter 26, "Using Models Together," contains a more thorough discussion about all related models.

- **Decision Trees** These are used to define complex decision logic that is embedded inside a system or decision step of a System Flow.
- **Data Flow Diagrams (DFDs)** These show the flow of the business data objects between data stores and process steps that manipulate the data.
- **Ecosystem Maps** These are used to show the systems depicted in swim lanes.
- **Feature Trees** These are used to identify steps of a System Flow.
- **System Interface Tables** These might reference System Flows for error handling.
- **Process Flows** These show user activities and can trigger a System Flow. After the System Flow is complete, it might return to a step in a Process Flow.

Exercise

The following exercise is intended to help you to gain a better understanding of how to use this model. The exercise is open ended, and therefore the answer you come up with could be substantially different than the answer that we have provided. There are potentially many correct solutions. The answer provides an explanation of how we arrived at our solution. You will gain the most out of the exercise by attempting to do it yourself before looking at the solution. The answers for the exercises can be found in Appendix C.

Instructions

Prepare an L2 System Flow for this scenario.

Scenario

In this project, you are helping to build an online eStore for customers to order flamingos and other lawn accessories from Wide World Importers. The process is currently initiated when the customer calls a sales representative directly. The sales representatives fill out Microsoft Excel order forms that are manually input into the system. You have met with stakeholders and elicited an overview of the new automated process, as follows:

Product managers will build a product catalog with all of the available flamingos and lawn accessories. The product prices will be synced in the catalog from a pricing list. A customer will come to the eStore to buy products. When the order is submitted, it is processed, the product is shipped, and the inventory system is updated.

The order submission triggers a series of automatic system steps to process the order for shipping. The system evaluates which warehouses have the products on the order. If there are multiple warehouses with the products, the system picks the one(s) closest to the shipping address. Products can be shipped from multiple warehouses if needed. After the warehouse is selected, for each product, the warehouse robotic system pulls the product from the shelf and packs it in a box. The system minimizes the number of boxes to be shipped for an order.

Additional Resources

The best resources for System Flows are the same ones that are found in for Process Flows, in Chapter 9.

CHAPTER 14

User Interface Flow

When you visit a theme park, your experience has been designed by the park creators. At the main entrance, you'll be given a choice of a limited number of sections of the park that you can reach directly. When you choose a section and arrive there, you will have an additional set of options: you can eat, shop, see a show, or go on a ride. From the entrance of the section, you will have to navigate to your choice. Let's say you choose to go on a ride, but when you get there, the line is really long. From the line, you can see three food options: a sit-down restaurant, a fast-food window, and a snack cart.

The choices presented to you are not accidental: the theme park experts designed each set of options in a way that they hope will maximize your enjoyment of the park. There was a definite rationale for each of these design decisions, and the way that the designers visualized the big picture for the park was by creating a map to show the full park and the visitors' experiences as they navigate each section.

The User Interface Flow (UI Flow) is an RML systems model that shows how the user will navigate the user interface, much like a designer's theme park map. A UI Flow contains the screens and the navigation paths between them.

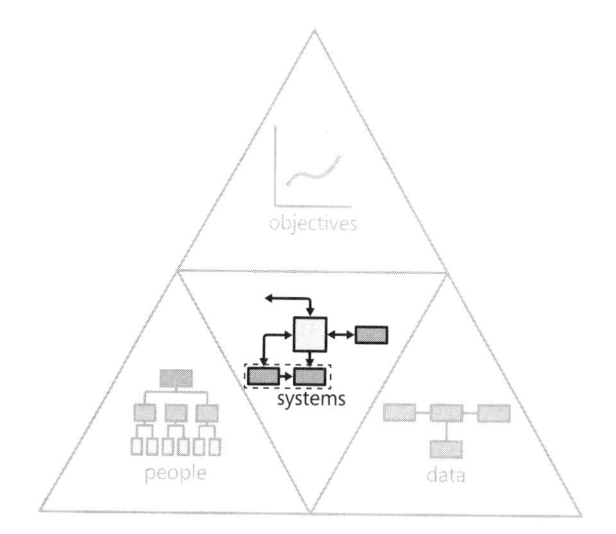

A software solution's usability often determines the efficiency and satisfaction of its users. Even if all of the features exist in the solution, if the path to access them is awkward, users might not adopt the new system. The flow of the UI directly effects an organization's ability to get value from a new system, thereby justifying a model to help optimize the UI experience.

There are two primary uses for UI Flows. One is to show the path a user would take through the screens to complete his tasks. Another is to make sure that the system logic is correct so that it is clear how each screen is accessed from other screens.

UI Flows differ from Process Flows (see Chapter 9, "Process Flow") in that they describe the user's physical experience while navigating the system, rather than the user's tasks. Although UI Flows represent screens to which users navigate, they do not capture the users' goals and tasks.

UI Flow Template

UI Flows have two basic required elements: screens and the directional arrows that connect them. A third element is the decision symbol, which is optional and represents decision logic that the system executes to determine which screen to display based on an action taken by the user. Finally, the grouping symbol can improve readability by grouping related screens together. The elements of a UI Flow are described in Table 14-1.

TABLE 14-1 User Interface Flow Elements

Element	Meaning
Screen	The screen box contains a name that represents the nature of the screen. The screen is typically a screen, but it could be a pop-up window, a dialog box, or a group of screens. Pop-up windows and dialog boxes are typically not included because they create clutter in the diagram and generally don't modify the flow.
UI trigger	The directional arrow connects screens to one another. The direction of the arrow shows the order of the flow between screens. The text on the arrow indicates the action that triggers the transition to the next screen.
Decision	The decision step represents system branches in the UI Flow, based on different states.
Grouping	Groupings allow you to divide your UI Flow into smaller sections for readability. Typically, they surround a set of screens with common functionality that is not split out into its own UI Flow.

A UI Flow template must at a minimum include screens and the arrows that represent the navigation path between the screens. Each screen should have at least one arrow coming into it and at least one arrow leaving it; otherwise there would be no way to access or leave that screen. The exceptions to this are the initial screens that a user sees, which might have no arrows coming in, and the last screens he sees in a normal flow, which might have no arrows leaving. The UI Flow template is shown in Figure 14-1, though there can be as many screens and arrows as needed.

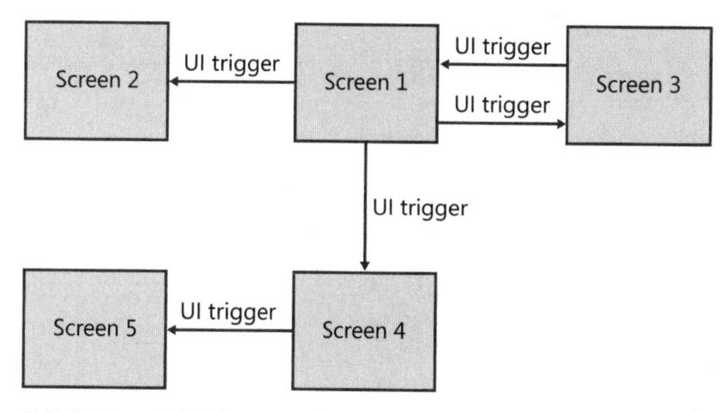

FIGURE 14-1 A UI Flow template.

You can add grouping symbols to your diagram when the number of screens begins to make it difficult to analyze the flow. Add decision symbols to your diagram to show decisions that the system makes to control which screen the user sees. Generally, you shouldn't show user choices, because every screen that connects to other screens has an implied user choice. Figure 14-2 shows an example template with those symbols added to it.

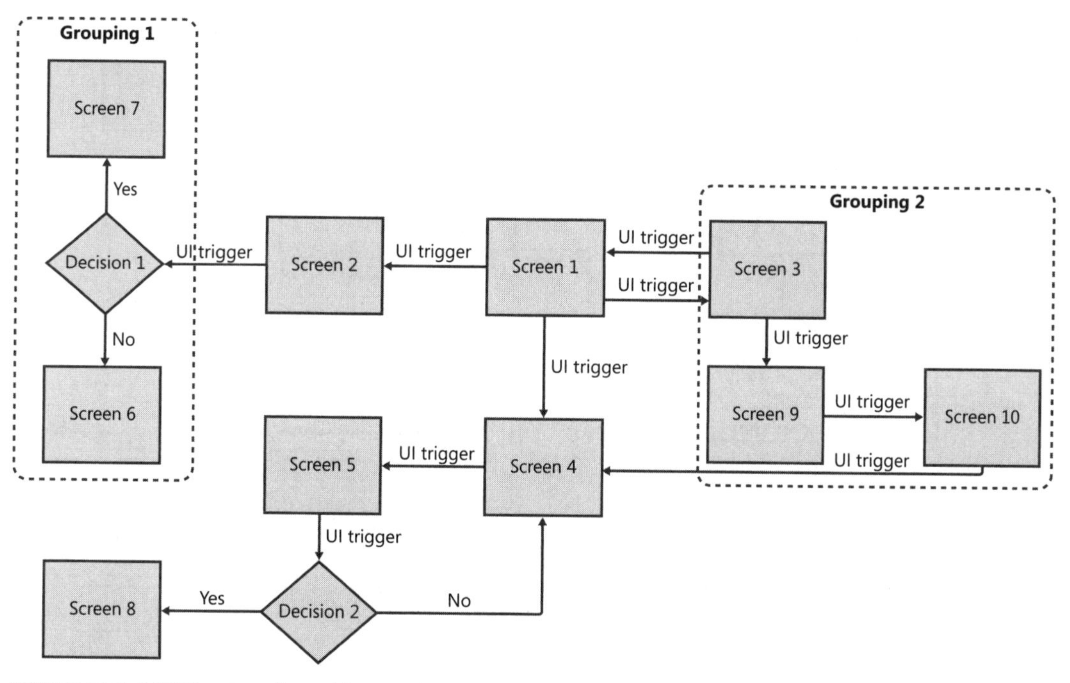

FIGURE 14-2 A UI Flow template with groupings and decisions.

Tool Tip UI Flows should be created in a tool that allows easy manipulation of the shapes. The most common tool is Microsoft Visio, though some requirements management tools allow flows to be created and manipulated easily.

Example

Figure 14-3 shows the UI flow for a trivia system in which users take quizzes with trivia questions.

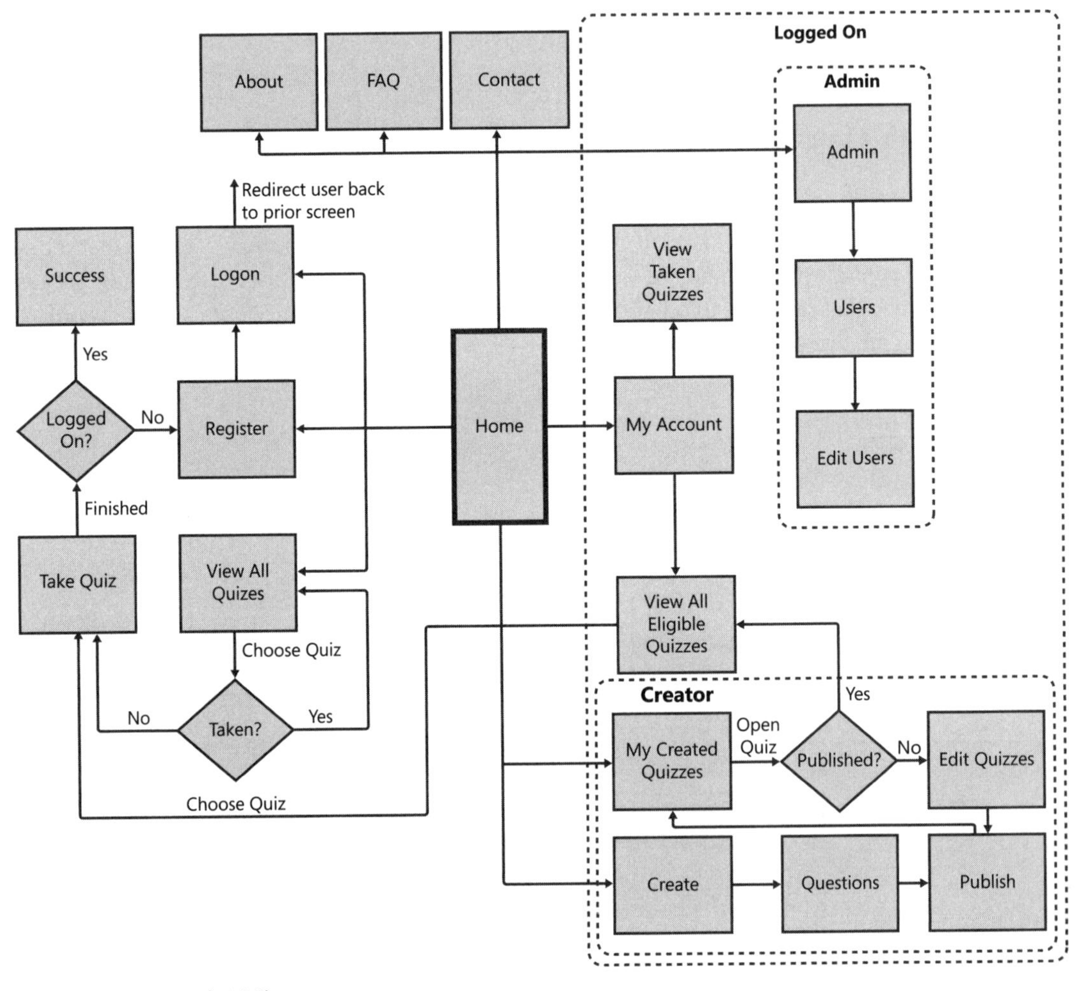

FIGURE 14-3 Example UI Flow.

There is a home screen at the center of the diagram. From it, users can navigate to log on, register, view all quizzes, read about the company, read frequently asked questions (FAQs), and find contact information. Users on the home screen can also navigate to their account information and view quizzes specifically available to them after they log on. Finally, users can create quizzes and administer other users if they have access. A Roles and Permissions Matrix (see Chapter 11, "Roles and Permissions Matrix") would further describe the accessibility of functions by roles.

Creating UI Flows

Figure 14-4 describes the process of creating a UI Flow. Although we suggest an order for these steps, they are iterative, and you might find yourself doing a few of them at the same time, such as identifying screens and the transitions between them.

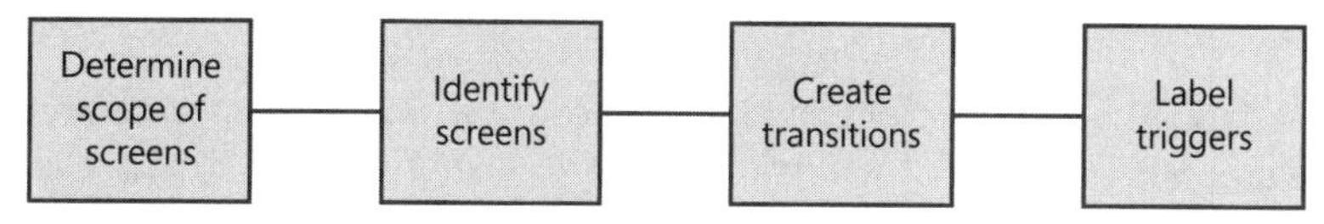

FIGURE 14-4 The process for creating a UI Flow.

Determine Scope of Screens

UI Flows do not usually need to cover every screen in the system. Start by identifying those screens that have complex logic to navigate between them and high-value user tasks that require the user to navigate many screens. You could decide that a task has high value because the navigation path is not trivial, because the tasks are executed frequently, or because they are the most important user tasks to be executed, so the UI navigation has to be clean for the solution to be successful.

Some sets of screens and navigation should not be included in your UI Flow because the flow is unimportant or obvious. For example, you might have error screens that you do not need to include. You can capture those by using Display-Action-Response (DAR) models (see Chapter 15, "Display-Action-Response") as variations of screens that caused the error. Wiegers describes a related model, dialog maps, for which he suggests omitting any standard screens that are common throughout the system, such as help menus that can be launched from any screen, because such screens will clutter your diagram without adding any value (2003).

Choosing which sections of the system to include on each UI Flow is an iterative process. We recommend that you break your UI Flows into sections that cover no more than 7+/-2 screens. You can accomplish this by using grouping symbols or additional UI Flows. The example earlier in this chapter used grouping symbols to show screens specific to the user's logged-on state, screens accessible to users with administrator access, and screens relevant to creating quizzes. Most importantly, think about the system from a user's perspective, and pick logical groupings to model the user experience of a specific Process Flow or Use Case (see Chapter 10, "Use Case"). This allows the business stakeholders to gauge the usability of common tasks by focusing on that section of the full UI Flow.

You can also use a hierarchy of UI Flows, as explained for Process Flows. You might need multiple levels of UI Flows to capture the full set of screens for your system and still make the diagram consumable in size. If you are using levels, you probably will only need two levels: level 1 (L1) and level 2 (L2). L1 UI Flows show the UI screens for the entire system, though sometimes sets of screens with common functionality are grouped together as one screen. L2 UI Flows show screens for a portion of the system, typically those screens that you grouped in the L1 UI Flow. In the earlier example, we could have created one screen box labeled "Create Quiz" and used an L2 UI Flow to capture the screens needed to create a quiz.

Identify Screens

After you decide the scope of your UI Flow, identify all of the relevant screens and include them in the diagram as screen boxes.

There are multiple ways to identify screens:

- Identify the top-priority Process Flows or Use Cases and consider what screens will be required to execute those user tasks.
- The business stakeholders probably have a good idea of what screens the users need to efficiently accomplish their tasks. The initial drafts of the UI Flow can be based on their input.
- If you are migrating or enhancing an existing system, you can start by putting the existing screens in your UI Flow.
- If you already have DAR models, you can create screen boxes for all of the screens in those models.
- If you identify complicated system logic that drives screen display, you should create the screens around that logic.

As you iterate through this process and identify transitions and triggers, you are likely to find more screens to add to your UI Flow.

Diagramming

Use descriptive names for the screens that business stakeholders will understand. If UI design work exists, use those screen names. If you have DAR models, use the same names for screens in both models. Finally, if you make up a new screen, name it something obvious to describe the functionality on the screen, using nouns and as few words as possible (for example, "Take Quiz" for the page to take quizzes or "Success" for the page that displays a success message to the user after he takes a quiz).

The UI Flow templates and the example given earlier in this chapter all have main screens at the center with arrows leading to other screens. In many systems, users do not proceed through the screens in a consistent order (consider a website with menus that allow you to jump to new top-level functionality at any point), so you do not want to imply an order that does not exist. If you create the UI Flow with a main starting screen at the center, you might want to make that main screen box larger than the other screen boxes, to make it visually stand out to the readers, as in the example.

If there is a consistent flow through all of the screens, you can order them from left to right as you would with a Process Flow. This is more common in an L2 UI Flow. Figure 14-5 is an example of a flow that shows the order in which screens are viewed through a registration process.

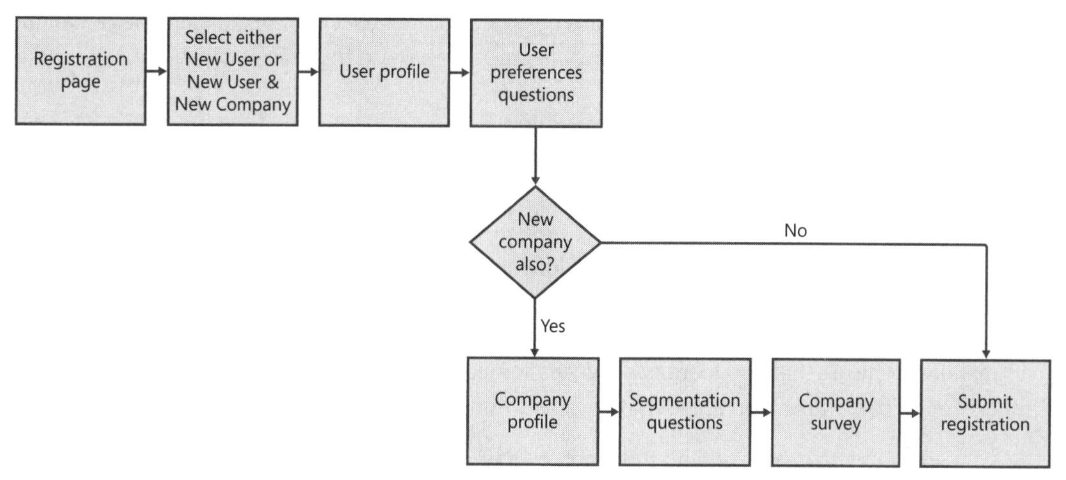

FIGURE 14-5 A UI Flow with order.

What Constitutes a Screen?

If you are using a UI Flow to help identify screens for a new UI, you need to consider how much functionality an individual screen should have. These considerations affect the system's usability.

- If you put too much functionality in a single screen, the screen might be confusing for users.
- If you put too little functionality in a single screen, users will have to click through too many screens to accomplish their tasks, which might negatively impact the adoption of the system.

In the end, you might need to prototype the screens and test them with users in order to find out their preferences. Mapping screens to Process Flows will help you measure the usability of your proposed screen layout.

When including screens in a UI Flow, we recommend that you not include every screen variation. For example, a UI designer might have three versions of a quiz question creation screen based on the types of questions the user wants to create, but you can include just one screen for creating questions in your UI Flow. The variations on the screen can be described in a DAR model. However, in some cases, a particular screen might vary significantly depending on the state of the system. In those cases, you can make separate screens in the UI Flow. For example, the screen that lists all of a user's quizzes might look different if that user can create quizzes as compared to just being able to take quizzes. Don't get hung up on making the screen boxes in your UI Flow an exact replica of the system screens in the implementation.

Create Transitions

Many screens have multiple navigation paths to them, and you will typically want to include them all, at least for the most common navigation paths. Draw arrows between the screens to represent the direction of flow. Organize related screens near one another to minimize crossing lines and improve readability. As you create transitions, you will probably have to move screens around in your diagram.

Identifying the Transitions

To identify transitions, you can consider each screen in your UI Flow and determine what other screens can be reached from it.

You should also walk through Process Flows or Use Cases to identify the screens users will access to execute their tasks, and the order in which they will access them. As mentioned previously, do this for the high-value flows first, but you can walk through all of the Process Flows and Use Cases in this manner to ensure that you identify all navigation paths. Remember to consider alternate paths and exception paths when you are identifying transitions (Gottesdiener 2005, Wiegers 2003).

If you are replacing or adding functionality to an existing system, you can walk through the existing system screens to create the initial UI Flow. Then work with users to understand how the flow should change in the new system.

Keep in mind that UI design is a specialized skill, and many systems require the input of UI designers to ensure usability. If that is the case, the UI designers should be involved in creating the UI Flow.

Adding Transitions to the Diagram

Remember that most screens contain at least one arrow coming in and one coming out. The starting screen or screens might have no arrows coming in. To indicate these on the diagram, use a larger bolded box, as in the example UI Flow. Screens from which a user will exit the system or return to the main screen can have no paths exiting the screen box.

If you choose to include screens that can be reached from anywhere and from which you can navigate to anywhere, be careful about adding too many transitions to the UI Flow. Include one primary navigation path to access the screen. In the example, the quiz company's website has a "Contact Us" link in the header that can always be reached, so the UI Flow includes one navigation path from the main screen to the contact screen. But specifying navigation from every screen to "Contact Us" or from "Contact Us" to any other screen adds unimportant clutter to the diagram. You can further clarify these types of details in the requirements.

If you have screens for which the outgoing navigation path depends on where the user came from, you can add transition arrows out of the screen that go nowhere and just label them accordingly. For example, if you have a logon screen that the user can enter from multiple screens, and you want the user to go back to where she came from after logon, you would create a transition line like the one shown in Figure 14-6.

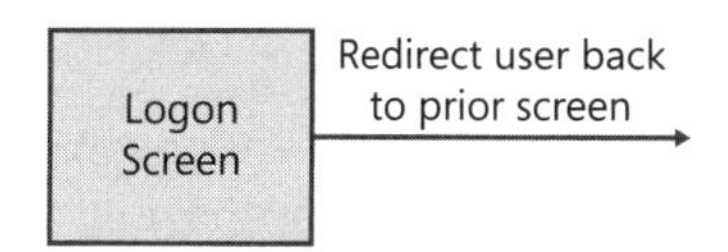

FIGURE 14-6 Example screen that redirects back to where the user was.

Branching

Any screen can have multiple lines leaving it, going to multiple other screens. This indicates that a user can choose any of those navigation paths. If the reason for a user's choice between multiple navigation paths is not obvious, you need to add trigger labels to clarify the user's intent.

In some cases, the system will decide which screen to take a user to, based on the state of the system. If this logic is not obvious from the diagram, you need to add decision symbols to show what the system is evaluating. In the quiz example, after a user takes a quiz, the system evaluates whether the user is logged on and directs the user to either a success screen or a logon screen, accordingly. The labels on the transition lines from the decision indicate the system's evaluation logic, as shown in Figure 14-7.

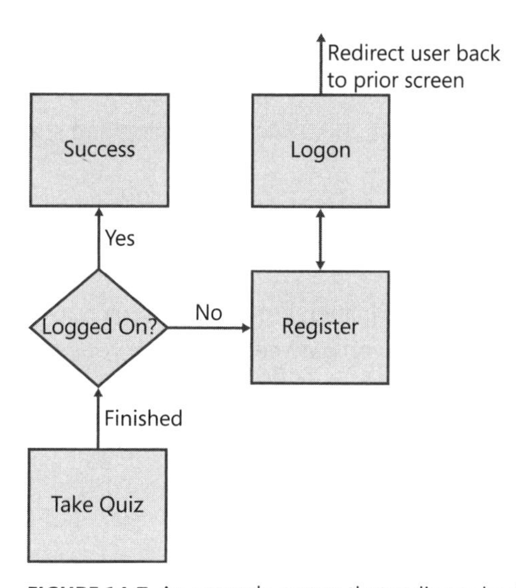

FIGURE 14-7 An example screen that redirects back to where the user was.

The reason UI Flows do not use decisions to represent choices that a user is making as she navigates the screens is that they are not meant to show the user's thought process. UI Flows show what the system is doing to determine which screen it shows. To consider the user's thought process, use the UI Flow in conjunction with Process Flows or Use Cases.

Label Triggers

Each transition arrow might be labeled with the trigger that causes the transition. The trigger will be generated either by a user action or by a system action. If the transition is initiated by the user, the trigger should be labeled with a verb that describes what the user is doing, such as, "Open quiz."

Arrows do not need triggers to be labeled if the trigger is obvious. For the example, going from the Home screen to the About screen is obvious; there is no need to say, "Click About."

If you are using trigger labels and the user can navigate back and forth between two screens, use two lines to label the trigger—one for each direction. Figure 14-8 shows an example of this.

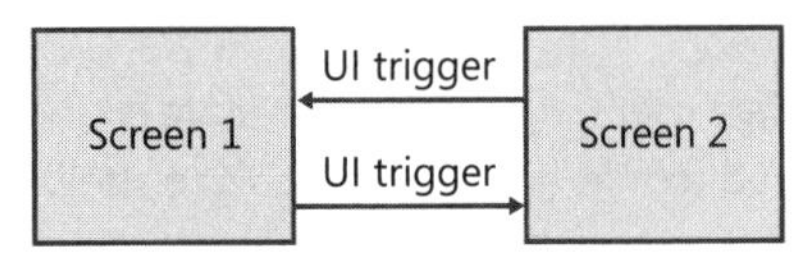

FIGURE 14-8 Multiple triggers show user movement back and forth between screens.

Using UI Flows

A UI Flow is a good model for communicating to business and technical teams how users will navigate through the entire system. UI Flows help to identify navigation, validate navigation paths, and optimize usability.

Identifying Navigation

If you are designing a UI, you can use UI Flows to decide on navigation between the screens. Walk through your Process Flows and Use Cases to create the navigation between screens. If you have existing screens, you can use UI Flows to answer questions such as, "When I am here, where can I go?" Without the view of the navigation that a UI Flow offers, it would be very hard for someone to answer such a question.

Validating Navigation

If you already have a proposed UI Flow, you can still walk through Process Flows and Use Cases to see what screens a user would see. This will help you identify any confusing paths or missing screens and the transitions necessary for executing the user tasks. Identifying these issues early in a project will help avoid potential usability issues in the future (Gottesdiener 2005). This is particularly useful if a UI designer created the navigation and you want to validate it with the business.

Without needing to understand why a user's tasks cause her to navigate the screens, you can also look at a UI Flow and notice inconsistencies or screens that go nowhere. For the quiz example discussed earlier, if you notice that there are screens with no arrows coming out of them, you can validate that this is correct either because those navigation paths are obvious (such as paths going back to the main screen) or they truly are end screens for a user.

You can also use UI Flows to validate that system logic is set up in a way that allows the user to get to all screens.

Optimizing Usability

A UI Flow presents an opportunity to look for efficiencies that can optimize usability. If there are many screen transitions required to complete a single task, you might be able to find ways to streamline those tasks and reduce the number of screens required.

Each UI Flow also shows the range of choices that a user has from any particular screen. You might determine that users need additional paths to access screens. For example, on a Confirm Order screen, if there are no options to get to the Cart screen, the transition to that screen might have to be added to allow a user to quickly edit an order before it is confirmed. Usability enhancements like this would be hard to detect from a long list of requirements about the navigation, or by just looking at individual screens.

Developing Test Cases

Each UI Flow can be used to determine how to test the solution, because it shows the important navigation paths to complete tasks. The test cases can be very specific about what screens a user should see (Gottesdiener 2005).

Deriving Requirements

UI Flows are not used to directly derive requirements, but they might help identify missing screens or navigation paths that cause you to create new DAR models with new requirements. UI Flows can also help ensure that Process Flows and Use Cases are complete. If there are screens that don't map to a Process Flow, it might be because the corresponding Process Flow is missing.

When to Use

UI Flows are helpful as soon as you have users interacting with a system to perform tasks that cross multiple screens. Some appropriate applications of UI Flows are for designing a new UI, describing existing UIs, and validating navigation paths.

If you or other teams are creating new screens, create the UI Flow as you identify screens. However, UI Flows can also be created after the screens are already identified and mocked up. If you are also creating DAR models, create the UI Flow first, then use it as you create DARs to help tie the DARs together and make sure you have full coverage across all screens.

When Not to Use

You do not always need to create a UI Flow. If you have no UI, if you have very few screens, if the UI is not very complex, or if very few users access it, then you might not need one. For example, embedded systems often will not have UI Flows.

Common Mistakes

The following represent the most common mistakes that we have seen with UI Flows.

Including Too Much Detail

When creating a UI Flow, do not include too much detail when describing the screens and the transitions. The UI Flow is not intended to give a full description of each screen—use DAR models for that. Further, do not include every transition between screens if it does not help readers understand how the system will work. If you have transition lines connecting to every possible screen, even the obvious transitions, your diagram will probably become unreadable.

Including Unimportant Details

You will have to use your judgment about whether two screens are unique or not, whether to include a screen in the UI Flow, and whether a transition between screens is worthy of inclusion. To make these decisions, consider what the screen or transition is helping by being in the UI Flow; whether it is identifying, validating, or improving a navigation path.

Not Using a UI Expert When Needed

Lastly, it is important to leave complex UI designs to the expert UI designers. These team members will be able to help create a usable navigation path for users.

Related Models

Dialog maps, navigation maps, and storyboards are similar to UI Flows, though their notation and scope might vary (Wiegers 2003). Dialog maps are sometimes created to focus on just a few Process Flows or Use Cases, as opposed to the entire set of screens (Gottesdiener 2005). Storyboards also show a flow through screens for a specific scenario, and they show more detailed information about the screens in the diagram.

The following list briefly describes the most important models that influence or are enhanced by UI Flows. Chapter 26, "Using Models Together," contains a more thorough discussion about all related models.

- **Process Flows and Use Cases** These describe the tasks users will execute as they navigate screens.
- **Display-Action-Response (DAR) Models** These provide detailed requirements about screen display and behavior.
- **Roles and Permissions Matrices** These provide detailed requirements about which roles can access screens, functions, or menus.

Exercise

The following exercise is intended to help you to gain a better understanding of how to use this model. The exercise is open ended, and therefore the answer you come up with could be substantially different than the answer that we have provided. There are potentially many correct solutions. The answer provides an explanation of how we arrived at our solution. You will gain the most out of the exercise by attempting to do it yourself before looking at the solution. The answers for the exercises can be found in Appendix C.

Instructions

Prepare a UI Flow for the following scenario.

Scenario

You are on a project to launch a new eStore to 2 million worldwide users. This eStore will have browse and search functions so that users can find flamingos and other lawn accessories. Additionally, there will be a cart in which the user can view her selected items, and a checkout process to complete the order. The eStore will also contain My Account information, from which the user can see her profile information and past orders, as well as an order tracking screen. There will also be a screen of FAQs and a Contact Us screen.

Additional Resources

- *The Software Requirements Memory Jogger* has a description of dialog maps in Section 4.8 (Gottesdiener 2005).
- *Software Requirements,* Chapter 11 also summarizes dialog maps (Wiegers 2003).
- In his web article, Ambler summarizes UI Flows from his book *The Object Primer,* particularly as they relate to Agile (Ambler).
- Chapter 12 of *Managing Software Requirements: A Use Case Approach* is about storyboarding (Leffingwell and Widrig 2003).

References

- Ambler, Scott W. *User Interface Flow Diagrams (Storyboards). http://www.agilemodeling.com /artifacts/uiFlowDiagram.htm.*
- Gottesdiener, Ellen. 2005. *The Software Requirements Memory Jogger.* Salem, NH: Goal/QPC.
- Leffingwell, Dean, and Don Widrig. 2003. *Managing Software Requirements: A Use Case Approach. (2nd Edition).* Reading, MA. Addison-Wesley Professional.
- Wiegers, Karl E. 2003. *Software Requirements, Second Edition.* Redmond, WA: Microsoft Press.

CHAPTER 15

Display-Action-Response

When you decide to build a house, your architect will begin by asking you questions about the way you live, to get a better understanding of how you might use the house. She might ask how old your children are, what kinds of activities you do, and what your daily routine looks like. During the schematic phase, the architect generates a series of rough sketches based on your answers, to give you an idea of what she is thinking of for your house.

After you decide on the general plan, you enter the design development phase. During this phase, the architect creates more detailed drawings with accurate scale, floor plans, and the materials to be used. When you have approved the design development document, the architect has construction documents with detailed structural measurements prepared, as well as electrical and mechanical schematics, also known as blueprints.

Each phase requires more effort, and changes become more costly. Some architects create hand-drawn renderings during the design development phase, and others create 3-D digital models that you can walk through in a virtual reality environment. When you virtually walk through the space, you can get a feel for the scale, especially if the virtual space is populated with furniture and decorated with the correct materials. You can open doors to help determine which way the doors should open, you can test lines of sight, and you can even experience the sunlight throughout the day and through all seasons.

The Display-Action-Response (DAR) model is an RML systems model that enables you to systematically document the valid ways in which a system displays the following:

1. The data-dependent user interface (UI) elements in screens
2. How the system responds to the actions that a user can take

DAR models are used to derive requirements and business rules associated with the UI. You can use them to define all possible valid actions and responses between a user and the UI elements in the system. By describing all the UI elements on a screen, you can ensure completeness of the requirements derived from the UI.

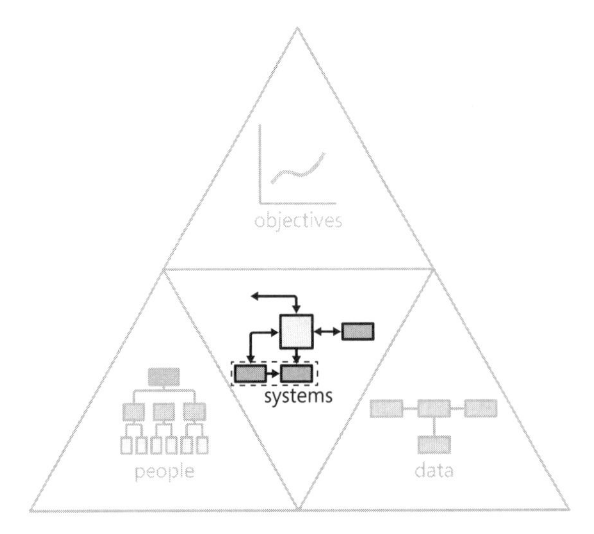

The quality of your UI can make or break the success of your software. From a requirements perspective, business analysts and business stakeholders should care a great deal about the usability of a UI, with an emphasis on ensuring that the software completely supports the business process and ultimately the business objectives of the organization.

A common method of documenting UI requirements is to use screen shots marked up to call out the non-obvious elements. Sometimes, if you're lucky, you'll see a list of requirements in the form of "shall statements" accompanying the screen shots. Typically, the UI and the requirements are not linked in the documentation, making it difficult for the reader to interpret and check that all the details are defined correctly. Figure 15-1 shows an example of a screen shot and a set of corresponding requirements, showing how difficult it would be to read that list and make sense of it well enough to know if anything is missing.

Software UI displays and actions are often driven by preconditions of objects in the system. For all elements, the DAR model captures both how they display and how the system responds to user actions with those elements, based on preconditions. The following statements are examples of simple display rules: If the state of a user is "not logged on," then a "logon" link displays. If the state of the user is "logged on," the "logoff" link displays. A corresponding example of element behavior would be that when the user "clicks the logon link," that changes the UI further, perhaps taking the user to a logon screen.

Process Flows (see Chapter 9, "Process Flow"), Use Cases (see Chapter 10, "Use Case"), and UI Flows (see Chapter 14, "User Interface Flow") all show threads of actions through what can be many different screens in the system. The DAR model shows a single screen and how the UI behaves immediately after particular user actions on that screen.

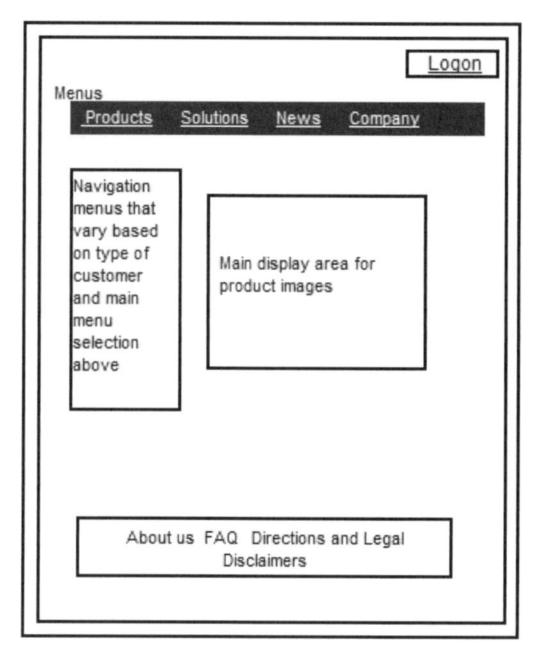

Requirements Document

- System shall display left navigation menu based upon user type if user is logged on.
- System shall display "My Profile" in left navigation menu for all logged-on users.
- System shall display company profile in left navigation if user is a business user.
- System shall display invoices due in left navigation if user is a business user.
- System shall display featured product based on user type.
- System shall display default featured product if user is not logged on.
- System shall display logon button if user is not logged on.
- System shall display logoff button if user is logged on.
- System shall display "Track Packages" in left navigation for all logged-on users.
- System shall display default left navigation menu if user is not logged on.
- System shall display featured product based on user's purchasing history for all logged-on users.
- System shall have a submit option.

FIGURE 15-1 A small sample of UI requirements for the wireframe—challenging to read!

DAR Model Template

The DAR model is composed of a combination of UI screen layout and corresponding element tables. A UI element is any entity of the UI that has a data-dependent display or behavior attributes (such as a button, a display table, an image, or a check box). Each UI element that has requirements should have its own element table. The screen layout can be in the form of anything from a low-fidelity wireframe to a high-fidelity screen design. Figure 15-2 shows examples of each of these.

The appropriate level of detail in the screen layout is determined by the type of project and the resources available (Rudd and Isensee 1996). DAR models work equally well with any level of screen detail.

The DAR model element table template is shown in Figure 15-3. Within each UI element table, there are three sections: UI element descriptions, UI element displays, and UI element behaviors, described in detail in the remainder of this section.

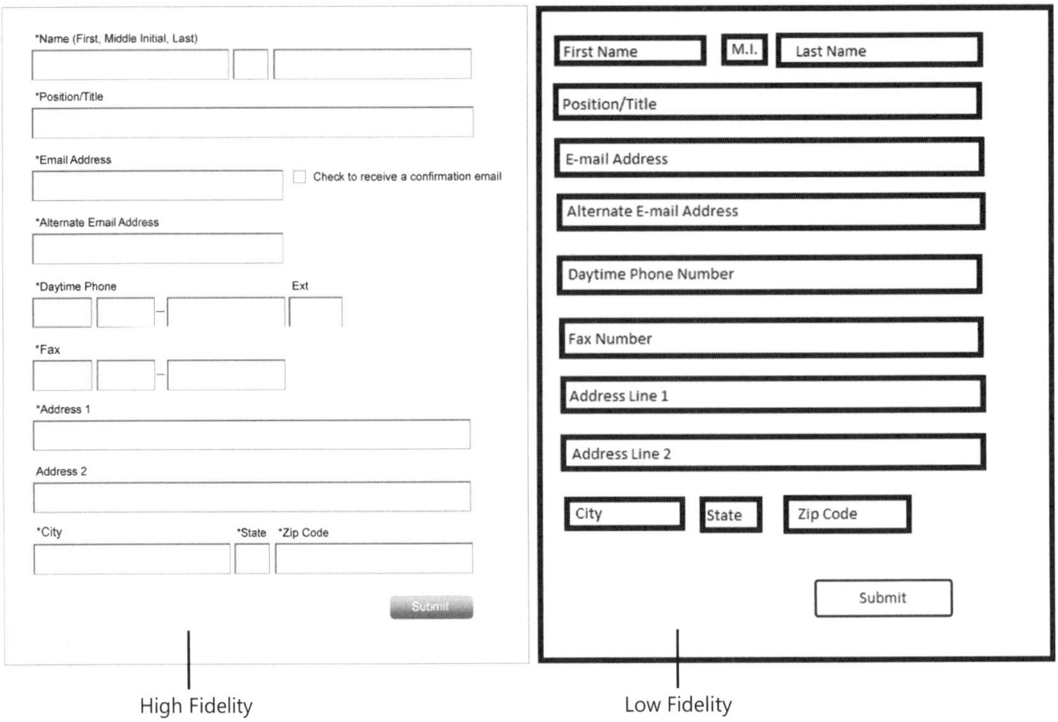

High Fidelity

Low Fidelity

FIGURE 15-2 High-fidelity and low-fidelity screen layouts.

UI Element: <element name>		
UI Element Description		
ID	<Unique ID for the element on the wireframe>	
Description	<Description of the element; can include a screen capture of the element>	
UI Element Displays		
Precondition	**Display**	
<Precondition 1>	<Display of the element under precondition 1>	
<Precondition 2>	<Display of the element under precondition 2>	
UI Element Behaviors		
Precondition	**Action**	**Response**
<Precondition 1>	<User action 1>	<System response under precondition 1>
<Precondition 2>	<User action 1>	<System response under precondition 2>
<Precondition 1>	<User action 2>	<System response under precondition 1>
<Precondition 2>	<User action 2>	<System response under precondition 2>

FIGURE 15-3 The UI element table template.

If the element tables will be in a document format, then each element table must be named in such a way to make it obvious which UI element it refers to. Alternatively, a screen capture of the element can be included in the element table. Further, if the model is created in documents, it is best to include the corresponding element tables directly after the image.

UI Element Description

The UI element description section of the table is used to identify the element with a unique identifier and a brief description of the screen element. The element also has a simple name at the top of the table, which is useful if the IDs are not meaningful at first glance. The unique ID schema should be consistent across all UI element tables.

UI Element Displays

The UI element displays section of the table is used to describe how the element appears on the screen under various preconditions. Each row within this section includes the element's display properties corresponding to a specific precondition. Preconditions could include states of users, prior actions the user took, values of particular business data objects, or run-time decisions that influence how the element is displayed. The only display elements that should be documented with an element table are those that either show data or have preconditions that affect how the elements are displayed. Static elements that are always displayed the same way should not be documented in an element table, because the screen layout shows them sufficiently.

UI Element Behaviors

The UI element behaviors section of the table is used to define the behavior of the system as the result of a user action with the element based on preconditions. Similar to the UI element displays section, each row of this section includes a precondition and an action by the user in relation to the element. The action property identifies the action taken by the user. The response property describes the corresponding system response to the action.

Tool Tip Element tables are most commonly created in Microsoft Word, Microsoft Excel, or in a requirements management tool. Screen layouts can be created in any image software, in Microsoft PowerPoint, or as a scan of an image. Ideally, the screen layout and all of the element tables will eventually end up in a requirements management tool so that the element tables can be linked to their elements in the screens directly.

Example

A team of analysts has created requirements for a quiz site redesign. The original site had a high volume of user traffic; thus, the business engaged a usability team to help create the UI screens. It was imperative that the development team build the user interface correctly. The developers could get the correct visual design directly from the wireframes, but they also had to understand how the user interface functioned, and this was not obvious from the wireframes alone. The analysts developed DAR models to capture the details that the implementation team needed. Figure 15-4 shows an example wireframe from this project.

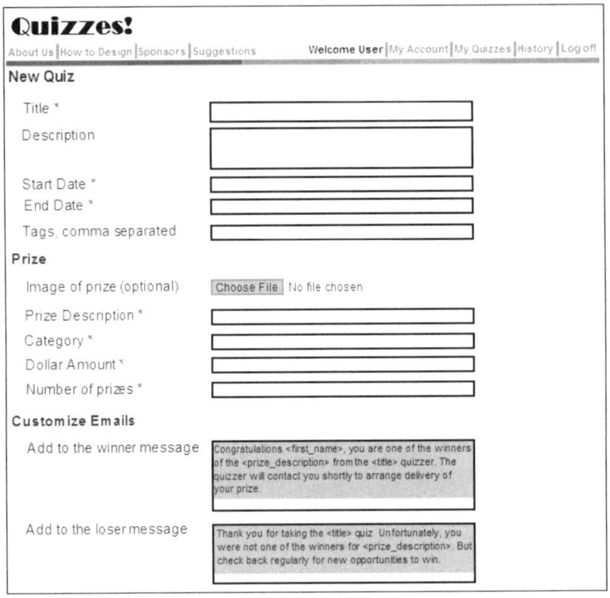

FIGURE 15-4 An example UI screen layout.

The following images show examples of DAR element tables for elements in the previous screen layout that have different displays and behaviors based on the type of user. Figure 15-5 shows the UI element table for the navigation bar. The navigation bar displays differently depending on whether the user is a quiz taker, administrator, or quiz creator. Figure 15-6 shows the quiz creation text input UI element. The text boxes have interesting behavior. Figure 15-7 is the element table for selecting the start and end dates for quizzes.

UI Element: Navigation Bar		
UI Element Description		
ID	ELMT_0045	
Description	Navigation bar with links to various user information and functions	
UI Element Displays		
Precondition	**Display**	
Always	Company Logo "About Us" link "How to Design" link "Sponsors" link "Suggestions" link "Welcome " <user's name> "My Account" link "My Quizzes" link "History" link "Log on" or "Log off" link	
<User.role> is administrative	Add "Admin" link to left of "Log off" link	
<User.role> is creator	"Create Quiz" link to the right of "My Quizzes" link	
UI Element Behaviors		
Precondition	**Action**	**Response**
Always	Select any link	User taken to corresponding page

FIGURE 15-5 An example DAR for the navigation bar.

UI Element: Create Quizzes Text Fields		
UI Element Description		
ID	ELMT_0046	
Description	Text fields for the creation of quizzes	
UI Element Displays		
Precondition	**Display**	
Always	"Title" text field "Description" text field with default text: "Enter description here" "Start Date" text field "End Date" text field "Tags, comma separated" text field "Image of prize (optional)" choose file icon "Prize Description" text field "Category" text field "Dollar Amount" text field "Number of prizes" text field "Add to the winner message" text field with suggested default message "Add to the loser message" text field with suggested default message	
UI Element Behaviors		
Precondition	**Action**	**Response**
Always	User types in text field without default messages	User's text displays in box
Always	User clicks in text field with default text	Default text is deleted and the user's text appears in the text box as it is typed.
Always	User types in text field with suggested default message	Suggested default message is retained, and the user's newly entered text is appended to the end of the message.

FIGURE 15-6 An example element table for text fields on the quiz creation page.

<table>
<tr><th colspan="3">UI Element: Start Date and End Date Fields</th></tr>
<tr><th colspan="3">UI Element Description</th></tr>
<tr><td>ID</td><td colspan="2">ELMT_0047</td></tr>
<tr><td>Description</td><td colspan="2">Calendar for selecting Start Date and End Date</td></tr>
<tr><th colspan="3">UI Element Displays</th></tr>
<tr><td>Precondition</td><td colspan="2">Display</td></tr>
<tr><td>Always</td><td colspan="2">Start Date and End Date text boxes and calendar to select dates
September 2011
Su Mo Tu We Th Fr Sa
1 2 3
4 5 6 7 8 9 10
11 12 13 14 15 16 17
18 19 20 21 22 23 24
25 26 27 28 29 30</td></tr>
<tr><th colspan="3">UI Element Behaviors</th></tr>
<tr><td>Precondition</td><td>Action</td><td>Response</td></tr>
<tr><td>Always</td><td>Select Start Date or End Date</td><td>Dynamic calendar is displayed for current month</td></tr>
<tr><td>Always</td><td>Date selected in calendar</td><td>Date text box is populated with selected date in the format YYYY-MM-DD</td></tr>
</table>

FIGURE 15-7 An example element table for start date and end date fields.

Creating DAR Models

To create DAR models, decompose each screen layout into its component elements. Then describe each data-dependent or interactive screen element in an element table. Screen elements can include blocks of text, buttons, links, tables, rows and columns of tables, and icons.

The process for creating a DAR model is shown in Figure 15-8. Start with the ID and description sections of the UI element table, and then proceed with the displays and behaviors sections. This process is repeated for each element on each screen.

Prepare the Screen

If you have a UI Flow already, you can use that to determine which screens need DAR models. It is likely that every screen in your UI Flow should have a DAR model associated with it.

You will have to decide whether two screens are different enough to warrant treating them as separate screens. Often, minor variations in display between two screens means that you can treat them as one screen and capture the display differences by using DAR models. For example, if multiple customer types have similar screen layouts with subtle differences, one screen layout can be used to represent them all, with callouts on the wireframe to denote variations by user type. The variances in display and behavior for these user types will then be described in the same element table together.

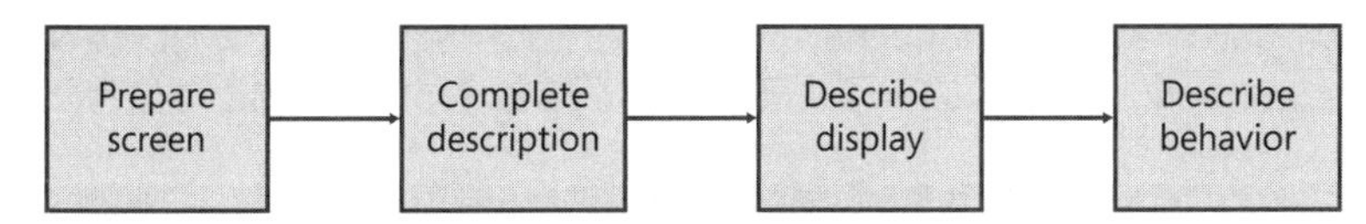

FIGURE 15-8 The process for creating a DAR model.

The screen layout does not have to be aesthetically designed for the DAR model to be useful. Even whiteboard drawings can be scanned and used for the model. Ideally, one team can be iterating on screen designs, and then when the screens are reasonably close to a final state, they are handed to the requirements team, who will elaborate on the UI requirements in DAR models.

If you do not have more than 7+/-2 screen elements, you can leave your screens as one unit and analyze each element of the full screen. However, if you have more than 10 screen elements, you might need to subdivide the full screen into major chunks to be analyzed. If you subdivide the screen, include one image of the full screen layout, marked to show the sections, as shown in Figure 15-9. Then handle each section of the screen layout as though it is its own screen, grouping element tables with the section of the screen.

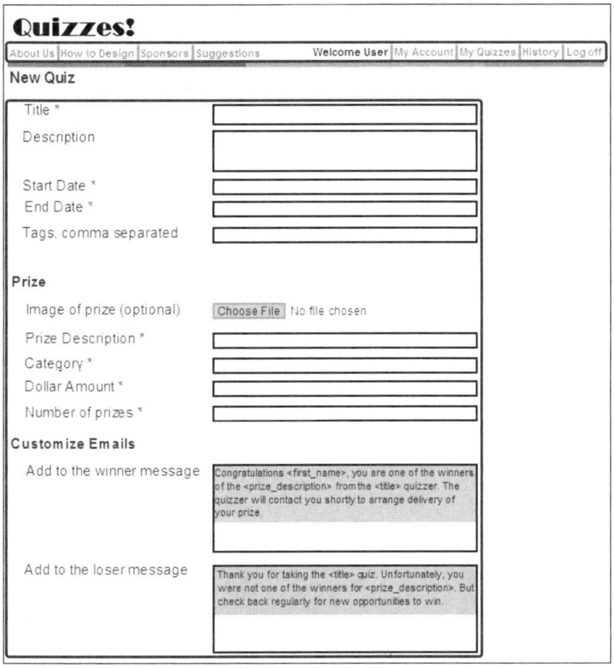

FIGURE 15-9 A subdivided screen layout.

Create a UI Element Description

The name of the element should be something obvious so that it can be easily referenced and discussed. Give each element table a unique identifier. You can determine a unique identifier (ID) format or let a requirements tool generate these, and apply the ID schema to all element tables. For example, the ID might be formatted something like *ELMT_xxxx*, where *xxxx* is the next available unique number. The description property should be a simple sentence that explains what the element is and does. Figure 15-10 shows the UI element description portion of the table.

UI Element: Start Date and End Date Fields	
UI Element Description	
ID	ELMT_0047
Description	Calendar for selecting Start Date and End Date

FIGURE 15-10 The UI element description.

The header properties are largely descriptive; the most important properties in the table are those that describe how the element is displayed or behaves under specific preconditions.

Create the UI Element Displays Section

The UI element displays section of the table shown in Figure 15-11 is used to define how the element displays under various preconditions. Each row within this section should describe the display under a different precondition. The data that goes in the precondition property is any information that causes the display to vary. For example, if the user is one of three different types, and each type of user has a different display of an element, then three rows would be created in this section of the table. The data in the display property might be a text description of how the element displays, or it might be a screen shot of the specific screen element. You can find preconditions by looking for states in State Tables and State Diagrams. In addition, the Business Data Diagram and Data Dictionary will list business data objects or fields that might be present in preconditions.

UI Element Displays	
Precondition	**Display**
Always	Company Logo "About Us" link "How to Design" link "Sponsors" link "Suggestions" link "Welcome " <user's name> "My Account" link "My Quizzes" link "History" link "Log on" or "Log off" link **Quizzes!** About Us | How to Design | Sponsors | Suggestions **Welcome User** | My Account | My Quizzes | History | Log off
<User.role> is administrative	Add "Admin" link to the left of the "Log off" link Admin | Log off
<User.role> is creator	"Create Quiz" link to the right of "My Quizzes" link My Quizzes | Create Quiz | History | Log off

FIGURE 15-11 The UI element displays section showing different preconditions.

Sometimes a display has a nested data element such as a table of data, with rows of records and columns with individual fields. In this situation, create a UI element table that describes how the rows are displayed. That table would describe how the rows are filtered and sorted, and how many elements are shown by default. Also, create a table for each field that is displayed differently based on preconditions. For example, a numeric field might show a leading zero in front of the decimal point if the number is between -1 and 1, but no leading zero otherwise.

Create the UI Element Behaviors Section

The UI element behaviors section of the table describes the immediate response of the system after a single action is taken by a user under various preconditions. As in the UI element displays section, each row of this section of the table represents a different combination of precondition and action by the user in relation to the element. The precondition is any information in the system that might cause variations in the UI behavior. The action property documents possible actions by the user. The response property describes the system response to the action by the user under the specified precondition. Figure 15-12 shows the UI element behaviors portion of the table.

UI Element Behaviors		
Precondition	**Action**	**Response**
Always	User types in text field without default messages	User's text displays in box
Always	User clicks in text field with default text	Default text is deleted and the user's text appears in the text box as it is typed
Always	User types in text field with suggested default message	Suggested default message is retained, and the user's newly entered text is appended to the end of the message

FIGURE 15-12 The UI element behaviors section.

Guidelines for Creating Element Tables

Here are some additional guidelines and tips for creating element tables:

- For elements that do not vary their display or behavior based on a precondition, the precondition value should be marked as "Always" to indicate that it always behaves the same. Keep in mind that you should only create DAR models for screen elements that show data or whose display or behavior varies by precondition or action. Fixed text or other unchangeable objects generally do not need element tables.

- For elements that have data-dependent displays but no behavior, put "N/A" for all columns in the behavior section.

- If an element has exactly the same display or behavior under multiple preconditions, it is appropriate to list those preconditions in one row by listing multiple preconditions together.
- The business rules around validation of fields are contained in the Data Dictionary. It is better to refer to the data fields by using the *<object.field>* notation described in Chapter 21, "Data Dictionary," rather than copying the validation rules to the DAR model. Also, if you refer to any field values in the model, use the *<object.field>* notation.

Using DARs

The old saying, "a picture is worth a thousand words" is applicable to DAR models. As mentioned earlier, often UI requirements are captured solely as a list of requirements supplemented by a screen shot. There are many problems with this approach. Readers have trouble determining whether there is anything missing because there are too many unorganized items to review. They also find long lists of requirements hard to understand, because the full essence of the UI can't be distilled from such a large number of items. Finally, because there is typically no mapping of the requirements to the UI itself, readers can't verify completeness of the requirements. It's challenging to develop software from just a basic list of UI requirements because such lists are typically disjointed or missing levels of detail.

Driving Completeness

The DAR model is a model that can effectively be bound for completeness. This means that you have a good chance of having a completely correct model. The reason for this is that each screen shows every element. There is only a small chance that the team will fail to document any particular element. The DAR model further bounds the scope of the UI specification by including all possible preconditions of the users, systems, and data that will interact with the UI, and then documenting the possible actions and responses for each precondition. In these ways, the model provides a self-documenting checklist against which the UI can be compared for accuracy and completeness, ensuring coverage of user-facing functionality within the UI.

Deriving Requirements

DAR models are used to capture UI requirements, by using a representation of the UI to frame the requirements. They help you ensure that all elements of the UI are considered and therefore no UI display or behavior requirements are missed. They are advantageous in that they are easy for stakeholders and developers to read to gain an understanding of what the system will look like and how it will behave. They are complete because they help you systematically analyze every user interface element.

The actions that the user can take translate directly to functional requirements. These actions will either map to existing functional requirements or will identify new functional requirements. Each row in the display or the behavior section of an element table or the behavior section will map to at least one, but sometimes several, functional requirements and business rules. In most cases, the behavior and display rows actually can become the requirements, and you can simply copy them to your complete list of requirements. The preconditions translate directly to business rules and modify display and behaviors based on system data.

When to Use

You should use a DAR model when you have significant concerns about the negative impact of a UI that does not work as expected. If a Commercial Off the Shelf (COTS) system is being deployed, these are still useful models because tables can be created for each element in the UI that is configurable, to help capture the configuration requirements. If this level of detail in the requirements does not exist, decisions about how the UI works will be made by the development team during the development process, when the business stakeholders might not be available to make decisions.

When Not to Use

DAR models can be extremely time consuming to create, because they document how the system will behave under every precondition. For some systems, this level of detail is important because there is a specific vision of how the software needs to work that is critical to its success. If an application has only a few users, DAR models might not be needed because the costs associated with a poor UI are not that significant. In this case, you can allow the developers to create the UI as long as the functional requirements are met. Many systems have no user interface, so it wouldn't make sense to use DAR models. Finally, some systems, such as help pages or data entry screens, have minimal amounts of data-driven data elements, so DAR models might not be useful.

Common Mistakes

The following represent the most common mistakes that we have seen with DARs.

Modeling Too Much

There are many preconditions or behaviors that are obvious, and it is not necessary to document them. For example, the default behavior of a drop-down box and the default behavior of a text box are well known. A DAR model is meant to communicate the concepts that might be confusing or that are complex, not to document exactly how the system behaves in every possible case. If your text box functions such that entering text causes something else to happen, then it would be worthwhile to document that.

Modeling Elements with No Data-Driven Behavior or Display

Static text, pictures, or other objects are better shown with a picture than with a DAR model.

Using Only UI-Based Models or Prototypes

There has been a push in the analysis industry to attempt to use only screen shots or prototyping applications. Similar to the movement to use only Use Cases to analyze a solution, this is doomed to fail because this view of the system, though critical, is not complete. For example, if a business has more than a hundred business processes, but chooses to only develop prototypes or screen-based models, it will become almost impossible for them to systematically ensure that every business process is completely supported by the screens. Moreover, if there are thousands of business rules and they are only contained within a prototype, the test organization will have no way to determine what the complete set is that they should be testing.

Focusing on the User Interface Too Early

For many business stakeholders, the solution isn't real until they can actually see pictures of it. You can feel the excitement the first time they see DAR models. However, DAR models are only one view of the system. Even more important is the value that the system is generating and the process that the system needs to support. It is very easy for teams to get caught up debating what the screen should look like instead of focusing on how the solution creates value. We recommend that the DAR model be one of the last models that you create.

Including Too Much Fidelity in the Screen Layout

High-fidelity screen layouts are exciting because they really show what the system will look like. However, many times they can be a distraction—for example, if the stakeholders don't like the colors, fonts, and even the spacing between elements. The purpose of the DAR is to help stakeholders understand what data will be shown on the screen and how users will interact with the screen to accomplish their goals.

Related Models

The DAR model is similar to an event-response table, in which the system detects external events (such as "user clicks on logon link") and responds based upon the state of the system at the time of the event (Wiegers 2003). The DAR model extends the event-response table model by linking the preconditions (which can be states), events, and responses of each UI element directly to the UI screen layout.

The following list briefly describes the most important models that influence or are enhanced by DARs. Chapter 26, "Using Models Together," contains a more thorough discussion about all related models.

- **Use Cases and Process Flows** These map to the user interfaces and therefore can help determine the behavior of elements.
- **Business Data Diagrams (BDDs)** These are used to understand the major system objects that have states that might affect the UI display and behavior.
- **State Tables and State Diagrams** These are used to identify the possible states of the objects in the BDD that might affect the display or behavior of the UI.
- **Data Dictionaries** These are used to capture static field display requirements and business rules and should not be duplicated in DAR models. Use *<object.field>* notation to reference data in the DAR.
- **User Interface (UI) Flows** These are used to document how all the screens in the application fit together. A UI Flow can act as a checklist of screens for which to make a DAR model. The transitions between screens should be documented in the behavior sections of elements in the DAR. The DAR can help improve the UI Flow by identifying additional transitions that are missing from the UI Flow.

Exercise

The following exercise is intended to help you to gain a better understanding of how to use this model. The exercise is open ended, and therefore the answer you come up with could be substantially different than the answer that we have provided. There are potentially many correct solutions. The answer provides an explanation of how we arrived at our solution. You will gain the most out of the exercise by attempting to do it yourself before looking at the solution. The answers for the exercises can be found in Appendix C.

Instructions

Prepare a DAR model for the color selector as described in the scenario.

Scenario

You are on a project to launch a new eStore to two million worldwide users. This eStore will have browse and search functions to find flamingos and other lawn decorations, and there will be a standard checkout process, including a cart review, shipping, and payment information collection, and an order confirmation step before an order is sent for order processing. Before an order can be placed, the user must sign in to their account or create a new account.

Because the executive team has decided on a strategy to drive as much traffic as they can to the eStore site instead of the phones, it's imperative that the site be easy to use, be built correctly to the requirements, and work consistently across the site. The executives have engaged a design team and a usability team to mock up wireframes and test them with users to finalize the look and feel of the screens. That is good news, because you have relatively stable wireframes from which to write UI requirements. Figure 15-13 is one wireframe for the system for which you can create DAR models. Create a DAR model for the color selector in the wireframe.

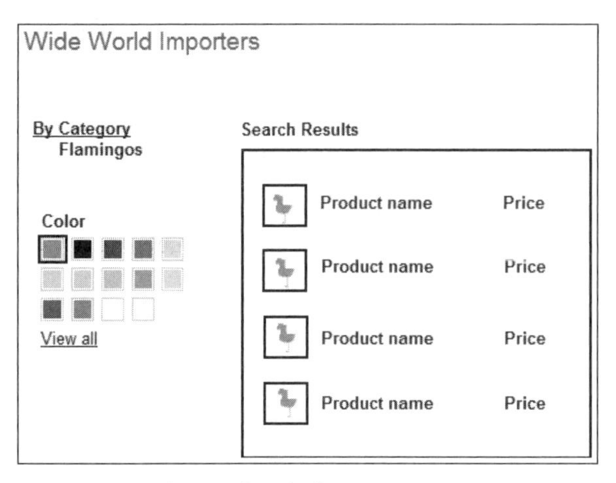

FIGURE 15-13 The exercise wireframe.

Additional Resources

- Section 4.4 of *The Software Requirements Memory Jogger* is a complete overview of event-response tables (Gottesdiener 2005).
- *Software Requirements* has a summary of event-response tables in Chapter 8 (Wiegers 2003).
- *Display-Action-Response Model for User Interface Requirement* includes a case study from our original creation of the DAR model (Beatty and Alexander 2007).

References

- Beatty, J., and M. Alexander. 2007. *Display-Action-Response Model for User Interface Requirements: Case Study.* New Delhi, India: Second International Workshop on Requirements Engineering Visualization. *http://www.computer.org/portal/web/csdl/doi/10.1109/REV.2007.3.*
- Gottesdiener, Ellen. 2005. *The Software Requirements Memory Jogger.* Salem, NH: Goal/QPC.
- Wiegers, Karl E. 2003. *Software Requirements, Second Edition.* Redmond, WA: Microsoft Press.
- Stern, K., Rudd, J. and S. Isensee. 1996. "Low vs. High-Fidelity Prototyping Debate." *Interactions 3:76-85.* New York, NY: ACM.

CHAPTER 16

Decision Table

The other day, I was trying to teach my friend how to play Texas Hold 'em poker. In the game, there are only a few actions that you can take: call, raise, fold, or check; yet the game is very complex, and it isn't at all obvious when you should take one of those actions.

I realized that there were just a few factors to consider, but that they created too many combinations to make me feel sure that I had covered all the important situations for my friend. Some of the factors going into the decision about your action are which seat you are in, how many other people have stayed in, how many have yet to act after you, the probability of improving your hand compared to the current pot size, and the type of each of the players.

For example, if the size of the pot compared to how much I have to put in is too small compared to my chances of improving my hand, then I usually fold regardless of any other factors. However, if everyone before me has folded and there are only one or two people after me, I might raise, unless I know that the players yet to act are the type to protect their antes (blinds). On the other hand, even if I have a good hand with good chances for improving it, if there are one or two really aggressive players still in, I might fold just to stay out of their way.

These kinds of multifactor decisions are very common in software development. The Decision Table is an RML systems model that helps you analyze all the permutations of complex logic in a comprehensive way. Decision Tables are used to answer the question, "Under what conditions will this outcome occur?" or "Given these conditions, what outcome should I choose?" The format of the model allows you to easily ensure that all possible conditions are being checked and acted upon properly. Decision Tables are used if there is no specific order to evaluating the decisions. If the decisions need to be made in any kind of order, a Decision Tree should be used instead (see Chapter 17, "Decision Tree").

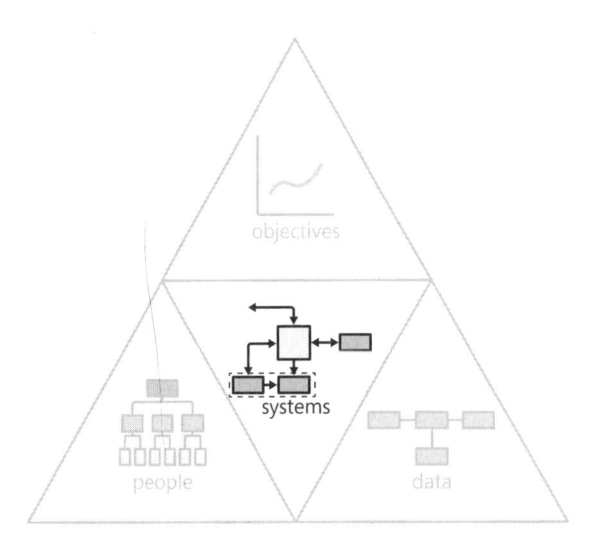

Decision Tables show all possible combinations of a set of conditions and their corresponding outcomes, represented in a grid. The Decision Table format allows you to ensure completeness. Because the full quantity of combinations is known, you can be 100 percent certain that you have looked at every permutation. It is easier for technical teams to use Decision Tables than tree structures because every option is shown in an organized format. A Decision Tree can get cumbersome when it attempts to show all possible conditions and outcomes.

The advantages of a Decision Table over a Decision Tree are visual traceability and speed. You can instantly trace an outcome back to the conditions that cause that particular outcome. You can also always trace all the potential outcomes from a condition. A table is faster to create than a Decision Tree, because with Decision Trees you have to rearrange your branches for every new branch that you add. If you decide to create both, it usually is best to create a Decision Table first, before you create your tree, so that you have an idea of what the layout should look like.

Decision Table Template

A Decision Table is represented as a grid, as shown in Figure 16-1. The top row contains labels for the business rules. The first column contains all the possible conditions and outcomes. Each of the remaining columns in the grid represents the outcomes valid for the specified choices. Collectively, the combination of choices and outcomes in a column make up each business rule.

Decision Table	Rule 1	Rule 2	Rule 3	Rule 4	Rule 5	Rule 6	Rule 7	Rule 8
Conditions								
Condition 1	choice 1a	choice 1b	choice 1a	choice 1b	choice 1a	choice 1b	choice 1a	choice 1b
Condition 2	choice 2a	choice 2a	choice 2b	choice 2b	choice 2a	choice 2a	choice 2b	choice 2b
Condition 3	choice 3a	choice 3a	choice 3a	choice 3a	choice 3b	choice 3b	choice 3b	choice 3b
Outcomes								
OC001 Outcome 1	-	-	X	-	-	-	-	X
OC002 Outcome 2	X	-	X	-	-	-	-	-
OC003 Outcome 3	X	-	X	-	X	-	X	X
OC004 Outcome 4	X	X	-	-	X	X	-	-
OC005 Outcome 5	-	X	-	X	-	-	-	-

FIGURE 16-1 The Decision Table template.

A condition is an individual check such as "Lives in the United States - Yes or No" or "Marital status - single, married, divorced, or widowed." We use the term "condition" instead of the more common term "decision" because "decision" implies that there is an order to the decision process, whereas "condition" does not.

The choices for a condition are the set of possible values for that condition. Choices can be binary, such as Yes or No or True or False; they can be multi-valued, such as ages 0-9, 10-21, 22-34, and 35+; or they can be a dash (-), meaning that the choice is irrelevant. The outcomes can have unique identifiers on them to help reference them from requirements.

Each outcome cell either contains an X, a number, a dash, or is left blank, as explained in Table 16-1.

TABLE 16-1 Outcome and Choice Intersection Elements

Element	Meaning
X	Outcome applies when the choices are valid
Number	Outcome applies when the choices are valid; the outcomes should be executed in a specified order
-	Outcome is irrelevant (does not apply) when the choices are valid
Blank	Outcome is unknown; follow-up is needed

A rule is the particular set of choices for each condition that have to match for the outcomes to apply. For example, the condition "lives in the United States = yes" and the condition "Marital status = single" could form the choices that make up a rule that says a specific outcome applies. The rules don't have names; they are just permutations of all the possible choices of all the conditions and valid outcomes. Rules eventually become business rules in your requirements. For example, in the template, if the choices choice 1a, choice 2a, and choice 3a are true, then outcomes 2, 3, and 4 apply.

Tool Tip Decision Tables are typically created as Microsoft Excel or Microsoft Word tables or in a requirements management tool that allows you to create tables of requirements.

Example

An insurance company has a formalized process for determining which homeowner policies a customer is eligible for. Their decision process is modeled in the Decision Table in Figure 16-2. The model provides the assurance that all possible combinations are considered, because every combination of choice for every condition is included.

Decision Table	Rule 1	Rule 2	Rule 3	Rule 4	Rule 5	Rule 6	Rule 7	Rule 8	Rule 9	Rule 10	Rule 11	Rule 12
Conditions												
Passed credit check	Y	Y	Y	Y	Y	Y	N	N	N	N	N	N
Existing policy	Y	Y	Y	N	N	N	Y	Y	Y	N	N	N
Total years as homeowner	>5	1-5	<1	>5	1-5	<1	>5	1-5	<1	>5	1-5	<1
Outcomes												
OC001 Policy A	X	X	-	X	-	-	-	-	-	-	-	-
OC002 Policy B	X	X	X	X	X	-	-	-	-	-	-	-
OC003 Policy C	X	-	X	-	X	X	-	-	-	-	-	-
OC004 Decline	-	-	-	-	-	-	X	X	X	X	X	X

FIGURE 16-2 The Decision Table for insurance policies.

For example, the Decision Table tells us that if a customer has passed a credit check, has an existing policy, and has been a homeowner for 20 years, then he is eligible for policies A, B, and C. If the same customer did not have an existing policy, then he would be eligible for policies A and B.

Looking at the complete table, you can see where unnecessary columns can be pruned. For example, being a homeowner and having existing policies with the company are irrelevant if the person fails the credit check. Figure 16-3 shows the simplified table.

Decision Table	Rule 1	Rule 2	Rule 3	Rule 4	Rule 5	Rule 6	Rule 7
Conditions							
Passed credit check	Y	Y	Y	Y	Y	Y	N
Existing policy	Y	Y	Y	N	N	N	-
Total years as homeowner	>5	1-5	<1	>5	1-5	<1	-
Outcomes							
OC001 Policy A	X	X	-	X	-	-	-
OC002 Policy B	X	X	X	X	X	-	-
OC003 Policy C	X	-	X	-	X	X	-
OC004 Decline	-	-	-	-	-	-	X

FIGURE 16-3 The simplified Decision Table for insurance policies.

Creating Decision Tables

The high-level steps for creating a Decision Table are outlined in Figure 16-4. We suggest an order to the steps; however, you might do this differently, as discussed later in this chapter, in the "Identify Outcomes" section. To illustrate how to create Decision Tables, this section continues with the example scenario from the previous section.

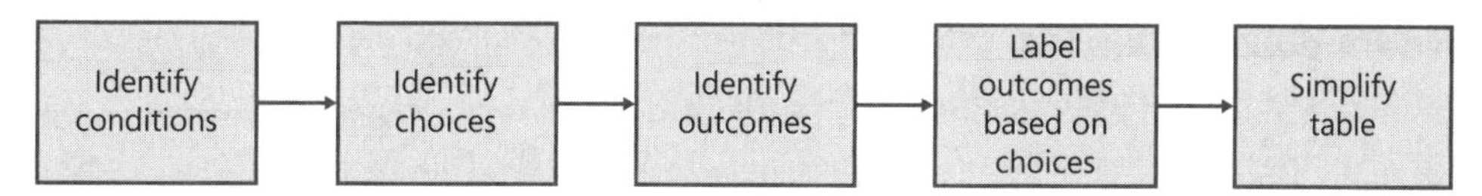

FIGURE 16-4 The process for creating a Decision Table.

Identify Conditions

Think about all the potential conditions that apply to the situation and list them in the first column of your table. Conditions can be decisions that people make, data attributes that trigger various business rules, or any other factor (Gottesdiener 2005). Each condition needs its own row in the table. If you combined multiple conditions, it would be very hard to check for completeness. Figure 16-5 shows the first part of the table with just the possible conditions. A condition will often reference specific data fields from a Data Dictionary. In those cases, use the *<object.field>* notation, as described in Chapter 21, "Data Dictionary."

Conditions
Passed credit check
Existing policy
Total years as homeowner

FIGURE 16-5 The conditions.

Identify Choices

When you identify choices, you first need to determine what the choices are, then you might re-order your conditions in the table based on the choices, and then you enumerate the choices to build the rules columns.

Determining Valid Choices

After you have the conditions, consider the possible choices for each condition. Look at your Data Dictionary to identify valid values for the field. Some conditions will have binary choices of Yes and No or True and False, but the choices can be more complex, such as a range of numbers or matching words. There is no requirement that the conditions all be binary; in fact, the table can be simpler if a single multi-choice condition is used instead of several binary conditions. For example, if the condition is "Years as a homeowner," you might have three potential choices for that condition that should be modeled: more than five years, one to five years, and less than one year.

Make sure that the choices you use reflect all possible choices for the condition. If you miss any possible choices, your table will be incomplete and you cannot guarantee that you have all of the requirements. For a particular condition, the choices must also be mutually exclusive, in that only one can exist at a time. A condition cannot have overlapping ranges such that each could simultaneously match because they share values. For example, the ranges 0–1 and 1–5 overlap because each includes the number 1. If you need to specify ranges like this, use the following type of range definitions instead: <1 and 1–5, or <=1 and >1–5.

Reordering Conditions

You do not need to list the conditions in any specific order; however, it is generally easier to make a table when they are listed in the order of number of choices. The condition that has the fewest choices should be the first condition. For example, if you have a rule such as, "If the customer failed the credit check, then automatically decline him," then you can cut out half of your permutations. You don't need to do any work to evaluate the rest of the conditions; they just don't matter. The condition that has the most choices should be the last condition listed. This order puts the most constraining conditions at the top of the list, which aids you in reviewing and simplifying the table.

Enumerating Choices

Now you add rules (columns) to enumerate all possible combinations of choices for all conditions. If you multiply the number of choices together for each condition, you can determine how many columns you need. If you have just one condition with two choices, you will need only two columns. If you have three conditions with two choices each, you will need eight columns (2 x 2 x 2 = 8). In this example, there are two choices for the first condition (Y or N), two for the second condition (Y or N), and three for the third condition (>5, 1–5, or<1), so there are 12 columns (2 x 2 x 3 = 12).

In addition to each choice being mutually exclusive, each rule needs to be mutually exclusive. This means that you should have no columns with the same set of choices.

The order of the rules should make it easy to recognize that all possible choices of conditions are being examined. In the first row, group all the like choices together. In the example, for the first condition, half will be Y and half will be N, so make the first four columns Y and the second four N, as in Figure 16-6.

Decision Table	Rule 1	Rule 2	Rule 3	Rule 4	Rule 5	Rule 6	Rule 7	Rule 8	Rule 9	Rule 10	Rule 11	Rule 12
Conditions												
Passed credit check	Y	Y	Y	Y	Y	Y	N	N	N	N	N	N

FIGURE 16-6 The first condition with choices.

For the second condition, half of the Ys from the first condition will be Y and half will be N. This results in the pattern in Figure 16-7.

Decision Table	Rule 1	Rule 2	Rule 3	Rule 4	Rule 5	Rule 6	Rule 7	Rule 8	Rule 9	Rule 10	Rule 11	Rule 12
Conditions												
Passed credit check	Y	Y	Y	Y	Y	Y	N	N	N	N	N	N
Existing policy	Y	Y	Y	N	N	N	Y	Y	Y	N	N	N

FIGURE 16-7 The second condition with choices.

Finally, in the third condition, alternate the three choices again to get the pattern in Figure 16-8. When you complete the conditions and choices of a Decision Table, you will get a result that looks like this. Remember that you will have more columns if you have more conditions or valid choices for conditions.

Decision Table	Rule 1	Rule 2	Rule 3	Rule 4	Rule 5	Rule 6	Rule 7	Rule 8	Rule 9	Rule 10	Rule 11	Rule 12
Conditions												
Passed credit check	Y	Y	Y	Y	Y	Y	N	N	N	N	N	N
Existing policy	Y	Y	Y	N	N	N	Y	Y	Y	N	N	N
Total years as homeowner	>5	1-5	<1	>5	1-5	<1	>5	1-5	<1	>5	1-5	<1

FIGURE 16-8 All conditions with all choices enumerated.

Identify Outcomes

The combinations of choices lead to one or more outcomes. Outcomes are the decisions, conclusions, or actions that occur when the choices are valid. Add the outcomes to the first column of your table, below all of the conditions. Figure 16-9 shows our same scenario with outcomes added.

Decision Table	Rule 1	Rule 2	Rule 3	Rule 4	Rule 5	Rule 6	Rule 7	Rule 8	Rule 9	Rule 10	Rule 11	Rule 12
Conditions												
Passed credit check	Y	Y	Y	Y	Y	Y	N	N	N	N	N	N
Existing policy	Y	Y	Y	N	N	N	Y	Y	Y	N	N	N
Total years as homeowner	>5	1-5	<1	>5	1-5	<1	>5	1-5	<1	>5	1-5	<1
Outcomes												
OC001 Policy A												
OC002 Policy B												
OC003 Policy C												
OC004 Decline												

FIGURE 16-9 Outcomes.

You might find it easier to identify the outcomes first. If you know your outcomes and want to determine the conditions under which they are valid, start with the outcomes part of the table and then identify conditions and choices. It is possible that you might start with a few business rules, so creating the table with just a few rules filled in can quickly show where there are gaps in your information.

Label Valid Outcomes by Choice Combinations

Each column now represents a possible combination of choices for the conditions. Label the valid outcomes under the combination of choices. If you know that an outcome is not valid, mark it with a dash, and if you are not sure, leave it blank to follow up later. Figure 16-10 shows the resulting Decision Table for the scenario.

Decision Table	Rule 1	Rule 2	Rule 3	Rule 4	Rule 5	Rule 6	Rule 7	Rule 8	Rule 9	Rule 10	Rule 11	Rule 12
Conditions												
Passed credit check	Y	Y	Y	Y	Y	Y	N	N	N	N	N	N
Existing policy	Y	Y	Y	N	N	N	-	-	-	-	-	-
Total years as homeowner	>5	1-5	<1	>5	1-5	<1	-	-	-	-	-	-
Outcomes												
OC001 Policy A	X	X	-	X	-	-	-	-	-	-	-	-
OC002 Policy B	X	X	X	X	X	-	-	-	-	-	-	-
OC003 Policy C	X	-	X	-	X	X	-	-	-	-	-	-
OC004 Decline	-	-	-	-	-	-	X	X	X	X	X	X

FIGURE 16-10 The complete Decision Table.

Simplify the Decision Table

Because so many columns are necessary even with just a few conditions, it is best to try to simplify your table as early in the process as feasible. If there are specific rules that are only dependent on a few of the conditions, that means that you do not need to evaluate other conditions. You should combine the rules to remove the ones that differ in conditions and not in outcomes.

When a condition is irrelevant to the outcome, put a dash in the cell for that condition. Do not just haphazardly delete columns, though! You must ensure that all combinations are included in the table, using the dash to represent those conditions whose choices do not matter. For example, you know that when a customer fails the credit check, she is declined, so you do not need to evaluate the existing-policy or years-as-a-homeowner conditions. Figure 16-11 shows the example after it has been simplified.

Decision Table	Rule 1	Rule 2	Rule 3	Rule 4	Rule 5	Rule 6	Rule 7
Conditions							
Passed credit check	Y	Y	Y	Y	Y	Y	N
Existing policy	Y	Y	Y	N	N	N	-
Total years as homeowner	>5	1-5	<1	>5	1-5	<1	-
Outcomes							
OC001 Policy A	X	X	-	X	-	-	-
OC002 Policy B	X	X	X	X	X	-	-
OC003 Policy C	X	-	X	-	X	X	-
OC004 Decline	-	-	-	-	-	-	X

FIGURE 16-11 The simplified Decision Table.

In simplifying your table, you might discover that some conditions are always irrelevant. You can remove those conditions and further condense your table. Finally, if, after you complete your table, you see that certain outcomes are always executed in tandem, you can combine those outcomes into a single outcome.

Using Decision Tables

Decision Tables can make very complex decisions appear orderly and complete because the table communicates a lot of information in a very compact format.

Making Decisions

A business can use a Decision Tree for training users how to make decisions, but a Decision Table is hard to read for these purposes. More commonly, a Decision Table is implemented in the system to make the decisions automatically.

Driving Completeness

The value provided by Decision Tables stems from the ability to walk through all possible combinations of choices. Assuming that every outcome, condition, and possible choice is identified, you can literally see that all the potential choices have been considered, and therefore your requirements for the decision scenario can be considered complete.

When you are analyzing Decision Tables, if you have any cells you do not know about, leave them blank and track them for follow-up.

Using Decision Tables with Decision Trees

Decision Tables are used to identify all possible conditions and choice combinations and their resulting outcomes. You can also use them to eliminate combinations that are not relevant. Finally, you can use the Decision Table to build a corresponding Decision Tree to better visualize the decisions and look for additional opportunities to simplify the logic. Generally, if you plan to create an ordered Decision Tree, you should order the conditions in the Decision Table by using the same order that you use to make the decisions in the ordered Decision Tree.

Deriving Requirements

A complete Decision Table indicates that you have modeled all of the requirements and business rules related to a particular set of decisions. You might also need to write out individual statements from your table for developers and testers to work from. Each complete column of the Decision Table represents one business rule you need to write; the rule describes the conditions under which the outcomes occur. Decision Tables can sometimes act as stand-alone requirements for developers and testers.

When to Use

Decision Tables are best when the order of the decisions does not matter. If the order does matter, you can use Decision Tables to identify all combinations of conditions and simplify them before you create a Decision Tree, but you still must create an ordered Decision Tree.

If you are in an elicitation session and have no time to prepare in advance, use a Decision Table with your business stakeholders to elicit an initial draft of the logic, because you can create Decision Tables very quickly.

Modeling Complex Logic

Decision Tables are usually supplements to System Flows (see Chapter 13, "System Flow"), UI Flows (see Chapter 14, "User Interface Flow"), Process Flows (see Chapter 9, "Process Flow"), or Use Cases (see Chapter 10, "Use Case"). The Decision Table model is used to simplify any of these models by removing the complex decision logic from the main flow. This allows the audience to focus on the overall picture of the flow in those models without getting lost in the details.

It is very useful to use Decision Tables alongside these other models when there are validation steps. For example, in a Process Flow to create an order, there might be complex logic to check that the proper fields are completed and formatted correctly, with different error paths if they are not. These validation steps can be represented in a Process Flow, but if there are many of them, it would be easier to read both the Process Flow and the logic steps by putting the validation into a Decision Table. Instead of putting them all in the Process Flow, the analyst can include one simple decision box in the Process Flow, such as, "Are order fields valid?" and can then reference the Decision Table, where that logic is further analyzed.

A Decision Table should be created any time you have a scenario with a series of nested "if" statements. If you find you need to write two to three "if" statements in a row in a Process Flow or Use Case, you probably should use a Decision Table to model them instead.

Particularly if the order of the decisions is not relevant, a Decision Table is usually the best choice, especially if each combination of choices leads to a different set of outcomes. The visual structure of a Decision Table allows you to quickly see the logic represented by your decisions. A five-by-five table is much easier to understand and review than the 25 separate "if" statements that would have to be written up to describe the information in the table.

When Not to Use

Decision Tables are not ideal for documenting decisions that cause you to move around in your decision hierarchy. If you need to show any order to your decision-making process, you simply cannot use a Decision Table as your only model, because these models do not show order. Similarly, you cannot use a Decision Table if you want to show any loops in your logic. You can use a Decision Table to do your initial analysis to prune the tree, and then follow up with the Decision Tree to show the order of the decisions.

Common Mistakes

The following represent the most common mistakes we have seen with Decision Tables.

Missing Permutations

Make sure you calculate the number of possible rules to ensure that you gather them all.

Overlapping Choice Ranges

Ensure that your boundary conditions for ranges don't overlap; be explicit by using >=, <=, >, and < symbols.

Not Combining Rules

Decision Tables can easily become large and unwieldy if you don't reduce the total number of rules. Make sure that you have identified any conditions that are not important for a rule, and then remove the rules that vary by that condition and not by outcome.

Modeling a Sequence of Decisions

Decision Tables should not be used if you are trying to model a sequence of decisions that occur in order; a Decision Tree is more appropriate.

Related Models

Decision Tables outside of RML sometimes call the conditions *factors* and the outcomes *actions*. Most Decision Table nomenclature allows you to have a blank cell when an outcome does not apply, but we recommend that you do not leave cells blank, because you will not be able to tell whether blank means "not valid" or "I haven't determined whether this is valid."

The following list briefly describes the most important models that influence or are enhanced by Decision Tables. Chapter 26, "Using Models Together," contains a more thorough discussion about all related models.

- **Decision Trees** These are used to visually show the decision logic in a tree structure. Also, the Decision Table can help you to create a Decision Tree.
- **Process Flows, System Flows, Use Cases, and User Interface (UI) Flows** Decision Tables are used to model complex logic found in them.
- **Data Dictionaries** The valid choices for conditions are based on data in the Data Dictionary and should use the *<object.field>* notation.

Exercise

The following exercise is intended to help you to gain a better understanding of how to use this model. The exercise is open ended, and therefore the answer you come up with could be substantially different than the answer that we have provided. There are potentially many correct solutions. The answer provides an explanation of how we arrived at our solution. You will gain the most out of the exercise by attempting to do it yourself before looking at the solution. The answers for the exercises can be found in Appendix C.

Instructions

Create a Decision Table for the following scenario.

Scenario

You are on a project to launch a new eStore to sell flamingos and other lawn decorations. You are capturing the rules for handling payment information. You decide a Decision Table will be the best model to capture the rules the system must implement to handle the different forms of payment. You know that the customer can store credit cards in his profile, but he can also choose to pay with a new credit card, check, or gift card. If he pays with a gift card, he will have to pay any balance with another payment form if there isn't enough money available on the gift card. Use this information and your general knowledge about online payment options to create a Decision Table.

Additional Resources

- *The Software Requirements Memory Jogger* has an overview of Decision Tables with a good example in Section 4.11 (Gottesdiener 2005).
- Wiegers's *Software Requirements* has an example of a Decision Tree and Decision Table (Wiegers 2003).
- Chapter 4 of Davis's *Software Requirements Revision* has a description of Decision Trees and Decision Tables (Davis 1993).

References

- Davis, Alan M. 1993. *Software Requirements: Objects, Functions, & States*. Upper Saddle River, NJ: PTR Prentice Hall.
- Gottesdiener, Ellen. 2005. *The Software Requirements Memory Jogger*. Salem, NH: Goal/QPC.
- Wiegers, Karl E. 2003. *Software Requirements, Second Edition*. Redmond, WA: Microsoft Press.

CHAPTER 17

Decision Tree

Does this sound like a familiar call to you?

Pleasant operator voice: *Thanks for calling the phone company. Press 1 for English, press 2 for Spanish, press 3 for French.*

<You press 1.>

Operator voice: *For automated information about your account, press 1. For billing information, press 2. For technical assistance, press 3. To change your account settings, press 4. To order new service, press 5.*

<You press 1.>

Operator voice: *For balance due, press 1. To make a payment, press 2. For the billing address, press 3. For a history of your last payment, press 4. To go back to the prior menu, press 5.*

<You press 1.>

Operator voice: *Please enter your account number followed by the pound sign.*

<You enter a series of digits you think is the correct account number.>

Annoying operator voice: *This is not a valid account number. Please enter it again.*

<Again, you enter a series of digits you think is the correct account number.>

Annoying operator voice: *This is not a valid account number. Please enter it again.*

<Again, you enter a series of digits you think is the correct account number, with increasing force on each keypress.>

Annoying operator voice: *This is not a valid account number. Please enter it again.*

<You press 5, in hopes of going back.>

Annoying operator voice: *This is not a valid account number. Press 9 to go back to the previous menu.*

<You press 9 with more hope.>

Operator voice: *For balance due, press 1. To make a payment, press 2. For the billing address, press 3. For a history of your last payment, press 4. To go back to the prior menu, press 5.*

<You press 5, hoping it takes you back a level and not back to where you just came from.>

Annoying operator voice: *For automated information about your account, press 1. For billing information, press 2. For technical assistance, press 3. To change your account settings, press 4. To order new service, press 5.*

<You press 4, because now you are mad and just want to cancel your entire service.>

Annoying operator voice: *To add a service, press 1. To cancel a service, press 2. To change your address, press 3. To change your online user name, press 4.*

<You press 2.>

Annoying operator voice: *To cancel your long-distance option, press 1. To cancel your digital option, press 2. To cancel your wireless option, press 3. To cancel your basic service, press 4. For more options, press 5.*

<You start pounding the 0 key on your phone, in the hope that you will finally just get to a person, completely forgetting why you called in the first place!>

Live person: *Hello, this is Luka, can I have your account number?*

Nearly everyone has been stuck in these automated menus before, where you often give up and either hang up or press 0, hoping for human help. This automated help line needed to be simplified to improve the experience for the user.

The Decision Tree is an RML systems model. Decision Trees allow you to model complex logic, allowing you to analyze a series of decisions. It is significantly easier to validate the logic visually in a Decision Tree than from a description in a list of statements. Decision Trees are also used to identify opportunities to simplify the logic in scenarios such as the call center story. Decision Trees can be ordered or unordered. *Ordered Decision Trees* are used if there is an implied order in which the decisions are made and are the most common type of Decision Tree. *Unordered Decision Trees* are used to simplify a set of decisions when there is no implied order.

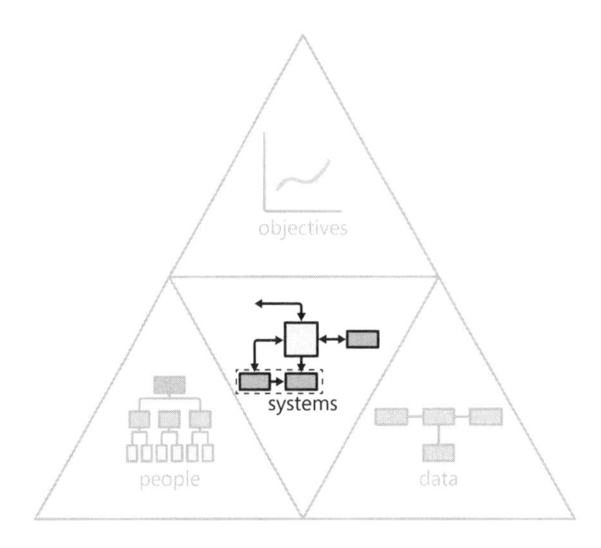

It is very difficult to ensure that all decisions have been captured in a Decision Tree alone; instead, you should use a Decision Table, which captures every permutation of decisions (see Chapter 16, "Decision Table"). However, by examining each decision and focusing only on the direct results of that decision, you will have a much higher chance of capturing all the choices than if you just create a list of the decisions and choices. In addition, a visual model enables you to literally see whether there are missing loops or dead ends that you had not considered before.

Although decisions are often made by people, the Decision Tree is an RML systems model because typically when decisions are complex enough to warrant the creation of the model, they are automated in the system.

Decision Tree Template

A Decision Tree has only three types of elements: decisions, outcomes, and connector lines between them. The elements are described in Table 17-1.

TABLE 17-1 Decision Tree Elements

Element	Meaning
Decision	The decision shape shows the decision to be made, phrased as a question.
Outcome	The outcome shows the result of taking a decision choice pathway. An outcome can be one or more actions or a reference to another model.
Decision Choice →	Connector lines with arrows are used between any of the decisions and other decisions or outcomes to indicate the order the decisions are evaluated. Their labels are phrased as answers to the questions asked in the decisions.
Decision Choice ———	Connector lines without arrows are used between any of the decisions and other decisions or outcomes when there is no order to the choices. The labels are phrased as answers to the questions asked in the decisions.

The Decision Tree template strings the decisions and outcome elements together with connector lines. The labels on the connector lines represent the possible decision choices emerging from the decision box. There will always be at least two decision choices from each decision point, and each line will be labeled with a different decision choice. An arrow indicates the direction of the flow from one decision to the result of the choice. The result is either another decision or an outcome. The outcome is a rectangle and represents a decision, conclusion, or action that is the result of a series of decisions. There should not be lines coming out of any outcomes; outcomes are end points in the Decision Tree. Figure 17-1 illustrates this concept in the format of a Decision Tree template.

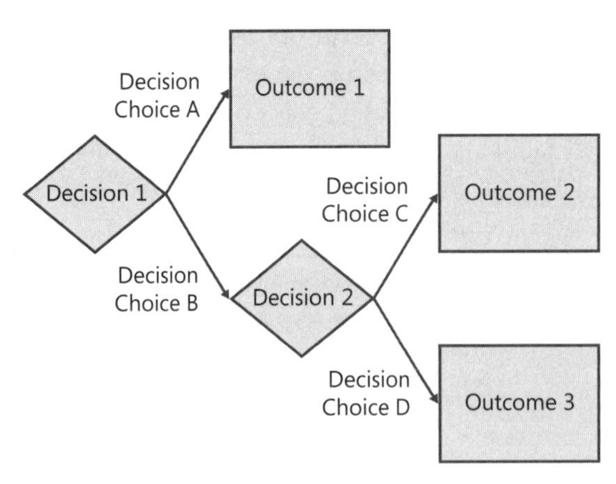

FIGURE 17-1 The Decision Tree template.

In this template, decision choices A and B must be different values. Decision choices C and D must be unique from each other, but they can repeat choices A and B. For example, choices A and B could be Yes and No. Choices C and D could also be Yes and No. There can be more than two choices for Decision 1 or 2. Also, Outcome 1 can be the same as Outcome 2 or Outcome 3, or it can be unique.

Decision Trees should be drawn from left to right or top to bottom, for readability.

Tool Tip One of the tricky things about Decision Trees is that they are challenging to manipulate after they have been created. It is best to use a whiteboard or sticky notes for early drafts before committing them to software. Typically, Decision Trees are created in a visual modeling tool such as Microsoft Visio or a requirements management tool, but they can also be created in Microsoft PowerPoint.

Example

A team of analysts was tasked to analyze an automated phone menu in a call center, much like the one at the beginning of this chapter. The analysts originally documented the existing system with a Decision Tree. This brought many dead ends and complex pathways to the surface that they were able to eliminate after they identified them visually. By rearranging the decision and outcomes, the analysts were able to reduce the call center application from 10 to 4 levels of logic, which allowed the company to cut call times and measurably improve customer satisfaction. They were also able to ensure that every choice allowed some path out for customers.

The example in Figure 17-2 includes only part of the tree; for example, other languages are left out and some of the menu options are not shown. However, those would look similar to one another and have been omitted for readability in this text.

The example Decision Tree was created such that most decision points have more than two decision choices coming from them, reflecting the customer's actual experience on the phone.

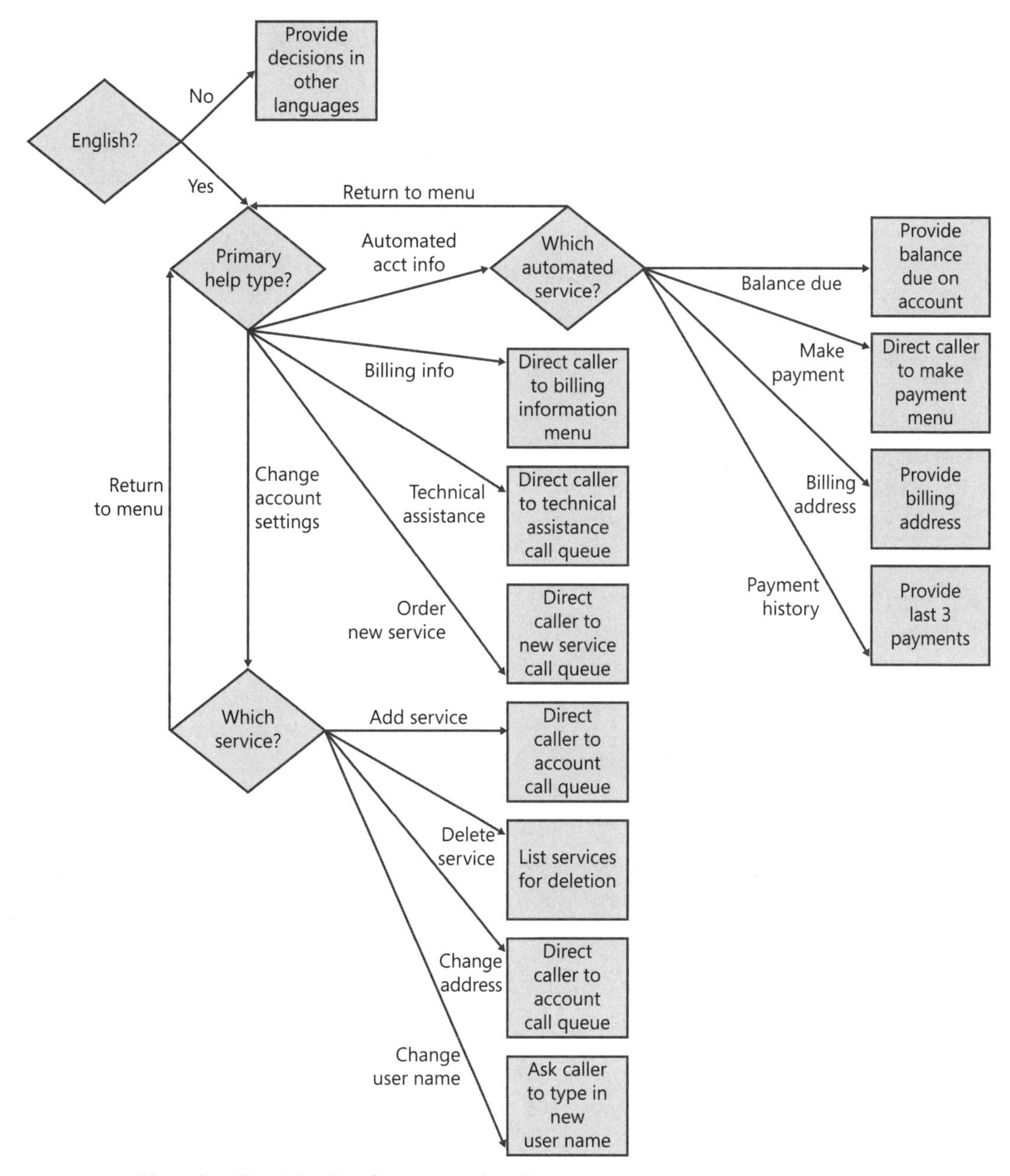

FIGURE 17-2 The ordered Decision Tree for an example call center.

Now consider a different example of a Decision Tree, in which the order of decisions does not matter. This is an example of a system that applies customer credits to orders. The type of credit is determined by several attributes, and the sequence in which the attributes are evaluated does not matter. Additionally, there are some attributes that cannot be paired together, which means that there are some branches that do not contain all possible conditions. Figure 17-3 shows the Decision Tree.

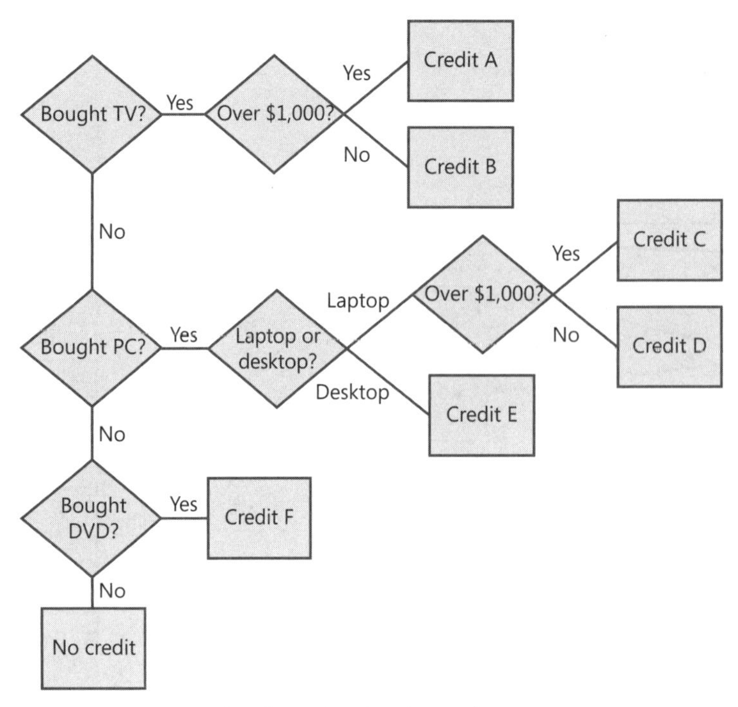

FIGURE 17-3 An unordered Decision Tree for credits.

Creating Decision Trees

The high-level steps for creating a Decision Tree are outlined in Figure 17-4. To illustrate how to create Decision Trees, we use the scenario from Chapter 16 about an insurance company's process to determine eligibility for home insurance policies. The Decision Tree for this scenario is an unordered Decision Tree.

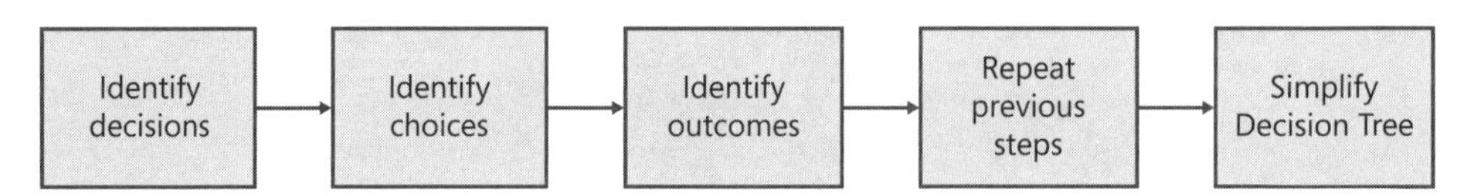

FIGURE 17-4 Process for creating a Decision Tree.

Identify Decisions

To build the Decision Tree, start by drawing a diamond for the first decision, and write the decision to be made in the shape, as shown in Figure 17-5.

FIGURE 17-5 The first decision.

Write the decisions in the form of questions, and simplify the question wording as much as you can so that it fits inside the diamond. If you have a lengthy question, you will have to use a smaller font to have it fit in the shape. The decision in this example is shortened to say "Passed credit?" but the full question is really, "Did the customer pass the credit check?"

Identify Choices

After you have identified a decision, think about all of the possible choices for answering that question. For this diamond, the possible choices are Yes or No. Figure 17-6 shows the different choices that can come from the decision "Passed credit?"

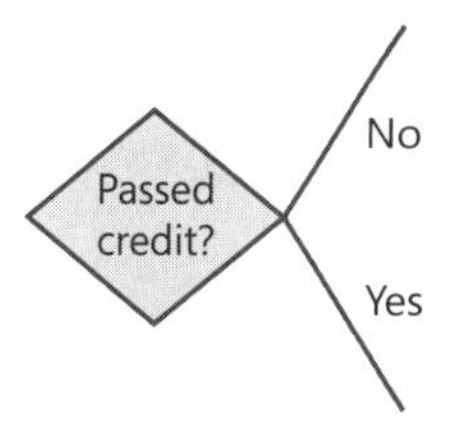

FIGURE 17-6 Decision choices.

The number of connector lines coming out of a decision is dependent on the type of decision being made. For True or False decisions or Yes or No choices, there will always be two connections coming out of each decision. For more complex decisions, there can be more choices. For example, there are three possible choices for the decision "No. of years as a homeowner?": <1, 1-5, or >5. There will never be just one choice, because then there is no decision being made.

When you model the decision choices, think about what is realistic for the scenario you are in. In the call center example, all of the decision choices could have been modeled as Yes/No decisions. However, that would not mimic what the users would experience when they called into the call center. Furthermore, it would have made for a much more complex Decision Tree. So although a series of Yes/No decision choices is logically equivalent to the multi-choice decisions in the call center Decision Tree, it would not represent the actual scenario.

If you can, make all of the decision choice lines come out of a Decision Tree from one point on the diamond. This will make it easier for the reader to notice all possible decision paths at once. Finally, decide whether to include arrows on your connector lines or not. If there is an order in which the decisions must be evaluated, then include arrows on the lines. If there is no order and, in fact, the decisions could be evaluated in any order, then do not include arrows.

Identify Outcomes

Every decision choice connector line must go to a result, which can be either another decision or an outcome. For each choice, decide whether there is another question to be asked or whether a final outcome is reached. Ordered Decision Trees allow one level of the Decision Tree to loop back to a previous level, whereas unordered Decision Trees do not. A full Decision Tree for the example is modeled in Figure 17-7, showing that some of the choices lead to new decisions and others lead to outcomes.

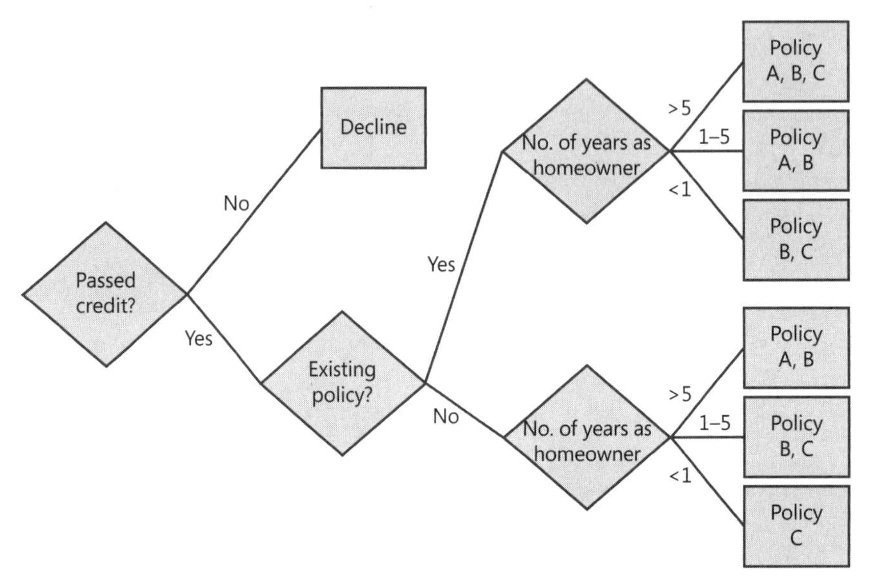

FIGURE 17-7 The full Decision Tree.

In this scenario, if the choice for the first decision is No, the resulting outcome is to decline to provide the customer a policy, and there are no more decisions to be made. If the question answer is Yes, there are two additional layers of decisions before an outcome is reached. The additional decisions are represented by creating a string of decision points branching off the Yes line. In this example, the next decision is "Existing policy?"

Repeat Until Every Branch Ends in an Outcome

Any connector line that does not end in a decision must end in an outcome. An outcome indicates that you have reached the end of the decision pathway. Repeat this process until you have reached outcomes at the end of each branch of the tree.

If you need to link an outcome to another decision or another outcome, then you are really building a Process Flow (see Chapter 9, "Process Flow") or combining multiple Decision Trees together. This is not ideal, and just note that when you do this, the model is no longer a pure Decision Tree.

Simplify the Decision Tree

If your tree does not have order, or if the order of decisions is flexible, then you can use your Decision Tree to find opportunities to simplify the tree.

Notice whether any decisions are repeated throughout the tree. If so, then you have an opportunity to move the duplicate decisions "up" the tree and combine them so they are made earlier in the tree, eliminating the total number of decisions and branches.

Typically, you will have a sense for which decisions are most constraining. Look for the decision you know is most constraining and put it at the top. For example, if you have a decision where you know one of the choices literally eliminates all other decisions, it should go first, so you can prune out a significant chunk of the tree underneath it. The decisions that don't constrain significantly should go at the bottom of the tree. Any decisions that link straight to outcomes will not be able to be reordered.

Using Decision Trees

Decision Trees can greatly simplify your software requirements gathering process when you use them to model complex logic to keep Process Flows, System Flows, and Use Cases simpler. In addition, Decision Trees can help you discover that something that seems very complex is actually more straightforward than you originally anticipated.

Driving Completeness

The value provided by Decision Trees stems from their visual branching structure. The key to creating a complete Decision Tree to represent a logic scenario is to identify all of the possible decisions and all possible choices for each of those decisions.

Decision Tables are discussed in more detail in Chapter 16, though they are mentioned here because they work well with Decision Trees. You can model a scenario in a Decision Table first to identify all possible decision and outcome combinations. You can also look to eliminate combinations that are not relevant. Then you can build the Decision Tree from that data to better visualize the decisions and look for more opportunities to simplify the logic.

Simplifying Logic

The structure of Decision Trees allows you to quickly "prune" them. If you model the logic in a Decision Tree, you can look for common decisions, choices, and outcomes that can be combined. You can also eliminate parts of the tree that will never be needed.

A Decision Tree can also help you identify usability problems in the system. If there are more than 10 decisions a user has to make manually in a system before an outcome is reached, then it's almost guaranteed that the end users will be frustrated with the system (and probably with more than just 5 or 6 decisions). As in the example, if there are 10 points at which the user enters her response to the automated questions, she will be likely to give up and abandon the automated phone menu before the end. On the other hand, if this level of complexity is handled entirely within a system, then it might not be worth trying to simplify it.

Modeling Nested "If" Statements

Scenarios for Decision Trees are often identified during the elicitation process when you hear someone using repeated "if" statements. Consider again the call center example: when eliciting requirements for the call center application, the analysts listened to the subject matter expert explaining what would happen when a customer called in: "If the caller wants English, press 1; if the caller wants Spanish, press 2; and then after they choose the language, if the caller wants technical help, press 1," and so on. You can quickly recognize that a Decision Tree is appropriate.

The visual structure of a Decision Tree allows you to quickly see the logic represented by the decisions. For the example scenario, if the analysts had written "if" statements instead of diagraming the decisions, the list of statements would look like this:

- Offer five types of primary help: automated account information, billing information, technical assistance, an action to change account settings, and an action to order new service.
- If the user selects automated account information, offer the following automated services: balance due, make a payment, retrieve the billing address, retrieve payment history, and return to the previous menu.
- If the user selects balance due, have the user enter her account number.
- If the user selects previous menu after choosing automated account info, take her back to the main help menu.
- If the user chooses to add a service, take her to an account call queue.
- If the user enters 0, take her to a call queue.
- If the user selects the option to make a payment, take her to the make a payment process.

Note that this is an incomplete list, but it is sufficient to show how difficult it is to use something like this to understand what the user's experience would be in navigating the automated phone menu.

Training Users

The logic in a Decision Table is commonly implemented in the system to automate the decisions. However, the business can use a Decision Tree to train users about the decision logic that the users need to use in their job. They can read a Decision Tree quickly to determine which rules apply in a scenario by determining which choices are valid.

Deriving Requirements

If your Decision Tree is complete, you can be reasonably confident that the requirements and business rules for the logic scenario being modeled can be identified. The decisions, choices, and outcomes or the combination of a string of decisions, choices, and outcomes are your business rules.

Developers and testers work best from a checklist of items, so although it can be helpful to give them the diagram, they will still most likely use the list of requirements and business rules to ensure that they developed everything. A tool that maps requirements and business rules to the model can save you a significant amount of time when you need to manage the traceability. If you are manually tracing requirements and business rules, use a unique identifier in the decisions and outcomes so that you can trace your requirements and business rules to them.

When to Use

Decision Trees are usually supplements to System Flows (see Chapter 13, "System Flow"), User Interface (UI) Flows (see Chapter 14, "User Interface Flow"), Process Flows, or Use Cases (see Chapter 10, "Use Case"). Just like the Decision Table, the Decision Tree model is used to simplify any of these other models by removing the complex decision logic from the main flow. A Decision Tree is a better model to visually show the branching and can simply be referenced from within these other models.

One indication that a Decision Tree should be created is when your scenario has a series of nested "if" statements. If you find that you need to model two or three "if" statements in a row, you probably should use a Decision Tree.

Ordering

If you need to show order to your decisions, as in the call center example, you have to use a Decision Tree. A Decision Table does not allow you to show any order to the decisions.

Looping

One value of Decision Trees over Decision Tables is they do allow you to include loops in the decision logic. In the call center example, there were cases in which it was easiest to show that if a caller wanted to return to the previous menu, it just took her back to that previous decision point. You often will not need looping logic like this, but if it represents the decision thought process that a user will go through, it's better to include it. Decision Tables simply do not allow you to do this.

When Not to Use

Decision Trees alone are challenging to use if you need to identify all possible permutations of a series of decisions. A Decision Table is better suited to this task because Decision Tables are designed to enable you to easily see the outcomes of all combinations of decisions choices.

Decision Trees should not be used if you are trying to model a series of activities. If you find that you have a lot of looping in your Decision Tree or outcomes leading to other outcomes or decisions, you should probably use a Process Flow.

Common Mistakes

The following represent the most common mistakes that we have seen with Decision Trees.

Modeling Process Steps

Decision Trees should not be used if you are trying to model a series of actions that occur; a Process Flow or Use Case is more appropriate.

Making All Yes or No Choices

Though you can model all decisions to have Yes or No choices, this is usually not the best approach. If you can model a particular decision to have multiple descriptive choices, you can create the same Decision Tree with fewer decisions (one decision with three choices as compared to three decisions with two choices each). When people think about decision making, they consider the actual descriptive choices, not just a series of Yes/No questions and answers.

Related Models

You might be familiar with the general term *decision tree*, which is a visual model used for decision analysis. RML Decision Trees use a different set of visual elements than decision analysis decision trees. However, the main difference is that decision analysis decision trees are used to identify requirements and business rules.

The following list briefly describes the most important models that influence or are enhanced by Decision Trees. Chapter 26, "Using Models Together," contains a more thorough discussion about all related models.

- **Decision Tables** These are used for completeness, to identify all combinations of decisions and outcomes that would show up in a Decision Tree.
- **Process Flows, System Flows, Use Cases, and UI Flows** These are supplemented by Decision Trees, which model complex logic that can be found in them.

Exercise

The following exercise is intended to help you to gain a better understanding of how to use this model. The exercise is open ended, and therefore the answer you come up with could be substantially different than the answer that we have provided. There are potentially many correct solutions. The answer provides an explanation of how we arrived at our solution. You will gain the most out of the exercise by attempting to do it yourself before looking at the solution. The answers for the exercises can be found in Appendix C.

Instructions

Create a Decision Tree for the following scenario.

Scenario

You are on a project to launch a new eStore to sell flamingos and other lawn decorations. You are capturing the rules for handling payment information. You decide that a Decision Tree will be the best model to capture the rules the system must implement to handle the different forms of payment. You know that a customer can store credit card numbers in his profile, but he can also choose to pay with a new credit card, a check, or a gift card. If he pays with a gift card, he will have to pay any balance with another form of payment if there isn't enough money available on the gift card. Use this information and your general knowledge about online payment options to create a Decision Tree.

Additional Resources

- Chapter 2 of *Requirements by Collaboration* discusses how Decision Trees are useful (Gottesdiener 2002).
- *The Software Requirements Memory Jogger* has an overview of Decision Trees with a good example in Section 4.11 (Gottesdiener 2005).
- The BABOK describes Decision Trees as they are used in decision analysis (IIBA 2009).
- Wiegers's *Software Requirements* has an example of a Decision Tree and Decision Table (Wiegers 2003).
- Chapter 4 of Davis's *Software Requirements* has a description of Decision Trees and Decision Tables (Davis 1993).

References

- Davis, Alan M. 1993. *Software Requirements: Objects, Functions, & States*. Upper Saddle River, NJ: PTR Prentice Hall.
- Gottesdiener, Ellen. 2002. *Requirements by Collaboration: Workshops for Defining Needs*. Boston, MA: Addison-Wesley.
- Gottesdiener, Ellen. 2005. *The Software Requirements Memory Jogger*. Salem, NH: Goal/QPC.
- International Institute of Business Analysis (IIBA). 2009. *A Guide to the Business Analysis Body of Knowledge (BABOK Guide)*. Toronto, Ontario, Canada.
- Wiegers, Karl E. 2003. *Software Requirements, Second Edition*. Redmond, WA: Microsoft Press.

CHAPTER 18

System Interface Table

These days, schools have gone high tech. The amount of communication between parents and teachers is so much higher than when I was a child. At the beginning of the school year, my daughter's teacher handed me a communications schedule. The schedule contained a listing of when I should expect to receive updates, the nature of the updates, and what information would be contained in those updates. I gave the teacher my email address and a phone number at which I could receive phone calls and texts. Each day I would receive the list of homework for that night by email. Each week I would receive a summary of the grades for that week and the quiz schedule for the following week. Finally, if there was an emergency, I would receive a text message and a phone call alerting me. At the end of each semester, I would receive a request to schedule a parent-teacher conference, and at the end of the year, I would receive the final grades. This schedule, detailing when I would receive communications and the information contained within those, helps tremendously in our efforts to plan out our weekly schedule and stay on top of our daughter's schoolwork.

The System Interface Table is an RML systems model that is similar to the school's communication plan. A System Interface Table details the communication between two systems. After you have completed an Ecosystem Map (see Chapter 12, "Ecosystem Map"), you might eventually want to document the information that is sent between systems.

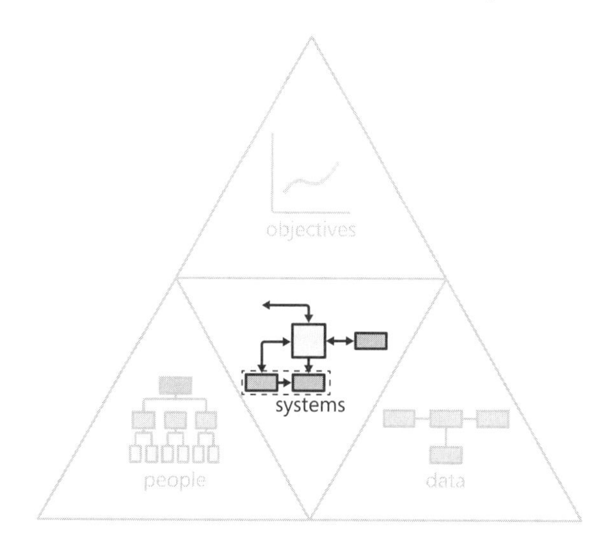

The System Interface Table shows the details of the interaction between two systems from a business stakeholder's point of view rather than from a technical point of view. This means it does not include message formats, character encoding, protocols, or any of the other information that describes exactly how the transactions occur. Instead, the System Interface Table describes the information that is transferred, how often it is transferred, and how much of it is transferred. The purpose is to give the technical team an understanding of the business constraints around the interface that might influence design decisions. For example, they need to understand whether the data is needed on a real-time basis and how much load the interface is expected to receive.

System Interface Table Template

A System Interface Table contains metadata about the requirements of the interface between two systems and does not include the exact nature of the technical protocol or messaging flow. The template is shown in Figure 18-1 and includes descriptions of each field.

System Interface			
Source	System information is flowing from		
Target	System information is flowing to		
ID	Unique Identifier		
Description	Short description about the nature of the interface		
Frequency	How often the information needs to be passed (real-time, once per day, monthly, etc)		
Volume	Total units in an interval (number/unit)		
Security Constraints	Refers to any security or privacy needs on the business object (encrypting fields in the data)		
Error Handling	Reference to a System Flow to describe how errors are handled		
Interface Objects			
Object	**Field**	**Data Dictionary ID**	**Validation Rule**
Business Object	Field within business object	Reference to Data Dictionary that defines business object	Specific rules on validating data; leave blank if the Data Dictionary business rules suffice

FIGURE 18-1 The System Interface Table template.

Tool Tip System Interface Tables are most easily created in a tool such as Microsoft Word or Microsoft Excel that allows a table with rows and columns to be easily manipulated. We prefer Excel because the worksheet functionality makes it easy to navigate between interfaces. In fact, each System Interface Table should go in its own worksheet. You can also use a requirements management tool that has a table structure.

Example

The order management system Ecosystem Map example from Chapter 12 is repeated again in Figure 18-2. It shows the relationship between the systems: The Order Routing and Tracking System (ORTS) interacts with the Order Entry, Fraud Services (FSS), Order Fulfillment, Accounts Receivable (ARS), and the Super Data Warehouse (SDW) systems. The data warehouse system also interacts with the accounts receivable system. The Ecosystem Map shows the major business data objects being passed between the systems, but it does not give details about the interactions.

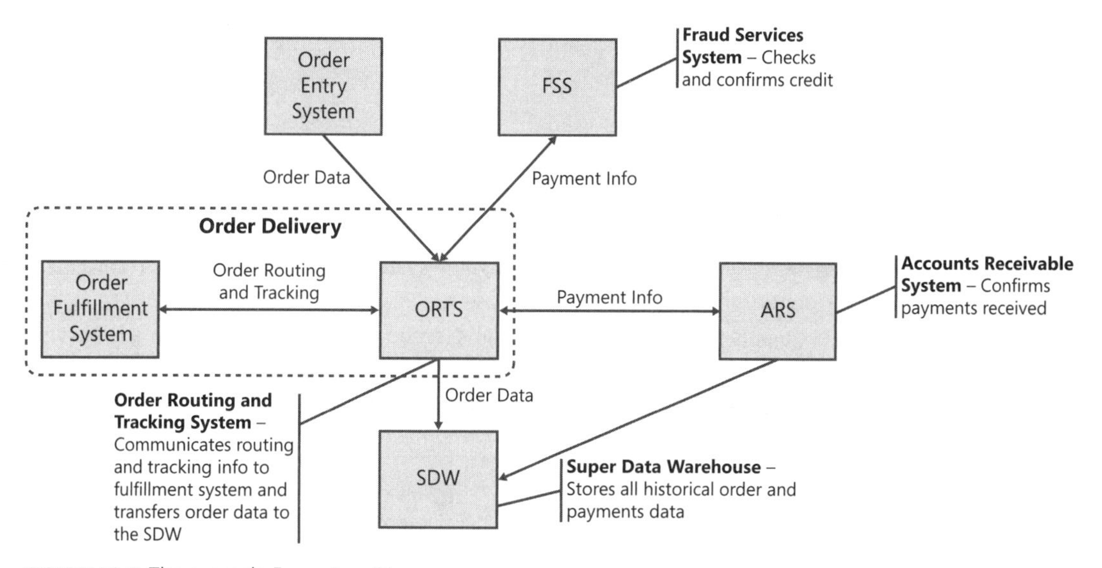

FIGURE 18-2 The example Ecosystem Map.

The business stakeholders have explained that they want the ORTS to be updated as soon as orders are placed. They expect 20,000 orders to be placed every day. These details are captured in the System Interface Table for this example, shown in Figure 18-3. Notice that the validation rule is to not validate the discounts. There is a business rule in the customer Data Dictionary (see Chapter 21, "Data Dictionary") on the discounts field that describes how to validate those discounts, and this field of the System Interface Table indicates that the interface should not validate the discounts. The empty validation rule field for the Order and Customer Name rows means that any business rules specified for validating those fields in the Data Dictionary should still be applied in this interface.

System Interface			
Source	Order Entry System		
Target	ORTS		
ID	SI001		
Description	Business wants the ORTS system to be updated with order information as soon as orders are placed		
Frequency	Real-time		
Volume	20,000 per day		
Security	Encrypt payment information		
Error Handling	Reference System Flow 1.3		
Interface Objects			
Object	**Field**	**Data Dictionary ID**	**Validation Rule**
Order	All fields	DD001	
Customer	Name	DD001	
Customer	Discounts	DD001	Do not validate discounts

FIGURE 18-3 An example System Interface Table.

Creating System Interface Tables

You create an Ecosystem Map by considering all possible systems that connect, so you can use the Ecosystem Map to identify the interfaces. You can use the Business Data Diagrams (BDDs) to identify which business data objects pass between the systems (see Chapter 19, "Business Data Diagram"). By using the Data Dictionaries associated with the objects, you can ensure that the table is complete. Figure 18-4 shows the process for creating a System Interface Table.

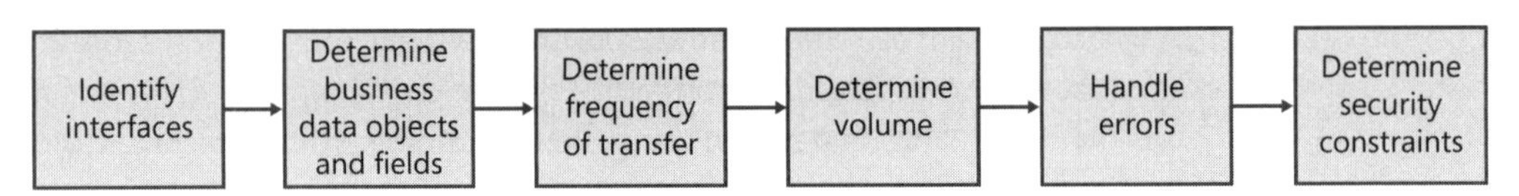

FIGURE 18-4 The process for creating a System Interface Table.

Identify System Interfaces

Not every interface needs a System Interface Table. Usually, the interface between systems is described by a technical model rather than a requirements model, because business stakeholders usually have no interest in the details of where data comes from or how it is passed. However, when the business stakeholders do care about the details of a data interface, you might be asked to specify things such as how current the data needs to be and which system it should come from. It is then the responsibility of the technical team to determine how to get the data from one system to another.

However, sometimes technical teams will ask you to document interface "requirements." Although the phrase has the word "requirements" in it, they technically aren't something the business wants or needs, so they really aren't requirements. However, we have often ended up gathering interface "requirements" at the behest of technical teams, so we developed this model to help ensure that the interfaces are documented consistently.

If you are asked to provide interface requirements, start by using the Ecosystem Map to identify all the systems that will need to transmit data to or receive data from your system. For each interface in which there are requirements about the information being passed, create a System Interface Table. Fill in the source system, target system, a unique ID, and a short description for each interface.

Determine Business Data Objects and Fields

Use the BDDs or Data Dictionaries to identify which business data objects are being transferred from the source system to the target system. It is possible that only some fields within an object should be transferred, so use the Data Dictionaries to help you identify the specific fields. For example, your order system might only need to pass the products and quantities for an order to the inventory system, because the inventory system does not need the full order object.

You can also use Display-Action-Response (DAR) models (see Chapter 15, "Display-Action-Response") to determine the data that you need in a system. If a piece of data is needed in the user interface (UI), then you need to ensure that that data is populated in your system. You can find the UI data fields in the Data Dictionary to identity their source system for the System Interfaces Tables.

For the interfaces, document every business data object and field that is transferred. Some objects will never leave their home system; usually just a few will be transferred to another system.

Data Dictionaries describe the business rules and validation required on a particular piece of data. The standard is to not duplicate the business rules and validation on business data objects in the System Interface Table. However, there might be cases for which you want to override the default business rules validation. For example, during the automated transfer of data between systems, you might want to relax the rules for business rule validation and simply allow the data to be transferred from one system to another as is. If this is the case, document the relaxed rules as part of each data field in the System Interface Table. You should also include a reference to the appropriate Data Dictionary for each object and field.

Determine Frequency of Transfer

There are many ways for data to be transferred, including batch processing, polling, and real-time event-based transfer. The method of transfer affects how often data is synchronized between systems. Work with the business stakeholders to understand how up to date the data needs to be. Real-time connections can be very expensive and dramatically increase the load on systems and networks.

You can use Display-Action-Response (DAR) models to talk through how the users use the data in the UI, to determine whether the data must be updated in real time. Process Flows can also help business users think about how often they execute a task, which will help them determine how fresh the data really needs to be. For example, if a task is performed only once per day, then it might not make sense to have a real-time update of the data. However, if the user needs to respond immediately to an event, then a real-time interface might be necessary. If the data is used by a report described by a Report Table (see Chapter 24, "Report Table"), then the Report Table will indicate how often the report will be used to make decisions, which will influence how often the data transfer needs to occur.

Determine Volume of Data

To appropriately design the system, developers need to understand how much data is passing through the interface. To determine the data volume, you can look at the Key Performance Indicator Models (KPIMs) (see Chapter 5, "Key Performance Indicator Model") or Data Dictionaries. The KPIM describes KPIs, which document how often a task occurs and by how many people it is performed. This can be used to determine the amount of data produced. The Data Dictionaries should also include information about estimated volume of a particular type of data, although not all of the data will necessarily be transferred across the interface. In the example earlier in this chapter, if the system is being designed to take up to 20,000 orders per day, then you would indicate that 20,000 orders/day are expected to pass across the interface between the order entry and the order routing and tracking system.

Determine Error Handling

Error handling usually involves a System Flow (see Chapter 13, "System Flow"). Rather than document the entire error-handling process in the System Interface Table, use a System Flow diagram and refer to it from the System Interface Table. Error handling is usually related to the need to maintain the integrity of transactions as they pass across the interface. You should primarily be concerned with whether it is acceptable for only a portion of the objects to make it across the interface or whether it is an all-or-none process. For example, it might be OK for 1 out of 10 orders to make it across, but not acceptable for half of the items in an individual order to make it across. Also, if the interface is validating data by using business rules, the System Flow should describe what kind of notifications or actions the system will automatically take in the event of validation failure. Finally, if an interface is not working, you should determine the impact to the user experience on both sides of the system interface.

Determine Security Constraints

Because the system is going to transfer data between systems, you need to consider any additional security constraints for the transfer. For example, if there are privacy concerns on information such as Social Security numbers or credit card numbers, the business might want to ensure that those numbers are encrypted.

Using System Interface Tables

Whenever possible, technical teams should document interface requirements. However, the technical team might not always understand the full set of data needs required by the user interface or the Data Dictionaries.

Deriving Requirements

The System Interface Table helps you ensure that interface requirements are captured completely because it provides a structured set of fields to fill out, instead of requiring you to write a list of requirements. Because the System Interface Table essentially lists the requirements, it is not necessary for you to derive separate requirements from the System Interface Table. However, any error handling documented by a System Flow in the system should have requirements derived from it.

When to Use

Because technical teams are not experts in how the business needs to use the data, and because that information can be spread among multiple models, it can be helpful for you to consolidate that information into the System Interface Table. Developers will use the table directly to create technical designs.

When Not to Use

These models should be completely eliminated from scope if your business stakeholders do not have specific requirements about how information is passed between systems. In these cases, the technical team can define interface requirements by using their own models.

Common Mistakes

The following represent the most common mistakes that we have seen with System Interface Tables.

Including Information That Is Too Technical

You do not need to focus on the technical aspects of the interface, such as technology used to pass the data. In fact, sometimes business stakeholders think they care about this when they really do not need to.

Documenting Every Interface

These models should only be created for the interfaces that have business requirements associated with them. There is no need to create them for every interface.

Not Understanding User Needs

The only reason to create a System Interface Table is to capture the business requirements for an interface. If you fail to understand how the users on the receiving end will use the data being transferred, then you will misunderstand their true needs in terms of frequency and volume.

Related Models

The following list briefly describes the most important models that influence or are enhanced by System Interface Tables. Chapter 25, "Selecting Models for a Project," contains a more thorough discussion about all related models.

- **System Flows** These can represent the error-handling process.
- **Ecosystem Maps** These provide maps of systems that interact.
- **Business Data Diagrams (BDDs)** These are used to identify which business data objects might need to be passed across the interface.
- **Data Dictionaries** These are used to provide the list of all fields and business data objects for the target and source systems. They also might provide business rules and volume of data.
- **Process Flows** These help users think about how fresh data in the system needs to be.
- **Key Performance Indicator Models (KPIMs)** These provide information about how often activities occur and how many people perform them, which drives the data volume needs.
- **Display-Action-Response (DAR) Models** These provide information about the data used in the target system. Identifying where those fields come from can help you to determine which data must be transferred across the interface.
- **Report Tables** These provide information about the data used in the target system. Identifying where those fields come from can help you to determine which data must be transferred across the interface.

Exercise

The following exercise is intended to help you to gain a better understanding of how to use this model. The exercise is open ended, and therefore the answer you come up with could be substantially different than the answer that we have provided. There are potentially many correct solutions. The answer provides an explanation of how we arrived at our solution. You will gain the most out of the exercise by attempting to do it yourself before looking at the solution. The answers for the exercises can be found in Appendix C.

Instructions

Prepare a System Interface Table for the following scenario.

Scenario

In this project, you are helping to build an eStore to sell flamingos and other lawn decorations. Customers access the eStore directly. The eStore sends orders to the order processing system, which sends the final orders to the fulfillment system. The inventory system provides product inventory information to the order processing system and the eStore so those systems can show availability on all 500 products. It is updated by the fulfillment system after an order is shipped. The credit system receives credit card information from the eStore and sends approval status back to the user in the eStore and to the order processing system. Document the System Interface Table for the interface between the inventory system and the eStore.

PART V

Data Models

CHAPTER 19

Business Data Diagram

When I shop online, I have noticed that most e-commerce sites allow me to create an account to store information such as my name, address, and email, and to access information about my past orders. On some sites, when I purchase products, I can add multiple products to my shopping cart, but they all have to be shipped to one address together, so if I want to ship to two addresses, I need to complete two purchases. Other online shopping sites actually allow me to split my order across multiple shipping addresses. And almost always, I also have a billing address that is different than the shipping address. Also, I've noticed that some sites allow me to enter only one form of payment, whereas others allow me to split an order across as many forms of payment as I want.

The Business Data Diagram (BDD) is an RML data model that shows the relationships between business data objects. Most software systems exist solely to create, manipulate, store, and output data. Users think about and organize the data that they use to perform their tasks in a way that makes sense for them. In some cases, the tasks are related to jobs, but for consumer software, the task might be a personal task, such as balancing a checkbook. The way users think about their data might be very different from how that data is represented in a database by a technical team. The BDD describes how users think about their data. BDDs also show how many of one object can be related to another object, such as how many addresses or forms of payment an order can have. This is known as the *cardinality* of the relationship.

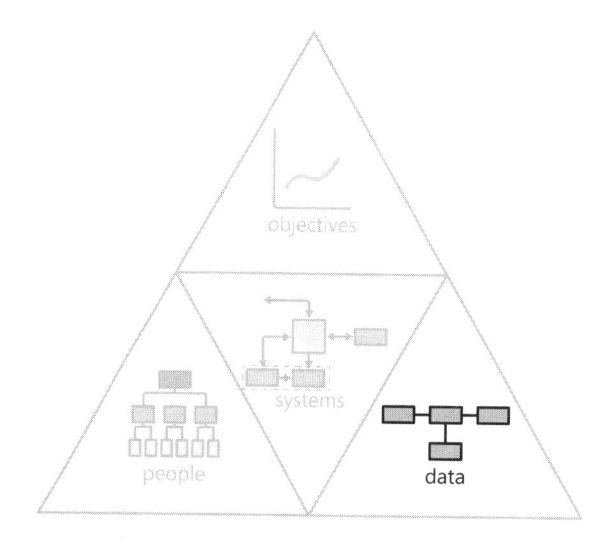

BDDs look very similar to a common technical model called an entity relationship diagram (ERD); however, BDDs are conceptual data models that show *business data objects* from a business stakeholder's perspective, whereas ERDs more commonly show the actual implementation of objects in a database schema. BDDs contain the business data objects, which are composed of either fields or other business data objects. They are focused exclusively on objects the user cares about and therefore only represent the business's view of the data. We use the BDD name to avoid confusing those of you who might be familiar with ERDs; the BDD does not imply a database design.

Misunderstandings about the cardinality of relationships between business data objects are very common between development teams and business teams, and cardinality is one of the biggest factors affecting software architecture. It might seem like a small thing, but the software's ability to handle a user account with only one shipping address versus multiple shipping addresses has huge implications throughout the application and business process. If you purchase a Commercial Off the Shelf (COTS) system that has a data model that is too limited for what you need, it might be virtually impossible to extend the data model.

BDDs can be complicated for business stakeholders to read, so we have extended this model with a variation called a Business Data Example Diagram. A Business Data Example Diagram shows a portion of the BDD using samples of the business's actual data.

BDD Template

A BDD template in its simplest form contains boxes, lines, and labels to denote the cardinality of the relationships. Table 19-1 shows the elements used in a BDD.

TABLE 19-1 BDD Elements

Element	Meaning
Business Data Object	The boxes represent business data objects and are labeled with names that are easily understood by the business stakeholders.
———	Boxes are connected with lines if the objects in those boxes are related.
n	The relationship cardinality is labeled on the line. The cardinality n means "many." There can be zero to an unlimited number of the objects in the relationship.
1	This represents one object in the relationship.
1..n	This represents one or more objects in the relationship. This label specifies that there cannot be zero objects.
0..1	This represents zero or one object in the relationship.

Element	Meaning
1..X	This notation specifies one to X relationships, where X is a number you specify. For example, X could be 5, which would mean that there are as few as one and as many as five objects in the relationship.
0..n	This notation is the same as n alone and represents an unlimited number of objects in the relationship.
Grouping	Groupings allow you to divide your BDD into smaller sections for readability. Typically, they surround a related set of data.

Figure 19-1 shows the BDD template. You can include as many business data objects and lines as you need in your diagram.

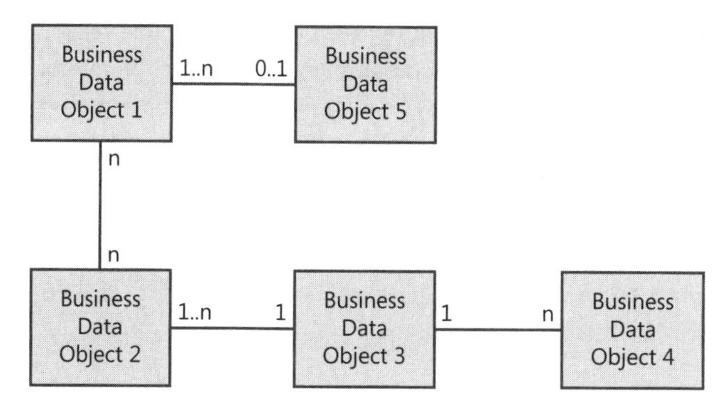

FIGURE 19-1 The BDD template.

The cardinality elements can be combined in various ways to show the cardinalities needed. The relationships shown in the diagram are described here.

- Business data object 1 relates to zero or one of business data object 5.
- Business data object 5 relates to one or more of business data object 1.
- Business data object 1 relates to zero to many of business data object 2.
- Business data object 2 relates to zero to many of business data object 1.
- Business data object 2 relates to exactly one of business data object 3.
- Business data object 3 relates to one or more of business data object 2.
- Business data object 3 relates to zero to many of business data object 4.
- Business data object 4 relates to exactly one of business data object 3.

Notice that the "one" cardinality means "exactly one," so an object with this cardinality cannot have zero or more than one of those objects related to it. Also, the many relationship is defined to mean any number, including zero. It is the same as the zero-to-many relationship. If zero is not allowed, you need to use one-to-many. We include the n element as the default to mean zero-to-many, because it is easier to write than 0..n. However, if you are concerned that your readers will not understand, you can just use 0..n or include the definition of *n* in a legend.

Finally, if you have more than 7+/-2 business data objects in your BDD, consider using the grouping element to organize the most closely related objects together. However, it might be easier to just create separate BDDs with fewer objects.

Business Data Example Diagram Template

Similar to BDDs, Business Data Example Diagrams use boxes and lines. However, in Business Data Example Diagrams, boxes represent actual or hypothetical examples of the business data objects and are labeled as such. Instead of using cardinality labels to denote the number of possible related objects, the relationships are mapped explicitly by using the number of lines to denote the number that can be related. For example, one line connecting to one box means a one-to-one relationship (1 to 1). Multiple lines from one object represent a one-to-many relationship (1 to n). The many relationship can mean zero are related, and this zero relationship is shown with no connecting line. Business Data Example Diagrams can be very complicated, so we generally recommend that you use them only if you have primarily 1..n or 0..n relationships. It's very hard to use them to show *n..n* relationships without making them too cluttered. Figure 19-2 shows the possible cardinality relationships in a Business Data Example Diagram format.

These basic relationships can be strung together to form a tree structure that shows the relationships for multiple objects in the BDD. Figure 19-3 shows the BDD relationships in a Business Data Example Diagram format for three of the business data objects. The placement or direction of the lines attaching the boxes is not important, but the diagrams are easier to read if you consistently connect from top to bottom or left to right throughout the diagram.

Tool Tip BDDs are most easily created in a tool such as Microsoft Visio, which allows you to move the objects and lines easily. You might want to create your first draft using sticky notes that you can maneuver quickly by hand.

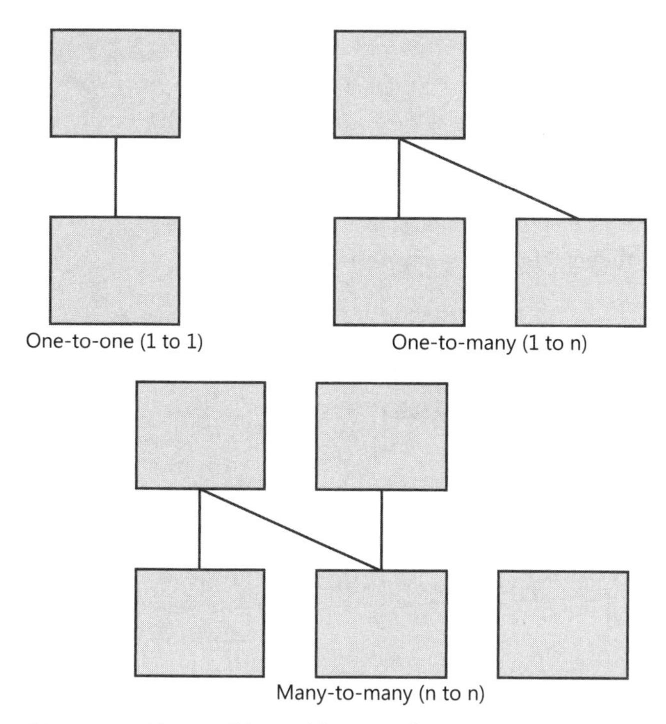

FIGURE 19-2 The possible combinations of objects in a Business Data Example Diagram.

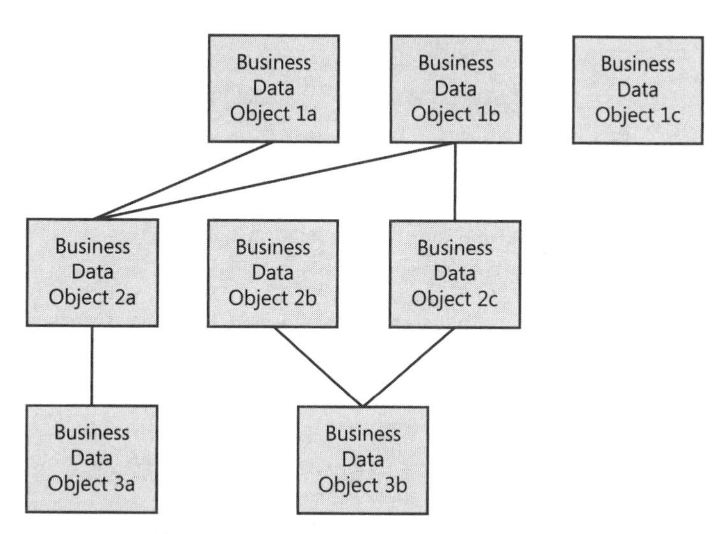

FIGURE 19-3 The Business Data Example Diagram template.

Example

A business is implementing an online training site. The subject matter experts (SMEs) describe their business terminology by using words such as curriculum, courses, quizzes, catalogs, students, transcripts, and incentives. The team needs to quickly learn their language to help ensure that the solution is designed correctly. They focus on creating a BDD that only includes the structure of the training itself as it relates to a basic student. The BDD is shown in Figure 19-4.

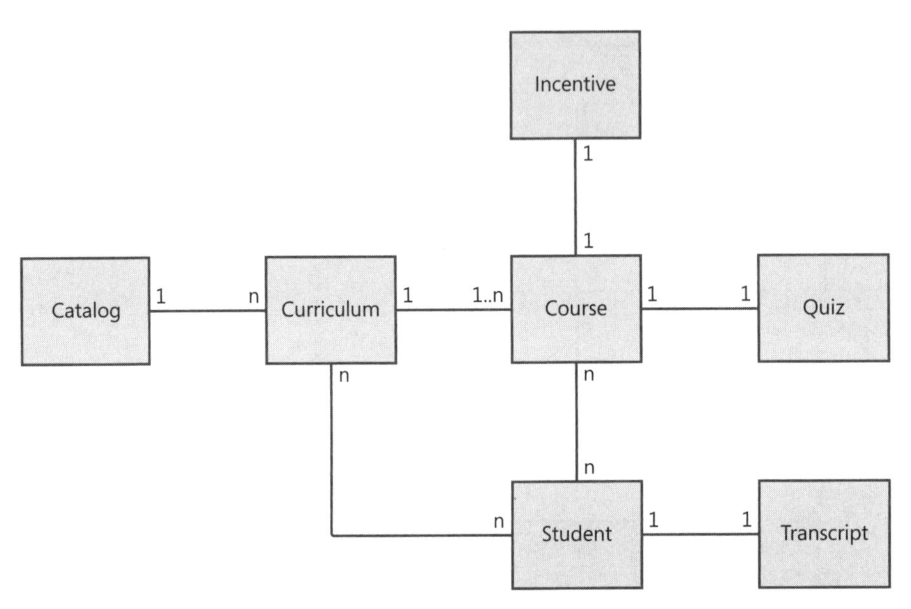

FIGURE 19-4 An example BDD.

This BDD defines several relationships: a curriculum has one or more courses, but a course can only belong to one curriculum; courses and quizzes have a one-to-one relationship; students can take zero to many courses; and courses can be taken by zero to many students.

Figure 19-5 is a Business Data Example Diagram that shows the catalog, curriculum, course, student, and transcript relationships from the BDD. You might need to add labels next to the boxes to clarify the object types. Enumerating all of the BDD relationships in a single Business Data Example Diagram can become complex and unwieldy.

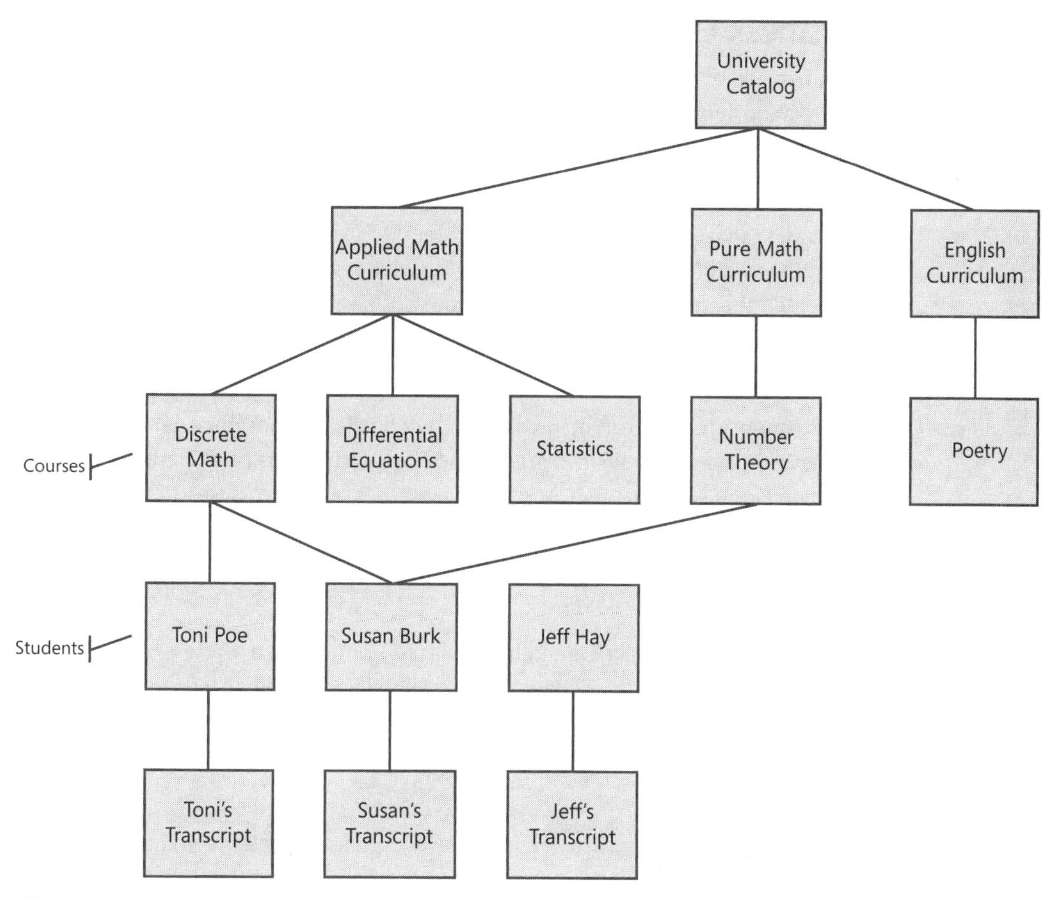

FIGURE 19-5 Business Data Example Diagram relationship examples.

Creating BDDs

This section describes the process for creating BDDs first and then explains how to create a Business Data Example Diagram from a BDD. Figure 19-6 shows the high-level BDD process.

FIGURE 19-6 The process for creating BDDs.

When creating BDDs (keeping the 7+/-2 rule in mind), if you do not want to try to group objects in your BDD, you can divide your objects across BDDs by functional areas of the solution. The example in the previous section is for a set of training objects; however, you could create another BDD for that same solution that is for the student and account objects.

Identify Business Data Objects

You start by identifying all of the known business data objects and writing them down without worrying about their relationships to each other. There are three primary methods for discovering which objects should go in BDDs: listen to SMEs, look at other visual models, and look at data models for existing systems.

- When the SMEs talk about their business, they tend to use business terms in their discussions about what they want the solution to do. The business terms they use often refer to their data. You can identify these terms quickly because the business data objects are the nouns that the SMEs use. Your notes from your sessions with them will be useful in identifying potential business data objects.
- Other requirements models can help you identify objects for consideration in your BDD. You can discover business data objects by reviewing Ecosystem Maps (see Chapter 12, "Ecosystem Map"), System Flows (see Chapter 13, "System Flow"), Process Flows (see Chapter 9, "Process Flow"), and DAR models (see Chapter 15, "Display-Action-Response") to determine what data is passed between systems, which data users need to perform tasks, and what data is displayed in user interface (UI) screens.
- If there are existing systems that are being replaced or integrated, these existing systems can be evaluated to see what data will need to be manipulated in the new system. Though it is important not to create BDDs that focus on database-level design, looking at existing databases can be useful in identifying objects that the business stakeholders might care about but forget to tell you about.

If you look at existing systems and UI screens of newly purchased systems, you can ensure that you have identified all of the possible objects to help bound the full scope of the data for your solution.

When you create the BDD, put the identified objects in boxes and label them with singular nouns that the business stakeholders will understand. In the example, "Course" and not "Courses," was used because the multiplicity is represented in the cardinality.

It is important to decide which objects are relevant to the diagram and which are not. In a first draft of the BDD, start with the basic objects; later revisions can add more detail. In the training system example, the business might have wanted to add objects related to the student, such as region and corporate account, but for a first draft, they did not need that information.

BDDs are meant to show the core business data objects only and not database schemas, so data fields do not belong in the BDD. Furthermore, if you find that two business data objects have a one-to-one relationship, it is possible that one of them might be a field of the other, and not another object. In the example, the business stakeholders think about courses and quizzes as distinct objects, so you should keep them as separate objects. However, if they had told you that a course has one title and one unique identifier, those are fields of a course, because they have a single one-to-one relationship and have no fields themselves. If an object relates to more than one object or has fields itself, then it is an object; otherwise it is a field.

When creating BDDs, don't think in terms of designing a database. You only construct BDDs to reflect how the business thinks about the data, and leave the data design to the database architects.

Relate Business Data Objects

After you think you have most of the business data objects identified, add lines to connect objects that are related to one another. Do not model indirect relationships (relationships that go through another object). This is not as trivial as it might sound. In the example, the quiz is linked to the course directly and is related to the student through the course. There is no need to also show the quiz linked to the student because the student to quiz relationship cannot exist without the course. However, sometimes that link is important to show if there are specific requirements and business rules about the relationship that should be implemented. For example, suppose that the student, course, and curriculum objects are all related to one another. The reason to show all three relationships could be the business has a requirement that a student can sign up for a full curriculum of courses or individual courses, and the business wants to restrict which curricula the student has access to based on his corporate account. Without these two requirements, the curriculum is just an aggregation of courses, and the relationship from curriculum to the student isn't important to show.

Deciding whether to link objects is one of the most difficult aspects of creating a BDD. An analogy might be that your grandparents, your parents, and you all have relationships with each other. For purposes of the BDD, you would link your grandparents to your parents and your parents to yourself. Your relationship with your grandparents is through your parents. Another way to think about it is to determine whether the relationship between two objects can exist without the relationship to the third.

After you have related the objects, remove any disconnected objects that you have determined are not important to the BDD. Also, as you add the lines, add any missing objects you might have identified.

As you create relationships, you are not trying to capture all of the business rules that further restrict the relationships. For example, the BDD can show that an incentive is related to a course and a student is related to a course, but it cannot show that there is a business rule that the student only has the opportunity to get some of the incentives depending on his company.

Add Cardinalities

Now you need to add the cardinality to the object relationships. Remember that the cardinality represents how many of the objects can relate to one another. In the example discussed earlier, a student has one and only one transcript, and a transcript has one and only one student, so you would show that as a one-to-one relationship, as in Figure 19-7.

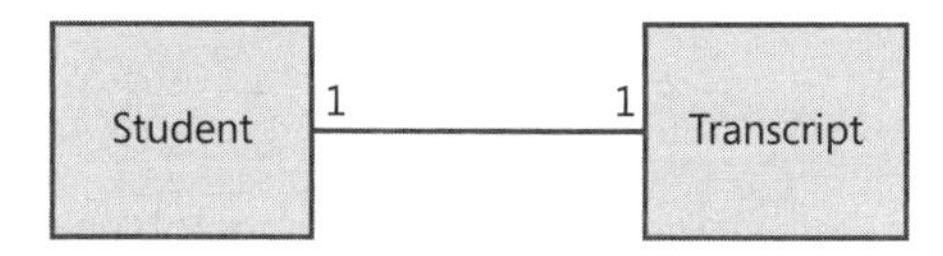

FIGURE 19-7 The student-to-transcript one-to-one relationship.

Similarly, a student can take as many courses as she wants, and a course can have zero to an infinite number of students signed up for it, so you would show the many-to-many relationship between student and course, as in Figure 19-8.

FIGURE 19-8 The student-to-course many-to-many relationship.

The "many" cardinality means "greater than or equal to zero." However, in some cases, you might want the cardinality to indicate a specific number. For example, if you know that a student always has between one and five courses but never more, you can label the cardinality on the course object as 1.5.

Creating Business Data Example Diagrams

If you decide to create a Business Data Example Diagram, start by deciding which objects in your BDD warrant this type of diagram. You might be able to fit all of the objects from the BDD in one Business Data Example Diagram, or you might need multiple models, or you might just need one Business Data Example Diagram for some of the key object relationships. This decision is based upon which relationships are most important for the business to understand and get correct.

When you know which objects you are going to model, pick the first two by identifying the most important objects in the BDD or the top-level objects if there is a hierarchical relationship. In the example, you would not start with student and transcript, but rather the catalog, curriculum, or course. Put the main object at the top and the related one below it (or use a left-to-right structure). When naming these objects with examples, you can use something that is real and meaningful to the business, such as "Math 101" for a course. Or you can use something generic, such as "Course A," to communicate that the object is an example of a course.

If the relationship is one-to-one, show only one example of each, as in Figure 19-9.

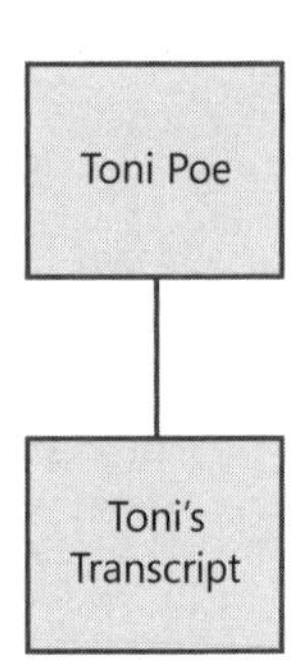

FIGURE 19-9 A one-to-one relationship in a Business Data Example Diagram.

If the relationship is one-to-many, show multiple examples of the second object, as in Figure 19-10. When you want to show many, you need to have at least two objects, but you can have more if that is helpful. If you are trying to communicate an exact number, you can show that number of example boxes; however, the BDD will more clearly communicate this detail in its cardinality label.

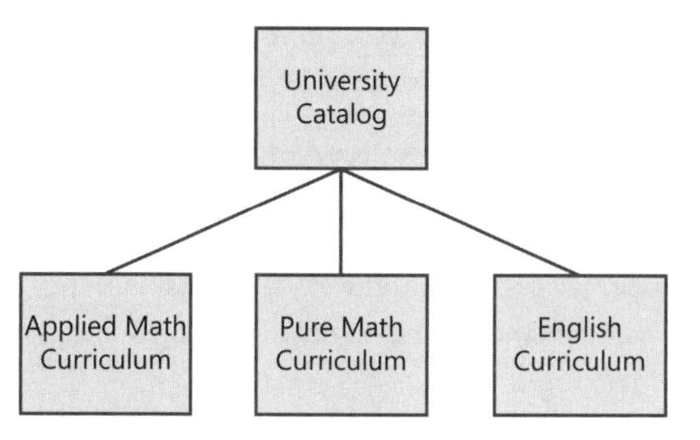

FIGURE 19-10 A one-to-many relationship in a Business Data Example Diagram.

If the relationship is many-to-many, add multiple examples of both and show a variety of connecting lines between them, as in Figure 19-11.

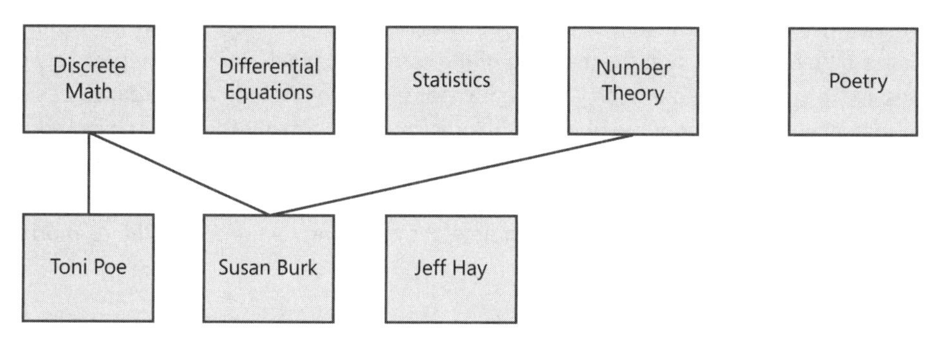

FIGURE 19-11 A many-to-many relationship in a Business Data Example Diagram.

Continue this process, adding one object at a time to your diagram until you have captured all of the relevant objects. Notice in this example that you can show a zero relationship (as in "zero-to-many") by including in the diagram an example object that does not link to anything.

Using BDDs

Typically, the BDD is the first data model created. BDDs can be used to fully bound the scope of the solution from the data perspective by identifying every business data object. The business data objects are used as the foundation for creating Data Dictionaries (see Chapter 21, "Data Dictionary").

Understanding the High-Level Business Data Objects

In learning about new subject matter, you might find yourself juggling terminology that is common to the business stakeholders, but completely foreign to you. You cannot focus on the detailed requirements until you understand the objects that the business stakeholders are talking about. A BDD helps you visually relate the words the business is talking about. Usually a very short conversation with the SMEs is enough to enable you to draft a BDD to be reviewed and corrected.

Not only can BDDs help you understand the business terminology, they also help you crisply define the language you are going to use in defining the requirements. For example, if some people in the business talk about "courses" and others talk about "classes," when you model both of these on a BDD, your experts will be able to spot the error and tell you both terms mean the same thing. Then you can decide which term is better and use that as the name for the object in your BDD and the rest of the requirements.

One value of BDDs is that they show the business data objects from the perspective of the business, not the technical team. However, BDDs are not intuitive to read if you don't understand the elements. Expect to have to read them to the business stakeholders to teach them how to understand a BDD.

BDDs are helpful because they show at first glance which objects are related. However, you might have to think a bit more to interpret the meaning of the cardinality labels. In fact, you probably read the relationships to yourself in your mind because it is not simple to just look at a cardinality and know what that label implies about the objects. So, for example, you might find yourself saying things such as, "A curriculum can have many courses" and "A course can belong to one curriculum" when you create and use BDDs. That being said, it is still better to diagram the relationships than to try to write them in a list of requirements alone. For example, the following text describes the relationships defined in the example for this chapter:

- A catalog can have zero or more curriculums.
- A curriculum belongs to exactly one catalog.
- A curriculum has one or more courses.
- A course belongs to exactly one curriculum.
- A course has exactly one quiz, and a quiz has exactly one course to which it belongs.
- A course has exactly one incentive, and an incentive has exactly one course to which it belongs.
- A student can take zero or more courses.
- A course can be taken by zero or more students.
- A student and a transcript have a one-to-one relationship.
- A student can take zero or more curriculums.
- A curriculum can be assigned to zero or more students.

This list alone is almost incomprehensible for understanding how all of the objects relate to one another or for finding incorrect or missing relationships.

Driving Completeness

BDDs can help you identify missing business data objects because you can look at the relationships between the objects. Analyzing the BDD should prompt a series of questions about the diagram to consider or ask the SMEs. You can display a draft of this diagram and ask questions such as the following:

- **Do we really need to have both catalogs and curriculums to group courses?** From the answer, you might be able to remove unnecessary objects to simplify the diagram, or you might gain a better understanding of the detailed requirements around what a catalog and curriculum actually are.
- **Is a curriculum really just a grouping of courses?** This helps you understand the terminology better. Capture responses to these kinds of questions in a glossary.
- **Why would you ever have a curriculum with zero courses? Or should there at least be one? Does a course have to have a quiz?** Responses to these types of questions might require you to update to the cardinality of relationships in your diagram.
- **Are incentives ever attached to a curriculum instead of just courses?** This question has to do with analyzing objects that are not already related. The answer to this question might identify new relationships and new sets of functionality.
- **What other objects are related to students?** The answer to a question such as this might cause you to consider whether those objects belong in this BDD or perhaps whether there should be an additional BDD; for example, one that that shows the relationship between students and accounts.

Identifying Processes

Analysts use BDDs to identify Process Flows and Use Cases (see Chapter 10, "Use Case") by looking at six actions that might happen to each object in a BDD: create, update, delete, use, move, and copy. Each of those actions should be described in Process Flows or Use Cases. For example, assume that you want to know how a training course is created, and this question leads to a "Create Course" Process Flow or a step in a Process Flow. Similarly, asking about updating courses might tell you that you need an "Edit Course" Process Flow. In addition, there could be a "Take a Course" process, which would represent how the course is used. In considering the "delete" action, you might realize that the business does not want anyone to delete courses but rather mark them as "Inactive." Finally, you might determine that moving a course is not relevant in this case, and copying courses is not a high-priority feature.

Helping Technical Teams with Database Design

Though we cannot stress enough that BDDs do not represent database design directly, it is important that you do deliver the BDDs to the database team. The database team can use BDDs to understand the relationships that will need to be supported in their technical design. Furthermore, BDDs will be easy for them to understand because they are similar to ERDs.

Using Business Data Example Diagrams to Review BDDs

Stakeholders new to BDDs often have difficulty understanding the cardinality of the relationships modeled in a BDD. Business Data Example Diagrams can be used to help facilitate the BDDs review with the business. Business stakeholders might understand Business Data Example Diagrams better than BDDs because these stakeholders can visualize the real examples from their day-to-day activities, which makes the BDD come to life. We often start with a BDD and create a Business Data Example Diagram only when the business stakeholders have difficulty understanding part or all of the BDD, and even then we will only create one for the portion of the BDD that is difficult to understand.

As an extension of BDDs, Business Data Example Diagrams can be used to identify missing or incorrect relationships. A Business Data Example Diagram is in essence a trial version of the BDD that enables you to see whether the BDD holds up to practical intuitions about the relationships. Business Data Example Diagrams can also improve the development of Process Flows and Use Cases, because the stakeholders might start thinking of specific exceptions to relationships, which could help define alternate paths.

Deriving Requirements

The relationships and cardinalities in a BDD are requirements and business rules. You do not have to write the relationships and cardinality in a list, but you might want to do so, to make those requirements and business rules explicitly clear to the technical team. Also, the BDD objects will be further detailed in a Data Dictionary, where additional business rules about the data will be described.

When to Use

Any project that has databases will use BDDs, which means that most projects will need them. You might not have to create one for every object in your solution, just for the major business data objects the business cares about.

When Not to Use

If your project has no database, that's a good indication that you probably do not need to use a BDD. Software that only performs stateless calculations (computations) but that does not store anything or that just passes data straight through (such as an API) might not have any objects to model in a BDD.

BDDs show relationships; they don't show all of the business rules that further restrict the relationships. For example, a BDD could show that a customer is related to a tier and a course is related to a tier. What it does not show is that there is a business rule that customers can take courses only for their tier.

Common Mistakes

The following represent the most common mistakes that we have seen with BDDs.

Including Fields As Objects

Don't include any fields in the model. If you model an object that has only one direct relationship and its cardinality is one, it might be a field. If that object has no other fields itself, it is probably a field.

Creating Middle-Man Objects

It can be hard to know whether to include an object or not. Sometimes analysts put unnecessary objects to act as containers in their diagrams. Try to make your object-selection decisions based upon how the business thinks about the objects and their relationships, as well as whether they have any requirements or business rules related to them.

Thinking in Terms of a Database Design

You are not trying to create a normalized database design. Instead, make sure you understand and document how the business thinks about data in the system.

Related Models

Entity relationship diagrams (ERDs) are similar to BDDs (Richardson 2007). There are a variety of notations for denoting the cardinality of relationships (SmartDraw), including the common notation, *crow's feet*. Some similar models also label relationships between objects on the lines. BDDs do not typically use these labels, instead explaining the relationship in the requirements if necessary.

The following list briefly describes the most important models that influence or are enhanced by BDDs. Chapter 25, "Selecting Models for a Project," contains a more thorough discussion about all related models.

- **Data Dictionaries** These are used to show additional field-level detail on each of the objects in the BDDs and can also be used to come up with examples to use in the Business Data Example Diagram.
- **Process Flows, System Flows, and Use Cases** These are partially derived by considering the six actions for each object in the BDDs.

- **Ecosystem Maps** These are used to identify business data objects that are passed between systems.
- **Display-Action-Response (DAR) Models** These can be used to identify additional business data objects that need to be added to the BDD.

Exercise

The following exercise is intended to help you to gain a better understanding of how to use this model. The exercise is open ended, and therefore the answer you come up with could be substantially different than the answer that we have provided. There are potentially many correct solutions. The answer provides an explanation of how we arrived at our solution. You will gain the most out of the exercise by attempting to do it yourself before looking at the solution. The answers for the exercises can be found in Appendix C.

Instructions

Using the following scenario, prepare a draft BDD.

Scenario

You are building an eStore to sell flamingos and other lawn decorations, including items such as gnomes, dwarfs, ornamental giraffes, birth baths, and statues.

Your customers for the first release are companies that have multiple users and individual customers shopping from home. Customers will be able to browse and search for accessories, add them to a cart, put an order through a full checkout process, save their information as registered users, and automatically send their orders to a back-end order processing system.

During checkout, only credit cards will be accepted for payment, and customers can only pay with one credit card. The address must allow for two lines of a billing address (because businesses have long addresses), city, state, and postal code. In addition, it is important that you capture the user's county, in case there are tax implications for shipping the order. Allow the customer to ship the items in a single order to multiple addresses.

Additional Resources

- Section 4.9 of *The Software Requirements Memory Jogger* is an overview of this model, though the author calls it a "Data Model" (Gottesdiener 2005).
- Chapter 11 of *Software Requirements* has a summary of ERDs (Wiegers 2003).
- Richardson provides information on ERDs and crow's feet notation (Richardson 2007).

References

- Gottesdiener, Ellen. 2005. *The Software Requirements Memory Jogger.* Salem, NH: Goal/QPC.
- Richardson, Lee. 2007. "An Entity Relationship Diagram Example." *http://rapidapplicationdevelopment.blogspot.com/2007/06/entity-relationship-diagram-example.html*
- SmartDraw. "Software Design Tutorials: Entity Relationship Diagrams." *http://www.smartdraw.com/resources/tutorials/cardinality-notations/#/resources/tutorials/Introduction-to-ERD.*
- Wiegers, Karl E. 2003. *Software Requirements, Second Edition.* Redmond, WA: Microsoft Press.

CHAPTER 20

Data Flow Diagram

I love to cook and have many recipes. Each recipe has a set of ingredients and a set of steps that I need to follow. Most of the time, I have an idea of what I want to cook, so I pull out the recipe and go to the store to buy the ingredients. The recipe tells me which cooking equipment and techniques I will need to prepare the dish. Sometimes, though, I'm not exactly sure what I want to eat. Sometimes, I only know that I want something grilled or maybe I just want a recipe that will work with ingredients that I already have on hand. I wish I had a way to look at all the recipes that use the grilling process, a particular set of ingredients, or even a cooking technique.

The Data Flow Diagram (DFD) is an RML data model that provides a graphical representation of the flow of information through a solution, focusing on how data is transformed as it is manipulated or used in processes. A DFD shows a view of the solution that ties many disparate Process Flows (see Chapter 9, "Process Flow"), System Flows (see Chapter 13, "System Flow"), or Use Cases (see Chapter 10, "Use Case") together as a particular business data object is used across many processes. A DFD does not show decisions, and it does not show a sequence of processes. DFDs only show how data flows between processes and is transformed by processes.

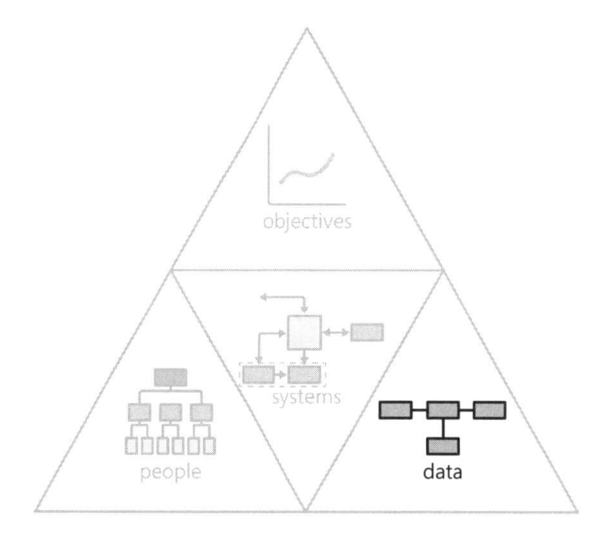

DFDs originated from a set of analysis techniques called *structured analysis*, which was defined in the 1970s and 1980s (DeMarco 1979). In structured analysis, software developers create DFDs from context diagrams and then decompose the DFDs to create the functional modules of the solution (Yourdon 1986). We use RML DFDs to help gather requirements rather than to design the technical architecture. A DFD is a data-oriented view of the solution that allows you to develop the big picture of how data moves through the solution.

In many cases, Process Flows share data with other Process Flows; however, those processes are not necessarily executed by the same groups of people. Each group explains how they use the data, but there is no single Process Flow that captures every process that uses the shared data and shows how these processes are related by the data that they use.

In structured analysis, the DFD was one of the most critical diagrams because the earliest analysis methods emphasized the operation of the system instead of the tasks that users were trying to accomplish. Today, analysts take a more balanced approach, looking at how the users intend to get value from the solution as well as how data flows through the systems. When you are listening to an MP3 or watching a digital movie, it is easy to forget that the sole action that any computer system is responsible for is taking input, processing it, and providing output. The Data Flow Diagram helps you model that view of your systems.

DFD Template

A DFD is a visual diagram that uses four types of elements, as shown in Table 20-1.

TABLE 20-1 DFD Elements

Element	Meaning
Data Store	Data stores or places where data is held temporarily or permanently.
External Entity	External entities such as people or other systems that feed data to or take data from the system. If the external entity is a system, remove the person from the box.
Process A	A process that manipulates data.
Data	The flow of data between data stores, external entities, and processes.

The data flow lines must go from data stores or entities through processes, because external entities and data stores cannot pass data between each other directly. The diagram in Figure 20-1 is a DFD template.

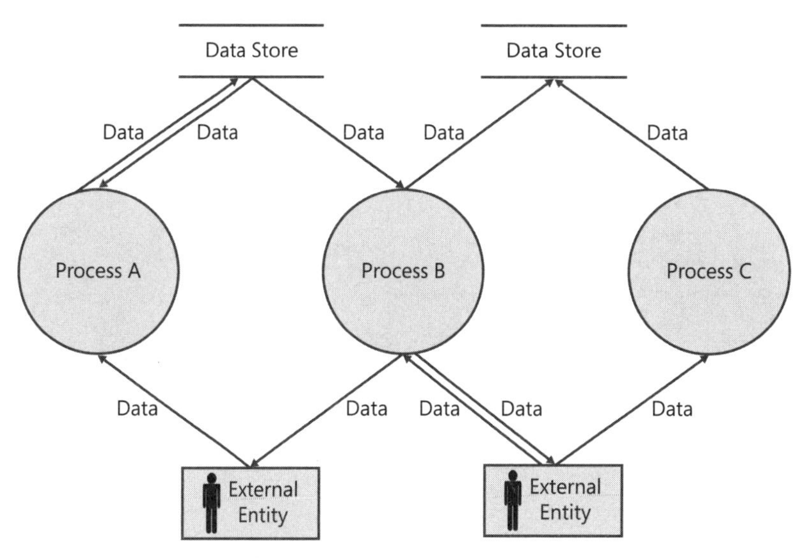

FIGURE 20-1 A DFD Template.

Tool Tip DFDs are most easily created in Microsoft Visio or a similar visual modeling tool.

Example

The example DFD shown in Figure 20-2 is for an order placement system. This diagram shows several high-level pieces of information, including: sales reps update customer data, the finance staff maintains the rules for the tax calculations, and orders flow to the order fulfillment system after they have been processed. In general, this diagram is useful for beginning a conversation about creating an order. It visually shows that customer data, plus product data, plus input from sales rep, plus taxes result in a complete order. Teams can easily validate this type of information with the business stakeholders and from which the developers can quickly get context.

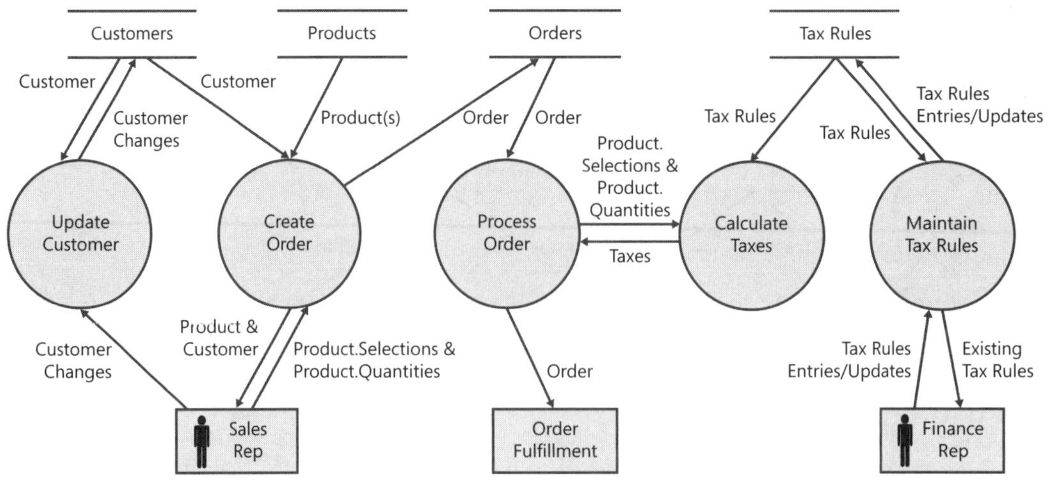

FIGURE 20-2 A DFD Example.

Creating DFDs

You create DFDs by considering all of the business data objects and what actions the system might take using those business data objects. By identifying all the data input and data output of the systems, you will have completely bounded the solution's data. In practice, this can be very difficult. When you are creating DFDs, talk with the business stakeholders to understand how they create data and how they use the output. Then focus on their understanding of how data is processed throughout the systems. It is not reasonable to expect that the business stakeholders will be able to create a DFD on their own, but they should be able to review a DFD, particularly if you walk them through it. Your goal is to create a picture to enable everyone to agree how data is entered into the system, processed, and used. Figure 20-3 shows the steps for creating a DFD.

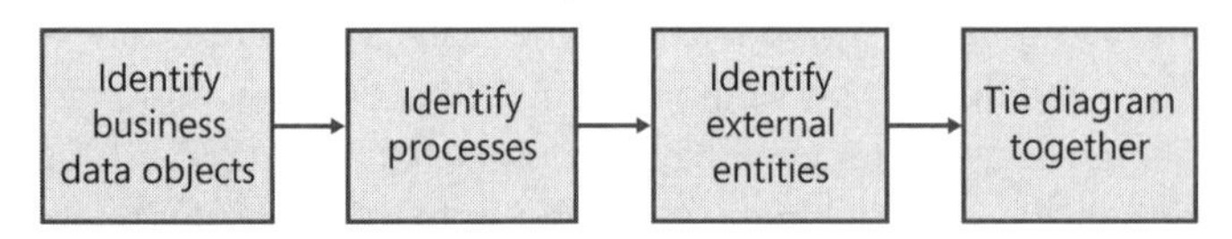

FIGURE 20-3 The process for creating a DFD.

Identify Business Data Objects

Because a DFD is a diagram that is focused on the flow of data, it is useful to start by identifying the business data objects. Use existing Business Data Diagrams (BDDs) (see Chapter 19, "Business Data Diagram") to trigger identification of the business data objects for a DFD. Ecosystem Maps can also help identify business data objects if you showed data flowing between systems in that diagram. Keep in mind that the business data objects are not necessarily actual database objects. In the order management example in the previous section, the obvious business data objects that would be identified include Customers, Products, and Orders. Tax rules might not be identified at first.

The data stores are conceptual and might not represent actual physical data stores in the solution. At this point, it's also helpful to determine which logical data stores these business data objects reside in. You don't necessarily care whether two types of business data objects such as customer and order are in the same physical data store. Instead, just refer to the external storage as the "customer data store" and "order data store." Although DFDs primarily focus on business data objects, it is possible that only particular fields of an object are passed. In those cases, it is sometimes useful to articulate which fields from a Data Dictionary are being passed by using the *<object.field>* notation. In the example, the sales rep passed the Product.Quantities to the Create Order process. If there are too many fields, it is better to simply document the business data object flow.

Identify Processes

After you have identified the important business data objects for the DFD, identify the processes that manipulate the data. Use existing Process Flows to identify the names of processes that might be relevant to the business data objects in your DFD. Generally, every process circle in the DFD will be the same as a process step in a Process Flow or System Flow diagram, so use Process Flows and System Flows to identify the steps for which you want to model the data flows. The primary actions that can apply to data are create, update, delete, use, move, and copy, so each of these actions should be considered in identifying the processes that can manipulate data. Name the processes something simple in the form of a verb followed by an object, if possible, for readability and consistency with other diagrams. DFDs do not have decisions; the diagram is simply a representation of every data flow and all the processes, with input and output.

A DFD should have at most 7+/-2 processes in it so that it is a consumable size for the audience. As with all other models, this number is just a guideline. When you start putting more than 10 processes into a DFD, consider grouping them into groups of 7+/-2. Alternatively, it might be appropriate to create a level 1 (L1) DFD for high-level functional information and to break out more details in additional level 2 (L2) or level 3 (L3) DFDs for subfunctions. In the order management example earlier, you could remove "calculate taxes" and have the tax rule feed directly into "create order." You could then have a "create order" DFD that shows more detailed processes for creating the order.

The processes in the diagram do not imply any order. If you label them with numbers, you will create confusion, because your business stakeholders will begin presuming an order. If a DFD must be labeled with an identifier for later use, carefully explain that the order is not important. It might be helpful to show the processes in DFDs from left to right if there is an obvious order, for readability, but it's critical that your audience understand that DFDs are not meant to show an exact order of execution. The processes simply show transformations of the data, and other models such as Process Flows should be used to show sequential ordering. DFDs are more akin to Ecosystem Maps (see Chapter 12, "Ecosystem Map"), which show all connections simultaneously.

Identify External Entities

You can identify external entities by looking at systems in the Ecosystem Map and roles in Org Charts (see Chapter 8, "Org Chart"). Look in these models for any entities that manipulate the data by executing the processes, bring data into the system, or take data out for consumption outside the system. Again, it is useful to remember that data is only ever created, updated, deleted, used, moved, or copied, so each of these actions should be considered in identifying systems or people that can manipulate data. For this example, an obvious question is, "Who creates the order?" which triggers the identification of the Sales Rep entity.

Tie the Diagram Together

After the major building blocks of a DFD are identified, you must tie them together with arrows representing the appropriate flow of the data. A data flow must go through a process in a DFD; it cannot just flow from an external entity to a data store, for example. After the major obvious objects are connected with flow arrows, consider whether any additional business data objects, processes, or external entities should be part of the diagram, and update it accordingly. Also, as you add processes, notice whether any of them have data only flowing in, or data only flowing out, because this is a trigger that something is missing. Processes are meant to use and/or transform data; therefore, there should be at least one input and output business data object for each process.

In the example discussed earlier, after the "create taxes" process step was identified, it was apparent that there was a tax rule business data object that was moving from the tax rules data store to the "calculate taxes" process. If "maintain tax rules" hadn't already been discovered, the external data store would have helped identify the missing process step to "maintain tax rules." The "maintain tax rules" process would then have triggered identification of another external entity, the finance rep, who is responsible for those tax rules.

DFDs do not have to be perfect to be useful. The technical implementation team will be able to understand the DFD in this conceptual format and build their design appropriately from it.

Using DFDs

DFDs can be used in systems such as transaction processing systems, in which there are many business data objects and data processing events, to help track data as it flows through the solution. More generally, though, DFDs should be used in any situation in which you are trying to show conceptually how multiple business data objects come together in the execution of a process to produce output. They are helpful for showing how business data objects transform as systems or people interact with them. For example, a DFD could show the processes that transform a quote to be a cart, and then a cart to be an order. In the example in this chapter, the DFD could help answer questions such as the following:

- Are these all of the processes that can be used to update orders?
- Are these all of the inputs and outputs of those processes?
- Are these all of the systems involved?
- What data is being stored?

The DFD shows you the inputs and outputs of a process, whereas a Process Flow shows you the steps or decisions to complete the process.

Representing Data Used Across Multiple Processes

In many cases, Process Flows share data with other Process Flows; however, those processes are not necessarily executed by the same groups of people. Each group explains how they use the data, but there is no single Process Flow that captures every process that uses the shared data and shows how these processes are related by the data that they use.

For example, if you are developing an e-commerce system, you might have product managers who define the products to be sold on the website. They might have extensive processes for creating the electronic representation of a product with pictures, descriptions, and other metadata. Your marketing organization creates promotions, advertisements, and layouts that position those products. Customers come to the site and view the products, put them in their shopping carts, and then purchase them. Fulfillment customizes the physical products, packages them, and ships them. Business intelligence analyzes the data created by the orders and has business processes and reports that determine which products, promotions, and advertisements were the most successful. These processes might be seen together in an L1 Process Flow that loosely ties the processes together, as shown in Figure 20-4.

FIGURE 20-4 An L1 Process Flow for an e-commerce system.

At the L2 and L3 Process Flow levels, the details of these processes do not appear concurrently. All of these Process Flows use the product business data object, but the Process Flows do not offer a single view of the life cycle of the product and the associated processes that transform it. The DFD is a different slice of your solution that enables you to see the data that ties each of the processes that use related data together. This is important because it enables you to understand how a particular business data object is used throughout the entire solution. This understanding, in turn, can help you understand how that particular business data object is transformed or manipulated throughout the life cycle of the solution. By understanding all of the data input and output, you can completely bound your solution. Everything else is simply processing data within the system.

Using DFDs to Help with Readability

It might help to think in terms of how business data objects are used together and combine to make new business data objects, such as "customer + product + sales rep input + taxes = order." This is obviously not a complete description, and in this format, it does not explain what systems or actors are necessary to create these objects, or what processes they perform on the data. For example, it does not capture the facts that a sales rep updates customer data, the finance staff maintains the rules for the tax calculations, and orders flow to the order fulfillment system after they have been created. However, a DFD does show all of that information, as in the example DFD in this chapter. Notice, though, that the simple equation is actually the central process "create order" in our DFD, and the objects in the equation are all very much related to the data flowing into and out of that process. For this reason, the business analyst "equation" can be a helpful place to start when creating a DFD.

Driving Completeness

A DFD might trigger some interesting questions for follow up that can help you make the diagram and other requirements more complete. DFDs can help you identify missing process steps. If you have inputs with known outputs, you need to identify all the process steps required to transform the data into its final form. This means ensuring that you understand all of the data inputs that are required to make the processing possible. In addition, a DFD can help you identify additional external entities as you determine how data is being created.

DFDs are primarily used alone to allow the audience to visualize data transformation; however, they can also be used to identify missing Process Flows. Each of the process steps should be a stand-alone Process Flow or part of a greater Process Flow. It's also helpful to remember that data is only created, deleted, edited, used, moved, or copied. Looking at all the data elements in this way can identify missing Process Flows, including some that should actually be in the DFD.

DFDs are also helpful to ensure that all users and systems are accounted for in other models, such as Org Charts and Ecosystem Maps. Most obviously, the external entities and data stores in the DFD might exist in those models. If the system is a conceptual system or a data store, though, it might just prompt you to think about where the data flow is coming from, to identify new systems and users.

In the example used in this chapter, the following questions might be identified and are worth asking a subject matter expert about:

- **How is customer data initially populated?** The answer to this question can help you determine whether there is a missing process, such as "create customer."
- **Where does the product data come from?** This question is similar to the previous question. It might also trigger identification of an external system, such as a product catalog, that should be on this diagram.
- **Does the order fulfillment system update the order store with information about the fulfillment of the orders?** The answer to this question would identify another missing process. If the answer is yes, add a process that updates the orders data store with an arrow flowing from the order fulfillment external entity, through the process, back into the orders data store.
- **Are all of the tax rules manually entered, or is there also an electronic source for them?** This answer will determine whether there is another external entity that updates tax information to the tax rules data store and pushes existing tax rules through the "maintain tax rules" process.
- **Is updating customer data really a separate process?** This answer would tell you whether you have an incorrect process identified. Perhaps, in this case, the "customer updates" need to automatically flow out of changes made when the order is created and are not a separate process.
- **What happens to data in each process?** This question can probe whether the processes are automatic or manual, which would further drive requirements for each process.

Deriving Requirements

DFDs are primarily useful for visualizing the transformation of data and the processes that transform it. However, they can be used to identify which processes must be further analyzed for functional requirements that support what the solution needs to do to transform data.

DFDs are useful if you are changing processes or data in the systems or integrating systems; you can check to see what downstream activities depend on the data. For example, if you change the structure of the order object, it's helpful to realize that you also have to decide whether it affects the cart, the order, and the other processes that touch it later, to see if those must also be updated.

When to Use

Use a DFD to model your key business data objects as they are processed from inputs to outputs. DFDs give you an alternate view to Process Flows by potentially linking many Process Flows together. DFDs are very useful when you have many stakeholders performing a variety of processes using the same core set of data.

When Not to Use

If you are using a Commercial Off the Shelf (COTS) product and are simply configuring it, it might not make sense to use a DFD. If the solution has a mostly linear set of processes with a simple BDD, then it is probably not valuable to construct a DFD. If the processes are simple or there is just a single user group, then the alternate view that the DFD provides is much less useful. For example, a digital signal processor that takes input and provides output probably wouldn't benefit from a DFD.

Common Mistakes

The following represent the most common mistakes that we have seen with DFDs.

Trying to Articulate Order in a DFD

DFDs have no order, although it is tempting to imply an order. The problem with this is that many processes can occur at completely unrelated times, especially when a data store is involved. Time has no meaning with a DFD, and it can be a challenge to communicate this.

Trying to Document Every Single Data Flow

A complete DFD would actually completely describe any solution. However, it is much more difficult for business stakeholders to think in terms of data flow versus the tasks that they will execute. Use the DFDs to explain the flow and the processing of key objects in the solution, such as a mortgage application in a mortgage system or a product in an e-commerce system.

Related Models

Some modeling approaches consider the DFD to be a type of detailed context diagram. RML separates DFDs from the model most similar to context diagrams, Ecosystem Maps, because they serve different purposes. Ecosystem Maps are used to identify the interactions between systems, whereas DFDs show the life cycle of data.

The following list briefly describes the most important models that influence or are enhanced by DFDs. Chapter 26, "Using Models Together," contains a more thorough discussion about all related models.

- **Business Data Diagrams (BDDs)** These are used to identify business data objects that might show up in a DFD.
- **Data Dictionaries** These capture the detailed fields for the business data objects flowing in a DFD.
- **Process Flows, Use Cases, and System Flows** These can represent the details within and around the processes of a DFD.
- **Ecosystem Maps** These show the systems represented by external entities and how they interact with other systems.
- **Org Charts** These can provide missing external entities.

Exercise

The following exercise is intended to help you to gain a better understanding of how to use this model. The exercise is open ended, and therefore the answer you come up with could be substantially different than the answer that we have provided. There are potentially many correct solutions. The answer provides an explanation of how we arrived at our solution. You will gain the most out of the exercise by attempting to do it yourself before looking at the solution. The answers for the exercises can be found in Appendix C.

Instructions

Prepare a DFD for the following scenario.

Scenario

In this project, you are helping to build an eStore to sell flamingos and other lawn decorations. Product Managers are responsible for updating products in the product data store. A shopper adds products to her cart, and then the cart is confirmed to form an order that goes for fulfillment. Shoppers have to add their own personal information to the order. After the order is placed, the shopper can view the shipping information as part of the order history.

To understand the processes, you might find it helpful to look at the Process Flows created in the exercise for Chapter 9.

Additional Resources

- The Structured Analysis wiki contains a great explanation of DFD symbols and how to create them: *http://yourdon.com/strucanalysis/wiki/index.php?title=Chapter_9*.
- Chapter 2 (2.3.3.1) of *Software Requirements Revision: Objects, Functions, & States* covers an extensive overview of DFDs with some examples (Davis 1993).
- *Software Requirements & Specifications* has some history of DFDs and a couple of examples that are similar to RML DFDs (Jackson 1998).
- Wiegers's *Software Requirements* summarizes DFDs and has a complete example (Wiegers 2003).

References

- Davis, Alan M. 1993. *Software Requirements Revision: Objects, Functions, & States*. Upper Saddle River, NJ: PTR Prentice Hall.
- DeMarco, Tom. 1979. *Structured Analysis and System Specification*. Englewood Cliffs, NJ: Prentice Hall.
- Jackson, Michael. 1998. *Software Requirements & Specifications: A Lexicon of Practice, Principles and Prejudices*. Reading, MA. Addison-Wesley Publishers.
- Wiegers, Karl E. 2003. *Software Requirements, Second Edition*. Redmond, WA: Microsoft Press.
- Yourdon, Edward. 1986. *Managing the Structured Techniques: Strategies for Software Development in the 1990s*. Yourdon Press.

CHAPTER 21

Data Dictionary

When I shop online and am finishing my order, there are several fields I have to fill in before I can submit my order. For example, I usually have to enter my phone number and shipping address, select a type of shipping, and provide a billing address and payment information. The shipping address and billing address are similar in that they both require me to give a street address, city, state, and postal code. Some online stores ask for more information, such as the country I'm in, which would probably change the address fields. Because the city of Austin, Texas, exists in two counties, sometimes the store asks what county I live in because sales taxes can vary by county. As I fill in the values for the order fields, sometimes I get errors on the screen because I have entered my values in the wrong format. This happens a lot in phone number fields because some websites expect me to enter dashes, whereas others put them in for me.

The Data Dictionary is an RML data model that captures field-level details about the data in your system.

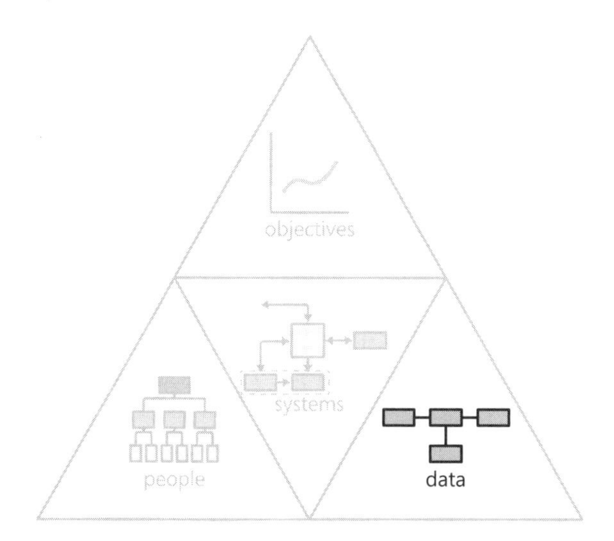

Business Data Diagrams (BDDs) (see Chapter 19, "Business Data Diagram") show the relationships between business data objects. Data Dictionaries model the fields that make up the business data objects.

During the requirements phase, your primary focus is not on the actual data in the database or the technical design required to implement the business data objects within the database. Instead, your focus should be on how the business stakeholders group fields into business data objects. To that end, the following are the elements of a Data Dictionary:

- **Business data objects** These are representations of the real-world objects that business users encounter while performing their jobs. Examples include a credit application, a purchase order, a product, or any other information that the system will process. These are modeled in a BDD.
- **Fields** These are the characteristics or attributes that describe or define a business data object. For example, an order might have an ID, products, shipping address, billing address, payment information, order date, and estimated ship date. A field can be an individual field or it can be a reference to single business data object or a collection of business data objects.
- **Properties** A field has properties that specifically define the field and business rules that govern the field.

Capturing all of this information in a Data Dictionary allows you to look at the properties of all the data in your system in a very analytical, centralized, and structured fashion. The table format allows you to manipulate the model quickly; for example, you can quickly populate values common to many fields or sort on properties. In addition, the Data Dictionary provides a consistent way to reference each field within requirements, business rules, and other models.

Data Dictionary Template

A Data Dictionary lists the business data objects and fields along with their properties in a table structure, as shown in Figure 21-1. Each row of the table is an individual field. Each column is a property of the fields. Although some Data Dictionary properties are a necessity, most are tailored to meet the system's needs.

ID	Business Data Object	Field Name	Property 4	Property 5	Property 6	Property 7	Property ...

FIGURE 21-1 The Data Dictionary template.

Properties List

Table 21-1 is a list of properties commonly found in a Data Dictionary with a description and example for each property. The table explains what each property is used for and suggests whether the property's use is necessary, recommended, or optional. The table starts with the properties that define the business data objects and fields, progresses to the properties for the business rules that govern the data, and ends with administrative properties.

TABLE 21-1 Data Dictionary Elements

Property	Description	Example	Notes	Usage
Properties That Define the Business Data Objects and Fields				
ID	A unique identifier for the field. Use a numbering convention that is consistent with the requirements ID numbering convention.	DD001		Necessary
Business Data Object	The name of the business data object that the field is part of.	Customer	The Last Name field is part of the Customer business data object.	Necessary
Field Name	The name the business uses to refer to the field.	Last Name		Necessary
Description	Defines the field. Provides any relevant information beyond the name.	Last Name is a family name or surname of the customer. If the customer only has one name, use the Last Name field.	This is a possible description of the Last Name field.	Optional
Alternate Names	Other names this field is known as. Ideally, you only have one name for each field. However, when you are merging systems or creating a system that is used by multiple groups, a field might have two different, well-established names. If a common name is not clearly understood by all, use this property. This also happens when the names are not synonyms in everyday language but have specific usage within the company. These names can be included in the description if you want to exclude this property. Also, note that this property is provided for reference only; business rules and requirements that refer to the field should use the field name, not the alternate names.	Family Name	An alternate name for the Last Name field could be Family Name.	Optional
Associated Business Data Object	When a field is another business data object, use this reference and do not repeat the object's information in this row.	Name	Any other business data object. In this case, there might be a Name business data object that has the field's first name, middle name, and last name.	Optional
Data Field	The name under which the data is stored in the system's data store.	LName		Optional

Property	Description	Example	Notes	Usage
Unique Values?	Whether or not the value for the field has to be unique. This is used if the field is a unique identifier that can be used to differentiate between business data objects of the same type.	No	Multiple customers could have the same last name. This property would be Yes for a field such as social security number.	Optional
Data Type	The type of data used to populate the field. It is best to create and use a set of standard types defined outside an individual Data Dictionary across all of your objects. Also, include formatting information such as patterns for phone numbers or number of decimal digits for real numbers.	Alpha	Basic standard types: Alpha, Numeric, Alphanumeric, or Boolean. More elaborate types: Integer, Real Number, Percent, ZIP/Postal Code, or Phone Number. Alternatively, include formatting information: 3-digit code number, 9-digit number (999.999.9999), or 5 digits plus optional 4 digits (99999-8888).	Recommended
Length	The maximum number of digits or characters of the field.	50		Recommended
Properties for the Business Rules That Govern the Data				
Valid Values	Values that the field is allowed to have. If the value doesn't fit within the criteria, it can never be a value for the field. This is stated by using ranges, minimums, maximums, a list of specific values, a reference to a list of specific values, or other rules. It provides the restrictions on the data in and of itself, not how it relates to other data fields. Use the business rules property to indicate needed relationships to other fields. If there are no further restrictions beyond data type and length, then set this field to "Any."	All two-character state codes	This example is the valid value for a State field. Other examples for other fields include: 1..100 > 1900 "Dog", "Cat", "Bird", "Other" 10 digits 10 characters, which must be letters, digits, hyphens, or periods Any	Recommended
Default Value	The value to assign to the field when the business data object is created.	TX	When creating an Address business data object, the default for the State field is "TX."	Recommended
Calculation	If the value of the field is populated by the system, this describes the calculation or rules for populating the value. If the value is user input or user override, use N/A in this field. If the calculations are maintained separately, this field can be omitted or used to provide a reference to the calculations.	If Score > 70 then "Pass", otherwise "Fail"	The example is for a Pass/Fail field on a test. Another example for a Percent Change field: ((Current Year – Prior Year) / Prior Year) * 100, rounded to the nearest integer	Recommended

Property	Description	Example	Notes	Usage
Required?	Whether or not a value for the field must be provided when the business data object is created or updated.	Yes	A value for the ZIP/Postal Code field of an Address business data object is required, but a value for the Address Line 2 field is not.	Recommended
Business Rules	The business rules that apply to the field. These can be validation rules, access rules, or other business rules. If the business rules are maintained separately, this can be omitted or used to provide a reference to the business rules.	Must be on or after Start Date	This is an example rule for a Finish Date field.	Recommended
<Role>	Create a property for each role in the system and define the level of access users with the role have to the field. The access levels are typically "None," "View," or "Edit." If you have data that is extremely restricted at the field level, this property is more efficient than using a Roles and Permissions Matrix to specify the permissions. However, if the data is generally accessible to all roles, you should use the Roles and Permissions Matrix instead of this field.	View	For an Approval Status field, you might add a column for Individual Contributor and one for Manager to the Data Dictionary. Then the property value for the Individual Contributor role is View access and the one for the Manager role is Update access.	Optional
Track Changes?	Whether or not changes to the value for the field need to be tracked.	Yes	Changes to values for the Last Name field must be tracked, but changes to values for Secondary Phone do not need to be.	Optional
Sequence	If values for the fields of a business data object are presented or processed in a specific order, this property defines the order. You would use this property instead of a Report Table or DAR if there is an order to the fields that always applies every time the fields display. The corresponding Report Table and DAR models would simply say to use the default order displayed in the Data Dictionary.	3	Use if the fields appearing on a data entry page for a business data object should appear in a specific relative order. Use if the fields for a business data object can appear as columns or rows on reports; this property specifies the order in which to display the fields. Use if the data for business data objects can be exported and the fields should appear in a specific order. This example means that the field will be third in the sequence of all fields.	Optional
Administrative Properties				
Owner	The person or department who makes decisions about the properties of the field.	John Smith	This could also be a department, such as Finance Department.	Recommended
Status	The current status of the field. Status values are typically the same values used for requirements status.	Draft	Other example values for this property are: Reviewed Approved Deferred Obsolete	Recommended

Property	Description	Example	Notes	Usage
Notes	Other relevant information about the field that should be available to people reviewing the fields.	Data migrated from the legacy system is all caps, but that isn't required.	A Last Name field might contain this note.	Optional

Tool Tip You should create Data Dictionaries in a tool that supports structured data, such as Microsoft Excel, which allows you to easily create, filter, search, and navigate tables with a large number of rows and columns.

Example

In an online shopping system, an order has a variety of fields, including Shipping Address and Billing Address. Figure 21-2 through 21-4 show some of the the Data Dictionary for the Order business data object. We broke the Data Dictionary into three tables because the full table is too wide; these tables would typically be one table with the rows continuing across the table.

The first Data Dictionary properties, shown in Figure 21-2, identify and define the fields of the Order object. The Associated Business Data Object property indicates that both the Shipping Address and Billing Address fields are actually Address business data objects. This means that they are the same type of data (addresses), and therefore have the same types of fields.

ID	Business Data Object	Field Name	Description	Alternate Names	Associated Business Data Object	Data Field	Unique Values?	Data Type	Length
DD001	Order	Shipping Address	The entire shipping address for the order	Ship-to Address	Address	shipping address	N	Alphanumeric	50
DD002	Order	Billing Address Same As Shipping	An indicator of whether the shipping address and the billing address are the same		N/A	billing address same	N	Boolean	N/A
DD003	Order	Billing Address	The entire billing address for the order		Address	billing address	N	Alphanumeric	50
DD004	Order	Coupon Code	Payment can be made in full or partial with use of valid promotional coupon or codes.	Valid system coupon	N/A	payment coupon	N	Alphanumeric	15
DD005	Order	Payment Info Subtotal	Subtotal of price of items in cart	Cart subtotal	N/A	payment subtotal	N	Currency	10
DD006	Order	Payment Info Sales Tax	Sales tax added to the order subtotal depending upon customers location	Sales Tax $	N/A	payment tax	N	Currency	10

FIGURE 21-2 The first part of an example Data Dictionary for an Order business data object.

Figure 21-3 shows most of the properties that describe the rules that govern the data for the Order object.

ID	Business Data Object	Field Name	Valid Values	Default Value	Calculation	Reqd?	Business Rules
DD001	Order	Shipping Address	May only contain letters, digits, and periods May not contain a "PO" or "P.O." as a word Case insensitive	Customer's preferred Shipping Address if returning customer, otherwise null	N/A	Y	N/A
DD002	Order	Billing Address Same As Shipping	True/False	Customer's preferred setting if returning customer, otherwise TRUE	N/A	N	N/A
DD003	Order	Billing Address	May only contain letters, digits, and periods	Customer's preferred Billing Address if returning customer, otherwise null	N/A	Y	N/A
DD004	Order	Coupon Code	Any	null	N/A	N	Must be a legitimate coupon code that is still valid (not expired) and not redeemed previously
DD005	Order	Payment Info Subtotal	0.00...999,999.99	null	If a "Dollar Off" coupon code is entered: Sum of the price of all items in the cart minus the coupon amount. If result is < 0, then 0.	Y	Subtotal must be in USD
DD006	Order	Payment Info Sales Tax	0.00...999,999.99	null	Tax calculated using Payment Info Subtotal and Shipping Address; see tax calculations	Y	See "tax calculations"

FIGURE 21-3 Additional properties in the example Data Dictionary.

The final set of properties, shown in Figure 21-4, contains the remaining properties for data governance and the administrative information about the fields.

The *<order.shipping address>* and *<order.billing address>* fields are Address business data objects. We have included the first set of properties for the Address object to show some of the fields of the Address business data object. in Figure 21-5. Note that the Address business data object fields can go in the same file with the Order object; we have just split them up for readability here.

In the example Data Dictionary, there are five values for the data type. Instead of specifying exactly what those data types are in the Data Dictionary, you can create a separate table as a reference. The data type definition table in Figure 21-6 would be included with the Data Dictionary.

ID	Business Data Object	Field Name	Customer Role	Sales Rep Role	Track Changes?	Sequence	Owner	Status
DD001	Order	Shipping Address	View, Edit	View, Edit	Yes	1	Purchase Team	Reviewed
DD002	Order	Billing Address Same As Shipping	View, Edit	View, Edit	No	7	Purchase Team	Reviewed
DD003	Order	Billing Address	View, Edit	View, Edit	Yes	8	Purchase Team	Reviewed
DD004	Order	Coupon Code	View, Edit	View, Edit	Yes	14	Business SME	Draft
DD005	Order	Payment Info Subtotal	View	View, Edit	Yes	15	Finance	Draft
DD006	Order	Payment Info Sales Tax	View	View	Yes	16	Finance	Draft

FIGURE 21-4 Administrative properties in the example Data Dictionary.

ID	Business Data Object	Field Name	Description	Alternate Names	Associated Business Data Object	Data Field	Unique Values?	Data Type	Length
DD001	Address	Address Line 1	The first line of the address; will contain house or building address and street name	Address House number and Street Address 1		address line1	N	Alphanumeric	50
DD002	Address	Address Line 2	The second line of the address; will usually contain apartment or suite number	Address Apt/suite # Address 2		address line2	N	Alphanumeric	50
DD003	Address	City	The city to which the items are to be shipped/billed			address city	N	Alphanumeric	50
DD004	Address	State	The state/province/region to which the items are to be shipped/billed			address state	N	Alphanumeric	30
DD005	Address	ZIP Code	The ZIP code or postal code to which the items are to be shipped/billed	Postal Code		address zipcode	N	ZIP Code	10
DD006	Address	Country	The country to which the items are to be shipped/billed			address country	N	Alpha	50

FIGURE 21-5 A portion of the Data Dictionary for the Address business data object.

Data Type	Definition
Alphanumeric	Letters, numbers, and special characters; characters other than letters and numbers may be limited in Valid Values property; formatting will vary
Alpha	Letters only; formatting will vary
Boolean	Data attribute can be either true or false; no formatting
Currency	Data is in US currency format: $0.00 - $999,999.99
ZIP Code	10 characters. Only allow digits and hyphens. First 5 characters must be digits. 6th character is optional, may only be hyphen. Last 4 characters must be digits, but are optional as a group--all must be entered or none

FIGURE 21-6 Data type definitions.

Creating Data Dictionaries

The structure of the Data Dictionary is set, with fields as rows and properties as columns. You should determine which properties are necessary to meet the project's needs before you populate the Data Dictionary. However, as you progress, you might need to add properties. Figure 21-7 shows the process for creating a Data Dictionary.

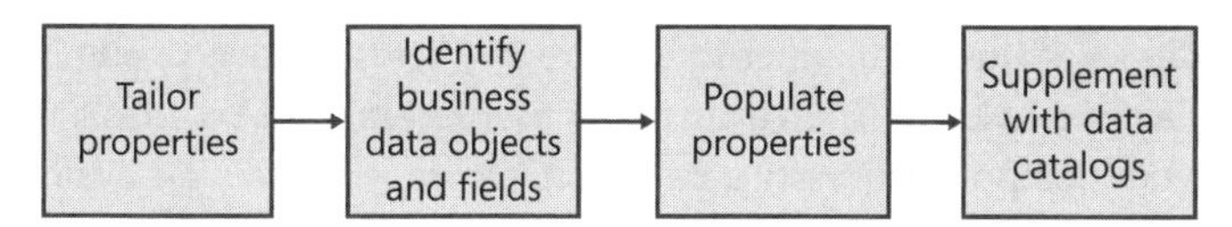

FIGURE 21-7 The process for creating a Data Dictionary.

Tailor Properties

When you are creating a Data Dictionary, the first step is to review the list of properties in the template section and determine which you need. The properties are classified as Necessary, Recommended, or Optional to help you with this decision. For example, you might not use the data field property if actual database names are not available or not useful. Conversely, you could add a property to capture whether the field is populated by the user or by the system.

When you are entering the user interface (UI) design phase of a project, it can be useful to add properties to the Data Dictionary that capture which screens a field appears on.

Finally, if there are properties that the business does not care about and that are strictly technical design properties, you generally should not include them in the Data Dictionary because it is a requirements model. However, if the development team asks for properties just for their use, you might add those properties if it does not cause issues. Just be sure to communicate additions as development-specific information, especially if they are not important for the business stakeholders to review.

Identify Business Data Objects and Fields

Next, begin populating the Data Dictionary. Start by populating the business data object property by using all the business data objects listed in the BDD. This is a very crucial step in the process. It is tempting to think in terms of system objects and database tables, but that is not what you should be focusing on in a Data Dictionary. Instead, think about the real-world objects the system deals with that are diagrammed in the BDD. For example, a shipping management system focuses on the tracking and routing of packages. Those packages are real-world objects that have tangible fields such as weight, dimensions, recipient address, and return address. Focusing on these objects drives you toward the real business requirements and not some predefined implementation concept. Also, you can use your Data Flow Diagrams (DFDs) to ensure that the business data objects passed throughout the DFD are covered in the Data Dictionary.

There are many sources for determining the fields of the business data objects. When you are working with an existing system, look at existing screens to find candidate fields for the Data Dictionary. Also consider the existing database fields, but don't directly model them; the focus of the Data Dictionary is the business needs. When you are creating a new system, look at any paper forms that are going to be automated. Looking at existing reports is often one of the most useful ways to identify the fields required, because the reports simply list fields that are displayed as part of the report. Additionally, Process Flow, System Flow, or Use Case steps can be used to identify necessary data fields; look at the data required to complete a step. Wireframes or existing screen shots can provide long lists of fields. State Tables and State Diagrams can be used to identify any business data objects that should have a field such as State or Status. Remember to capture any fields needed to administer the system. For example, if there's a need to know when a customer user last logged on, then Last Logon Date is probably a field of your Customer business data object. Obviously, interview business stakeholders to identify fields; however, taking a draft list of fields will help them think of other fields. Regardless of the source of your information, be sure to map the fields back to the business data objects in the Data Dictionary.

If you are using Excel, the entire Data Dictionary can exist in a single worksheet, but that might be too unwieldy if the list of fields becomes very long. However, splitting each business data object into its own worksheet can also be unwieldy when the number of business data objects increases above 20-30. If a single worksheet is too crowded, then group fields for related objects together into worksheets that each contain less than 300-400 fields.

Populate Properties

Finally, it is important to note that the creation of Data Dictionaries is usually iterative. The first iteration might simply provide the business data object and names of the fields. That is usually sufficient information for developers to estimate their work. They'll need more detail to actually create the system, but you can provide that later. Finish filling in information for additional properties as it becomes available. It is common to complete the Data Dictionary collaboratively. The analyst might create the initial draft of it, and then the business stakeholder might write descriptions and indicate which fields are required. Or the developer might fill in the data field property. In many cases, you will be able to infer what the values for some fields and properties should be based on past experience or on what you know about other systems. Just be sure that you validate those inferences with the business stakeholders.

If a field is another business data object, you should document that business data object name in the Associated Business Data Object property in the Data Dictionary. Also, if a cell is left blank in a Data Dictionary, it means that the property does not apply for that field.

Supplement with Data Catalogs

If the valid values for a field are a specific list of values, such as a list of states, it can be hard to read the list in a single cell of a Data Dictionary. Furthermore, if the same list of valid values applies to multiple fields, maintaining it in multiple places causes unnecessary work. Similarly, long calculations can be hard to read, and if the same calculation method is used on multiple properties, maintaining it in multiple places is inefficient.

In situations like this, use a data catalog. A data catalog is a set of lists and/or calculations that apply to the data. When a property for a field is based on a list or calculation, enter a reference to the catalog in the cell, rather than including the list or calculation itself. For example, the Valid Values property of a Salutation field might say "Use the Salutations list from the data catalog." The corresponding data catalog contains the values in Figure 21-8. You can see the "Salutations" list in the data catalog, in addition to a few other lists.

Data Catalogs			
Salutations	**Gender**	**Countries**	**Job Title**
Mr.	Male	Canada	Business Analyst
Mrs.	Female	United States	Product Manager
Ms.		Mexico	Project Manager
Miss			Quality Assurance Analyst
			Developer
			Other

FIGURE 21-8 A data catalog corresponding to a Data Dictionary.

If you use a spreadsheet tool such as Excel to create the Data Dictionary, put the Data Dictionary and the data catalog in the same workbook, using separate worksheets. Some people prefer to create a separate worksheet for each list or calculation in the catalog, which is also fine.

Using Data Dictionaries

Data Dictionaries are helpful when you are well into a project and need to create consistent terminology to talk about the data. Their structure allows you to be thorough when defining the data and the rules that govern it. The table format of the Data Dictionary allows you to quickly populate a lot of information across multiple fields. Given this, it is often more efficient to document data information in a Data Dictionary than in other models, such as Display-Action-Response (DAR) models. For example, you could create the rules for validating fields in the behavior section of a DAR model, but you would have to create an individual table for each field and repeat the validation rules. Capturing that information in a Data Dictionary is much more efficient.

Promoting a Consistent Data Nomenclature

One of the key values of the field definitions is that you can use them to present a consistent nomenclature throughout all other documentation to uniquely refer to the fields in the Data Dictionary, so that it is completely unambiguous as to which piece of data is being used. The recommended notation is <*object.field*> or, in the case of a business data object that contains a collection of objects, <*object 1.object 2.field*>. In this notation, *field* is the Field Name property because that is the one that the business is familiar with. Also, *object 2* is the Field Name that *object 1* uses to refer to the object. For example, if an order has a ship-to address and you want to use the ZIP Code to calculate shipping costs, you would refer to the field as <*order.ship to address.zip code*>. There might be many other ZIP Codes in the entire solution, but by using this reference, you are absolutely clear as to which ZIP Code you mean. Using this notation, you can be sure that you are absolutely clear which piece of data you are referring to from other parts of the documentation. Keep in mind that this notation has nothing to do with the actual underlying database table structure and refers purely to business data objects that business stakeholders are familiar with.

Driving Completeness

The benefits the analyst gets from using the Data Dictionary are also realized by the business stakeholders, developers, and testers. It gives them a structured approach for reviewing and using the information. Without this structure, reviewers would be hard pressed to determine whether the information is complete, and other consumers of the requirements might find it difficult to find specific pieces of information. For example, Data Dictionaries give the testers one location to determine what fields are required without having to dig through requirements statements. Finally, the development team can use the Data Dictionary directly to create the database design.

Deriving Requirements

A structured format such as a Data Dictionary ensures that all business data objects and data fields are considered and that consistent details about each are captured. When your system is heavily data driven, a thorough analysis of data can lead to many hard-to-find requirements.

Unlike most models that decompose into more granular requirements, the Data Dictionary is associated with higher-level requirements. Don't go through each cell of the Data Dictionary and ask, "Is there a requirement for that?" The Data Dictionary *is* the requirement for that! Instead, go through each property of your Data Dictionary and ask if the property implies expected system behavior. If it does, be sure there's a requirement for the behavior. For example, defining data validation rules in a Data Dictionary implies a need to apply the validation rules. However, it does not tell how to apply them. Are records with invalid data rejected? Does the system accept any data but provide a list of errors in the data? The requirements must address the expected system behavior. The requirements associated with the Data Dictionary typically include a reference to the Data Dictionary; for example, "The system prevents the user from saving invalid data (please see the Data Dictionary for validation rules)."

When to Use

Use a Data Dictionary anytime you have business data objects with fields that have validation criteria. The Data Dictionary is most useful in situations in which the system has a database back end, rather than some kind of real-time processing system. The model provides depth, rather than breadth, so if you are short on time, prioritize appropriately. Rather than eliminating it altogether, a good strategy is to limit your Data Dictionary to a few essential business data objects and limit the properties that you define.

When Not to Use

A Data Dictionary might not be necessary if the solution has no databases, has a very simple set of data models, or the data set is well understood. If there is no user input, then it might be less important to specify validation criteria. In addition, in many Commercial Off the Shelf (COTS) implementations, you will be configuring a system to meet business process needs. In those cases, you might not need the Data Dictionary because the fields are already defined by the COTS software. You still might want to use the *<object.field>* notation for testing purposes.

Furthermore, the Data Dictionary does not model the relationships of the data; use the BDD for that. For example, a corporation can have multiple employees. Employee is not a field of the Corporation business data object, but rather a separate business data object that is related to the Corporation business data object. The BDD, not the Data Dictionary, shows this relationship. Also, the Data Dictionary is not the project glossary. The Data Dictionary defines only the data used in the solution. The project glossary includes any terms related to the solution, including acronyms. These two should not be combined.

Common Mistakes

The Data Dictionary captures many of the less interesting data requirements, so you have to be careful in creating and reviewing it. The following represent the most common mistakes we have seen with Data Dictionaries.

Becoming Overwhelmed by the Size

One very common mistake is to become overwhelmed with the large volume of data. The Data Dictionary can be very time consuming to make and very boring to review with stakeholders. In some cases, generating an approximate Data Dictionary is sufficient. As new fields are discovered, they can be added to the Data Dictionary. Unlike with a BDD, additions to the Data Dictionary rarely have far-reaching architectural implications. Fields can usually be added easily and without much impact.

Not Articulating Important Validation Rules

Often analysts will assume that the validation business rules are obvious. This can result in major changes to the system if other parts of the system depend on and expect certain ranges of values.

Related Models

The following list briefly describes the most important models that influence or are enhanced by Data Dictionaries. Chapter 26, "Using Models Together," contains a more thorough discussion about all related models.

- **Business Data Diagrams (BDDs)** These are used to show the relationships between the business data objects defined in the Data Dictionary.
- **Data Flow Diagrams (DFDs)** These show how the values for the fields of business data objects are supplied. The data that flows into and out of processes in the DFD should be business data objects and/or fields of business data objects defined in the Data Dictionary.
- **Display-Action-Response (DAR) models** These are used in conjunction with Data Dictionaries for considering which fields should be displayed and how they should behave for a user. Wireframes have lists of fields that will probably be described in the Data Dictionary.
- **State Tables and State Diagrams** These define the states a business data object can obtain. There is usually a field, such as Status, that indicates the state of the business data object. The valid values for the status typically correspond to the states.
- **Report Tables** The rich lists of fields in reports most likely need to be included in the Data Dictionary.
- **Process Flows, System Flows, and Use Cases** These can help identify data fields by showing what data is needed to complete the steps.

Exercise

The following exercise is intended to help you to gain a better understanding of how to use this model. The exercise is open ended, and therefore the answer you come up with could be substantially different than the answer that we have provided. There are potentially many correct solutions. The answer provides an explanation of how we arrived at our solution. You will gain the most out of the exercise by attempting to do it yourself before looking at the solution. The answers for the exercises can be found in Appendix C.

Instructions

Prepare a draft Data Dictionary for the scenario, using your experience to populate the table when information is not provided.

Scenario

In this project, you are helping to build an eStore to sell flamingos and other lawn decorations, including statues, dwarfs, elves, and bird baths. Each product has a cost, list price, discount price, SKU, quantity, and flag indicating whether it is in or out of stock. Information for each product is initially populated based on a data feed. The discount price is always 80 percent of the list price.

Additional Resources

- Chapter 10 of *Software Requirements* by Karl Wiegers has an explanation and examples of Data Dictionary elements (Wiegers 2003).
- Data Dictionaries are explained in Al Davis's *Software Requirements* as repositories of all the data items from DFDs. His Data Dictionaries have fewer properties but otherwise are similar (Davis 1993).

References

- Davis, Alan M. 1993. *Software Requirements: Objects, Functions, and States*. Upper Saddle River, NJ: PTR Prentice Hall.
- Wiegers, Karl E. 2003. *Software Requirements, Second Edition*. Redmond, WA: Microsoft Press.

CHAPTER 22

State Table

My daughter is applying to college. The application process is pretty straightforward, but we have to go through the process for each of the 10 schools she wants to apply to. For each school, she must complete the application and submit it, after which it goes through an initial evaluation by the college to make sure all of the information has been submitted, and finally it is accepted or rejected. If for some reason she submits an incomplete application, she is notified and gets a chance to resubmit it. We realized that at any given point, an application can be in only one of a few states: incomplete, submitted, accepted, or rejected. Further, we saw that it could only go backward in the process if she made an error. We used this information to set up a simple system to track the state of each of her applications.

The State Table is an RML data model that is used to identify all states and all possible single-step transitions between the states for a particular business data object or objects. A *state* describes a stage of an object's life cycle. An object's states must be mutually exclusive, and an object has to exist in exactly one of the states at any time. States can usually be determined by a field or unique combinations of a set of fields of an object. States influence the behavior of the system in significant ways, such as program flow, available user actions, and information that is displayed on the screen. A *transition* is an object's movement from one state to another. State Tables can capture the events that trigger transitions. The events can be user or system events, the conditions under which the transition is allowed, or simply the fact that the transition is allowed (Gottesdiener 2005).

State Tables are used to ensure that all transitions are identified, showing which transitions are allowed and not allowed and what triggers or conditions are required for the transitions. If a business data object has more than a few states, it is almost impossible to identify the complete set of state transitions without a State Table structure to ensure that they are all considered.

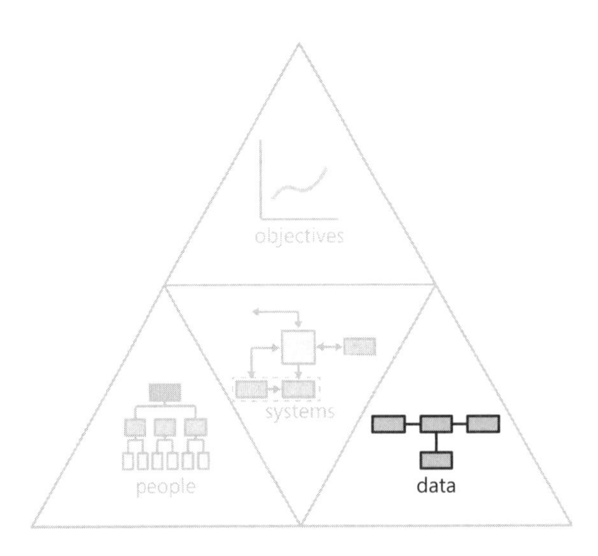

State Table Template

A State Table is represented as a grid, as shown in Figure 22-1, with all states listed across the top row and repeated in the first column. The value in each of the cells in the grid represents whether there is a valid transition from the state in that row to the state in that column. The set of states in the first column are labeled "Initial State," and the set of states in the top row are labeled "Target State" to demonstrate the order of the flow of transitions. State Tables are read by starting with the initial state in the first column, finding the desired final state, and then determining the value in the intersecting cell. For example, in this template, the two cells containing Yes in the row labeled "State C" denote that transitions from state C to state B and from state C to state D are both allowed.

		Target State						
		State A	State B	State C	State D	State E	State F	State G
Initial State	State A	no	yes	no	yes	no	no	no
	State B	no	no	yes	yes	yes	no	no
	State C	no	yes	no	yes	no	no	no
	State D	no	no	no	no	no	no	no
	State E	no	no	no	no	no	yes	yes
	State F	no	no	no	no	no	no	yes
	State G	no	no	no	no	no	no	no

FIGURE 22-1 The State Table template.

If there is an obvious order to the states, then it is helpful to list the states in the table in the order that they occur in the solution (from top to bottom and left to right). If the states can appear in different sequences depending on user actions, use your judgment to determine the most understandable order.

Each cell can contain a simple Yes if the transition is valid or No if the transition is not valid. Also, instead of Yes, you can note the transition event that initiates the transition or the condition that is required to allow the transition to occur, as shown in Figure 22-2. For example, "Transition from A to B" is an event that causes the transition from state A to state B.

Initial State \ Target State	State A	State B	State C	State D	State E	State F	State G
State A	no	Transition from A to B	no	Transition from A to D	no	no	no
State B	no	no	Transition from B to C	Transition from B to D	Transition from B to E	no	no
State C	no	Transition from C to B	no	Transition from C to D	no	no	no
State D	no	no	no	no	no	no	no
State E	no	no	no	no	no	Transition from E to F	Transition from E to G
State F	no	no	no	no	no	no	Transition from F to G
State G	no	no	no	no	no	no	no

FIGURE 22-2 The State Table template with transitions.

However, if additional requirements information about the transitions is necessary, if the state transition events are complex to describe, or if multiple events cause the same transition, then Yes can be replaced by unique IDs as references, such as REQ001, REQ002, and so on, as Figure 22-3 shows. The requirements would further detail the transitions, separate from the table, to provide the additional necessary information. The preferred method is to put the state transition event in the cell directly for easier readability, if it fits.

Initial State \ Target State	State A	State B	State C	State D	State E	State F	State G
State A	no	REQ001	no	REQ002	no	no	no
State B	no	no	REQ003	REQ004	REQ005	no	no
State C	no	REQ006	no	REQ007	no	no	no
State D	no	no	no	no	no	no	no
State E	no	no	no	no	no	REQ008	REQ009
State F	no	no	no	no	no	no	REQ010
State G	no	no	no	no	no	no	no

FIGURE 22-3 The State Table template with requirement IDs.

Tool Tip Typically, State Tables are created in a tool such as Microsoft Excel, which provides a grid as part of its typical spreadsheet.

Example

The example shown in Figure 22-4 is a State Table from a loan application system. As an applicant works with her mortgage broker, the broker might tell the applicant, "Your loan application is in underwriting" or "Your loan application is in funding now."

	Target State							
Initial State	**Prequalified**	**Submitted**	**Processing**	**Underwriting**	**Set to Close**	**Closing**	**Funding**	**Non-close**
Prequalified	no	Property address entered	no	no	no	no	no	Prequalification denied
Submitted	no	no	Application is submitted	Application is sent to underwriting	no	no	no	Application denied
Processing	no	no	no	Application is sent to underwriting	Application is sent to underwriting and closing simultaneously	no	no	Application denied
Underwriting	no	no	no	no	Underwriting approved	no	no	Underwriting denied
Set to Close	no	no	Underwriting process suspended	no	no	Closing date set	Funding number assigned	Closing canceled
Closing	no	no	An application field needs to be modified	no	no	no	Funding number assigned	Closing canceled
Funding	no	no	no	no	no	no	no	no
Non-close	no	no	no	no	no	no	no	no

FIGURE 22-4 A State Table example.

The State Table in this example allows you to consider every possible transition of a loan application. For this scenario, every loan application starts in a "prequalified" state and can move into a "submitted" state if the property address is entered or "non-close" if the application was immediately denied. Similarly, if the loan application is denied while in an "underwriting" state, then it moves to "non-close"; otherwise, it moves into the "set to close" state. In this example, the State Table can drive discussion around questions such as, "Are there any circumstances under which a non-closed loan application can be reopened to any other state?" Also, you might discover interesting transitions. For example, perhaps when an applicant is approved with a high enough score, the application goes to a "set to close" state with a simplified underwriting process that happens in that state. Further, you can deduce from the table that both "funding" and "non-close" are end states because there are no transitions out of them.

Creating State Tables

You create State Tables by following the process shown in Figure 22-5. The first step is to identify the business data objects that need to be analyzed, after which you must identify the states. Finally, you should analyze the transitions between states to determine whether they are allowed, and if so, what conditions and triggers are required for the transitions.

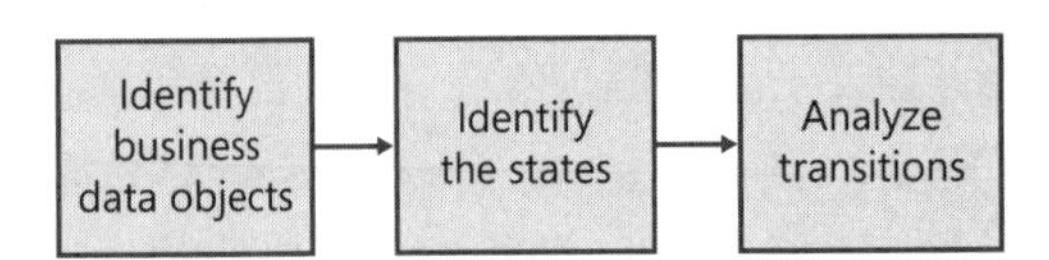

FIGURE 22-5 The State Table creation process.

Identify the Business Data Objects

First and foremost, decide which objects need State Tables. As a starting point, look at each business data object in the Business Data Diagrams (BDDs) (see Chapter 19, "Business Data Diagram") to consider each of the objects to determine whether any have more than a few states. Remember, a field of a business data object represents a state if it causes significant changes in the behavior of the solution, such as program flow, available user actions, and information that is displayed on the screen. For example, if the business data object has a field defined in its Data Dictionary (see Chapter 21, "Data Dictionary") to capture something such as state or status, the object probably also needs a State Table.

The states in a State Table usually represent the different values of a single field of a single business data object. However, there might be situations where the state is actually represented by multiple fields from the same or even different business data objects. Each state represents a unique set of values of each of the fields. Be careful when creating a state from more than three or four fields, because any system that has too many states will become very difficult to test.

If an object can only exist in two states, it is not generally necessary to create a State Table, because there are only four possible transitions, which is well below the 7+/-2 pieces of information that an individual can analyze at one time. For example, if there is a light switch object and the two possible states are "on" and "off," a State Table is uninteresting because it is just obvious that you can go from "on" to "off," and possibly you can also go from "off" back to "on." However, when three states are present, there are nine possible transitions, which is just on the edge of manageability without a model.

Identify the States

After you have selected a business data object, identify all of the possible states that the object can have. In the example shown earlier, a loan application can be in one of eight different states. You might find it helpful to examine the Process Flows (see Chapter 9, "Process Flow") that interact with these business data objects, because the Process Flows might trigger identification of useful states to track. When you are working to identify states, remember that states are mutually exclusive: an object can only exist in one state at a time.

States are most often described with an adjective to represent the condition of an object. Transitions between states are initiated by actions; however, the actions themselves are not states. Consider the example of a dog at dinnertime. The subject is Diogo, a friendly cocker spaniel. In the evening, he trots to his bowl in eager anticipation of a hearty helping of kibbles. His starting state is "hungry." To Diogo's delight, his owner pours a shower of crunchy bits into his bowl, and he enthusiastically eats until he reaches a state of "full." Now that he has a full belly, he meanders around the family room until he recognizes that he is in a new state, "tired." He flops onto his bed and before long reaches a state of "asleep."

The example shows that Diogo transitions through states of "hungry," "full," "tired," and "asleep." Notice that the verbs *eat*, *meander*, and *flop* are not states that the dog is in, but rather actions the dog takes to move between states.

After determining what the states are and how they should be labeled, list all possible states in the State Table across the top row and down the left column. The states in the top row and the first column should be identical. If you are creating a State Table using more than one field or business data object, you need to list all combinations of objects and their states in the top row and left column. For example, say you have two business data objects, a user and a cart. Each has two states, logged on/anonymous and valid/invalid, respectively. You can list the user/cart state combinations in each row and column: logged on/valid, logged on/invalid, anonymous/valid, and anonymous/invalid.

Analyze the Transitions

A State Table facilitates consideration of every single transition, no matter how trivial or unlikely that transition might be. You must analyze literally every cell in a State Table to determine whether it is a valid transition, what the transition event is, what conditions are necessary for the transition, and what associated requirements are needed to allow for the transition.

A useful first-pass analysis that you can complete very quickly is to simply indicate Yes or No for whether each transition is valid. No cells in a State Table should be left blank in the final version, because a blank cell means that the validity of the transition is unknown and has to be determined. This first-draft State Table might actually exist as a stand-alone artifact on the project for a while, until additional details can be analyzed. A next-pass analysis of the State Table is to identify the transition events and conditions for all of the valid transitions, replacing the Yes with the transition event and/or conditions. In the final analysis, the detailed requirements are captured for the transitions and are referenced from IDs in the cells.

In the example earlier in this chapter, the transition between "submitted" and "underwriting" might lead to a whole set of requirements around the submission process, including identifying the data that is needed for the application to make it to "underwriting" directly and defining who takes ownership of the loan application at that "underwriting" state. All of that information can't fit in the table, but the table can serve as a pointer to additional requirements information for the transition.

Using State Tables

The states of the objects will constrain behavior in the solution. A State Table is used to visually communicate which transitions are allowed and to ensure that all possible state transitions are identified. State Tables help identify all transitions, because every single cell in the State Table is evaluated for whether it is a valid transition. These models can very quickly enable business stakeholders to visually determine whether there are errors in the team's understanding of states and then immediately link to the requirements to access details about how the transitions happen. Finally, they facilitate discussions around changes in the state model and the implications of those changes.

Enhancing Readability

State Tables are extremely useful to development and test groups because they aggregate all the permutations they need in a single location. The readability of State Tables is superior to that of text lists because State Tables provide a high-level visual view of the transitions, and they organize the requirements and business rules according to the state transitions.

The following text descriptions show the same information as in the first two rows of the State Table from the loan application example:

1. A loan application moves from "prequalified" to "submitted" when the property address is entered.
2. A loan application moves from "prequalified" to "non-closed" when the prequalification is denied.
3. A loan application moves from "submitted" to "processing" when the application is actually submitted.
4. A loan application moves from "submitted" to "underwriting" when the application is sent to underwriting.
5. A loan application moves from "submitted" to "non-close" when the application is denied.

Twelve additional statements like these would be required to complete the list of valid transitions, and none of these state what transitions are invalid. This is far more challenging to read. Further, it is virtually impossible to read this list and determine whether any transitions are missing. For example, in looking at the list, it is not possible to determine whether the loan application can move from a "non-closed" state back into another state or if the transition was just forgotten in the text list.

Driving Completeness

State Tables can help you identify a significant number of allowed transitions that were initially thought to be disallowed. Most often, these are transitions from a state that is thought to be final, such as a the state of a denied loan application. In the case of a denied loan application, if an applicant decides to come back at a later date and reapply, it might be useful to allow a broker to reopen, modify, and resubmit the original loan application rather than reentering redundant data, thereby saving hours of labor.

Analyzing a State Table should prompt a set of questions about the states and transitions for the business stakeholders. You can display a draft of the State Table and ask your prepared questions, such as:

1. **Is there intentionally not a state called "Approved?"** The answer to this question helps validate that the correct states were identified up front. If that state was missed, the State Table has to be adjusted for it. Otherwise, it can be helpful to examine the Process Flow for the application approval process and ensure that the movement between the states in the State Table is clean.

2. **Can you really skip the "Processing" state for some loan applications?** If so, in what cases is that allowed, and can the solution determine this? The answer to this question will help you ensure that you captured the transitions correctly and define the required fields and conditions on an application.

3. **After a loan application has gone to the "Funding" state, is there a way to stop it and send it back to another state?** This answer will again confirm that there are no missing transitions or requirements. Additionally, it might trigger some business processes to be revisited for what happens in this case.

Though State Tables clearly show all of the valid transitions and the transition events that triggered them, they do not visually show the flow of state transitions. For situations in which the visual sequences are necessary, a State Diagram is more useful. State Diagrams are described in Chapter 23, "State Diagram," in more detail, but Table 22-1 shows the key differences between these two models.

TABLE 22-1 Differences Between a State Table and a State Diagram

Model	Use
State Table	Use when you want to make sure you are able to ask about every state and possible transition.
State Diagram	Use when you are planning to leave out non-transitions and focus on visualizing the sequence of allowed transitions.

State Tables are far better for identifying transitions, because all possible transitions are obvious (that is, each one is a cell in the table). If you wanted to do the same thing with a State Diagram, you would have to consider a line from every state to every other state, which is more cumbersome. In Chapter 23, additional comparisons are made between State Tables and State Diagrams, though it is often more useful to use both models together to capitalize on both of their strengths.

Completing Other Models

The states in State Tables help you complete other models. When completing Display-Action-Response (DAR) models (see Chapter 15, "Display-Action-Response"), you can use states as possible preconditions to trigger display or behavior in a user interface. For example, an order review screen might be displayed differently based on the state of an order, so the different states of an order are the preconditions for the DAR models for that screen. Also, a business data object that has state transitions might identify the need for a Report Table (see Chapter 24, "Report Table"). For example, the business might want to run a report to see all orders in a particular state.

Deriving Requirements

After you have identified all state transitions, you can then analyze State Tables to define detailed requirements. The four main questions to ask about the transitions are:

- What conditions are required for the transition to occur?
- What action initiated the transition?

- What is the output of the transition?
- What actions or data transformations occur as a result of the transition?

If data is used or transformed during the state transitions, then those behaviors should be captured as requirements and potentially even in other models, such as Process Flows. The actions that trigger the transitions, by users or by systems, should be evaluated for whether they are covered in existing Process Flows, System Flows (see Chapter 13, "System Flow"), or Use Cases (see Chapter 10, "Use Case"), or whether perhaps there are gaps in those. These actions can directly translate into software requirements. Consider that if there is no requirement related to one of the transitions in the table, there will be no way to transition from one state to the other in the final solution. In the example State Table, a loan application can go from either "submitted" or "processing" to "underwriting." Specific requirements must be defined about which data fields have to be completed on the loan application for it to move to "underwriting," and specifically what conditions allow it to skip "processing."

When to Use

State Tables should be used for all objects that go through complex state changes. Business data objects that go through workflow are the most common source of State Tables. These include objects such as e-commerce orders, test cases, online registrations, and the example in this chapter—loan applications.

When Not to Use

Any solution that does not have behavior based on objects' states does not need a State Table. Similarly, if your business data objects have simple states—for example, only two or three states—then State Tables might not be useful.

If the transitions between states are linear without significant branching, then a State Table might not provide much value. However, often you can't determine that the solution is simple until you create the State Table and consider all possible transitions.

Common Mistakes

The following represent the most common mistakes we have seen with State Tables.

States That Are Not States

A challenge with State Tables is identifying states that are actually states. In State Tables created by analysts new to State Tables and State Diagrams, it is common to see states that are actions or transitions instead of states. When you try to label the transitions with transition events, it should become obvious that these are not states. A state is a field of a business data object that causes significant changes in decision logic based on the value of the field.

Missing States

If you create a State Table but fail to identify all of the states correctly, you will miss the value of the model. Identifying transitions between states can help identify missing states if the transition from one state to another does not seem correct.

Incorrect "No" Transitions

Sometimes everyone agrees that a transition is not allowed without actually thinking carefully about cases in which it does happen. By marking a transition No, the development team might specifically prevent that transition from ever happening. For example, in the case of a mortgage application, when an application reaches the "non-close" state, everyone might agree that it can never leave that state. However, upon further probing, you could discover that after a long period of time, customers often come back and want to restart the process. In the current system, the brokers actually set the status to open and begin editing the original application, against company policy. After further discussion, everyone could still agree that the transition is truly not allowed, but it can turn out that there is a requirement to be able to copy the information into a new record. The copy would save significant time by allowing brokers to avoid rekeying information that the system already has about the applicant. The new record would have all the original data and a new initial state, but no history.

Related Models

The following list briefly describes the most important models that influence or are enhanced by State Tables. Chapter 26, "Using Models Together," contains a more thorough discussion about all related models.

- **Business Data Diagrams (BDDs)** These are used to identify which business data objects should be considered for analyzing states in a State Table.
- **State Diagrams** These show a visual representation of the state transitions, which are easier to read if the flow of transitions is most important.
- **Process Flows, System Flows, and Use Cases** These are used to help look for events that trigger state transitions. Also, State Table transition events can be used to ensure that there are no gaps in these models.
- **Display-Action-Response (DAR) models** These use the states in State Tables as possible preconditions for user interface display and behavior.
- **Data Dictionaries** For the business data objects represented in State Tables, these contain the fields indicating the state of the objects.
- **Report Tables** The need for a Report Table might be triggered by a State Table when it is useful to see a full report on the objects by state.

Exercise

The following exercise is intended to help you to gain a better understanding of how to use this model. The exercise is open ended, and therefore the answer you come up with could be substantially different than the answer that we have provided. There are potentially many correct solutions. The answer provides an explanation of how we arrived at our solution. You will gain the most out of the exercise by attempting to do it yourself before looking at the solution. The answers for the exercises can be found in Appendix C.

Instructions

Prepare a State Table for the scenario.

Scenario

You are helping to build an eStore to sell flamingos and other lawn decorations. After a user browses the site for products, he adds his selections to his cart. After reviewing the cart and finalizing any updates, the user decides to proceed through the checkout process to purchase the items in the cart. Pricing is finalized, and then the system captures checkout information from the user, such as shipping and payment details. Finally, the order is submitted to the order system, where it is assembled and shipped to the user. Here are a few additional suggestions for creating the State Table:

- The cart can be updated while the user is continuing to shop. However, after talking through it with the stakeholder, it is determined that until the cart proceeds into checkout, it is essentially in the same state, which is a "draft" state. Therefore, no "updated" state is needed.
- The business stakeholders want the user to see the tax applied only after the user is really ready to purchase the order, because the stakeholders think that the tax calculation is complicated. Additionally, the user has the option to apply discounts after he proceeds to checkout. There might be some opportunities for process improvement here, but for draft purposes on the State Table, a "priced" state is suggested.
- The user enters shipping and payment information and then gets one last chance to confirm the order, so a "confirmed" state is suggested so that the user can still back out.
- After the products are assembled at the factory, the user cannot back out of the order. If the user is unhappy, he will have to go through a return process because the order is not allowed to be updated.

Additional Resources

- *Software Requirements: Objects, Functions, and States* has examples of what Davis calls Statecharts. They are similar in concept to State Tables but have a different structure (Davis 1993).

References

- Davis, Alan M. 1993. *Software Requirements: Objects, Functions, and States*. Upper Saddle River, NJ: Prentice-Hall.
- Gottesdiener, Ellen. 2005. *The Software Requirements Memory Jogger*. Salem, NH: Goal/QPC.

CHAPTER 23

State Diagram

I found a house that I was absolutely in love with and was very excited to purchase. I did not have enough cash on hand, so I had to take out a mortgage on the house. Because I was so eager to buy the house, I really did not want to have any issues during the finance process that would get in my way, so I checked in with my mortgage broker every week to determine the status of my loan application. I initially called him to ask, "Did you get all of my paperwork?" The next week I called to ask, "Is the appraisal complete?" followed by, "Did the appraiser find that the house was worth my offer price?" The most pressing status check was, "Did I get approved?" after which came, "Is the bank funding ready for closing?" At each stage, I also asked questions about the process, such as, "What is next?" and "What happens if the house is appraised for less than it needs to be?"

Each time I called my mortgage broker, I was actually checking on the state of my application. When I started the process, it would have been nice to have seen a full life cycle of the loan application so I would know all the stages it would go through and the possible things that could happen before I closed on the house.

The State Diagram is an RML data model that shows the transitions between states of objects in a solution. State Diagrams show the life cycle of an object's states, including any events that cause state changes. They only show valid transitions, the events that triggered the transitions, and the visual flow of the transitions.

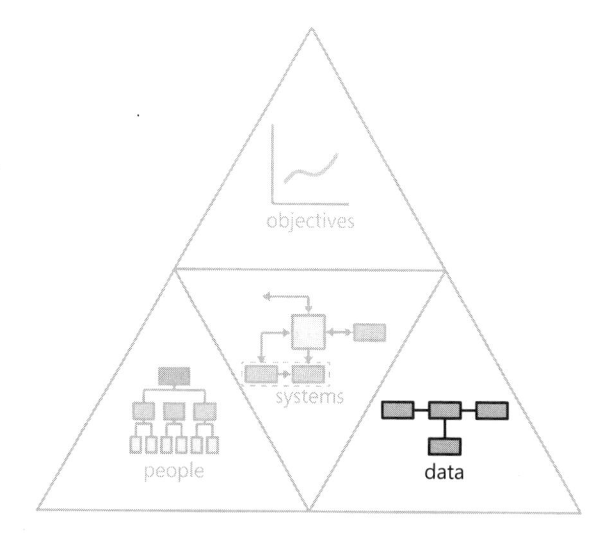

State Diagrams are better for visualizing transitions than State Tables (covered in Chapter 22, "State Table"), which are better for ensuring that you evaluate every possible transition. However, both models can be used together for capturing complete requirements. If you have a lot of transitions, and specifically transitions that loop back to previous states, then a State Diagram is much easier to read than a State Table.

State models were introduced in the State Tables chapter, which showed how these models can be used to discover requirements directly and how they can help you identify gaps in other models. There is significant overlap between State Tables and State Diagrams, particularly with creating and using them; therefore, these details will not be repeated in this chapter. For more information, refer back to the State Table chapter.

State Diagram Template

A State Diagram contains circles, transition arrows between states, and labels on the transitions. The elements are shown in Table 23-1.

TABLE 23-1 State Diagram Elements

Element	Description
State	A stage of a business data object's life cycle. The label in the circle is the name of the state.
Start State	The initial state that a business data object exists in prior to any transition events. This element is optional.
End State	The final state that a business data object exists in. The object cannot be affected by any events after it is in this state. This element is optional.
Transition Event	An object's movement from one state to another. The label indicates the event or condition that caused the transition to occur.

Transitions are shown by using a unidirectional arrow connecting one state to another to show the flow from the first state to the second state. Figure 23-1 illustrates the movement from one state to another. State 1 and State 2 are two different states, and the transition event triggers a valid transition from State 1 to State 2, but not vice versa.

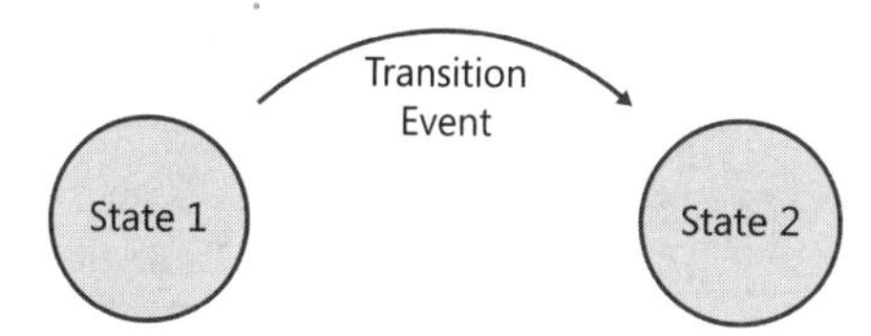

FIGURE 23-1 State transition.

Notice that the start state and end state have distinct symbols, separate from the standard state symbols. The start state element is simply an indicator to the reader where an object begins its life cycle. You do not have to include start states, but they can help with readability. A start state is one in which an object begins its life cycle, but it can also be transitioned to from other states if an object comes back to the start state in its life cycle. End states, by definition, are states at which the object comes to rest and never leaves again. There can be more than one end state if an object has more than one end to its life cycle. Though it is less common, you can have a State Diagram with no end states, if the object never reaches a final state. Figure 23-2 shows a State Diagram template, though you can have as many states as needed.

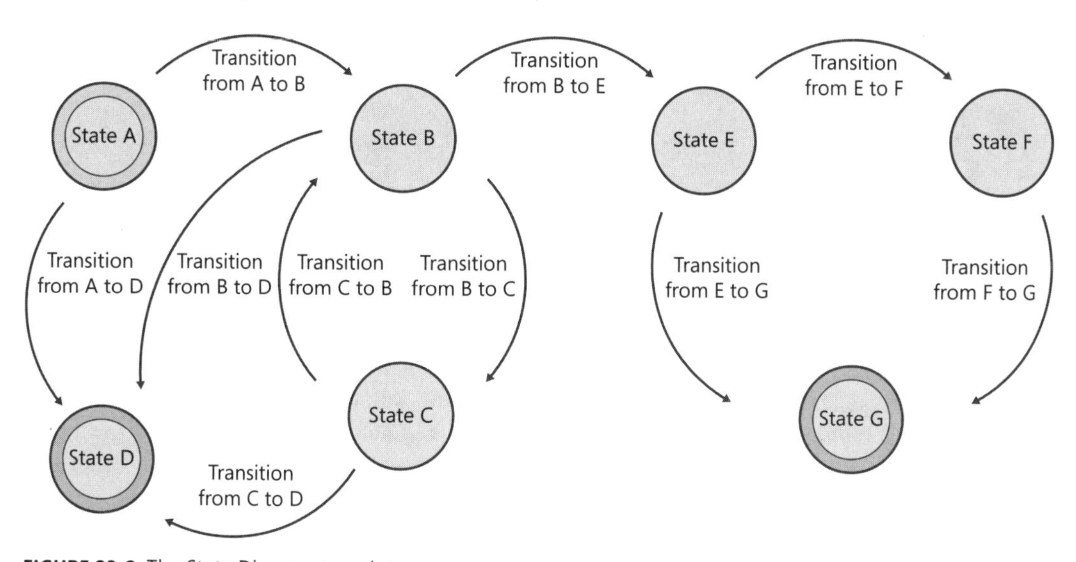

FIGURE 23-2 The State Diagram template.

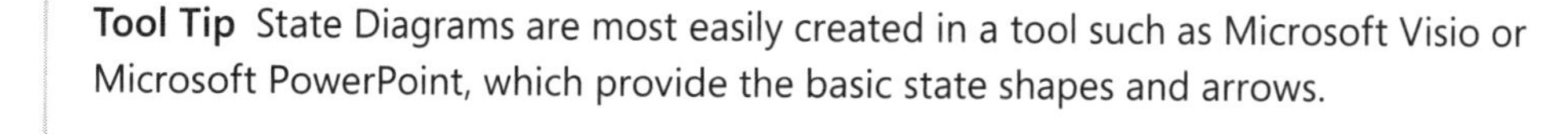

Tool Tip State Diagrams are most easily created in a tool such as Microsoft Visio or Microsoft PowerPoint, which provide the basic state shapes and arrows.

Example

This chapter uses the same loan application system project example that was used in the State Table chapter. The State Table shown in Figure 23-3 is the same loan application object State Table from Chapter 22.

		Target State							
		Prequalified	Submitted	Processing	Underwriting	Set to Close	Closing	Funding	Non-close
Initial State	Prequalified	no	Property address entered	no	no	no	no	no	Prequalification denied
	Submitted	no	no	Application is submitted	Application is sent to underwriting	no	no	no	Application denied
	Processing	no	no	no	Application is sent to underwriting	Application is sent to underwriting and closing simultaneously	no	no	Application denied
	Underwriting	no	no	no	no	Underwriting approved	no	no	Underwriting denied
	Set to Close	no	no	Underwriting process suspended	no	no	Closing date set	Funding number assigned	Closing canceled
	Closing	no	no	An application field needs to be modified	no	no	no	Funding number assigned	Closing canceled
	Funding	no	no	no	no	no	no	no	no
	Non-close	no	no	no	no	no	no	no	no

FIGURE 23-3 The State Table example from Chapter 22.

Although the State Table for the loan application allows you to consider every possible transition to decide if it is valid, the State Diagram allows you to see the flow of the loan application through the states. For example, Figure 23-4 tells you that every application starts in a prequalified state and can move into only a state of "submitted" or "non-close" if it is denied. Also, you can easily see that "funding" and "non-close" are end states that all loan applications flow to eventually and never leave.

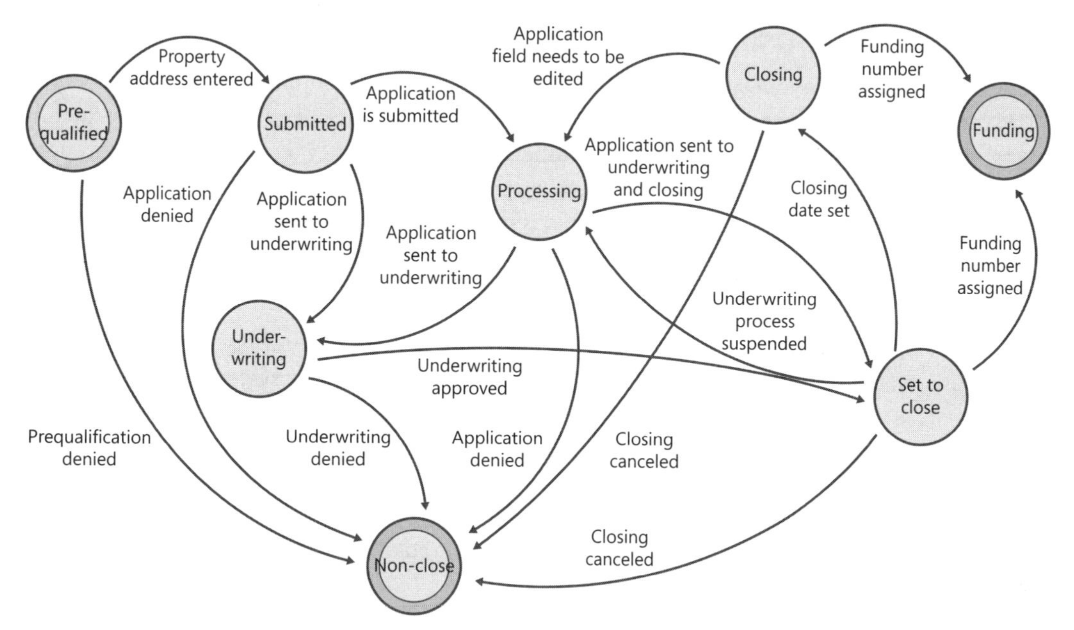

FIGURE 23-4 A State Diagram example.

Creating State Diagrams

To create a State Diagram for a business data object, identify the business data object, identify the states, and identify the transitions, as shown in Figure 23-5. Start by listing all states for the object, and then add arrows to indicate which specific transitions are allowed. If you are starting with a State Table, the steps are very simple to execute. A key difference between State Tables and State Diagrams is that transitions between states that are not allowed are simply not shown in State Diagrams, whereas in State Tables, they are explicitly labeled as "no."

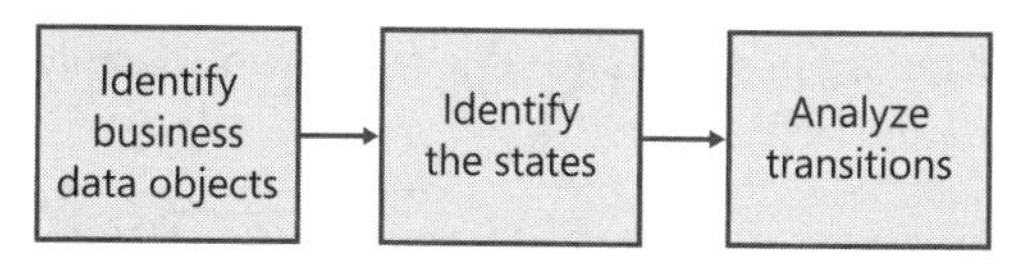

FIGURE 23-5 The process for creating a State Diagram.

Identify the Business Data Objects

First, you need to decide what business data objects need State Diagrams. This subject was described in the State Tables chapter in detail. Any object that has a State Table is a candidate for a State Diagram as well. It is very important to create both models if there are a lot of transitions or types of transitions that make the State Table hard to read. A State Diagram is necessary if you want to understand the flow of an object through states, because that is difficult to visualize from a State Table. State Tables are excellent for looking at individual transitions from or to a particular state. They are not good for looking at multiple transition steps; a State Diagram is better for that.

As a reminder, you can create a State Diagram for more than one field or business data object, because multiple objects can change state and affect the behavior of a system as a group.

Identify the States

State Diagrams are very easy models to create after a State Table exists for the object. Even if you don't create a State Table first, you can just identify all possible states for your identified business data object, considering models such as Process Flows to look for state changes. It's still appropriate to follow the same steps as for a State Table to name the states. If there is a State Table, all of the states in the grid are also states to include in the State Diagram. After the states have been identified, you should put them into the appropriate circles on the diagram, with the focus on just putting them on paper and not worrying about how to order them initially. Remember to label the states consistently; state names are typically adjectives that describe the object.

If you are including the states of more than one business data object in your State Diagram or you have multiple fields on a single object, you need to show every permutation of every state of each object or field. The state labels on the diagram must include the combination of states of those objects. For example, say you have two business data objects, a user and a cart. Each has two states, logged on/anonymous and valid/invalid, respectively. You can label the states in a user/cart format: logged on/valid, logged on/invalid, anonymous/valid, and anonymous/invalid.

Indicate the starting and ending states with the appropriate shapes. Usually, the first state in a State Table is the starting state, and the last state listed is the end state. End states are also easily identified as rows in a State Table that have no transitions in them.

After you have the states in circles in the diagram, try to order the states roughly in the order they occur, with start states on the left and end states on the right. You might want to move them around after you have added transitions.

Analyze the Transitions

It is usually best to identify the transitions in a State Table and then simply add them to your State Diagram. In your State Table, for every cell that has a transition event, draw an arrow from the circle containing the state listed in the row to the circle containing the state listed in the column, and label the arrow with the transition event from the cell. Figure 23-6 shows one example from the loan application object. In the State Table, the cell that contains "closing date set," is at the intersection of the row with the "set to close" state and the "closing" column. Based on this, you draw a transition arrow from "set to close" to "closing" in the State Diagram. Label the transition arrow "Closing date set" to indicate what event causes the transition.

	Target State					
Initial State	Prequalified	Submitted	Processing	Underwriting	Set to Close	Closing
Prequalified	no	Property address entered	no	no	no	no
Submitted	no	no	Application is submitted	Application is sent to underwriting	no	no
Processing	no	no	no	Application is sent to underwriting	Application is sent to underwriting and closing simultaneously	no
Underwriting	no	no	no	no	Underwriting approved	no
Set to Close	no	no	Underwriting process suspended	no	no	Closing date set

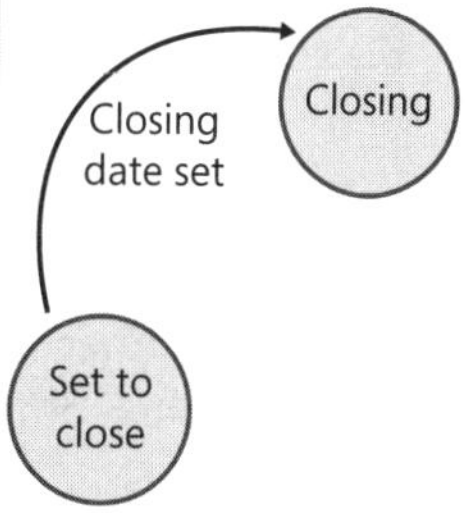

FIGURE 23-6 Using a State Table to label transitions in a State Diagram.

If there are no transitions already identified, follow the same process as described in the State Tables chapter (see the "Analyze the Transitions" section in Chapter 22). As with State Tables, for each state, you must individually consider whether the object can transition to each of the other states, and if so, draw the transition arrow. It can be more difficult to keep track of which transitions you have considered in a State Diagram than in a State Table.

One challenge in creating State Diagrams is trying to get all the shapes and transition lines to cleanly fit on the page so they are readable. As in the example, there will be times that lines have to cross if you have many transitions back and forth between states.

Using State Diagrams

A State Diagram is used to visually show complex state transitions in a solution. State Diagrams are valuable because they show a sequential flow of transitions that is hard to see in a State Table. They are less useful for ensuring that all state transitions are identified. State Tables are great for analyzing the set of all transitions from or to a particular state, but they are not very good for analyzing sequences of transitions through multiple states.

Visualizing Flow Between States

State Diagrams are helpful when you need to see how an object moves between multiple states. The State Diagram in the example visually shows these types of statements:

1. An application moves from "prequalified" to "submitted" when the property address is entered.
2. An application moves from "prequalified" to "non-closed" when the prequalification is denied.
3. An application moves from "submitted" to "processing" when the user actually submits the application.

It is far more challenging to read the text than it is to view the information in the model. Additionally, it is virtually impossible to read this list and understand how an object flows between states in order. Further, if you want to look at a particular state and see how to get to a state that requires going through other states, it is easier to see this in a State Diagram.

Though it contains mostly the same information as a State Table, a State Diagram is easier to read because it visually shows the full life cycle of an object, it only shows valid transitions, and the transition events and conditions are labeled directly on the transitions. Because State Diagrams are more visual, business stakeholders might find them easier to read than State Tables. Development and testing teams can use them as well, though they might also like the State Table to have the complete set of transitions identified as valid or invalid.

Driving Completeness

Although State Diagrams are not very good for ensuring that you have considered every possible transition, they are good for ensuring that the life cycle of the business data object matches how the business stakeholders think about the object. Analyzing a State Diagram is like looking at the forest, whereas analyzing the State Table is like looking at the trees.

Deriving Requirements

Identifying requirements from State Diagrams is the same as for State Tables, so that information will not be repeated here.

When to Use

As mentioned in the previous chapter, it's often appropriate to use both State Tables and State Diagrams. Table 23-2 is included again as a reminder of when you should use each of these models.

TABLE 23-2 Differences Between a State Table and a State Diagram

Model	Use
State Table	Use when you want to make sure that you consider every state and possible transition.
State Diagram	Use when you are planning to leave out non-transitions and focus on visualizing the sequence of allowed transitions.

You can opt to use only a State Diagram if you have just a few states (probably no more than three) and believe you can ensure completeness without a State Table. Similarly, you can use a State Diagram without a State Table if your object moves sequentially from one state to only one other state and there are few cases in which it loops back to previous states. For example, a subway might move from "stationary" to "in transit" to "slowing" and repeat the life cycle—this would be easy to model in a State Diagram without a State Table. But most commonly, you would use a State Diagram to supplement a State Table when you have transitions that loop back into previous states, so that you can see those more easily than in the grid format.

When Not to Use

Solutions without any business data objects that go through state transitions are uncommon. However, if you use a State Table to identify the states and do not need to visually show the transitions to the business, then you can avoid creating a State Diagram.

Common Mistakes

The following represent the most common mistakes we have seen with State Diagrams.

States That Are Not States

As with State Tables, sometimes the states in State Diagrams are not actually states. The states might be actions or transition events or a mix of dissimilar things, which makes the diagram hard to complete and understand.

Missing States and Transitions

If you did not create a State Table before the State Diagram, it is very hard to know that you have identified all of the possible states and the transitions between them.

Related Models

State Diagrams are more commonly used than State Tables. They are often referred to by different names, such as statecharts (Gottesdiener 2002) or state transition diagrams (Wiegers 2003).

The following list briefly describes the most important models that influence or are enhanced by State Diagrams. These models are related to State Diagrams in a similar manner as they are to State Tables; additional details about those relationships are included in Chapter 22. Chapter 26, "Using Models Together," contains a more thorough discussion about all related models.

- **Business Data Diagrams (BDDs)** These are used to identify the objects that should be considered for analyzing states in a State Diagram.
- **State Tables** These show the state transitions in a grid representation, which is better for identifying all the possible transitions before making a State Diagram.
- **Process Flows, System Flows, and Use Cases** These are used to help look for events that trigger transitions. Conversely, State Diagram transition events can be used to ensure that there are no gaps in these models.
- **Display-Action-Response (DAR) models** These use the states in State Diagrams as possible preconditions for user interface display and behavior.
- **Data Dictionaries** For the business data objects represented in State Tables, these contain the fields indicating the state of the objects.
- **Report Tables** The need for a Report Table might be triggered by a State Diagram because it is useful to see a full report on the object by state.

Exercise

The following exercise is intended to help you to gain a better understanding of how to use this model. The exercise is open ended, and therefore the answer you come up with could be substantially different than the answer that we have provided. There are potentially many correct solutions. The answer provides an explanation of how we arrived at our solution. You will gain the most out of the exercise by attempting to do it yourself before looking at the solution. The answers for the exercises can be found in Appendix C.

Instructions

Prepare a draft State Diagram by using the State Table you created in the Chapter 22 example.

Scenario

You are helping to create an eStore to sell flamingos and other lawn decorations. After a user browses the site for products, he adds his selections to his cart. After reviewing the cart and finalizing any updates, the user decides to proceed through the checkout process to purchase the items in the cart. Pricing is finalized, and then the system captures the checkout information from the user, such as shipping and payment details. Finally, the order is submitted to the order system, where it is assembled and shipped to the user.

Hint: If you completed the State Table in the previous chapter's example, use that State Table to create the State Diagram directly. If not, you can use the State Table shown in Figure 23-7.

Initial State \ Target State	Drafted	Finalized	Priced	Completed	Confirmed	Assembled	Shipped	Received
Drafted	no	Ready to checkout	no	no	no	no	no	no
Finalized	no	no	Taxes and discounts calculated	no	no	no	no	no
Priced	Edits made	no	no	Shipping and pricing info captured	no	no	no	no
Completed	Edits made	no	no	no	Order purchased	no	no	no
Confirmed	Factory cannot complete	no	no	no	no	Factory built	no	no
Assembled	no	no	no	no	no	no	Factory shipped	no
Shipped	no	no	no	no	no	no	no	Order arrived
Received	no	no	no	no	no	no	no	no

FIGURE 23-7 The State Table for the exercise.

Additional Resources

- Section 4.10 of the *Software Requirements Memory Jogger* contains a summary of State Diagrams (Gottesdiener 2005).
- Chapter 2 of *Requirements By Collaboration* has an overview of statecharts (Gottesdiener 2002).
- In Chapter 19 of *More About Software Requirements,* Wiegers talks about how State Diagrams are used (Wiegers 2006).
- *Software Requirements* has a summary of State Diagrams and a couple of examples (Wiegers 2003).
- *Applying UML and Patterns: An Introduction to Object-Oriented Analysis and Design and the Unified Process* has an introduction to statechart diagrams (Larman 2004).

References

- Gottesdiener, Ellen. 2002. *Requirements by Collaboration: Workshops for Defining Needs*. Boston, MA: Addison-Wesley.
- Gottesdiener, Ellen. 2005. *The Software Requirements Memory Jogger*. Salem, NH: Goal/QPC.
- Larman, Craig. 2004. *Applying UML and Patterns: An Introduction to Object-Oriented Analysis and Design and the Unified Process*. Upper Saddle River, NJ: Prentice Hall.
- Wiegers, Karl E. 2006. *More About Software Requirements: Thorny Issues and Practical Advice*. Redmond, WA: Microsoft Press.
- Wiegers, Karl E. 2003. *Software Requirements, Second Edition*. Redmond, WA: Microsoft Press.

CHAPTER 24

Report Table

Each month, I get a bill from the utility company, which charges me for gas, electricity, and water. When the Texas temperatures climb above 100°F, we end up using a lot more water to keep our landscaping alive and electricity to keep our house cool. To help mitigate the costs, I read our house's electricity and water meters and write down our usage every day. I create a running log and graph it to help my family understand how their behavior affects how much we spend for utilities. The log includes kilowatt hours of electricity and gallons of water, as well as a conversion to dollars spent based on our utility prices. With this information, we can make daily decisions to turn off lights and appliances and to water the yard less often.

In a software solution, all reports exist to support decisions by the users or other stakeholders. The Report Table is an RML data model that provides a structured way to capture all of the information needed to implement a report, including the data to be displayed, the output format, drilldown views, and requirements for manipulation of and interaction with report data. The Report Table describes the requirements for both the main view of a report and any layers that show additional drilldown views. Although Report Tables are suited to traditional reports, they are also useful for capturing requirements for any structured display of information that contains many data fields that need to be sorted, grouped, filtered, and/or aggregated.

Most importantly, Report Tables capture the decisions that users make when they use the reports, which first and foremost helps determine why the report is actually needed. This information can help drive the report requirements to the most important set of fields, interactions, and format in order to facilitate such decisions. Report Tables can help stakeholders understand and visualize the reports they are requesting. This assists the business in reviewing report requirements and is also helpful during prioritization, when it might turn out that some of the reports specified are actually slight variations of other reports that already exist.

Reports exist for many reasons, some of which are not always obvious. For example, some reports are produced day after day and don't seem to support any decisions, but at some point, a particular value might get out of range, triggering a decision. Similarly, some reports are produced for compliance purposes, and a reasonable argument can be made that from the point of the view of the organization, no decisions are being made from those reports. However, there are likely to be outside parties that will make decisions based on those reports. Finally, there might be reports for which you determine that no decisions at all are made. In these cases, you should evaluate whether the report really needs to exist before you create a Report Table for it.

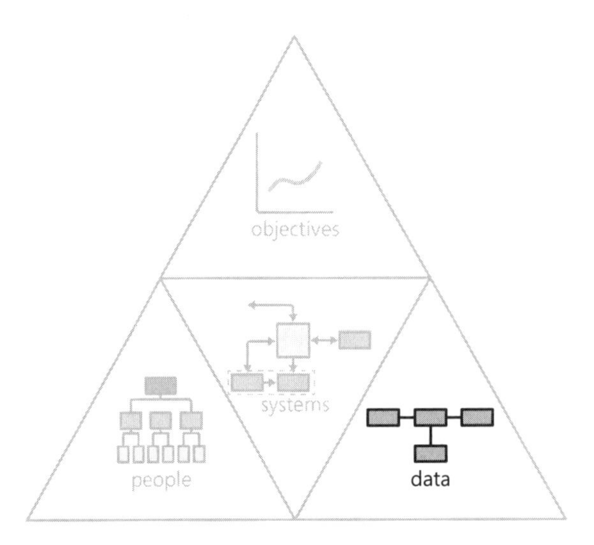

Report Table Template

Figure 24-1 and Figure 24-2 make up a Report Table template. (We split the template into two images for readability, but the template is one table.) The template contains descriptions for each of the model's elements. When you present this model to the stakeholders, it is often helpful to include the template with these descriptions as a key in the requirements document, so they understand the meaning of each Report Table element. In addition to the Report Table, you should include a sample of the report being specified to help stakeholders and developers visualize the final report.

Notice how the overall template is split: the elements that describe the report as a whole are at the top (in this chapter, they are in Figure 24-1, and the elements that describe the fields displayed in the report are at the bottom (in Figure 24-2). The columns show either the main view of the report or additional layers from drilldowns on the report. The template shows the Report Table elements as rows with element descriptions in the second column, where the values for the main view of the report would actually go. In actual Report Tables, you can also have additional columns to handle layers, as shown in the example in the next section.

Tool Tip Microsoft Excel is often the best tool in which to create Report Tables, but they can also be created in Microsoft Word or Microsoft PowerPoint.

	Element	Description
Top-Level Elements	**Unique ID**	Unique identifier of the Report Table
	Name	Simple report name, should be unique from other report names. For drill down layers, this is the layer name.
	Description	A short summary of the report for context.
	Decisions Made from Report	The business decisions that are made using the information in the report. Link to other models the context for the decisions (Process Flows).
	Objective	The Business Objectives Models or KPI Models that this report supports.
	Priority	The priority to implement this report. Priorities should be expressed as sequential numbers to order all reports against one another. The priority ordering should be based on the value the report contributes to meeting the business objective or KPI.
	Functional Area	The business processes or areas that use the report.
	Related Reports	List of any other reports that have similar data.
	Report Owner	Business user(s) who own approval of the report requirements.
	Report Users	Business user(s) who run or use report to make decisions.
	Trigger	What triggers report to run. If reports are scheduled, include the schedule.
	Frequency	How often the report is generated and accessed.
	Latency	How quickly report is delivered to users in relation to being requested. How current the data needs to be when run.
	Transaction Volume	How many transactions are pushed into the repository feeding the report.
	Data Volume	On average, how much data is expected to be read each time the report is accessed. You might define the maximum data allowed to be returned. Express the data volume in business terms such as number of orders rather than kilobytes or some other technical measure.
	Security	Security on the report or fields that varies from security specified on the fields in the Data Dictionary.
	Persistence	Expected persistence in report settings between report sessions.
	Visual Format	How the report is visually displayed, including type of graph, axes, rows, or column information.
	Delivery Format	How the report is delivered to users for viewing, and any related functionality. This includes whether it is displayed in an application, emailable, emailed to the user, printable, or viewable on mobile devices.
	Interactivity	Functionality within a report that allows the user to change views or other aspects of the data being displayed. This includes the ability to expand and collapse parts of the report, and hyperlinks that take you out of the report to a data entry screen. For complex interactions, link to DAR models.
	Drilldowns	Links to other related reports or, more commonly, layers of this report with expanded data. This element explains what the user can drill down on and which view he is taken to.

FIGURE 24-1 The Report Table template top-level elements, describing the report as a whole.

	Element	Description
Field Elements	**Filtered By**	The data fields that are used to filter out certain sets of data in the report (use the *<object.field>* notation). If the filter criteria is preset, state the criteria. If the filter criteria are determined by the system, state the rules for determining the criteria. If the filter criteria are user inputs, state the fields the user can select from. Specify whether the field filters are mandatory or optional. Specify whether there is a default value (or if the default is to have no filter for optional filters).
	Grouped By	Logical groupings of data into separate sections within the report by data fields (use the *<object.field>* notation). You can specify a hierarchy of grouping here. If the grouping criteria are preset, state the fields to group by. If the grouping criteria are user inputs, specify the fields the user can select from. Groupings are applied after filters. Might need to define how groupings interact with filters, including expected behavior if the filtered data set has no groupings.
	Sorted By	The data fields that are used to sort the data in the report (use the *<object.field>* notation). Specify if the user can choose the sort order and the default sort order, if there is one. If user can sort on any field displayed, say that. Sort order needs to specify whether to sort ascending or descending. You can specify a hierarchy of sorts to be applied. Sort is applied after filters and groupings. Note if the user can sort by more than one property. Might need to define how sortings interact with groupings.
	User Input Parameters	Fields that the user can define to generate the report different than filtering, grouping, and sorting (use the *<object.field>* notation if it is a field).
	Group Calculation	Data fields that are aggregated and on which a calculation applied. This includes counting, average, min, max, means, and std devs. Specify the grouping that the calculation applies to. This will be specified as a calculation applied by some unit of aggregation.
	Calculated Fields	Individual fields that have a calculation applied outside of the data prior to being displayed in the report. Format to specify it will follow <Calculated Field> = [Formula] where [Formula] should use *<object.field>* notation. Specify any rounding or display formats.
	Displayed Fields	All fields displayed in the report (use the *<object.field>* notation). Specify any formatting to apply to the information displayed and, if applicable, a rounding method (round to 2 decimals, commas in large numbers). If a report has a large number of fields, you can reference the Data Dictionary and specify in that model which fields to display.
	What If	Specifies which data fields are used for "what if" scenarios if forecasting is included in the report and how they impact the report. Specify any forecasting assumptions. This could include calculations, including how to handle rounding or zero denominators.

FIGURE 24-2 The Report Table template field elements.

Example

The report in Figure 24-3 is from a time and expense application. The report provides information about revenue earned and forecasted based on actual and projected time spent on projects. This sample report only shows a few of the rows and columns that would exist in the actual report.

Company Revenue							
		3/4/12	3/11/12	3/18/12	3/25/12	4/1/12	**Grand Total**
Client Name	Project	Actual	Actual	Actual	Projected	Projected	
Adventure Works	AW Q1 2012						**$24,156**
Adventure Works Total							**$24,156**
Alpine Ski House	Ski House Training	$175		$25,825			**$26,000**
Alpine Ski House Total		$175		$25,825			**$26,000**
Lucerne Publishing	Lucerne Marketing	$4,200	$3,623	$3,675	$3,360	$2,520	**$44,468**
Lucerne Publishing Total		$4,200	$3,623	$3,675	$3,360	$2,520	**$44,468**
Southridge Video	Southridge Marketing						**$17,545**
	Southridge Advertising	$6,126	$6,090	$5,873	$6,670	$5,510	**$63,111**
Southridge Video Total		$6,126	$6,090	$5,873	$6,670	$5,510	**$80,656**
Wingtip Toys	Wingtip Advertising						**$8,415**
	Wingtip Marketing						**$38,435**
	Forcasted Project					$12,203	**$120,000**
	Training Planning	$6,830	$10,456				**$17,286**
	Wingtip Training			$3,389	$12,330	$12,330	**$28,049**
	Wingtip Followup						**$102,600**
Wingtip Toys Total		$6,830	$10,456	$3,389	$12,330	$24,533	**$314,784**
Woodgrove Bank	Woodgrove Advertising		$95	$95			**$189**
Woodgrove Bank Total			$95	$95			**$189**
Grand Total		**$55,924**	**$66,393**	**$90,713**	**$152,401**	**$83,404**	**$1,659,142**

FIGURE 24-3 A report sample.

The top-level Report Table elements are shown in Figure 24-4, and the field elements are shown in Figure 24-5.

	Element	Example	Example Layer
Top-Level Elements	Unique ID	REP010	REP010_1
	Name	Forecasted Revenue	Project Revenue
	Description	Report shows forecasted revenue values by customer by project for a specified time period and time period unit	Report shows forecasted revenue values for a specific project for a specified time period and time unit. It is used when more information is needed about a specific project's actual and forecasted revenue.
	Decisions Made from Report	How many consultants should we assign to each project? Does the company need to hire more consultants?	How many consultants should we assign to this project?
	Objective	Business Objective 2 - Increase Revenue	N/A
	Priority	3 of 20 (Strategic initiative to increase revenue). See Objective Chain 010.	14 of 20 (Significantly less important than seeing all projects since it is accessed less often). See Objective Chain 010.
	Functional Area	Professional services	N/A
	Related Reports	Sales Forecast, Employee Utilization	N/A
	Report Owner	Services Manager	N/A
	Report Users	Services Manager, VP of Sales, VP of HR	Services Manager
	Trigger	Services Manager is prepping for weekly staff planning meeting	Services Manager is making a real-time staffing decision
	Frequency	Weekly	Weekly to Monthly
	Latency	Delivered on demand (within 30 seconds of requesting). Data should be real time.	N/A
	Transaction Volume	Each week 10,000 transactions about time spent are stored. 10 sales forecast transactions are entered or updated weekly.	N/A
	Data Volume	On average, the report returns 5,000 transactions	On average, the report returns 100 transactions.
	Security	Viewable by all employees of the company	N/A
	Persistence	All settings are saved between report executions by any user (User A sees User B's settings if User B last ran it)	N/A
	Visual Format	Matrix with Customers and Projects as rows, Time units as columns. Revenue amounts in cells. Bar chart format shows Customer and Projects in different colors on x-axis grouped by time unit and revenue on y-axis.	Matrix with Project as row, Revenue as a row, Resources as a row, Time units as columns. Revenue amounts in revenue cells. Resource numbers (integers) in resource cells.
	Delivery Format	Displayed in application and emailable as an Excel file. Within the application, the user can scroll to see the data that does not fit on the screen.	N/A
	Interactivity	The customer names can be expanded and collapsed to show or hide the projects by customer. Default to expanded.	N/A
	Drilldowns	User clicks on project name and is taken to the Project Revenue layer.	N/A

FIGURE 24-4 An example of the top-level elements of a Report Table.

	Element	Example	Example Layer
Field Elements	**Filtered By**	User can filter date range (default to <project.end date> within the last 12 months and through the next 3 months). User can choose to filter by customer name (select from all possible <customer.name> values). User can choose to filter by <project.status> (Actual, Forecasted, or Both. Default to Both)	System filters to <project.name> selected for drilldown. User can filter date range (default to <project.end date> within the last 12 months and through the next 3 months). User can choose to filter by <project.status> (Actual, Forecasted, or Both. Default to Both)
	Grouped By	Revenue grouped by <customer.name>, then by <project.name>, and by user input time unit.	Revenue and resources grouped by user input time unit.
	Sorted By	Sort by <customer.name>, then <project.name> alphabetically. Sort time unit chronologically.	Sort time unit chronologically.
	User Input Parameters	User can specify time unit (Year, Quarter, Month, Week. Default to Week)	N/A
	Group Calculation	Sum <project.revenue> per time unit by customer, by project, and with no filter (all revenue) for the data range specified in the filter. Round sums to the nearest dollar.	Sum <project.revenue> per time unit for the data range specified in the filter. Round sums to the nearest dollar. Count <project.resource> per time unit for the data range specified in the filter.
	Calculated Fields	N/A	N/A
	Displayed Fields	<customer.name> <project.name> <project.revenue> sum of revenue as defined in group calculations Display all currency as USD with 0 decimal places and commas for large numbers	<customer.name> <project.name> <project.revenue> sum of revenue as defined in group calculations count of <project.resource> defined in group calculations Display all currency as USD with 0 decimal places and commas for large numbers
	What If	Forecast revenue for future date ranges: forecasted total revenue = 80% x <project.remaining revenue>. <project.remaining revenue> = <project.total revenue> - <project.earned revenue>. Display forecasted revenue as total forecasted revenue / time unit.	N/A

FIGURE 24-5 An example of the field elements of a Report Table.

Creating Report Tables

The steps for creating a Report Table are shown in Figure 24-6.

FIGURE 24-6 The process for creating a Report Table.

Identify Reports

First, you need to gather all of the existing reports that are manually or automatically generated. Process Flows (see Chapter 9, "Process Flow") are helpful for identifying reports, because manual decision points will often require the user to look at a report before making a decision. In addition, Business Data Diagrams (BDDs) (see Chapter 19, "Business Data Diagram") and Data Dictionaries (see Chapter 21, "Data Dictionary") can be used to identify the business data objects and fields that need to be used in reports. You should also interview the stakeholders to determine what decisions they need to make that require reports.

Prioritize Reports

To prioritize the reports, rank them based on the decisions the stakeholders are trying to make. You can determine the value of the decisions by looking at the value of the process supported by the report and how those processes contribute to meeting the business objectives or key performance indicators (KPIs). Also, in many solutions, a system log will track how often users have requested or used a particular report; this can be a guide to how important a report really is.

Complete Report Table Elements

Each type of information in a Report Table is an element. For example, Title, Description, and Displayed Fields are all examples of elements of the Report Table. For each required report, create a Report Table, including a sample or mockup. You should create the reports in order of priority.

If there are existing versions of the report, use these as a starting point to reverse-engineer the report in the new solution. If the report is new with no previously existing version, ask stakeholders about the high-level categories of information the report users need to make the decision (use the BDD or Data Dictionary as a prompt), then drill down to field-level requirements. The Report Table can be used as a prompt when eliciting the various elements of a report. Providing a sample of the report can help stakeholders identify missing fields.

As you complete the Report Table, you should fill in every element of the table. If an element is not applicable, just put "N/A" rather than leaving it blank.

Report Table Top-Level Elements

The report name and description are at the top of the template to quickly provide context for the report. You also should include a unique ID so you can reference this report from other models. The top-level elements are explained in the template and most are self-explanatory. Some of the more challenging elements are described here.

Decisions Made from Report One of the most important elements of the Report Table is Decisions Made from Report. This element identifies the reason for the report's existence and should never be left blank under any circumstance. Often, stakeholders become focused on creating reports that have the ability to slice and dice data in every possible way without fully understanding the decisions that the information is supporting. This creates significant additional development effort without corresponding value. The Decisions Made from Report element can be used during elicitation to determine whether a stakeholder is providing requirements for a report that actually adds business value. In the process of elicitation, it might turn out that a report is not needed because no decision will be made from it, that the same decision could be made from another report that already exists, or that only a much smaller subset of the data is needed to make the decision. It is also possible that a single report can support many decisions. In the event that many reports might be required in order to make a decision, it might make sense to combine those reports to make it easier for the user to identify the correct decision. Asking "What decisions do you make from this report?" isn't really sufficient to get at the real answer—you might have to dig and try to understand how the report is related to the decision-making process (a Process Flow is helpful). Examples of questions used to elicit the decision include:

- How does this report help you make the decision?
- This report seems to contain a lot of the same information as an existing report—why can't the existing report be used to make the decision?
- How would it affect you if you did not have this report?
- Where in the business process do you use this report?

Interactivity and drilldowns Reports are often interactive in that you can manipulate controls on the report that change the way the report displays. Further, you can often drill down on the data. The template includes an element specifically to address what you can drill down on in a report and where it takes you. The user might go from this report to another report or to another layer of the same report. If the user goes to another layer, the layer can be described in the same Report Table with another column. You can include as many layers as needed.

The drilldowns are additional Report Tables that generally use the same data set but that are filtered based on the drilldown the user selected. For example, the top-level report might be a summary of historical closed deals for all sales representatives, with each sales representative's pipeline history being a line on a graph. A manager could determine which sales representatives might be struggling, and then have the ability to select a particular sales representative. The next level might show all historical opportunities for the sales representative with additional information to give the manager a more detailed idea of why deals did not close. Finally, the sales manager might have the capability of selecting a particular opportunity to view every contact the sales representative made to the client, including links to recordings of the actual calls.

Report Table Field Elements

For all data fields you list in the Report Table, you should use the *<object.field>* notation so it is clear exactly which data field is being referenced.

The User Input Parameters element includes any user-defined input to generate the report, other than parameters used in filtering, grouping, and sorting, because those parameters are captured in their respective elements separately.

Among the parameters that constrain the data, filters are applied first. Then the filtered data is grouped according to the Group By parameters. Finally, the data set is sorted within the resulting groups by the Sorted By parameters. Within each of those, you need to clearly explain any default values for the parameters, whether any of the parameters are mandatory or optional, and any hierarchy of groups. Also, be careful to consider and specify behavior about how filtering, grouping, and sorting work together. For example, your user might apply a filter that removes the default parameter value for Group By, so you need to describe how to handle that type of scenario.

Group Calculations describe any calculations performed on groups of data. For example, if you are grouping sales data by country, then region, then by district manager, the group calculations would represent any operations you make on the data as a group, such as counting, sums, standard deviations, averages, commission calculations, or any other types of calculations. The Displayed Fields element is the list of fields that are displayed in the report output. They should be specified by using the *<object.field>* notation.

Calculated Fields are fields that do not exist in the database but that exist only as calculations based on other fields. For example, if a report has fields for revenue and cost of goods sold, then a calculated field could be gross profit, which is calculated in real time as the report is generated, using the equation gross profit = revenue – cost of goods sold.

If your report has more than 7+/-2 data columns to be displayed, instead of listing them in the Displayed Fields element, it might be helpful to reference them in a report column within the Data Dictionary. If you do that, you might find it easier to specify some of the elements in that table instead, including the format or calculations.

Finally, the What If element captures any forecasting scenarios that the stakeholders want to display. You might need to specify additional parameters and values that the users can enter for these scenarios, as well as how the solution should calculate and display the information in the scenario.

Managing Report Scope

In order to prevent scope creep, gather requirements for each element in the Report Table in the context of the decisions made from the report. If a stakeholder asks for a lot of complex filtering and interactivity, ensure that such functionality is actually needed in order to make the decisions that the report facilitates.

Using Report Tables

Report Tables are needed if you are creating reports for your project. They are also helpful if you are creating structured output on a screen, even if it's not called a "report." The structure of Report Tables helps you be thorough when specifying reporting requirements.

Defining the Reports

A Report Table should be created for every report being developed. In addition, Report Tables can be created to capture detailed requirements on any table, grid, or other structured data view that is displayed in the user interface. Report Tables can link to other models such as Process Flows or Use Cases (see Chapter 10, "Use Case") to identify where in the process the users utilize the report. Typically, Report Tables can be used as the detailed requirements, so there is no need to further derive individual requirements statements from the Report Table. The person implementing the report should be able to read the Report Table and design the report without further written requirements. At minimum, he should have enough information to ask questions about how the report should be designed based on the constraints of the report tool he is using.

Checking Completeness and Consistency Against Other Models

Report Tables can also be used to identify new business data objects for BDDs. If a business data object is referred to in a report in order to make a decision, the existing BDDs should be checked to ensure that they include the referenced object. Further, each field that appears in the Report Table should be defined in a Data Dictionary. The Report Table refers to the field by using the *<object.field>* notation. Reports might be used as operations in Roles and Permissions Matrices (see Chapter 11, "Roles and Permissions Matrix") if access to the reports is driven by a role-based security model.

Unlike some of the other data models, it is difficult or impossible to be certain that you have identified all reports. However, if you have reports that map to every manual decision in the Process Flow, then you probably have the most important reports covered. You can create this mapping in a Requirements Mapping Matrix (see Chapter 7, "Requirements Mapping Matrix").

Deriving Requirements

Report Tables typically stand alone; you do not need to write additional requirements. The exception to this is if there are non-functional requirements related to the reports that are not captured in the top-level elements of the report.

When to Use

Report Tables should be used to document all reports, including interactive reports. This includes any screen on which business data object fields are displayed for use in decision making, or are displayed in a structured, aggregated, sorted, filtered, and/or grouped format. If you have a lot of business data object fields being displayed, that is another indication that a Report Table might be useful to organize their layout.

When Not to Use

You should not use Report Tables to capture complex business logic behind the display of information. Further, if your report has complex interactions, you should not use Report Tables to define those interactions. In both cases, you might use Report Tables for the requirements for the report, and supplement it in such cases with models including Process Flows, Decision Trees (see Chapter 17, "Decision Tree"), and Display-Action-Response (DAR) models (see Chapter 15, "Display-Action-Response").

Common Mistakes

The following represent the most common mistakes we have seen with Report Tables.

Not Relating Reports to Decisions Made

By not understanding the decisions made by a report, you cannot be sure that the stakeholders actually need that report. If they do need the report, you cannot be sure that the report has the right data to support a decision.

Documenting Unnecessary Reports

Business stakeholders often think they need hundreds of reports because they have them in an existing system. However, it is unlikely that they could ever use all of the reports that they request. It is important to understand which reports are truly going to be used to make decisions and only develop requirements for those.

Related Models

The following list briefly describes the most important models that influence or are enhanced by Report Tables. Chapter 26, "Using Models Together," contains a more thorough discussion about all related models.

- **Process Flows** These are used to identify where in a process a report is used to make decisions.
- **Use Cases** These are used to identify when a user needs a report during his interactions with the system.
- **Decision Trees** These can be used to identify where in a process a report is used to make decisions. They are also used to model any complex logic used in the information displayed in the report.
- **Business Data Diagrams (BDDs)** These are used to prompt questions about fields or business data objects being reported on.
- **Data Dictionaries** These are used to provide the field definitions for elements in reports.
- **Roles and Permissions Matrices** These are used to define the roles that have permissions to access the reports if the model is a role-based security model.
- **Display-Action-Response (DAR) models** These can be used for highly interactive reports in conjunction with Report Tables.
- **Requirements Mapping Matrices (RMMs)** These might be used to map Report Tables to manual decisions in Process Flows.

Exercise

The following exercise is intended to help you to gain a better understanding of how to use this model. The exercise is open ended, and therefore the answer you come up with could be substantially different than the answer that we have provided. There are potentially many correct solutions. The answer provides an explanation of how we arrived at our solution. You will gain the most out of the exercise by attempting to do it yourself before looking at the solution. The answers for the exercises can be found in Appendix C.

Instructions

Create a Report Table based on the information provided in the scenario.

Scenario

In this project, you are helping to build an eStore to sell flamingos and other lawn decorations, including items such as gnomes, bird baths, and statues. The eStore has helped increase the number of total sales that the company is making; however, inbound customer service calls have also increased, leading to more employees having to work overtime and becoming burned out. As a result, the director of call center operations has been tasked by the general manager with improving employee morale and has pulled you into this effort.

Employee turnover has been quite high, and the business must increase the retention rate to at least 80 percent or risk spending more money on new trainees. The director decides to institute a new retention policy and promote one high-performing customer sales representative (CSR) every quarter. In order to decide which employee should be promoted, the director needs to understand the average call-handling time for each CSR at the call center (average call-handling time is the average amount of time spent on each inbound phone call). The director will make a promotion decision using the average call-handling time report. Only the CSR director or her assistant should have access to the report. The director asks her assistant to design this report and to give her the results on the third Friday of every month.

Call center metrics about time spent on the phone with each customer are kept in a central database at the main office and are automatically populated by the company's internal phone exchange. The director's assistant tells you all of these details and asks you to design a Report Table to hand off to IT for implementation. Figure 24-7 is a mockup of the report.

CSR	Number of Calls per Day	Average Call-Handling Time
⊟CSR 1	**21**	**8.62**
3-1-2012	2	13.50
3-4-2012	1	16.00
3-5-2012	3	7.00
3-9-2012	2	4.50
3-11-2012	1	5.00
3-13-2012	1	13.00
3-19-2012	2	9.00
3-22-2012	3	8.33
3-24-2012	1	4.00
3-25-2012	1	3.00
3-28-2012	1	20.00
3-29-2012	1	7.00
3-30-2012	1	11.00
3-31-2012	1	2.00
⊞CSR 2	**54**	**9.37**
⊞CSR 3	**24**	**11.46**
⊞CSR 4	**15**	**9.60**
⊞CSR 5	**39**	**9.95**
⊞CSR 6	**21**	**8.71**
⊞CSR 7	**21**	**11.95**
⊞CSR 8	**30**	**11.03**
⊞CSR 9	**24**	**9.79**
⊞CSR 10	**18**	**10.56**
⊞CSR 11	**18**	**9.94**
⊞CSR 12	**27**	**11.04**
Grand Total	**312**	**10.13**

FIGURE 24-7 The report mockup for the call center.

PART VI

Models in the Big Picture

CHAPTER 25

Selecting Models for a Project

When I decide to work on a project around my house, I start by selecting the tools to use. I first consider what type of project I'm doing and then consider what step in the overall project I'm working on, so that I can pick the right tool. For example, if I'm cooking, I use tools such as a mixer, measuring spoons, a rolling pin, a frying pan, and a spatula. I can further narrow my tool selection by the type of cooking I'm doing. If I'm baking, I would more likely use a mixer than a frying pan. Finally, I pick the tools I need based on which steps in my cooking project I'm executing. Initially, I use measuring spoons and cups, then I use a mixer, then I might use a spatula or rolling pin, and finally I might use a baking dish and cooling rack near the end.

On the other hand, if my task is to build a bookshelf for the house, I would select different tools than those I use for cooking. I could use a hammer, a screwdriver, a saw, nails, and screws. Similarly, I can further narrow my tool selection at any point based on the step I'm at in the project. Early in the project, I might use a saw to cut the wood, but later I would use the hammer and nails to assemble the bookshelf.

To select tools for projects around my house, I determine what I'm trying to accomplish and then decide which tools best help me meet those goals. There are many RML models, and selecting the right models to use for specifying a solution is similar to selecting tools for home projects. The task can be overwhelming if all you have is a list of models without a framework to help you narrow the list.

This chapter will help you select models for your project based on the project phase you are executing and the project characteristics. For each of these factors, we overlay the model categories to ensure that you consider all types of models.

Selecting Models by Project Phases

Models are a key component of every stage of the software process. It's important not to lose sight of the overall project approach and become bogged down in the minutiae of creating models, but rather to understand how the models fit into the approach to ensure a complete set of requirements during the entire development cycle. Figure 25-1 shows a generic requirements process and the activities that occur within each phase. The phases are envision, plan, develop, launch, and measure. Within each phase there are requirements-based activities. These process phases map to phases in virtually any development approach (such as waterfall, iterative, agile, and custom approaches). The focus is on the activities within the phases rather than how the phases are executed. The key is that no matter what your development approach is, within each phase there are activities that benefit from using requirements models.

Using the appropriate models helps all stakeholders understand the requirements so that nothing important is missed and only the requirements that are important are implemented. The following sections further discuss the role of models in each phase of the requirements process. Although these are described in an order similar to a waterfall approach, they can be applied in any development methodology.

The information from the following sections is summarized in a table in Appendix A, "Quick Lookup Models Grids."

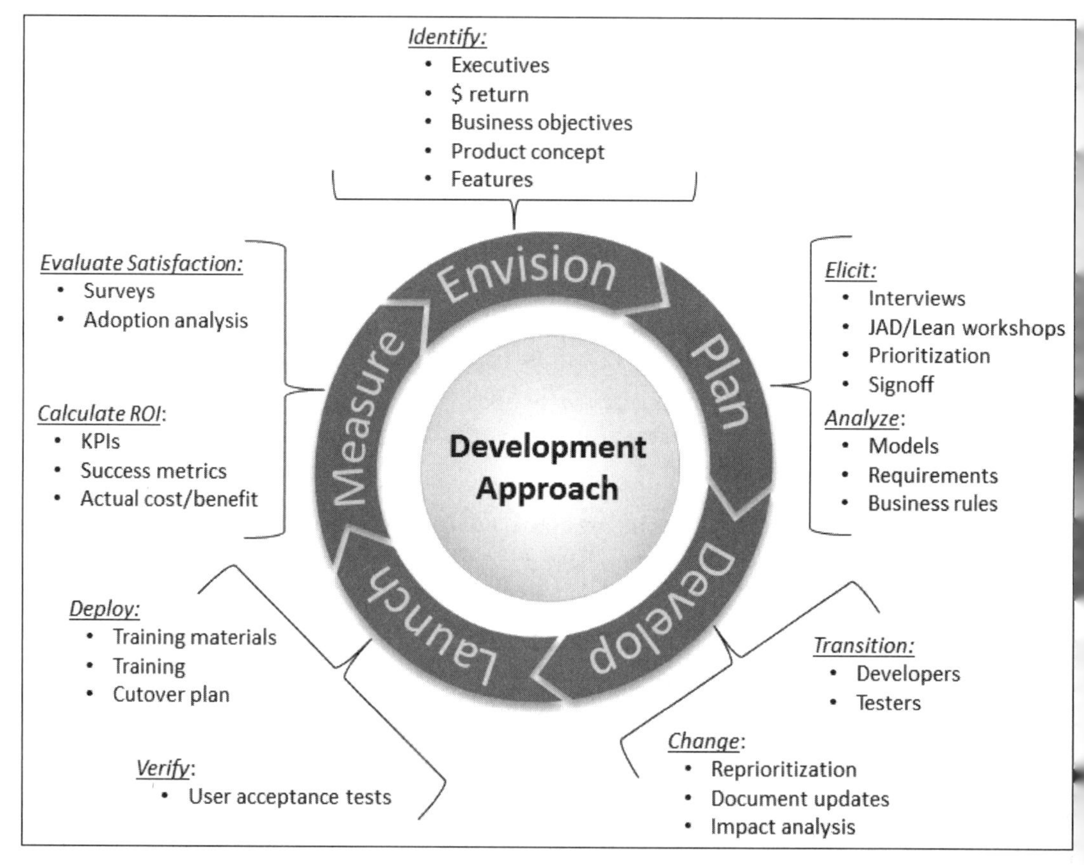

FIGURE 25-1 A requirements process.

Envision Phase

The Envision phase occurs before a project is actually chartered. Executives who own corporate strategy and manage a portfolio, program, or product roadmap have to determine which projects to fund based on the value they add to the organization. This phase determines how the project supports the corporate or program strategy, what value the business stakeholders will receive from it, and what high-level features the stakeholders need to achieve that value.

During the Envision phase, a business analyst helps executives explore the business problems, determine the business objectives that all requirements eventually map back to, develop the business case for the project, and set a broad scope for the project. The business problems and objectives are captured in a Business Objectives Model, and the highest-level features are captured in a Feature Tree. The business objectives enable business analysts to determine the project's priorities, which will be used throughout the entire project to help the team make decisions when cutting scope or when trying to decide which features to develop first.

You should also create initial high-level models such as Org Charts and Ecosystem Maps. Org Charts are a great starting point for creating people models, because they offer the opportunity to consider every single person or role that might affect or use the system. Though Ecosystem Maps do not identify specific requirements, they do identify the interfaces for which to elicit requirements and the systems that might be affected by the project. In addition to models, you should create an issues list to log every outstanding requirements-related unresolved issue or question. If you are not using a requirements management tool, then typical documents that you might produce during this phase might have names such as "business case," "business requirements document," "marketing requirements document," "product backlog," and "vision scope document."

Models in Agile

Many organizations try to depict agile methods as mini-waterfalls. Even the requirements process diagram in Figure 25-1 could be interpreted as a mini-waterfall. However, it should not be interpreted in that way. The diagram is simply intended to classify the activities that a business analyst would perform regardless of the development approach. In a waterfall approach, each phase would require signoffs before the project could enter the next phase. In an agile project, all of the phases could be executed simultaneously within a particular sprint. However, even when you are using an agile approach, at some level (perhaps at the individual story level) you have to figure out the value of the story first (Envision); then the details of the story, such as acceptance criteria (Plan); then your developers build it (Develop), potentially updating the story as you gain a better understanding of the project; and then you test and deploy what you have just built (Launch). Within a sprint these phases might be occurring every single day, simultaneously.

Even when you are using an agile approach, on very large projects with many teams that have to synchronize their work, develop some of the models up front before any development begins. This is the best way to ensure that each team has a shared understanding of the overall business goals and system requirements. Models such as the Business Objectives Model and the Objective Chain help to ensure that all teams really understand the value of the project. Org Charts, Ecosystem Maps, Business Data Diagrams, and Process Flows ensure that all teams have a shared understanding of how users will need to use the system and the environment that they are working in. A product backlog is great for managing the project, but it provides no framework for determining which things need to be in the backlog in the first place. Models can be used to populate the backlog and determine any detailed requirements and business rules within each sprint.

Plan Phase

During the Plan phase, you are trying to determine how the software needs to work so that it will achieve the value expected by the business. By listing out all the requirements, including the functions the software needs, the business rules that influence the functions, and the non-functional qualities, you will create a complete list of requirements that your business stakeholders, developers, and testers can use to build, configure, or test the system to ensure that the business value is achieved. Identify which models are needed based on the characteristics of the project, and define a requirements architecture (described in Chapter 26, "Using Models Together"). Finally, you might select tools to create and store models that support the requirements architecture, and create a requirements plan that outlines when each of the models will be created in relation to the others.

You should test out your requirements architecture and process on a portion of the project, adjusting it as you determine what works best for your organization. Project priorities can change; analysts might find that the choice of models is not sufficiently capturing requirements, or a variety of other reasons can force the team to alter the requirements architecture. In these scenarios, it's important to review the already created requirements and models to ensure that no additional artifacts need to be created or existing ones altered; changes to the requirements architecture often affect prior work.

This phase is where you will do most of the elicitation and analysis to complete models, working from a high level to more detailed models (see Chapter 26 for more about this). You also should derive requirements from models. In addition, you should continue to update your requirements issues list as you determine parts of models that you cannot yet complete.

During this phase, you might create a Key Performance Indicator Model (KPIM) to articulate how the project will improve or at least maintain the throughput of the business. You will also create Objective Chains to determine the scope of the requirements. You should create Business Data Diagrams (BDDs) and Process Flows to define and bound the project scope. The remainder of the models you need on the project will typically be created in this phase.

Further, you can use the Business Objectives Model to prioritize the analysis work you have to complete. If you are not using a requirements management tool, examples of documents that you might create during this phase include business requirements documents, system requirements specifications, software requirements specifications, functional requirements specifications, sprint backlogs, and user stories.

Develop Phase

After the models have been created, validated, and verified, the next step is to ensure that the development and testing teams understand what they need to build. Developers and testers will use models and corresponding requirements and business rules to build code, configure existing systems, and develop test cases. During your model creation, you should have derived requirements for most of the models. This is the phase for which it is most important to have done that step, because developers and testers have an easier time knowing that their job is done when they have a list of functional requirements and business rules that they can use as a "checklist" rather than just a model to build and test from.

During this phase it is important to fully explain the usage of the models to these teams; otherwise, the models might be interpreted and used in a manner for which they were not intended. For example, developers might use only the Use Cases and not look at the requirements if they do not understand how the two fit together. Further, they might look at only the requirements and not the models, missing the important context you set with the models.

It is common for this phase to also include steps for updating models that are now in a "locked" state as changes occur. This means that all changes to requirements and models must be approved and communicated to teams downstream of the business analysts because those teams might have created artifacts using those requirements and models.

During this phase, you should be maintaining your issues list as well as updating all documents and models as necessary. You should be engaged with the developers as they build the solution, and with testers as they ensure that the system is built properly. Your role is to clarify how the software should work, update priorities, and ensure that what is being built works the right way. No matter how well you document the requirements, there will always need to be verbal clarifications, especially as you get into the details of the business rules, usability, and detailed functionality of the system. As you explain the functionality, you will most often be using models to help other team members understand the context. For example, you could use a Process Flow to help the developers understand what the user is trying to accomplish, then use a BDD to explain how the business thinks about the data elements. During the development phase, you will be updating your existing documents and might create documents such as "user acceptance tests" or versions of previous documents tailored to specific development teams.

Launch Phase

During the Launch phase, the business stakeholders confirm that the solution meets their needs. They can use Process Flows and Use Cases to create user acceptance tests to perform this verification. When the system has stabilized to the point where the business evaluates and accepts the solution, it is ready to be deployed. Process Flows, Use Cases, Roles and Permissions Matrices, and Display-Action-Response (DAR) models can be used to create training materials for the new system. Typical documents created during this phase could include training manuals, user guides, help files, and any other materials that will ensure that users have high satisfaction and adoption rates.

Measure Phase

The Measure phase takes place after a new system is live and the users have adopted the system for their use. During this phase, analysts can measure the return on investment of the solution's business objectives and use key performance indicators (KPIs) to truly determine the value that the project brought to the organization. By using real data and a live measurement, it is possible to confirm that the business objectives set at the start of a project in the Business Objectives Model were actually achieved. Furthermore, the organization can measure individual business processes to ensure that they have met KPI targets described in KPIMs. Documents created during this phase might include presentations to executives describing the return, lessons learned documents, or retrospectives.

Selecting Models by Project Characteristics

In addition to the project phase, you should take into account the characteristics of the project when selecting which models to use. Typically, the first questions to ask are:

- Is this system being custom built from scratch, or will it be purchased from a vendor?
- Will the system replace an existing system entirely, result in a new implementation, or enhance an existing system?

There are several common project characteristics that can be used as guidelines to help determine which models to use. The list of project characteristics in the sections that follow is not meant to be comprehensive but is meant to give you a starting point for determining which models might be appropriate for your project. Project characteristics are not mutually exclusive, so you probably will have multiple characteristics that apply. For example, a project to replace an existing system can also be a cloud implementation. A system that will exist in a large ecosystem might also be an analytics system.

A Model to Select Models

Notice that we actually use a model to communicate how to select models by project characteristics. We use a grid that has all project characteristics down the left side and all models across the top. However, leaving the grid in that form would have given us 20 items in the list of characteristics, which is far more than 7+/-2 items. To make the grid more consumable, we further divided the characteristics into Objectives, People, Systems, and Data categories. Each project characteristic section in this chapter shows the relevant row of that grid. The complete grid is in Appendix A, for your quick reference later.

To select models using this section, first decide which project characteristics apply to your project, and then consider the suggested models for those characteristics (shown in rows in the grid in each section) to determine which models will be helpful on your project. The recommended models grid shown in each project characteristic uses the key in Table 25-1.

TABLE 25-1 Key for Models by Project Characteristic

Meaning	Cell Value
Likely to be needed	L
Might be needed	M
Not needed based on this characteristic alone	blank

The meaning of blank cells is tricky and is important to understand so that you can interpret this information correctly. If a cell is blank, it means that the particular characteristic alone does not indicate the need for that particular model. The project might still need the model, though, because of another relevant project characteristic. Conversely, if the cell is filled in, it means the characteristic alone is sufficient to indicate that the model is needed for that type of project. For example, you might notice that the Business Objectives Model is not indicated for most of the characteristics. That's because the use of a Business Objectives Model is dependent on a project having one of only a few of the characteristics; however, those characteristics are actually pretty common, and at least one of them will apply to almost all projects. Also, a project for implementing enhancements to replace existing systems functionality might need a KPIM, but it needs the KPIM because the project is replacing an existing system, not because it is an enhancement.

Objectives Characteristics

The following objectives characteristics help determine which objectives models are needed based on the type of project implementation.

Greenfield Projects

A greenfield project is one in which a brand new system is custom built from scratch because no system currently exists to provide the needed functionality. A primary consideration in these projects is scope, because it can easily balloon out of control. Many future users of these systems will offer input on features and requirements that they have for the system, and it is important to prioritize these requests in the context of a Business Objectives Model and Objective Chains. You should create a Feature Tree to show all planned features, and then tie each feature to a business objective so that the organization only builds the features that have the most value. A Requirements Mapping Matrix (RMM) is important to ensure that requirements ultimately map back to business objectives through other models.

	Objectives	Business Objectives Model	Objective Chain	Key Performance Indicator Model	Feature Tree	Requirements Mapping Matrix	**People**	Org Chart	Process Flow	Use Case	Roles and Permissions Matrix	**Systems**	Ecosystem Map	System Flow	UI Flow	Display-Action-Response Model	Decision Table	Decision Tree	System Interface Table	**Data**	Business Data Diagram	Data Flow Diagram	Data Dictionary	State Table	State Diagram	Report Table
Greenfield		L	L		L	L																				

Commercial Off the Shelf (COTS) Projects

The goal of a COTS project is to evaluate and select a third-party solution to solve a business problem and then implement it. We have broken the COTS project characteristic into two aspects, selection and implementation, because in many organizations they exist as completely separate efforts with differing model needs. Often the selection phase proceeds, but then COTS implementation does not occur because the team decides to build a new system or improve the existing system.

COTS selection The selection phase involves qualifying vendors, determining what the primary business objectives are, and ultimately selecting a system that meets an organization's needs. Creating a Business Objectives Model and Objective Chain might be important to ensure that the selection process focuses on the systems that provide the greatest return on investment (ROI) as defined by the business objectives.

During the selection phase of a COTS system, many organizations create a list of features that the organization needs. This method is extremely weak because it does not address how the software satisfies the business process. To resolve this, you should use Process Flows and KPIMs to prioritize the Process Flows and determine the features that support the most critical business processes. You should use an Org Chart to ensure that you are talking to all of the right people about their Process Flows. During interviews with the vendor, you can use the highest-priority Process Flows to have the vendor demonstrate exactly how those processes and KPIs would be satisfied by using their software. You might still want to create a Feature Tree to help you quickly summarize the features deemed to be most important. An RMM helps you keep your features prioritized. In addition, a BDD should be used to ensure that there are no major discrepancies in data models between the software and the business needs. A Data Dictionary might not be needed because the individual fields typically do not require major changes. Finally, an Ecosystem Map should be used to ensure that there is a good understanding of the integrations that the COTS system will need to support. The vendor should be prepared to address gaps between the models and the COTS system.

	Objectives	Business Objectives Model	Objective Chain	Key Performance Indicator Model	Feature Tree	Requirements Mapping Matrix	**People**	Org Chart	Process Flow	Use Case	Roles and Permissions Matrix	**Systems**	Ecosystem Map	System Flow	UI Flow	Display-Action-Response Model	Decision Table	Decision Tree	System Interface Table	**Data**	Business Data Diagram	Data Flow Diagram	Data Dictionary	State Table	State Diagram	Report Table
COTS selection		M	M	L	L	L		L	L				L								L		M			

COTS implementation The implementation phase of a COTS project could be part of an existing system replacement project, but it could also represent installation of a completely new system. If the COTS system is replacing an existing system, and there is little customization, KPIMs are better because they help ensure that business throughput is maintained at desired levels. If there is significant customization, then there are features that you can map to business objectives by using a Business Objectives Model and Objective Chain. If the COTS system is not replacing an existing system or is introducing a significant amount of new functionality, defining the business objectives and their relationship to features by using a Business Objectives Model and Objective Chain is crucial to prioritizing features.

Org Charts can help ensure that all existing users are represented. Process Flows ensure that those users' functionality needs are understood. The RMM is helpful for ensuring that all requirements of the business processes are implemented in the new system. A Roles and Permissions Matrix is useful because many COTS systems allow you to configure roles out of the box, so this helps you decide who should have those roles and what permissions those roles should have. Ecosystem Maps and System Flows are important if the COTS system will be deployed in an existing ecosystem, to help identify integration points. BDDs and Data Dictionaries help ensure that data used in existing systems or processes is considered, whether it is to be converted to a new type of data or not. Most COTS software comes with standard reports, so Report Tables are important to define how those are deployed. Use Cases might be used to describe how users will interact with the COTS software directly. DAR models might be useful because tables can be created for each element in the UI that is configurable, to help capture the configuration requirements.

	Objectives	Business Objectives Model	Objective Chain	Key Performance Indicator Model	Feature Tree	Requirements Mapping Matrix	People	Org Chart	Process Flow	Use Case	Roles and Permissions Matrix	Systems	Ecosystem Map	System Flow	UI Flow	Display-Action-Response Model	Decision Table	Decision Tree	System Interface Table	Data	Business Data Diagram	Data Flow Diagram	Data Dictionary	State Table	State Diagram	Report Table
COTS implementation		M	M	L		L		L	L	M	L		L	L		M					L		L			L

Enhancement Projects

An enhancement project makes a major change to an existing system by adding new functionality to the system's capabilities. Because enhancement projects tend to primarily focus on new capabilities, focusing on mapping features to business objectives is paramount to minimize gold plating. The Business Objectives Model and Objective Chain are extremely important, because they allow you specifically to restrict the solution's scope to the appropriate people, systems, and data. The RMM will help you continue the traceability by mapping requirements to other prioritized models to control scope. The Feature Tree can provide a quick view of all features that are in scope for implementation.

Because an existing system is being modified, often the data model is not changing. In these cases, a BDD is not necessary. By the same token, if the new features do not require additional integration, then an Ecosystem Map might not be necessary either.

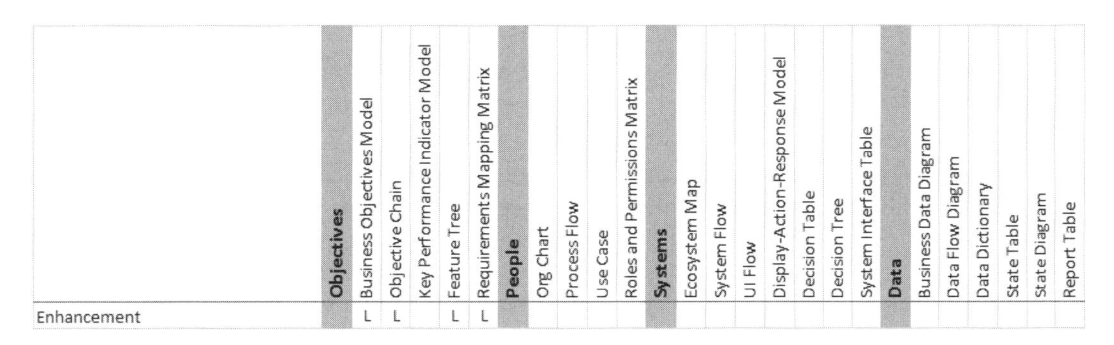

	Objectives	Business Objectives Model	Objective Chain	Key Performance Indicator Model	Feature Tree	Requirements Mapping Matrix	People	Org Chart	Process Flow	Use Case	Roles and Permissions Matrix	Systems	Ecosystem Map	System Flow	UI Flow	Display-Action-Response Model	Decision Table	Decision Tree	System Interface Table	Data	Business Data Diagram	Data Flow Diagram	Data Dictionary	State Table	State Diagram	Report Table
Enhancement		L	L		L	L																				

People Characteristics

The following project characteristics are related to the users who use the system.

Systems with Extensive User Interaction

Systems with extensive user interaction are defined as those that have many users performing many types of operations in the system. You should focus on people models first. Typically, Process Flows will be used in a project that is heavily driven by the user interface (UI). Use Cases might be helpful to further describe user interactions. Roles and Permissions Matrices are helpful if you have a limited number of roles or types of user and need to implement a security model in the user interface. UI Flows and Display-Action-Response (DAR) models will be two of the most important models, because they illustrate visual aspects of the solution that Process Flows and Use Cases cannot capture. Each step in the Process Flows can then be linked to a DAR model to illustrate the UI in the level of detail needed.

If you are replacing an existing system or automating a process, KPIMs will probably be helpful because of the increased focus on end-user throughput and completion of tasks. If your project is an enhancement with an extensive UI, these models will be key in order to allow you to keep a consistent look and feel with the current software.

	Objectives	Business Objectives Model	Objective Chain	Key Performance Indicator Model	Feature Tree	Requirements Mapping Matrix	People	Org Chart	Process Flow	Use Case	Roles and Permissions Matrix	Systems	Ecosystem Map	System Flow	UI Flow	Display-Action-Response Model	Decision Table	Decision Tree	System Interface Table	Data	Business Data Diagram	Data Flow Diagram	Data Dictionary	State Table	State Diagram	Report Table
Extensive user interaction									L	M	L				L	L										

Customer-Facing Systems

Customer-facing systems primarily have users that are external to the organization that is implementing the system. There are typically a few internal roles as well, such as administrative roles, but most users are from outside the organization.

Because the users are external, Org Charts are typically not helpful. Roles and Permissions Matrices might be used to define the type of permissions necessary for security in the system. Process Flows and Use Cases might be important to describe how the customers will use the system. UI Flow and DAR models should be created to ensure that the user interface is easily navigated and used by external users. This is important even if there aren't very many customer-facing screens.

	Objectives	Business Objectives Model	Objective Chain	Key Performance Indicator Model	Feature Tree	Requirements Mapping Matrix	People	Org Chart	Process Flow	Use Case	Roles and Permissions Matrix	Systems	Ecosystem Map	System Flow	UI Flow	Display-Action-Response Model	Decision Table	Decision Tree	System Interface Table	Data	Business Data Diagram	Data Flow Diagram	Data Dictionary	State Table	State Diagram	Report Table
Customer-facing									M	M	M				L	L										

Business Process Automation Projects

Business process automation projects either fully or partially implement the business's processes in a system. These projects use KPIMs because the performance of existing manual processes can be measured to ensure that the performance levels are either maintained or improved in the new system. Org Charts are important to ensure that you talk to all existing business stakeholders who execute the process. Process Flows can be used to document existing business processes that will be performed using the new system. Use Cases might help describe how those activities will occur in the system. Furthermore, future-state Process Flows and Use Cases can illustrate how the system should function and provide a basis for new training guides.

Roles and Permissions Matrices might be important for putting a security model in place. BDDs and Data Dictionaries will be necessary to describe the business data objects and fields used and manipulated in the process.

	Objectives	Business Objectives Model	Objective Chain	Key Performance Indicator Model	Feature Tree	Requirements Mapping Matrix	People	Org Chart	Process Flow	Use Case	Roles and Permissions Matrix	Systems	Ecosystem Map	System Flow	UI Flow	Display-Action-Response Model	Decision Table	Decision Tree	System Interface Table	Data	Business Data Diagram	Data Flow Diagram	Data Dictionary	State Table	State Diagram	Report Table
Business process automation				L				L	L	M	M										L		L			

Workflow Automation Projects

A workflow is a specific type of business process that has a heavy emphasis on approvals and routing of information between groups. A project that automates a workflow typically requires a Process Flow to describe context for the workflow. These projects usually have a BDD to show the business data objects that are manipulated during the workflow. State Tables and State Diagrams can help show how the objects change state during the workflow. Typically, these projects have security needs related to who can perform functions at different steps in the workflow, so Roles and Permissions Matrices are helpful.

	Objectives	Business Objectives Model	Objective Chain	Key Performance Indicator Model	Feature Tree	Requirements Mapping Matrix	People	Org Chart	Process Flow	Use Case	Roles and Permissions Matrix	Systems	Ecosystem Map	System Flow	UI Flow	Display-Action-Response Model	Decision Table	Decision Tree	System Interface Table	Data	Business Data Diagram	Data Flow Diagram	Data Dictionary	State Table	State Diagram	Report Table
Workflow automation									L		L										L			L	L	

Systems Characteristics

The following project characteristics are related to the type of system being worked on.

System Replacement Projects

A system replacement project replaces an obsolete solution with either a custom-built system or a COTS system. When an existing system is being replaced, the business objectives are often related to goals such as improving throughput, performance, reduction in license fees, or reduction in maintenance costs. These goals are often not achieved through implementation of specific new features. Even if there are new features, a majority of the functionality simply needs to be maintained as compared to the legacy system. The Business Objectives Model and Objective Chains aren't as useful because their purpose is to map the value (for instance, return on investment) of features to business objectives. Unlike projects that trace their value up to business objectives, existing system conversion projects should use KPIMs for business processes to prioritize requirements and business rules. At a minimum, the new solution must be able to maintain the KPIs at their current levels—there should be no degradation in overall efficiency from switching to a new solution.

The KPIM is one of the most critical models because it helps analysts demonstrate to business stakeholders that even if the new system behaves differently, the business outcomes will be the same or better. One common challenge with existing system conversions is that new software might cause a reduction in the KPIs of one group while improving the KPIs of another group. Even though overall the throughput and business value are positive, the group that is negatively affected might not approve the system unless they understand that the negative impact is in the context of an overall improvement to the business. You should use KPIMs to reassure the business stakeholders that the new system, though different, will still let them get their jobs done.

With the use of KPIMs, you will also need Process Flows against which to map the KPIMs. Org Charts, Ecosystem Maps, and BDDs are all valuable to an existing system conversion project as well, because they help you understand all current users, the existing system integrations that might need to be replaced, and the full set of data the business cares about. Process Flows are needed to describe the activities that users perform in the existing system. Report Tables are needed because existing systems almost always have reports that need to be converted to the new system.

	Objectives	Business Objectives Model	Objective Chain	Key Performance Indicator Model	Feature Tree	Requirements Mapping Matrix	**People**	Org Chart	Process Flow	Use Case	Roles and Permissions Matrix	**Systems**	Ecosystem Map	System Flow	UI Flow	Display-Action-Response Model	Decision Table	Decision Tree	System Interface Table	**Data**	Business Data Diagram	Data Flow Diagram	Data Dictionary	State Table	State Diagram	Report Table
System replacement				L	L	L		L	L	M	M		L	M	M				M		L	M	L			L

Real-Time and Embedded Systems

Real-time and embedded systems have significantly smaller or more primitive user interfaces than most user-facing systems. The goal of these types of projects might be to implement automation or controller systems. In real-time and embedded systems, System Flows are the dominant models. Ecosystem Maps and System Interface Tables might be helpful if the real-time system has interfaces with many other systems. Most people models will not be helpful, because a majority of the effort will focus on the steps within the system. Real-time and embedded systems often have very simple data models, so a BDD and a Data Dictionary might not be necessary. Although the system will obviously be dealing with data, it is most likely doing so at a technical level, so the business stakeholders are not concerned about the details of the data itself. State Tables and State Diagrams are commonly used, because these types of systems often have complex state changes that trigger behaviors.

	Objectives	Business Objectives Model	Objective Chain	Key Performance Indicator Model	Feature Tree	Requirements Mapping Matrix	**People**	Org Chart	Process Flow	Use Case	Roles and Permissions Matrix	**Systems**	Ecosystem Map	System Flow	UI Flow	Display-Action-Response Model	Decision Table	Decision Tree	System Interface Table	**Data**	Business Data Diagram	Data Flow Diagram	Data Dictionary	State Table	State Diagram	Report Table
Real-time and embedded system													M	L					M			M		M	M	

Large-Ecosystem Projects

Projects with large ecosystems have many existing systems that interact. You should focus on the systems first by starting with an Ecosystem Map. System Interface Tables might be needed to describe the interface requirements between systems. Identify the business data objects to create BDDs, and then use Data Flow Diagrams (DFDs) to show the flow of data between the systems. Data Dictionaries will be necessary to describe the fields and rules for the data.

	Objectives	Business Objectives Model	Objective Chain	Key Performance Indicator Model	Feature Tree	Requirements Mapping Matrix	**People**	Org Chart	Process Flow	Use Case	Roles and Permissions Matrix	**Systems**	Ecosystem Map	System Flow	UI Flow	Display-Action-Response Model	Decision Table	Decision Tree	System Interface Table	**Data**	Business Data Diagram	Data Flow Diagram	Data Dictionary	State Table	State Diagram	Report Table
Large ecosystem													L						M		L	L	L			

Internal IT Systems

Internal IT systems are systems in which all (or most) of the users are internal to the organization. These systems are deployed in one organization's environment. Org Charts will certainly be used because the users are internal, and Process Flows are necessary because they define how the business will use the internal system. Roles and Permissions Matrices will probably be used to describe the security model for users. Ecosystem Maps are helpful to show how the system fits in with other existing systems in the IT organization, and System Interface Tables might be helpful if the interface requirements are important to the business stakeholders.

	Objectives	Business Objectives Model	Objective Chain	Key Performance Indicator Model	Feature Tree	Requirements Mapping Matrix	People	Org Chart	Process Flow	Use Case	Roles and Permissions Matrix	Systems	Ecosystem Map	System Flow	UI Flow	Display-Action-Response Model	Decision Table	Decision Tree	System Interface Table	Data	Business Data Diagram	Data Flow Diagram	Data Dictionary	State Table	State Diagram	Report Table
Internal IT								L	L		L		L						M							

Hardware and Software

Systems that have both hardware and software components to be implemented typically have many inputs and outputs to be considered. Although people and data models are important, system models are the most critical to create for this characteristic. An Ecosystem Map shows how the components are related, System Flows show how the hardware and software interact, and System Interface Tables describe the inputs and outputs between each component. Keep in mind that although these models are similar to technical models, the purpose of these models is to derive the requirements—whatever the business stakeholders need. Leave the technical documentation to the technical team.

	Objectives	Business Objectives Model	Objective Chain	Key Performance Indicator Model	Feature Tree	Requirements Mapping Matrix	People	Org Chart	Process Flow	Use Case	Roles and Permissions Matrix	Systems	Ecosystem Map	System Flow	UI Flow	Display-Action-Response Model	Decision Table	Decision Tree	System Interface Table	Data	Business Data Diagram	Data Flow Diagram	Data Dictionary	State Table	State Diagram	Report Table
Hardware and software													L	L					L							

Packaged Software

Packaged software is software that is sold as stand-alone software. Packaged software should heavily use people and data models and will probably use few system models. Process Flows and Use Cases are helpful for showing how the users will interact with the software. Org Charts are not useful because the users are not common to one environment. Feature Trees are useful for actually building the "packaging" for the software. RMMs help control scope by mapping the requirements to Process Flow steps to ensure that extra features that are not anticipated to create significant value for the users are excluded. UI Flows and DAR models are important for modeling the user interface.

	Objectives	Business Objectives Model	Objective Chain	Key Performance Indicator Model	Feature Tree	Requirements Mapping Matrix	People	Org Chart	Process Flow	Use Case	Roles and Permissions Matrix	Systems	Ecosystem Map	System Flow	UI Flow	Display-Action-Response Model	Decision Table	Decision Tree	System Interface Table	Data	Business Data Diagram	Data Flow Diagram	Data Dictionary	State Table	State Diagram	Report Table
Packaged software					L	L			L	M					L	L										

Cloud Implementation Projects

In cloud implementation projects, you are implementing a cloud solution to solve a business problem. The fact that the project is a cloud implementation does not influence the selection of requirements models as much as other the other characteristics do. For instance, if the cloud implementation is part of a large ecosystem, then an Ecosystem Map will be useful to show how the cloud part of the solution interacts with other parts of the system, a System Flow can help describe the system steps, and System Interface Tables might be necessary to describe the interfaces. The Org Chart might be useful in identifying users, and Roles and Permissions Matrices can define security access in the cloud for the user types. Process Flows can be used to describe how users will interact with the cloud. Also, state models are often useful because cloud implementations typically are based on user states, such as logged on, logged off, online, or offline.

	Objectives	Business Objectives Model	Objective Chain	Key Performance Indicator Model	Feature Tree	Requirements Mapping Matrix	People	Org Chart	Process Flow	Use Case	Roles and Permissions Matrix	Systems	Ecosystem Map	System Flow	UI Flow	Display-Action-Response Model	Decision Table	Decision Tree	System Interface Table	Data	Business Data Diagram	Data Flow Diagram	Data Dictionary	State Table	State Diagram	Report Table
Cloud implementation								M	L		L		L	M					M					L	L	

Web App Projects

Web apps expose functionality and display data to users through a web interface. Because the web app is communicating to a back-end server, an Ecosystem Map is helpful for showing the architecture, but System Flows are most important for describing those interactions. Data models are important for showing what data exists in the system and is passed between the server and client, so you should create a BDD and a Data Dictionary. UI Flows and DAR models are often helpful for building the web interface, to ensure that it is usable.

	Objectives	Business Objectives Model	Objective Chain	Key Performance Indicator Model	Feature Tree	Requirements Mapping Matrix	People	Org Chart	Process Flow	Use Case	Roles and Permissions Matrix	Systems	Ecosystem Map	System Flow	UI Flow	Display-Action-Response Model	Decision Table	Decision Tree	System Interface Table	Data	Business Data Diagram	Data Flow Diagram	Data Dictionary	State Table	State Diagram	Report Table
Web app													L	L	M	M					L		L			

Mobile Systems

Systems with mobile capabilities are intended to be deployed at least partially on mobile devices. Mobile systems should have Use Cases that precisely describe how users will interact with the mobile device, and they might use Process Flows to describe users' goals with the device. Ecosystem Maps and System Flows might be helpful to show the interfaces and interactions between the mobile system and the servers it communicates with. Because mobile devices have limited screen size and sometimes slow interaction times, UI Flows and DAR models are helpful to ensure that the screens on the mobile device are designed efficiently and can be easily used.

	Objectives	Business Objectives Model	Objective Chain	Key Performance Indicator Model	Feature Tree	Requirements Mapping Matrix	People	Org Chart	Process Flow	Use Case	Roles and Permissions Matrix	Systems	Ecosystem Map	System Flow	UI Flow	Display-Action-Response Model	Decision Table	Decision Tree	System Interface Table	Data	Business Data Diagram	Data Flow Diagram	Data Dictionary	State Table	State Diagram	Report Table
Mobile									M	L			M	M	L	L										

Projects with Complex Decision Logic

Projects with complex decision logic automate a decision process. These projects typically have other characteristics that drive model selection. You should use Decision Tables and Decision Trees to model the complex logic. State Tables and State Diagrams might be needed because many decisions are based on states in the system.

	Objectives	Business Objectives Model	Objective Chain	Key Performance Indicator Model	Feature Tree	Requirements Mapping Matrix	People	Org Chart	Process Flow	Use Case	Roles and Permissions Matrix	Systems	Ecosystem Map	System Flow	UI Flow	Display-Action-Response Model	Decision Table	Decision Tree	System Interface Table	Data	Business Data Diagram	Data Flow Diagram	Data Dictionary	State Table	State Diagram	Report Table
Complex decision logic																	L	L						M	M	

Data Characteristics

The following project characteristics are related to the data needs of the system.

Analytics and Reporting Components

Systems that have analytics and reporting components are typically used in business intelligence to help people make decisions based on large data sets. In fact, these projects can be identified by their business strategy—any project that involves getting information to make a decision has significant data requirements.

Projects that involve significant volumes and use of data need several data models to accurately document the requirements. You can use the BDD to determine which types of data are involved in the project, DFDs to describe the flow of the data, and Data Dictionaries to further describe the data. Report Tables are a necessity if you are creating reporting requirements.

Often Process Flows and the other people models aren't needed at all for a pure analytics project. However, keep in mind that Report Tables include decisions that need to be made. For a very large business intelligence project, prioritizing reports might require Process Flows for determining which reports support the most important processes and for articulating the decisions that need to be made. Also, decision models might be helpful on analytics projects.

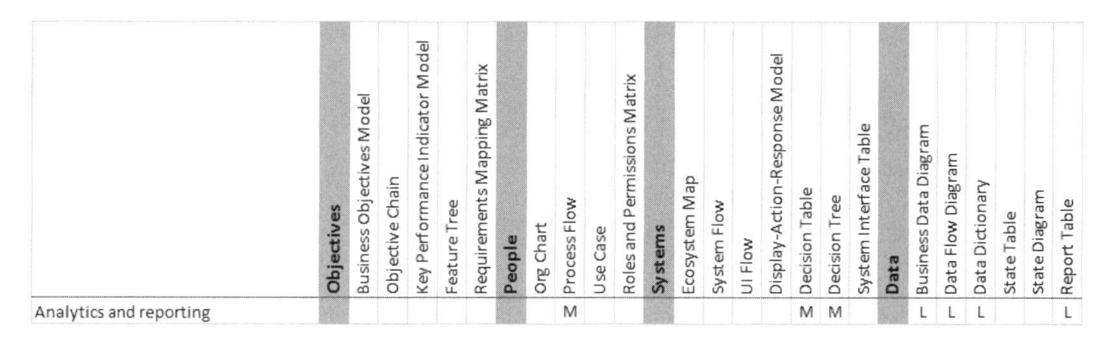

	Objectives	Business Objectives Model	Objective Chain	Key Performance Indicator Model	Feature Tree	Requirements Mapping Matrix	People	Org Chart	Process Flow	Use Case	Roles and Permissions Matrix	Systems	Ecosystem Map	System Flow	UI Flow	Display-Action-Response Model	Decision Table	Decision Tree	System Interface Table	Data	Business Data Diagram	Data Flow Diagram	Data Dictionary	State Table	State Diagram	Report Table
Analytics and reporting									M								M	M			L	L	L			L

Database Back-End Components

Many projects will have a database back-end component. These systems contain data that is used by and stored in the system. For these projects, you will need to identify all of the business data objects in BDDs and define their flow between processes, systems, and storage components in DFDs. You should also define the actual field-level details in Data Dictionaries. Keep in mind that you do not need to document the database schema or physical architecture of the database servers. Instead, focus on documenting how the business stakeholders think about the data.

	Objectives	Business Objectives Model	Objective Chain	Key Performance Indicator Model	Feature Tree	Requirements Mapping Matrix	People	Org Chart	Process Flow	Use Case	Roles and Permissions Matrix	Systems	Ecosystem Map	System Flow	UI Flow	Display-Action-Response Model	Decision Table	Decision Tree	System Interface Table	Data	Business Data Diagram	Data Flow Diagram	Data Dictionary	State Table	State Diagram	Report Table
Back-end database																					L	L	L			

Data Warehouse Components

Data-heavy systems contain many business data objects and pass a large volume of data between systems. You will probably use many non-data models, but you should focus on data first, by identifying business data objects to create BDDs, then completing DFDs. You can create Data Dictionaries to provide an increased level of detail for the data requirements.

	Objectives	Business Objectives Model	Objective Chain	Key Performance Indicator Model	Feature Tree	Requirements Mapping Matrix	People	Org Chart	Process Flow	Use Case	Roles and Permissions Matrix	Systems	Ecosystem Map	System Flow	UI Flow	Display-Action-Response Model	Decision Table	Decision Tree	System Interface Table	Data	Business Data Diagram	Data Flow Diagram	Data Dictionary	State Table	State Diagram	Report Table
Data warehouse																					L	L	L			

Project Examples

An existing financial services system is to be replaced with a heavily customized COTS product that will integrate to several other existing systems. The system will be used by hundreds of thousands of customers every day. The team works with several departments that handle the various regions that are transitioning to the new system. A majority of the functionality will be maintained. Figure 25-2 shows the appropriate characteristics and most useful models for this project.

Another project is to build a single-user game for a mobile device. Figure 25-3 shows the appropriate characteristics and most useful models for this project.

A final project is to select and implement COTS software to manage a loan approval process. Figure 25-4 shows the appropriate characteristics and most useful models for this project.

	Objectives	Business Objectives Model	Objective Chain	Key Performance Indicator Model	Feature Tree	Requirements Mapping Matrix	People	Org Chart	Process Flow	Use Case	Roles and Permissions Matrix	Systems	Ecosystem Map	System Flow	UI Flow	Display-Action-Response Model	Decision Table	Decision Tree	System Interface Table	Data	Business Data Diagram	Data Flow Diagram	Data Dictionary	State Table	State Diagram	Report Table
COTS implementation		M	M	L		L		L	L	M	L		L	L		M					L		L			L
Extensive user interaction									L	M	L				L	L										
Customer-facing									M	M	M				L	L										
System replacement				L	L	L		L	L	M	M		L	M	M				M		L	M	L			L
Large ecosystem													L						M		L	L	L			
Database back-end components																					L	L	L			
Selected models for scenario		x	x	x	x	x		x	x		x		x	x	x	x					x	x	x			x

FIGURE 25-2 Models for a financial services example project.

	Objectives	Business Objectives Model	Objective Chain	Key Performance Indicator Model	Feature Tree	Requirements Mapping Matrix	People	Org Chart	Process Flow	Use Case	Roles and Permissions Matrix	Systems	Ecosystem Map	System Flow	UI Flow	Display-Action-Response Model	Decision Table	Decision Tree	System Interface Table	Data	Business Data Diagram	Data Flow Diagram	Data Dictionary	State Table	State Diagram	Report Table
Customer-facing									M	M	M				L	L										
Mobile									M	L			M	M	L	L										
Complex decision logic																	L	L						M	M	
Selected models for scenario									x	x					x	x	x	x						x		

FIGURE 25-3 Models for an example mobile game project.

	Objectives	Business Objectives Model	Objective Chain	Key Performance Indicator Model	Feature Tree	Requirements Mapping Matrix	People	Org Chart	Process Flow	Use Case	Roles and Permissions Matrix	Systems	Ecosystem Map	System Flow	UI Flow	Display-Action-Response Model	Decision Table	Decision Tree	System Interface Table	Data	Business Data Diagram	Data Flow Diagram	Data Dictionary	State Table	State Diagram	Report Table
COTS selection		M	M	L	L	L		L	L				L								L		M			
COTS implementation		M	M	L		L		L	L	M	L		L	L		M					L		L			L
Workflow automation									L		L										L			L	L	
Complex decision logic																	L	L						M	M	
Selected models for scenario		x	x	x	x	x		x	x		x		x	x			x	x			x		x	x	x	x

FIGURE 25-4 Models for an example loan approval project.

Thinking About the Audience

Consider who the audience is when you select your models. All RML models are designed to be understood and used by all audiences. However, when you ask someone to review or use models, you should still select models that are most appropriate to them.

- Asking a vice president to review models that are very detailed might not be a good use of her time. Conversely, creating only very high-level models for developers and testers to use will not provide them with enough information to do their jobs.
- You might find that business stakeholders have a hard time telling you all of the systems and their integrations, whereas architects might not be very familiar with business processes or how the product manager intends users to use the system.

Regardless of who creates, reviews, and uses the models, you should make sure that your development teams are aware of the full set of models and requirements that you do create. Models linked to requirements provide additional information beyond just the checklist of requirements to be developed. Although models represent a way to organize and present information, it is still necessary to verbally communicate with all stakeholders to ensure that they understand the material. Handing over models without discussing them with the technical teams is a recipe for failure. You will never be able to capture every iota of information in the models.

Table 25-2 describes the most common stakeholder audience scenarios. The types of stakeholders who will directly help with creating a model are marked with a C, those who will be more likely to only review what you give them are marked with R, and those who probably won't use it at all are blank. The analyst is not listed in this table because it is assumed that he will help create and review all models.

TABLE 25-2 Model Use by Audience Type

Model	Business	Technical	Executive
Objectives Models			
Business Objectives Model	C	R	C
Objective Chain	C	R	R
Key Performance Indicator Model (KPIM)	C	R	R
Feature Tree	C	R	R
Requirements Mapping Matrix (RMM)	R	R	
People Models			
Org Chart	C	C	R
Process Flow	C	C	R
Use Case	C	R	
Roles and Permissions Matrix	C	R	

Model	Business	Technical	Executive
Systems Models			
Ecosystem Map	R	C	R
System Flow	R	C	
UI Flow	C	C	
Display-Action-Response (DAR) model	C	R	
Decision Table	C	R	
Decision Tree	C	R	
System Interface Table	C	C	
Data Models			
Business Data Diagram (BDD)	C	R	
Data Flow Diagram (DFD)	R	C	
Data Dictionary	C	C	
State Table	C	C	
State Diagram	C	C	
Report Table	C	C	R

Tailoring Models

When you are selecting requirements models, it is possible to get stuck trying to fit information into a structure that is not appropriate. It might be necessary to make small adaptations to the structure of some models based on the specific needs of a project. Each requirement model is flexible enough that the components can be tailored to the specific needs of the project.

The most common types of customization we see are the addition of coloring to highlight particular types of elements or the addition of elements, such as fields to a Data Dictionary or a particular shape from Business Process Modeling Notation (BPMN) to a Process Flow.

Avoid modifying the models unless it's absolutely necessary to communicate additional information that the model does not normally contain. If you do need to modify them, do it in such a way that an untrained user can still consume them easily. If a model must be modified, the tailoring should take place before the start of the project rather than during the requirements process, to reduce the amount of rework and to avoid inconsistency in the requirements documentation. Often you might not recognize that a model needs to be modified until you have done a significant amount of work. In those cases, you will have to use your best judgment as to whether it is worth it to go back and fix the prior work.

Exercise

The following exercise is intended to help you to gain a better understanding of how to use the information in this chapter. The exercise is open ended, and therefore the answer you come up with could be substantially different than the answer that we have provided. There are potentially many correct solutions. The answer provides an explanation of how we arrived at our solution. You will gain the most out of the exercise by attempting to do it yourself before looking at the solution. The answers for the exercises can be found in Appendix C.

Instructions

Identify the project characteristics and select the appropriate models for the scenario.

Scenario

You are on a project to launch a brand new eStore to sell flamingos and assorted lawn decorations, and you have to document all of the requirements. Currently, orders are only taken over the phone and manually entered into the order system by sales representatives. You expect to have thousands of customers visiting the website every day. You know that there will be servers that push catalog data to the website and send the orders on to fulfillment.

As you explore the high-level features, you also learn that the eStore orders will have various states, such as "New," "Received," "Packaged," "Billed," "Shipped," and "Returned." The president of Wide World Importers wants to view reports that show him metrics such as sales volume, inventory volume, and inventory costs by month. In addition, the training team wants to be sure that the process of shopping is well documented from the point at which a customer arrives at the website to when he receives an order confirmation after checkout.

CHAPTER 26

Using Models Together

In high school, you learn science, math, language, music, and social studies in separate classes. Each class teaches a specific subject area, and you learn about that area separately from the rest. However, as you progress, you learn that many fields cross disciplinary boundaries. For example, math heavily affects sciences such as biology, physics, and chemistry, and each of the sciences affect each other. Physics helps you to better understand chemistry, and chemistry helps you to better understand biology. The techniques and information that you learn in each area help you increase your understanding of many other areas.

After you have selected and created your models for a project, the next step is to use those models to improve each other—which is the true key to getting the most out of a models-based approach. The information in this chapter is meant to help you understand the basics of using models together. It can take years of practice before you can easily use the different models together. However, the practice is worth the reward because it helps you create a more valuable, targeted, and useful solution.

Many Different Views

No single requirements model will contain all of the information needed to sufficiently describe the business's needs. You can only represent a subset of the information in any individual model; therefore, multiple models are necessary for adequately modeling your requirements.

Consider different types of maps of Texas—one that shows driving routes to wineries across the state, and another that shows average annual precipitation. In fact, there could be many other types of maps of Texas, if you consider maps that show things such as counties, geological information, weather trends, voting districts, and school districts. None of the individual maps would show all of the possible information about the state. In fact, if one map tried to show all of this, it would be impossible to use. Each visual representation has a different purpose, and the user selects the view of Texas that is appropriate based on his need. If the user is trying to get to Coho Vineyard, the precipitation map would be useless, but the driving routes to wineries would be perfect!

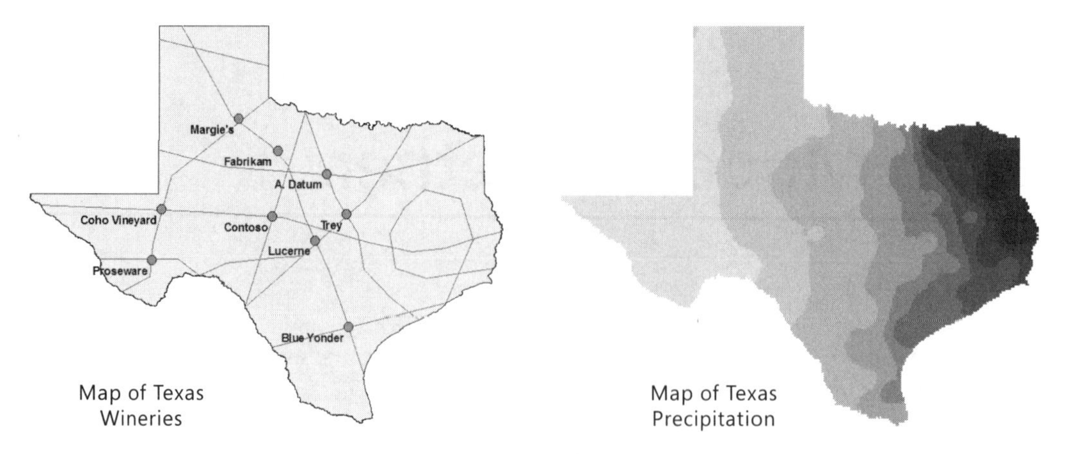

Map of Texas Wineries

Map of Texas Precipitation

As with maps, no individual requirements model can be used all of the time or by itself. It's important to understand the full set of RML models and select the appropriate models as needed.

Using More Than One Model

A key concept to remember is that all of the models are designed to be used in conjunction with each other. Each model presents a specific type of information, and you need to use more than one to convey all the information that the business and technical teams need to understand the solution.

Consider the following example: A company brought in an organization to train its analysts on use cases. This training organization presented use cases as the silver bullet to analyze software solutions. The analysts tried to create use cases as the only model in lieu of traditional requirements statements. Because these use cases were the only record of the requirements, each one was 30–40 pages long, and it was impossible to use them. This had disastrous consequences and use cases are now banned from that organization because of the poor outcome resulting from their exclusive use. The RML Use Case model is intended to describe the essence of what the user is trying to accomplish in the system, not to model every business rule and every aspect of the solution. There were many other models the team should have used in addition to Use Cases to capture the requirements.

RML models use the simplest possible nomenclature and are specifically designed to model requirements information. Because all models have limitations with respect to the information that they show, several must be used on any project to paint a complete picture. Using multiple, complementary models provides the team with greater insight into the solution, because one model might provide information that is missing in another. Additionally, every model can be used to find missing information in other models.

Consider another example: a project involved the replacement of an existing insurance underwriting system that took a long time to configure, when the business wanted to roll out new insurance products. The business had purchased a new system and identified gaps in the new system's functionality. They needed help prioritizing the requirements for an enhancement project to fill these gaps.

The team worked with the new system's vendor to help develop requirements models that would ensure that the new system met all of the business stakeholders' needs. The team started with Process Flows to document the as-is business process. Each step of the Process Flows had associated functional requirements and business rules. These, in turn, resulted in a comprehensive Data Dictionary that captured the data requirements for the system. These models and requirements were then combined to create wireframes and DAR models to visually represent what the enhancement would ultimately look like in the new system. Using these models together ensured that the enhancement was documented in a way that the business stakeholders understood what the new system would look like and the development team was able to build it correctly.

Requirements Architecture

A building architect uses multiple representations to communicate different types of information for a project. Each view can help the planners and builders make better decisions about the other views. A site plan or schematic design might lay out how the buildings sit relative to each other and to landscape features. For the interior of the building, there are electrical plans, window and door plans, plumbing plans, floor plans, and many other types of drawings. Finally, the architect might make a 3-D model to help clients visualize and walk through a simulation of the buildings. Each of the diagrams has a specific purpose; depending on the type of project, some plans might be used in different ways and some not at all.

Requirements architecture is the organization of requirements information; it includes how the requirements are structured, as well as the model-to-model relationships and model-to-requirements relationships. This chapter specifically focuses on the relationship between requirements models. The true goal behind a sound requirements architecture is to enable a team of analysts to have a shared understanding of how they will create requirements so that there is consistency and completeness across all requirements artifacts. A good requirements architecture helps ensure that:

- All needed models are considered and created over the course of the project.
- The appropriate number of models is used based on the complexity of the project.
- There is a consistent mechanism for working from one type of model to the next.
- Requirements are mapped to determine that they are complete and necessary.
- Requirements artifacts complement each other with minimal redundancy.
- Analysts can plan their approach early and not have to spend time during the project deciding how to organize the information.
- The entire requirements effort can be properly estimated.

A poor (or nonexistent) requirements architecture can cause the following problems:

- Traceability is superficial or unused, leading to a lack of ability to prioritize features.
- Requirements cannot be reused.
- Requirements reviews are on the wrong information.
- An inconsistent approach by multiple analysts leads to confusion among business and technical stakeholders about what to expect.
- The team is unable to forecast, plan, and estimate the effort required to complete the requirements.
- Reasons behind the requirements are not well understood or easy to find.

Relationships Between Models

You should create a requirements architecture to show all of the models you think you will use on the project and how they are connected. You can always add to it later or even change the relationships in it; however, that is more challenging after you have a lot of artifacts already created. Figure 26-1 shows one possible requirements architecture that includes all of the RML models.

There might be additional relationships beyond those specified here, but we have chosen to include the most common ones. Your requirements architecture can be simpler because you should not include models you are not going to create. The relationships you include in your requirements architecture are the same relationships you will use to reference models from one another and to ensure completeness of models. For example, if you want to reference business objectives from your Report Tables, you should have a link in your architecture from the Business Objectives Model to the Report Table. Also, if you want to ensure that your Data Dictionary is complete for all business data objects, it should link to the Business Data Diagram in your architecture.

A requirements architecture can also include more than just models. For example, you might find it helpful to include functional requirements, business rules, test cases, screens, or model elements such as Process Flow steps.

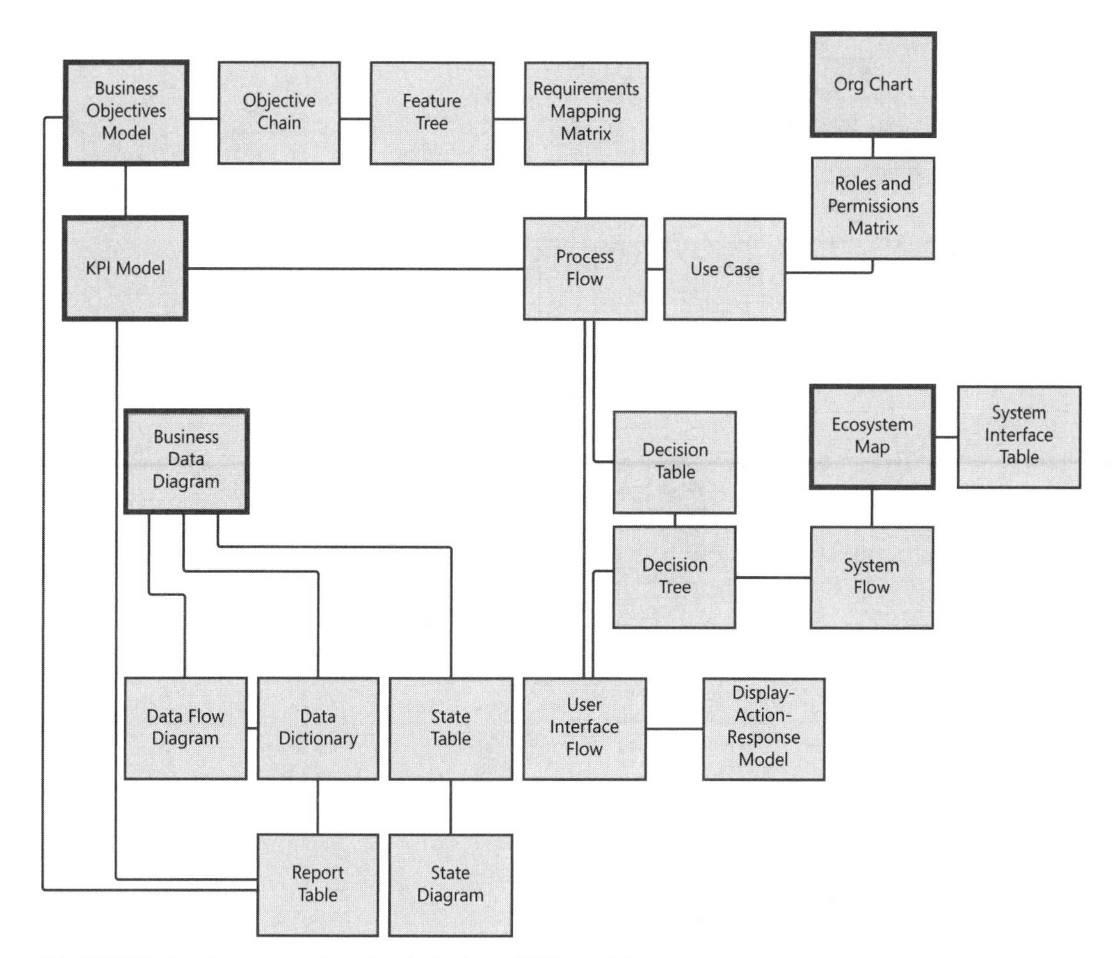

FIGURE 26-1 Requirements architecture including all RML models.

When you create a requirements architecture for your project, we suggest that you diagram it and share it with the business and technical teams so they understand all of the models and how they fit together. You might find it useful to just show pieces of the full architecture to a particular team, to focus on the aspects that are relevant to them. For example, Figure 26-2 is a requirements architecture for a project that implements a configurable system purchased by a business.

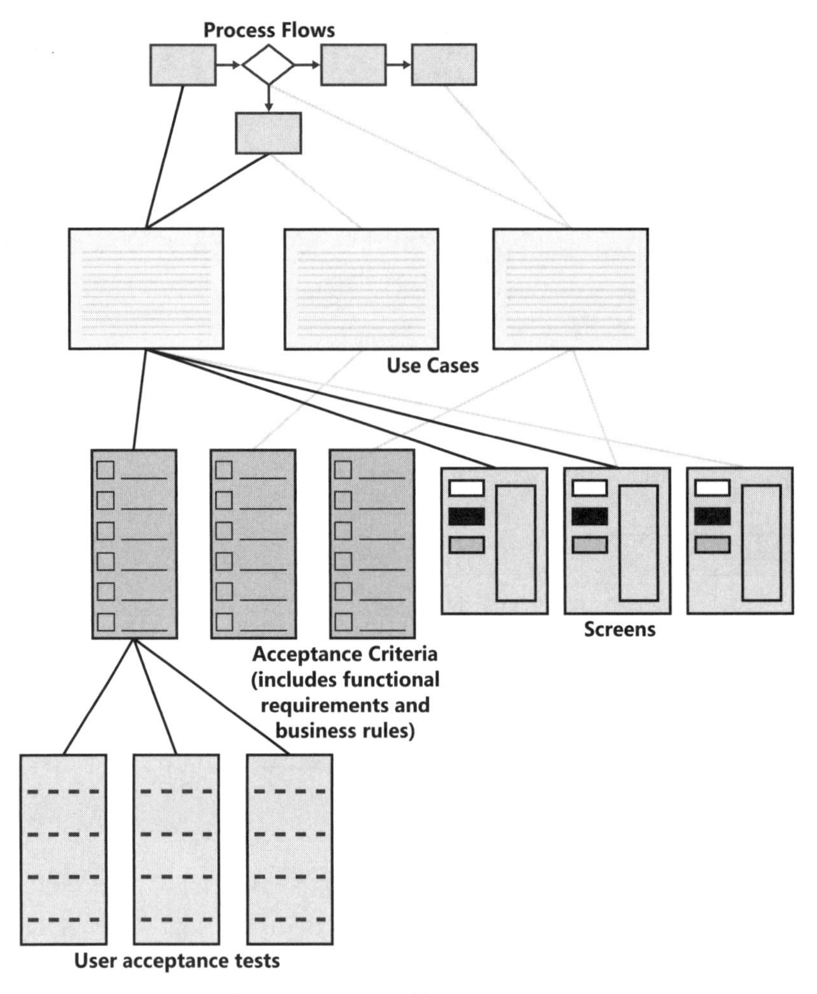

FIGURE 26-2 An example requirements architecture.

Where the Artifacts Live

Finally, you need to consider where all of the components of your requirements architecture will be created and stored. For example, you might decide that you will use a requirements management tool to create Process Flows and screen mockups for Display-Action-Response models (DARs), Microsoft Visio to create Decision Trees and Ecosystem Maps, and Microsoft Excel for State Tables and Decision Tables. Further, you might decide that all of the artifacts will live in the requirements management tool as images if the models cannot be created in the tool directly, and the source files for the models will live in a Microsoft SharePoint source control system, with a link from the tool to the file location.

A Models Plan

When you have a sense of which models you need to kick off a project and use as you get into the details (see Chapter 25, "Selecting Models for a Project," for a complete discussion about this), lay out a plan to show how you will progress through the models. This will help your business stakeholders understand how their participation at each step contributes to completing the requirements. Figure 26-3 shows an example of a plan.

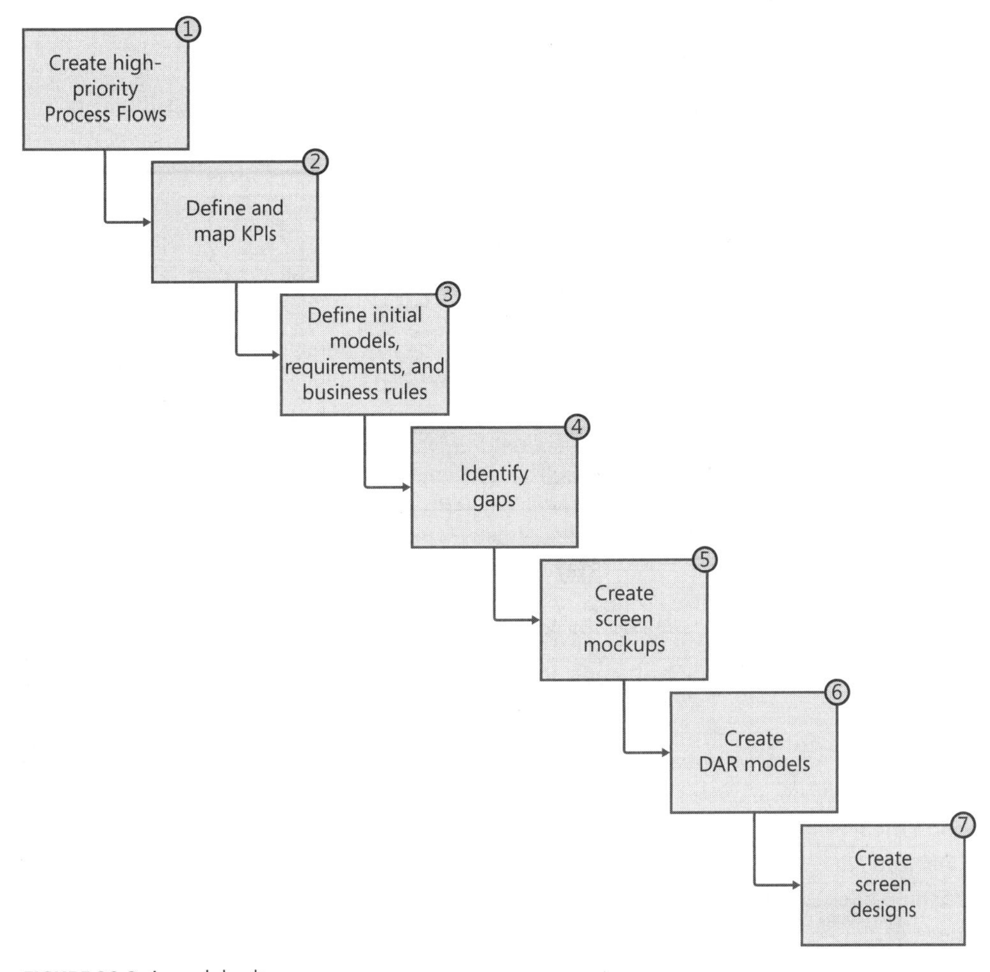

FIGURE 26-3 A models plan.

Related Models

You can realize the real power of models when you start relating them to each other. When you relate models, it becomes possible to ensure that the models are complete. Many models build upon one another, taking a set of information to the next level of detail. Others provide a list from which to select information to populate another model. For example, Requirements Mapping Matrices, Report

Tables, and Business Data Diagrams can provide the list of functions or data to be restricted by a Roles and Permissions Matrix, and an Org Chart can help to identify the roles that will have access to the information.

Figure 26-4 shows the most useful relationships between models that we have discovered by using them in hundreds of projects. To keep the table more useful, we have left out many possible theoretical relationships that just do not seem to occur in real projects. Instead, we have focused on the relationships that seem to come up most often on projects. Read this table by reading the model in the row to see what models it influences. Alternatively, if you are creating a model, find that model in a column and read down the column to see which models influence it and therefore help complete it. Note that the table only shows one layer of relationships; you can have multiple layers of relationships on your project, where one model relates to another model, which in turn relates to yet another model.

Influencing Model \ Influenced Model	Business Objectives Model	Objective Chain	Key Performance Indicator Model	Feature Tree	Requirements Mapping Matrix		Org Chart	Process Flow	Use Case	Roles and Permissions Matrix		Ecosystem Map	System Flow	UI Flow	Display-Action-Response Model	Decision Table	Decision Tree	System Interface Table		Business Data Diagram	Data Flow Diagram	Data Dictionary	State Table	State Diagram	Report Table
Business Objectives Model		X	X	X	X		X	X	X																X
Objective Chain	X		X	X	X		X																		X
Key Performance Indicator Model		X			X													X							X
Feature Tree	X	X			X			X	X	X			X							X		X			
Requirements Mapping Matrix				X			X	X	X	X			X							X		X			X
Org Chart	X							X	X	X											X				
Process Flow			X		X		X		X	X		X	X	X	X	X	X			X			X	X	X
Use Case					X			X		X			X	X	X	X	X			X		X	X	X	
Roles and Permissions Matrix							X	X																	
Ecosystem Map				X			X	X					X					X		X	X				
System Flow					X		X	X								X	X	X		X			X	X	
UI Flow					X			X		X			X		X	X	X						X	X	
Display-Action-Response Model					X			X		X			X	X						X		X	X	X	
Decision Table					X		X	X					X				X					X	X	X	X
Decision Tree					X		X	X					X			X						X	X	X	X
System Interface Table							X																		
Business Data Diagram								X	X	X		X						X			X	X	X	X	X
Data Flow Diagram								X	X			X	X												
Data Dictionary					X		X	X	X	X								X		X	X				X
State Table								X					X		X							X		X	X
State Diagram								X					X		X							X	X		X
Report Table		X		X			X	X		X					X							X			

FIGURE 26-4 Relationships between models.

Tables 26-1 through 26-22 describe how to improve your models by using information from one model with another. This list is not intended to be exhaustive; as you become more experienced with using models together, you will find relationships that might not occur often but that are still useful.

TABLE 26-1 Business Objectives Model

Model	How It Improves the Business Objectives Model
Objective Chain	When you identify features that are not mapped to any objectives, you might have identified new objectives that should be added to the Business Objectives Model.
Feature Tree	Use a Feature Tree to map the highest-level features to the Business Objectives Model to ensure that no objectives are missing.
Org Chart	Use the Org Chart to ensure that all objectives in the Business Objectives Model have a clearly identified executive stakeholder. Use the Org Chart to ensure all executives' business objectives are understood.

TABLE 26-2 Objective Chain

Model	How It Improves the Objective Chain
Business Objectives Model	Use the objectives in the Business Objectives Model to create the objectives for the Objective Chain.
Key Performance Indicator Model (KPIM)	Use the KPIs in the KPIM to identify objective factors and objective equations.
Feature Tree	Use the features in a Feature Tree to ensure that all the high-level features are accounted for in the Objective Chain and to identify any missing objectives based on features that don't map to objectives. Alternatively, any features in the Feature Tree that don't map to an objective might need to be cut.
Report Table	Looking at Report Tables can help you identify requirements associated with reports that help measure the business objectives.

TABLE 26-3 Key Performance Indicator Model (KPIM)

Model	How It Improves the KPIM
Business Objectives Model	Use the Business Objectives Model to identify which KPIs have the highest priority. Map the associated Process Flows to the Business Objectives Model to prioritize Process Flows associated with the KPIM.
Objective Chain	Use objective factors and objective equations to identify KPIs in the KPIM.
Process Flow	The KPIM is based on a Process Flow, so use the appropriate Process Flow as the basis for the KPIM.

TABLE 26-4 Feature Tree

Model	How It Improves the Feature Tree
Business Objectives Model	When first creating the Feature Tree, you will most likely start with the high-level features in the Business Objectives Model. In addition, if features in the Feature Tree don't map to business objectives, they might need to be cut from scope.
Objective Chain	Features in the Objective Chains will be used to populate the Feature Tree.
Requirements Mapping Matrix (RMM)	Often, you will create the RMM first and then use the features in the RMM to populate the Feature Tree. The Feature Tree is very effective at communicating features, but not necessarily at finding missing features.
Report Table	Reports often become a specific branch in the Feature Tree.
Ecosystem Map	Use the Ecosystem Map to ensure that there are features to support the exchange of data between systems based on system interfaces identified in the Ecosystem Map.

TABLE 26-5 Requirements Mapping Matrix (RMM)

Model	How It Improves the RMM
Business Objectives Model	Use the Business Objectives Model to prioritize features in the RMM by assigning the features with the highest value the highest priority.
Objective Chain	Use Objective Chains to prioritize features in the RMM by assigning the features with the highest value the highest priority.
KPIM	Use KPIMs to prioritize features in the RMM by assigning features with the highest value the highest priority.
Feature Tree	It is possible to use the Feature Tree to ensure that the RMM includes all features. This commonly occurs when the project has been kicked off with a feature list before most other work has been done.
Process Flow	Process Flows are the primary model used to organize requirements in an RMM. You assign requirements to each step in the Process Flow.
Use Case	You can use Use Case steps as the organizer for your RMM. Each requirement is mapped to a Use Case step.
System Flow	System Flows can be used to organize requirements. System Flow steps without business rules or requirements help to identify missing requirements.
UI Flow	UI Flows help to identify requirements that then go into the RMM. By looking at how the users transition between screens, you can identify the requirements that are needed to enable those transitions.
Display-Action-Response (DAR) Model	The DAR is one of the primary models to help elicit the requirements and business rules for the RMM. By looking at each element and identifying the functions on the screen as well as the business rules associated with each field, you will identify the requirements and business rules in the RMM.
Decision Table	Decision Tables provide business rules that populate the RMM.
Decision Tree	Decision Trees provide business rules that populate the RMM.
Data Dictionary	The fields from a Data Dictionary can be used in the business rules of an RMM.

TABLE 26-6 Org Chart

Model	How It Improves the Org Chart
Business Objectives Model	Use the Business Objectives Model to ensure that you have identified and assigned executive owners to each business objective. If the owner of an objective is not in the Org Chart, then she should be added.
Objective Chain	If you discover that some steps in the Objective Chains have missing owners, that might mean that you are missing critical stakeholders in the Org Chart.
RMM	Use the RMM to ensure that each Process Flow step has an owner who is in the Org Chart.
Roles and Permissions Matrix	The roles used to define permissions in a Roles and Permissions Matrix should all be in the Org Chart.
Process Flow	The users executing Process Flow steps should be individuals from an Org Chart.
Ecosystem Map	Identifying stakeholders who own each system can identify additional technical stakeholders in the Org Chart.
System Flow	Identifying additional stakeholders who own each System Flow can identify additional stakeholders for an Org Chart.
Decision Table	Identifying the users who make each decision can identify additional individuals for the Org Chart.

Model	How It Improves the Org Chart
Decision Tree	Identifying the users who make each decision can identify additional individuals for the Org Chart.
System Interface Table	Clearly identifying the owner of every System Interface Table can identify new stakeholders, especially technical stakeholders.
Data Dictionary	Identifying the users who create, update, use, delete, copy, and move data can identify additional individuals for the Org Chart.
Report Table	Mapping reports and report requirements to owners can ensure that you have spoken to all owners.

TABLE 26-7 Process Flow

Model	How It Improves the Process Flow
Business Objectives Model	The problems, objectives, and product concept for the project will narrow down which L1 Process Flows and steps are ultimately in scope.
Feature Tree	Features in the Feature Tree should be used in Process Flow steps, and if they are not, steps are probably missing from the Process Flows.
RMM	Find requirements in the RMM that are not mapped to Process Flows to identify potentially missing Process Flows or process steps.
Org Chart	Use stakeholders in the Org Chart to ensure that every Process Flow has an assigned owner that exists in the Org Chart. This will ensure that you speak to a representative from every group. Create a mapping of users to Process Flow to ensure that you have assigned an owner to every process step.
Use Case	Use Cases further define L2 or L3 Process Flow steps by describing the interactions between the user and the system to execute user tasks.
Roles and Permissions Matrix	The operations in a Roles and Permissions Matrix should correspond to parts of Process Flows.
Ecosystem Map	Use the Ecosystem Map when interviewing stakeholders, to ask them how they use a variety of different systems to execute their business process. The Ecosystem Map can jog a stakeholder's memory and remind him of Process Flows that go across multiple systems.
System Flow	A System Flow identifies the processes that are automatically executed by the system. Determining how the System Flow is set up, initiated, and triggers responses from users can help to identify missing Process Flows.
User Interface (UI) Flow	A UI Flow can help users to think about the process they go through as they encounter various screens in an existing or future application. Walk them through the UI to identify the business process they use.
DAR	You can walk business stakeholders through the actual fields in a screen in sequence to identify the very detailed Process Flows. Be careful not to include user interface element interaction in the Process Flow.
Decision Table	Decision Tables can be used to help clean up a Process Flow by moving complex decision making out of the Process Flow.
Decision Tree	Decision Trees can be used to help clean up a Process Flow by moving complex decision making out of the Process Flow.
Business Data Diagram (BDD)	All data is only ever created, updated, used, deleted, moved, or copied. Based on these verbs, you can use the BDD to ensure that you have Process Flows covering these actions for the most important business data objects.
Data Flow Diagram (DFD)	The processes in a DFD are described by Process Flows or parts of Process Flows.
Data Dictionary	The Data Dictionary can be used to provide the fields referenced in a Process Flow.

Model	How It Improves the Process Flow
State Table	Matching State Tables against Process Flows will help to ensure that the processes address every state in the State Table.
State Diagram	Matching State Diagrams against Process Flows will help to ensure that the processes address every state in the State Diagram.
Report Table	Identifying reports that are not yet mapped to any Process Flow can help you to identify missing Process Flows.

TABLE 26-8 Use Case

Model	How It Improves the Use Case
Business Objectives Model	Use the Business Objectives Model to complete the organizational benefit portion of the Use Case. The Business Objectives Model can also help prioritize Use Cases for completion.
Feature Tree	Feature Trees help identify Use Cases because features might need Use Cases to describe how they function in the solution.
RMM	Find requirements in the RMM that are not mapped to Process Flows or Use Case steps to identify potentially missing Use Cases or Use Case steps.
Org Chart	Use stakeholders in the Org Chart to ensure that you are using the correct nomenclature for the users in the Use Case.
Process Flow	The Process Flow might identify steps that warrant additional interaction details to be described in a Use Case. The Process Flow does not include system responses, whereas the Use Case does.
BDD	All data is only ever created, updated, used, deleted, moved, or copied. Based on these verbs, you can use the BDD to ensure that you have Use Cases covering these actions for the most important business data objects.
DFD	The processes in a DFD might be described by Use Cases.

TABLE 26-9 Roles and Permissions Matrix

Model	How It Improves the Roles and Permissions Matrix
Feature Tree	Use features in the Feature Tree as areas of ownership in the Roles and Permissions Matrix.
RMM	Use the RMM to identify functions that need restricted access. Often there are a few role-based security requirements that should be moved to the Roles and Permissions Matrix.
Org Chart	Use an Org Chart to identify the roles in the Roles and Permissions Matrix.
Process Flow	Use Process Flows as the areas of ownership in the Roles and Permissions Matrix.
Use Case	Use Use Cases as the areas of ownership in the Roles and Permissions Matrix.
UI Flow	The UI Flow identifies screens that might need permissions defined in the Roles and Permissions Matrix.
DAR	Use individual screens or areas of screens as areas of ownership in the Roles and Permissions Matrix.
BDD	Use the BDD to determine the business data objects that need to have restricted access.
Data Dictionary	Use the Data Dictionary to determine the attributes that need to have restricted access.
Report Table	Use reports as areas of ownership in the Roles and Permissions Matrix.

TABLE 26-10 Ecosystem Map

Model	How It Improves the Ecosystem Map
Process Flow	Stepping through Process Flows and identifying which system the users use to execute the process is one of the best ways to find missing systems in the Ecosystem Map.
BDD	Identifying which systems contain a particular piece of data is a useful way of identifying missing systems in the Ecosystem Map.
Data Flow Diagram (DFD)	Looking at each system that processes data is a good way to ensure that you have identified all systems in the Ecosystem Map.

TABLE 26-11 System Flow

Model	How It Improves the System Flow
Feature Tree	Features from the Feature Tree might be used in System Flow steps, and if they are not, then steps might be missing from the System Flows.
RMM	Requirements for the system to automatically process data that don't map to a System Flow can help to identify missing System Flows or System Flow steps.
Process Flow	Process Flows often result in the creation of a System Flow when you identify that the flow is executed by the system, not a user.
Use Case	Use Cases can help to identify System Flows if there are many consecutive system response steps in the Use Case.
Ecosystem Map	The interfaces between systems in an Ecosystem Map might warrant System Flows to describe them.
UI Flow	UI Flows often specify logic the system has to perform to determine how a user is allowed to go from screen to screen. This often results in a System Flow diagram.
DAR	DAR models often reference complex System Flows that occur after a user takes an action.
Decision Table	Decision Tables can be used to help clean up a System Flow by moving complex decision making out of the System Flow.
Decision Tree	Decision Trees can be used to help clean up a System Flow by moving complex decision making out of the System Flow.
System Interface Table	System Interface Tables might identify System Flows for error handling.
DFD	A DFD contains processes that manipulate data, and those processes might be represented as System Flows or parts of System Flows.
State Table	Matching State Tables against System Flows will help to ensure that the processes address every state in the State Table.
State Diagram	Matching State Diagrams against System Flows will help to ensure that the processes address every state in the State Diagram.

TABLE 26-12 UI Flow

Model	How It Improves the UI Flow
Use Case	Walking through Use Cases to see how they are executed in the UI Flow can be helpful for finding missing transitions in the UI Flow or usability issues with the transitions between screens.
DAR	DAR models are used as the screens referenced in a UI Flow. If you have a DAR model for a screen that is not in the UI Flow, it probably should be added.
Process Flow	Walking through Process Flows to see how they are executed in the UI Flow can be helpful for finding missing transitions in the UI Flow or usability issues with the transitions between screens.

TABLE 26-13 DAR Model

Model	How It Improves the DAR Model
Process Flow	Process Flows can be used to ensure that a DAR model contains all the functions and business rules to properly execute the Process Flow.
Use Case	Use Cases can be used to ensure that a DAR model contains all the functions and business rules to properly execute the Use Case.
UI Flow	The UI Flow shows all screens. This diagram can be used to ensure that you have a complete set of DAR models. The transitions between screens in the UI Flow might be documented in the DAR.
State Table	Matching State Tables against DARs will help to identify all the preconditions that influence the way the system displays and behaves.
State Diagram	Matching State Diagrams against DARs will help to identify all the preconditions that influence the way the system behaves.
Report Table	Report Tables that specify highly interactive reports could identify the need for DAR models to be created.

TABLE 26-14 Decision Table

Model	How It Improves the Decision Table
Process Flow	Decision Tables are often created when decision logic becomes too complex in a Process Flow.
Use Case	Decision Tables are often created when decision logic becomes too complex for a Use Case.
System Flow	System Flows are often used to identify Decision Tables when the decision logic becomes too complex.
UI Flow	Decision Tables are often created when decision logic becomes too complex for a UI Flow.
Decision Tree	Decision Trees can be used to directly create Decision Tables.

TABLE 26-15 Decision Tree

Model	How It Improves the Decision Tree
Process Flow	Decision Trees are often created when decision logic becomes too complex in a Process Flow.
Use Case	Decision Trees are often created when decision logic becomes too complex for a Use Case.
System Flow	System Flows are often used to identify Decision Trees when the decision logic becomes too complex.
UI Flow	Decision Trees are often created when decision logic becomes too complex for a UI Flow.
Decision Table	Decision Tables can be used to directly create Decision Trees.

TABLE 26-16 System Interface Table

Model	How It Improves the System Interface Table
KPIM	Use the KPIM to obtain information about how often activities occur and how many people perform them, which will drive the data volume needs in System Interface Tables.
Ecosystem Map	The Ecosystem Map is the primary model for determining the list of System Interface Tables.
System Flow	Use System Flows to describe error-handling processes in System Interface Tables.
BDD	Use BDDs to identify which business data objects might need to be passed across the system interface.
Data Dictionary	Use the Data Dictionary to provide the list of all fields and business data objects for the target and source systems in a System Interface Table. Data Dictionaries also provide business rules and the volume of the data passed between the systems.

TABLE 26-17 Business Data Diagram (BDD)

Model	How It Improves the BDD
Feature Tree	Features often mention business data objects. All business data objects in the Feature Tree should be in the BDD.
RMM	Requirements often mention business data objects. All business data objects in the RMM should be in the BDD.
Process Flow	Process Flows often refer to business data objects. In these cases, the Process Flow can be checked against the BDD to ensure that the BDD contains those business data objects.
Use Case	Use Cases often refer to business data objects. In these cases, the Process Flow can be checked against the BDD to ensure that the BDD contains those business data objects.
Ecosystem Map	Interfaces between systems in the Ecosystem Map describe business data objects that cross system boundaries. These should be in the BDD.
System Flow	System Flows often refer to business data objects. In these cases, the System Flow can be checked against the BDD to ensure that the BDD contains those business data objects.
DAR	The business data objects in a DAR are often directly used in a BDD.
Data Dictionary	Fields that are not associated with an object in a BDD might mean that objects are missing from the BDD.

TABLE 26-18 Data Flow Diagram (DFD)

Model	How It Improves the DFD
Org Chart	Use the Org Chart to help identify missing external entities in the DFD.
Ecosystem Map	Looking at how business data objects flow through the systems in the Ecosystem Map will form the basis for the DFD.
BDD	The business data objects in a BDD are the objects that are used in a DFD.
Data Dictionary	Often individual fields are transformed, so the fields in the Data Dictionary are the data that is transformed in a DFD.

TABLE 26-19 Data Dictionary

Model	How It Improves the Data Dictionary
Feature Tree	Features often mention fields. All fields in the Feature Tree should be in the Data Dictionary.
RMM	Requirements often mention fields. All fields in the RMM should be in the Data Dictionary.
Use Case	Use Case steps can help identify data fields that might be needed in order to execute the steps.
DAR	Almost all fields in a DAR need to be listed in the Data Dictionary. The DAR is a great way to find missing fields.
Decision Table	Decision Tables use data from a Data Dictionary. This can identify critical data missing from the Data Dictionary.
Decision Tree	Decision Trees use data from a Data Dictionary. This can identify critical data missing from the Data Dictionary.
BDD	All fields in a Data Dictionary should relate to an object in the BDD.
State Table	The state of an object is usually mapped to a specific field. This field is often overlooked in the Data Dictionary.
State Diagram	The state of an object is usually mapped to a specific field. This field is often overlooked in the Data Dictionary.
Report Table	Existing reports are one of the best ways to identify missing data elements in a Data Dictionary.

TABLE 26-20 State Table

Model	How It Improves the State Table
Process Flow	When a decision in a Process Flow is based on the state of an object, this can identify the need for a State Table.
Use Case	When a decision in a Use Case is based on the state of an object, this can identify the need for a State Table.
System Flow	When a decision in a System Flow is based on the state of an object, this can identify the need for a State Table.
UI Flow	When a branch in a UI Flow is based on the state of an object, this can identify additional states for the object.
DAR	When DAR preconditions are based on the state of an object, this can identify additional states for the object.
Decision Table	When a decision is based on the state of an object, this can identify additional states for the object.

Model	How It Improves the State Table
Decision Tree	When a decision is based on the state of an object, this can identify additional states for the object.
BDD	State Tables show the transition of business data objects in the BDD. You can use BDDs to help identify business data objects that might need a state model.
State Diagram	State Tables can be generated directly from a State Diagram.

TABLE 26-21 State Diagram

Model	How It Improves the State Diagram
Process Flow	When a decision in a Process Flow is based on the state of an object, this can identify the need for a State Diagram.
Use Case	When a decision in a Use Case is based on the state of an object, this can identify the need for a State Diagram.
System Flow	When a decision in a System Flow is based on the state of an object, this can identify the need for a State Diagram.
UI Flow	When a branch in a UI Flow is based on the state of an object, this can identify additional states for the object.
DAR	When DAR preconditions are based on the state of an object, this can identify additional states for the object.
Decision Table	When a decision is based on the state of an object, this can identify additional states for the object.
Decision Tree	When a decision is based on the state of an object, this can identify additional states for the object.
BDD	State Diagrams show the transition of business data objects in the BDD. You can use BDDs to help identify business data objects that might need a state model.
State Table	State Diagrams can be generated directly from a State Table.

TABLE 26-22 Report Table

Model	How It Improves the Report Table
Business Objectives Model	The business objectives or success metrics should be measured by a report. If the objectives cannot be directly measured, then potentially a proxy for the measurement from the Objective Chain should be used.
Objective Chain	All objective factors should be monitored in a report to enable the business to determine the actual value achieved by the solution. In the event that an objective factor cannot be directly measured, a proxy should be used.
KPIM	All KPIs should be monitored by a report to enable the business to ensure that the KPIs were met. In the event that a KPI cannot be directly measured, a proxy should be used.
RMM	Many requirements end up either being reports themselves or requiring reports. The RMM represents the full list of requirements and can be used to identify reports.
Process Flow	Each decision in a Process Flow will usually require a report that is used to make the decision. This can help to identify missing reports.
Decision Table	Each decision might require a report that the decision is based on. Looking at decisions can help to identify missing reports.
Decision Tree	Each decision might require a report on which the decision is based. Looking at decisions can help to identify missing reports.

Model	How It Improves the Report Table
BDD	Each report should reference business data objects from BDDs.
Data Dictionary	Each report should reference data elements using the <*object.field*> notation from a Data Dictionary.
State Table	Use the State Table to identify when it might be useful to see a full report on the objects by state.
State Diagram	Use the State Diagram to identify which business data objects might require a report to show the objects by state.

Exercise

The following exercise is intended to help you to gain a better understanding of the material in this chapter. The exercise is open ended, and therefore the answer you come up with could be substantially different than the answer that we have provided. There are potentially many correct solutions. The answer provides an explanation of how we arrived at our solution. You will gain the most out of the exercise by attempting to do it yourself before looking at the solution. The answers for the exercises can be found in Appendix C.

Instructions

Consider the scenario. Describe how you would use models together.

Scenario

You are on a project to launch a new eStore to sell flamingos and other lawn decorations, and you have to document all of the requirements.

You create a Process Flow for the wish list, a State Diagram for the shopping cart and wish list, a BDD for the key business data objects, a Data Dictionary for the cart, DAR models for the screens, and an RMM.

APPENDIX A

Quick Lookup Models Grids

This appendix can be used as a quick reference when you are trying to determine which models to use on your project. It summarizes the selection of models (see Chapter 25, "Selecting Models for a Project") in a simple grid format. You can download a copy of these grids to have them handy for times when you do not have the book handy. In fact, we like to keep a laminated copy at our desks so we have it as a tool to look at quickly when we are working on a project.

Figure A-1 shows the full grid of models by project characteristic. You use it by deciding which rows apply to your project. You should select as many of the characteristics as are appropriate. Then you read to the right to see which models are recommended for that project type and those characteristics. Keep in mind that we have not created a comprehensive set of project characteristics, so you will almost certainly have to create your own rows as you encounter project characteristics that we did not list.

If a cell is blank, it means that the particular characteristic alone does not indicate the need for that particular model. You might still need the model on your project, but it will be because your project has a different characteristic that applies to it that recommends the model. Conversely, if the cell is filled in, it means the characteristic alone is sufficient to indicate that the model is needed for that type of project. Table A-1 shows what the cell values in the grid mean.

TABLE A-1 Grid of Models by Project Characteristic

Meaning	Cell Value
Likely to be needed	L
Might be needed	M
Not needed based on this characteristic alone	Blank

Project Characteristics (pick one or more that apply)	Models																									
	Objectives	Business Objectives Model	Objective Chain	Key Performance Indicator Model	Feature Tree	Requirements Mapping Matrix	People	Org Chart	Process Flow	Use Case	Roles and Permissions Matrix	Systems	Ecosystem Map	System Flow	UI Flow	Display-Action-Response Model	Decision Table	Decision Tree	System Interface Table	Data	Business Data Diagram	Data Flow Diagram	Data Dictionary	State Table	State Diagram	Report Table
Objective characteristics																										
Greenfield		L	L		L	L																				
COTS selection		M	M	L	L	L		L	L				L								L		M			
COTS implementation		M	M	L		L		L	L	M	L		L	L		M					L		L			L
Enhancement		L	L		L	L																				
People characteristics																										
Extensive user interaction									L	M	L				L	L										
Customer-facing									M	M	M				L	L										
Business process automation				L				L	L	M	M										L		L			
Workflow automation									L		L										L			L	L	
System characteristics																										
System replacement				L	L	L		L	L	M	M		L	M	M				M		L	M	L			L
Real-time and embedded system													M	L					M			M		M	M	
Large ecosystem													L						M		L	L	L			
Internal IT								L	L		L		L						M							
Hardware and software													L	L					L							
Packaged software					L	L			L	M					L	L										
Cloud implementation								M	L		L		L	M					M					L	L	
Web app													L	L	M	M					L		L			
Mobile									M	L			M	M	L	L										
Complex decision logic																	L	L						M	M	
Data characteristics																										
Analytics and reporting									M								M	M			L	L	L			L
Database back-end components																					L	L	L			
Data warehouse																					L	L	L			

FIGURE A-1 The quick lookup grid of models by project characteristic.

Figure A-2 shows a summary of the models needed by project phase, which is described in more detail in Chapter 25. The grid is meant to help you get a feel for when in your project to create and use the models. Keep in mind that not all projects will follow these phases exactly. For example, if a project is already underway, you might create a Business Objectives Model in the Plan phase because there is no Envision phase. Table A-2 shows what the cell values in the grid mean.

TABLE A-2 Key for the Grid of Models by Project Phase

Meaning	Cell Value
Created	C
Used	U

Project Phase	Objectives	Business Objectives Model	Objective Chain	Key Performance Indicator Model	Feature Tree	Requirements Mapping Matrix	People	Org Chart	Process Flow	Use Case	Roles and Permissions Matrix	Systems	Ecosystem Map	System Flow	UI Flow	Display-Action-Response Model	Decision Table	Decision Tree	System Interface Table	Data	Business Data Diagram	Data Flow Diagram	Data Dictionary	State Table	State Diagram	Report Table
Envision		C			C			C					C													
Plan		U	C	C	U	C		U	C	C	C		U	C	C	C	C	C	C		C	C	C	C	C	C
Develop		U	U	U	U	U		U	U	U	U		U	U	U	U	U	U	U		U	U	U	U	U	U
Launch									U	U	U					U										
Measure		U		U																						

(Column group heading: Models)

FIGURE A-2 The quick lookup grid of models by project phase.

Additional Resources

- The quick lookup models grids can be downloaded for reuse from *http://go.microsoft.com/FWLink/?Linkid=253518.*

APPENDIX B

General Guidelines for Models

There are some aspects of models that are the same for every model and will help your stakeholders understand the models better. These guidelines apply to most of the models, though you should use your judgement as to when to apply them.

Metadata to Include in Models

Although the greater part of the model templates vary from model to model, there is some information that you might want to include in every model you create, as listed in the following table. If you use a requirements management tool, some of this information will be kept for you automatically.

Metadata	Definition
Title	Name of the model
Author	Person who created the model
Project	The project the model is for
Release	Which release of the project the model is for
Description	A short summary of what the model describes
Unique identifier	A unique identifier used to refer to the model from other models
Related documents	A list of other documents that are relevant to the model
Version history	A history of changes made to the model over time
Date created	When the model was created
Date modified	When the model was last modified
Approvers	The stakeholders who have read and will approve or have approved the model
Location	Where the model is stored, which allows people with hard copies to find the source document and people with local copies to find the most recent version

General Guidelines and Tips

These are some guidelines we recommend that you follow, to ensure readability in all models that you create.

- Make sure that all similar shapes are the same size. For example, Process Flow steps should all be the same size, and decision diamonds should all be the same size. The exception to this guideline is that if you need more space to fit text inside a shape, then you might want to make one instance of the shape larger than others if making them all bigger wastes a lot of space.
- Make sure that the text in all similar shapes is the same size. For example, if you change the font size in one box to have room for the Process Flow step, all the boxes might need to be changed to be consistent. At a minimum, you should try to make text the same size in similar shapes (for example, in Process Flow steps), but ideally you can make the text the same size in all shapes in a model (Process Flow steps and decision diamonds).
- When there are levels of models, number your models consistently within them. For example, label the L1 Process Flow steps numerically from left to right and then name and number the L2 Process Flows by referencing the step in the L1 from which they are called. Use the same numbering scheme across similar models on the same project, such as Process Flows and System Flows.
- When you use colors to differentiate elements within models, make sure to also differentiate by using a technique that will be evident if your models are printed in grayscale. For example, you could use patterns or change the type of outline on the shape.
- Try to keep aesthetic clarity by balancing the objects in your model with the white space. For example, don't clump your objects together; make use of the space you have.
- When the information has an underlying order, reinforce the order by presenting it from the upper left and flow to the lower right.
- Use active voice for all text in the models.
- Use consistent capitalization (sentence caps or title case) within similar models on a project. For example, capitalize the first letter of only the first word of all Process Flow steps in all Process Flows on your project.
- Present metadata in consistent locations in all models. For example, if you are creating a Microsoft Visio file for a set of Process Flows, and the Process Flows share metadata, create one page at the back of the Visio file to contain the metadata. Then create a similar page with the same name in the same location in all Visio files that contain models.

APPENDIX C

Exercise Answers

Chapter 3

The results of this exercise might vary greatly, depending on the questions you thought to ask and the answers you made up to those questions. The following list provides some reasonable questions and possible answers you might get if you ask them.

- *What problems are you trying to solve by building an eStore?* We think that another sales channel will increase our existing revenue.
- *What happens if you do not increase revenue?* Our executive team is hoping to sell the company within five years, and to do so, we have to reach $20 million in revenue.
- *How do you think an eStore will help to increase revenue?* We think many people out of our area will want to buy these products.
- *What is preventing you from selling to those people today?* Mainly they are not in our area and we have no cost-effective way to market to them.
- *How much do you want to increase revenue next year?* By the end of the year, we want to be at $12.5 million. By the end of five years, we want to be at $20 million in revenue per year.
- *Do you plan to convert phone orders to online orders?* We might convert some of our existing customers to buying online. However, we expect to attract new customers who are unwilling to make a phone call today to place an order, but who will buy from us if the entire order is completed online.
- *Is adding new customers the only way in which you expect to increase revenue?* No, we also expect to see our converted existing customers buy more online than on the phone because they will see more products that might interest them.
- *How will you attract new customers?* By marketing our eStore, we hope to attract new customers who would not shop with us via phone previously.
- *How will you increase existing customer purchases?* Our sales reps can tell existing customers about the new eStore when they talk to them on the phone. We will also send email campaigns to let them know about the eStore launch.

The preceding questions and answers help develop the Business Objectives Model in Figure C-1.

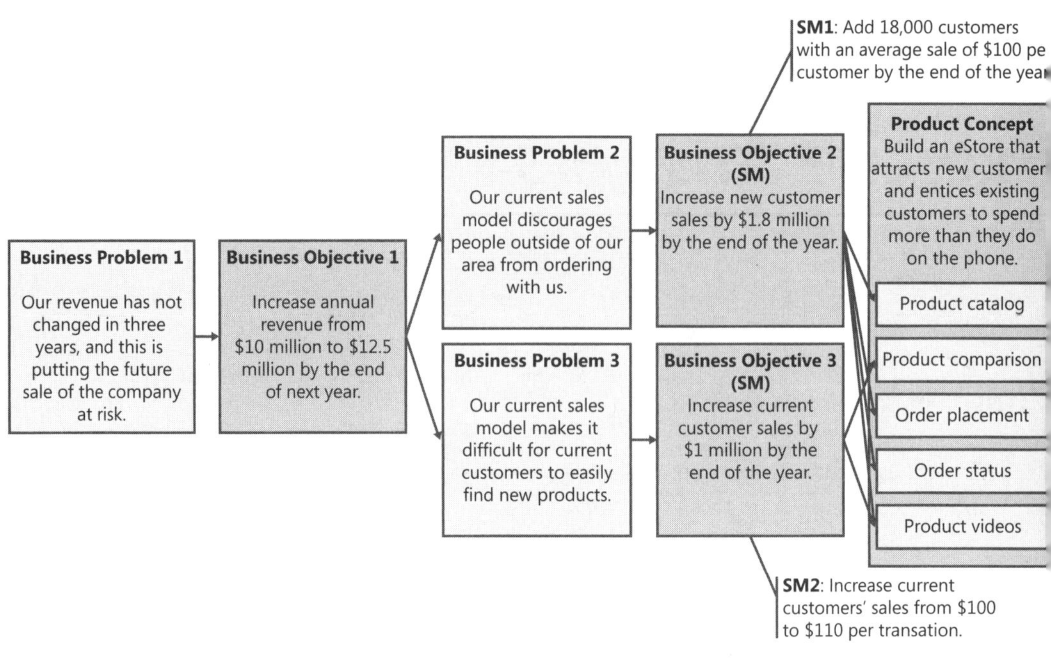

FIGURE C-1 The eStore Business Objectives Model.

Chapter 4

The business objective and features are suggested in the scenario, so the work is in creating the objective factors and objective equations to link them. To identify the objective factors, ask, "How does this feature increase revenue?" Some possible responses to this question include:

- Product catalogs make customers aware of more products than they would be exposed to by ordering on the phone, leading to an increase in the number of products purchased per order
- Cross-selling proposes products that might go well with the current purchases. Product ratings and reviews give the customers more information about the products and the comfort of knowing that other consumers have approved of the quality of the product.
- Adding an online purchase path attracts new visitors to the site, some of whom will become customers.

To complete the objective equations and calculate each feature's value, the team could make assumptions that might look like any of the following:

- New customers are expected to spend the same amount of money that existing customers would spend online.
- Online customers spend about the same amount of money as telephone customers.
- Cross-selling increases the average order size by 3 percent.
- Ratings and reviews increase average order size by 10 percent.
- Seeing additional products leads to one additional product purchased per customer.
- The additional product purchased by an existing customer is a $10 product.
- The eStore will attract 20,000 new online visitors per year.
- 90 percent of online visitors will place an order.

The resulting objective equations and feature values are calculated as follows:

- Adding a product catalog to the site increases each order from existing customers by one product, and each product is an additional $10. With 100,000 orders currently, that is $1,000,000 in additional revenue.
- The cross-sell and ratings and review features will generate 3 percent and 10 percent increases in the average order size, respectively. With $3 more per order for cross-sell orders and 100,000 orders, there is an increase in revenue of $300,000. With $10 more per order for ratings and review and 100,000 orders, there is an increase in revenue of $1,000,000.
- If 20,000 new potential customers visit the site and 90 percent of them purchase products within a year, there will be 18,000 new orders. At $100 per order, that amounts to $1,800,000 in new revenue.

The final Objective Chain is shown in Figure C-2. Based on the Objective Chain, the team can now work with the development team and stakeholders to determine the cost to implement each feature, and then prioritization will be straightforward.

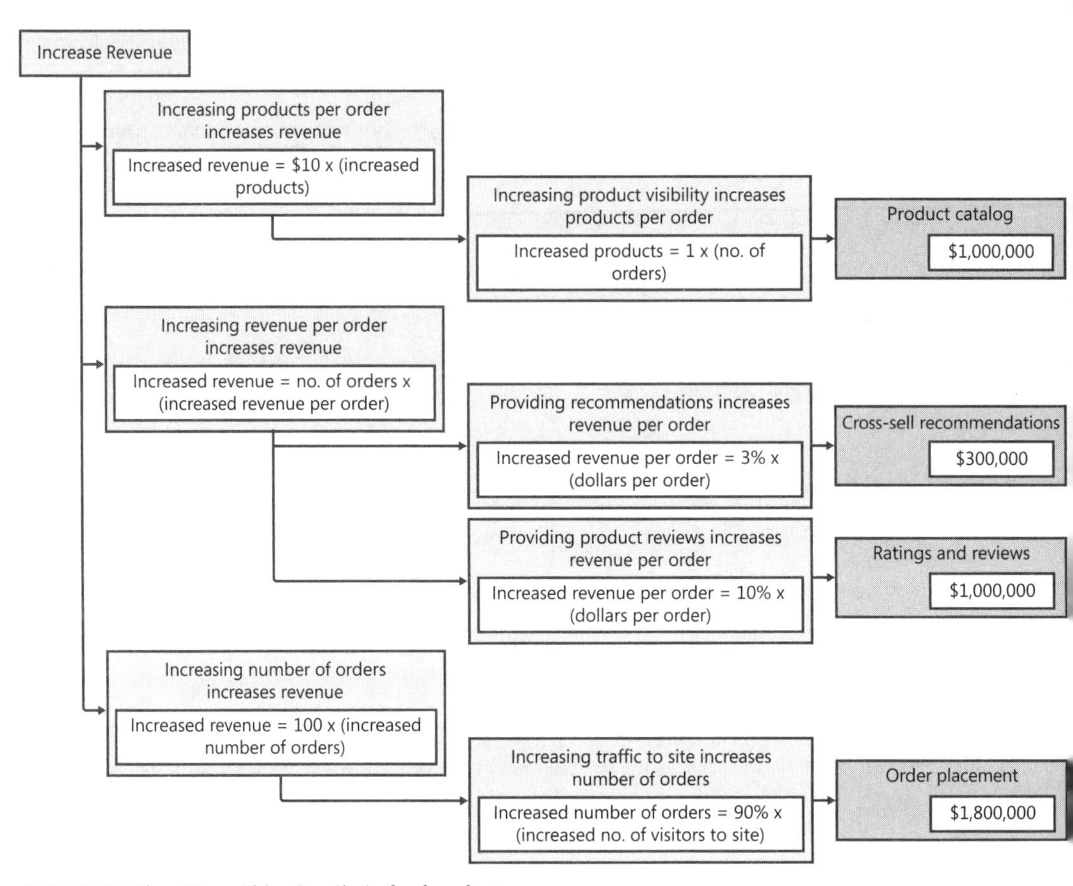

FIGURE C-2 The eStore Objective Chain for four features.

Chapter 5

There are three KPIs the sales managers measure currently and want to maintain in the new system. The KPIs are overlaid on the Process Flow to create the KPIM shown in Figure C-3.

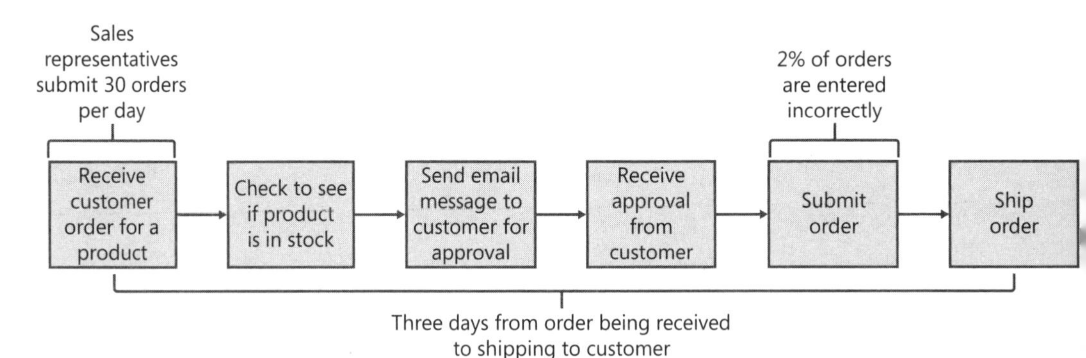

FIGURE C-3 The Key Performance Indicator Model for the process of preparing an order for shipment.

Chapter 6

In creating the Feature Tree, start by putting the features listed in the example scenario on sticky notes. You should identify features such as "Monitor load," "Related flamingos," "View system logs," "View site usage data," "Link cross-sell products," "Create account," "View site order data," "Update flamingo catalog," "Rate flamingos," "Browse flamingos," "Flamingo wish list," "Review flamingos," and "Purchase flamingos."

Then organize those features to form a first pass of groups of features, and add to the list of features based on those groups. For example, we identified the groupings "Shop for flamingos," "Flamingo wish list," "Manage account," "Manage flamingos," and "Monitor system." We can further look for features at this point and find we are missing a "Shopping cart" and an "Add flamingos to catalog" feature.

When there is a good draft list of features, move the features into a Feature Tree and continue to add features until it is complete, as shown in Figure C-4. Notice that at this point, the features were renamed to use noun phrases, for consistency. Finally, look for branches of the Feature Tree that are thin and ask about those. For example, is there any other type of account maintenance an administrator might need to do?

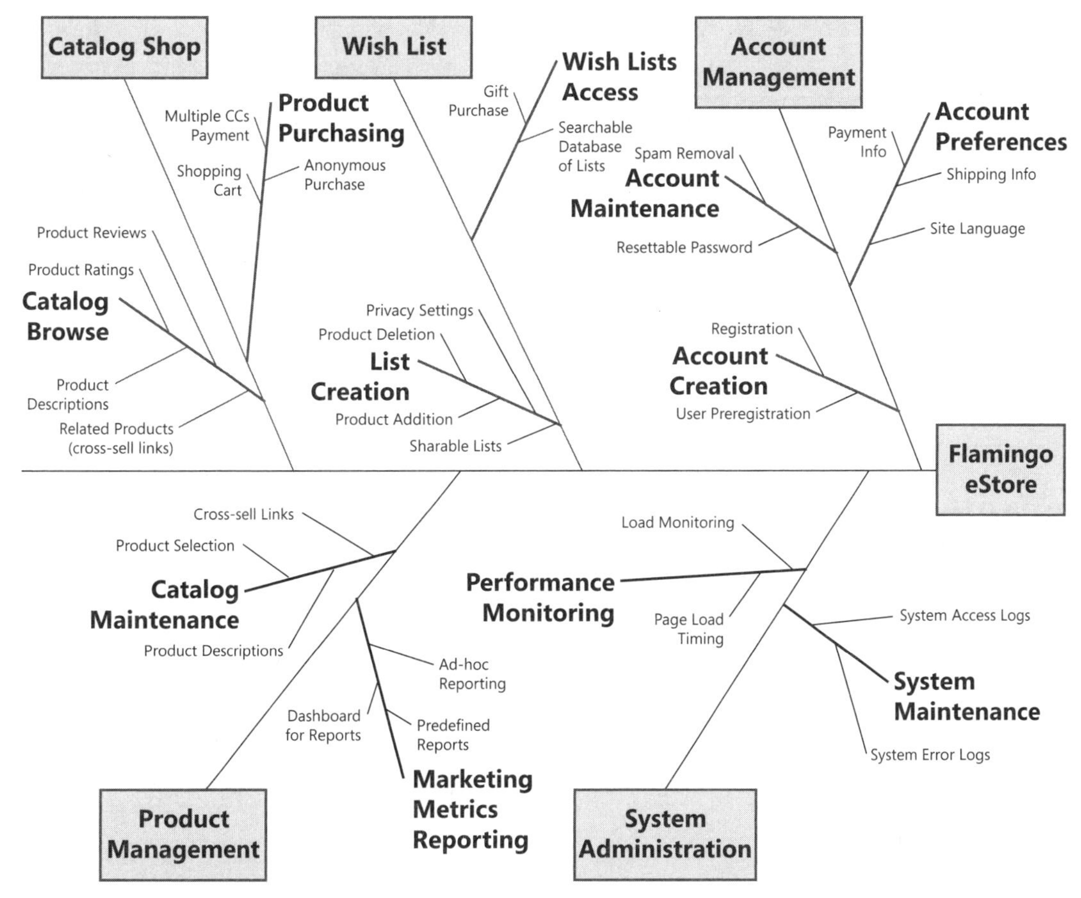

FIGURE C-4 A Feature Tree of eStore features.

Chapter 7

The L1, L2, and L3 Process Flow steps are mapped to one another, and a few examples of individual requirements for the exercise are mapped to the appropriate steps in the L3 Process Flow, as shown in Figure C-5. Business rules in this exercise are listed in the same row as the requirements.

L1 Process Step	L2 Process Step	L3 Process Step	Feature	REQID	Requirement	Business Rule
Determine products to restock	Determine how much to restock for each item	Product sells fast?	Restock	REQ001	Automatically compare historical sales rate against a predefined threshold	BR1: The default period is trailing three month
Determine products to restock	Determine how much to restock for each item	Product sells fast?	Restock	REQ002	Sales rate thresholds can be based on margin, units, or revenue	BR1: The default threshold is based on margin BR2: The default margin threshold is 5% lower than the trailing three month margin
Determine products to restock	Determine how much to restock for each item	Product sells fast?	Restock	REQ003	Sales rate thresholds can be compared over an arbitrary period	
Determine products to restock	Determine how much to restock for each item	Decide amount to restock	Restock	REQ004	System automatically restocks items below a threshold	BR1: Default threshold on all products is 20
Determine products to restock	Determine how much to restock for each item	Decide amount to restock	Restock	REQ005	System requests manual restocking when calculated automated restock exceeds the threshold	BR1: System checks stock inventory daily at midnight
Determine products to restock	Determine how much to restock for each item	More items to check?	Restock	REQ006	System shall be able to automatically determine which items need to be examined for restocking	

FIGURE C-5 A Requirements Mapping Matrix (RMM) for the eStore restocking process.

Chapter 8

To create the departmental Org Chart, create a second level under the president with each of the departments. Include the departments you know about for now, and follow up with stakeholders to identify any missing departments. For example, you might find that under Finance there is a Tax department that must be consulted to properly calculate tax for online orders. Be sure to include all branches so you can cut confidently as you determine that some of them are out of scope. What you might uncover is an overlooked department that you need to speak to about requirements; for instance, the IT branch of the company will certainly need to be understood. Figure C-6 shows the departmental Org Chart.

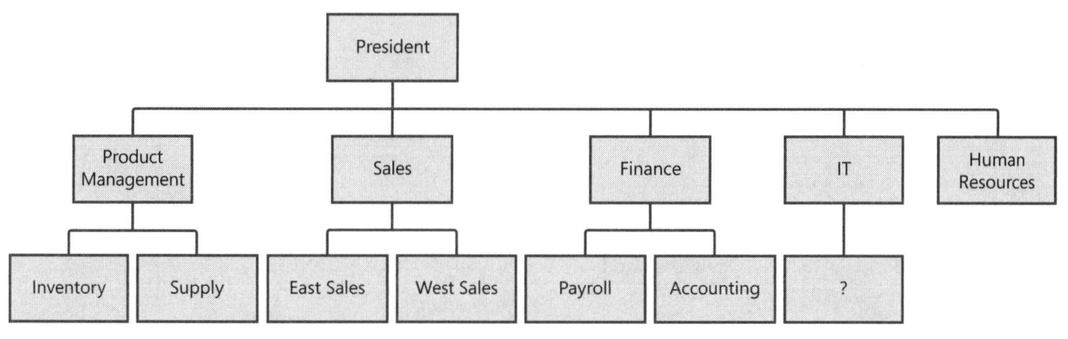

FIGURE C-6 The departmental Org Chart for the eStore team.

For the role Org Chart, shown in Figure C-7, label the actual roles that exist in each department. Ideally, maintain branches of the departmental Org Chart that are important to the project and cut the others. Keep in mind that the IT branch has not yet been defined and is a red flag for you to start speaking to stakeholders to understand who needs to be involved from that branch.

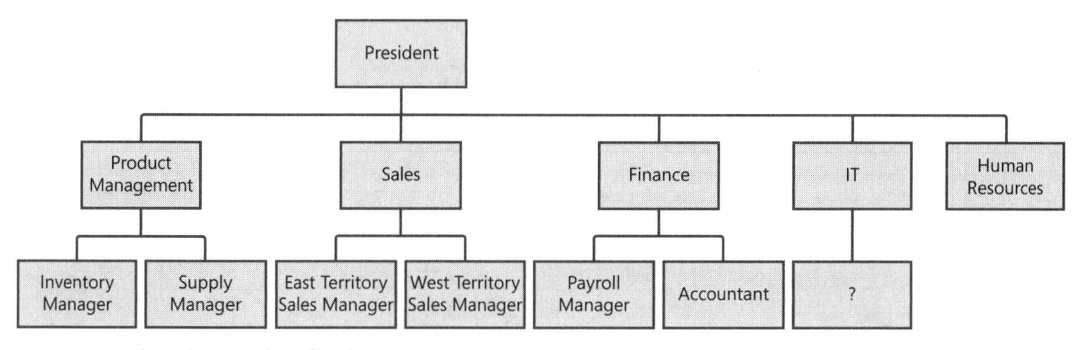

FIGURE C-7 The role Org Chart for the eStore team.

The individual Org Chart, shown in Figure C-8, can be created by putting the boxes on paper with the names and roles, then connecting them by their working relationship.

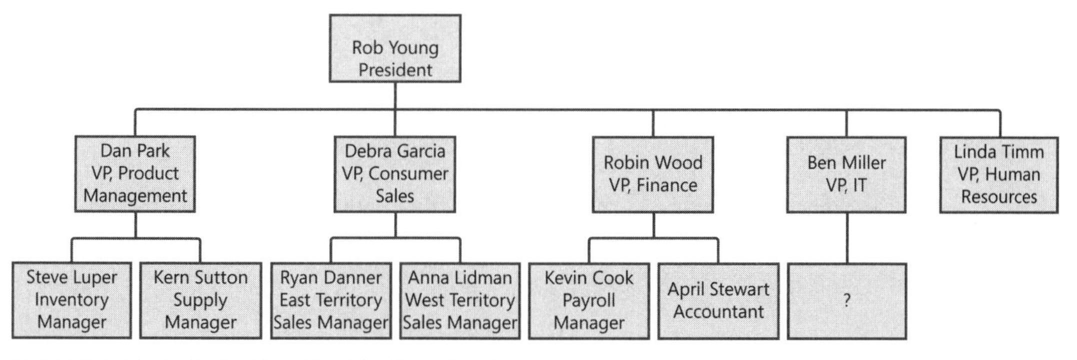

FIGURE C-8 The individual Org Chart for the eStore team.

Finally, you can see that the individual Org Chart still has an unknown under IT, so it is important to work with Ben Miller to understand his department to ensure that no one is left out of the meetings.

Chapter 9

The L1 Process Flow shows the end-to-end process at a very high level, as shown in Figure C-9.

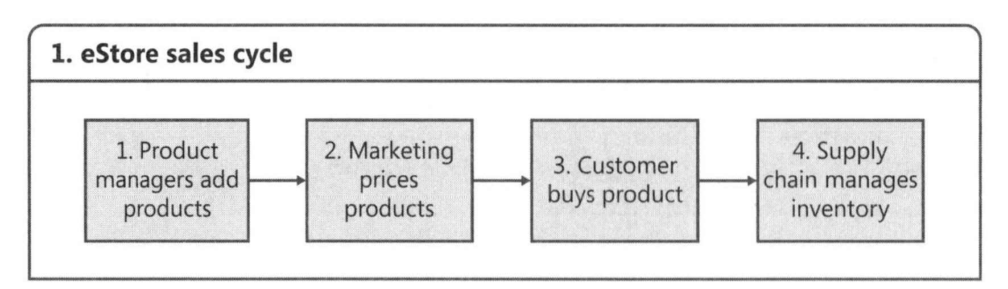

FIGURE C-9 L1 Process Flow for the eStore sales cycle.

You can then create an L2 Process Flow for the "Customer buys product" step in the L1 Process Flow. An example is shown in Figure C-10.

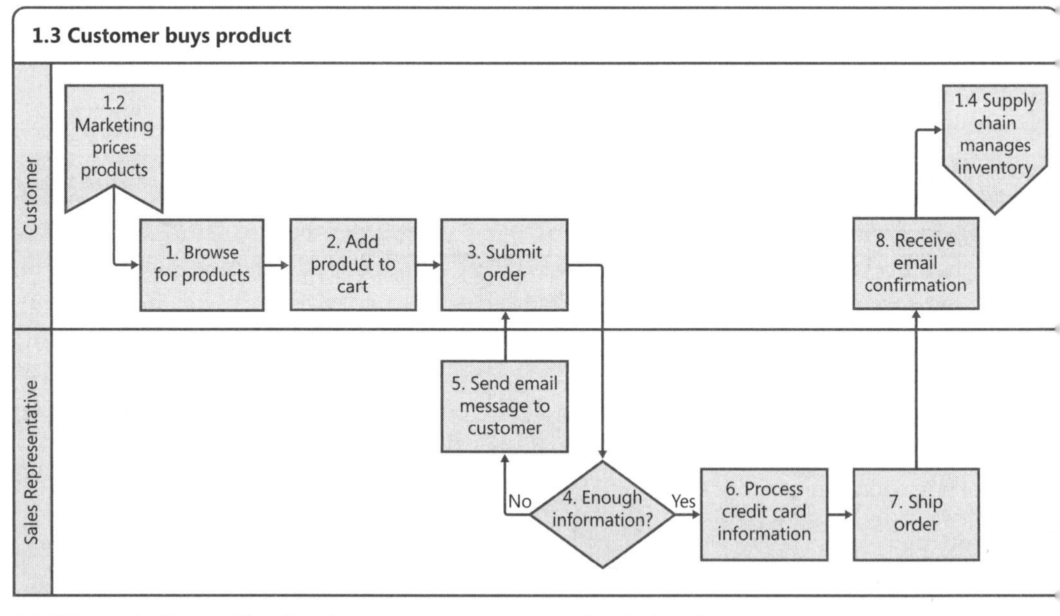

FIGURE C-10 L2 Process Flow for when a customer buys a product in the eStore.

And finally, you can create an L3 Process Flow to further detail the process of verifying that there is enough information to process the order (see Figure C-11 for an example).

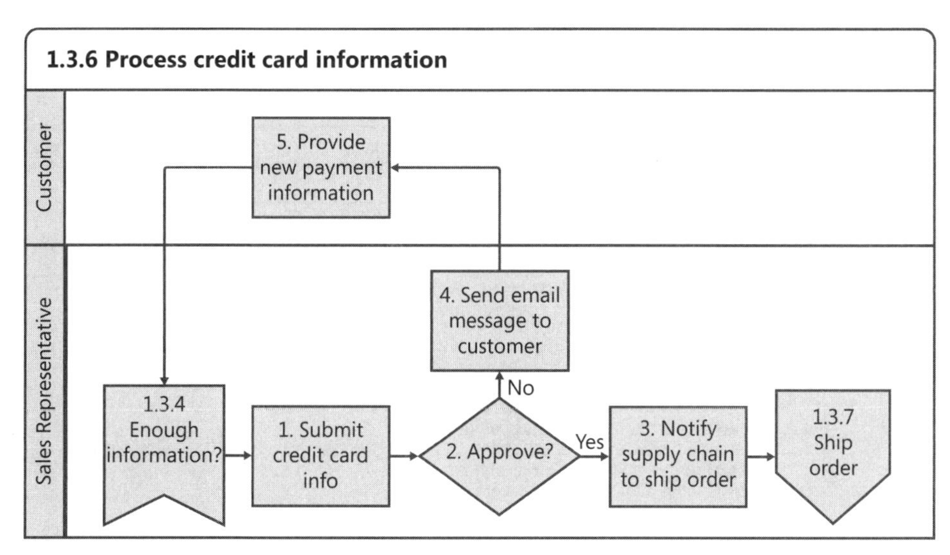

FIGURE C-11 L3 Process Flow for processing credit card information in the eStore.

Chapter 10

Figure C-12 shows an example Use Case for the scenario. This is a simple Use Case that does not include the search fields or product display fields within the Use Case. Those are requirements that are derived from the Use Case.

The following are sample requirements from this Use Case:

- From step 1: Products can be searched for by *<product.SKU>* or *<product.name>*.
- From step 3: Search results contain *<product.name>*, *<product.description>*, *<product.image>*, and *<product.date>*.
- From step 5: Products are displayed with the following fields from the product data system: *<product.name>*, *<product.description>*, *<product.image>*, *<product.datecreated>*, *<product.supplier>*, and *<product.colors>*.
- From step 5: User can choose to publish a product selected from the search results.

Also notice that an exception occurs if a product already exists in the eStore. This might prompt a conversation with the product managers to determine whether they really want those products to show up in the search results or if they want them to show up but with a flag to indicate that they are already in the eStore. The point is that in this example, the Use Case helped identity additional requirements by requiring the readers to think about the user's interaction.

Name	Add item to eStore.
ID	UC002
Description	An administrator adds an item to the eStore from the master product data set so it can be displayed for purchase online.
Actors	eStore Product Manager.
Organizational Benefits	Increase sales by making products readily available to online customers.
Frequency of Use	Twice a month during the eStore product and stock refresh, approximately 20 new products added each time.
Triggers	User selects the option to add a new product.
Preconditions	User is logged on with administrator credentials. All necessary information for the item is already stored in the product data system.
Postconditions	The item is visible in the eStore.
Main Course	1. System displays the SKU search parameters. 2. User enters all or part of the product SKU and chooses to search (see AC1). 3. System displays matching products from the product data system. 4. User selects product to be added to eStore (see AC2). 5. System displays the eStore product data system's information for that SKU and provides an option to publish the product to the catalog. 6. User chooses to publish product to catalog (see EX1). 7. System displays preview of product in eStore for review. 8. User chooses to finalize product (see AC3). 9. System redirects user to the new product in the eStore (see EX2).
Alternate Courses	AC1 User selects to add item by name. 1. System displays the name search parameters. 2. User enters in all or part of the name and chooses to search. 3. Return to Main Course step 3. AC2 Item not in results list or no search results returned. 1. Return to Main Course step 1. AC3 User does not like the product preview and wants to cancel. 1. Return to Main Course step 3.
	EX1: Item already exists in eStore catalog. 1. System displays error message. 2. Return to Main Course step 1. EX2: System fails to add product to eStore. 1. System displays error message. 2. Return to Main Course step 9.

FIGURE C-12 A Use Case for adding items to the eStore.

Chapter 11

Figure C-13 shows a Roles and Permissions Matrix that covers a few roles and the catalog, cart, and account functionality. Obviously, there will be more roles and permissions for the entire system; this is just an example of some of it.

After modeling the scenario, you can ask additional questions of the business team, such as:

- Are there custom sales reports? If so, who has permission to create sales reports?
- Who has permission to delete items from a catalog?
- Who can add items to the catalog—both a Product Manager and a Manager? The scenario was not clear about this.

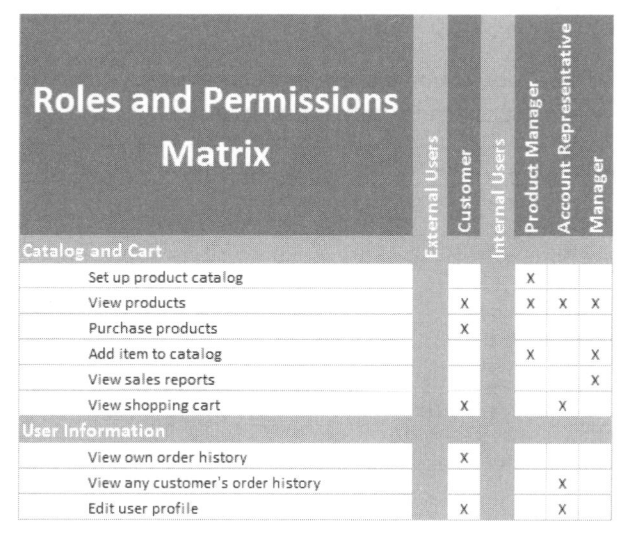

Roles and Permissions Matrix	External Users	Customer	Internal Users	Product Manager	Account Representative	Manager
Catalog and Cart						
Set up product catalog				X		
View products		X		X	X	X
Purchase products		X				
Add item to catalog				X		X
View sales reports						X
View shopping cart		X			X	
User Information						
View own order history		X				
View any customer's order history					X	
Edit user profile		X			X	

FIGURE C-13 A Roles and Permissions Matrix for eStore catalog, cart, and account functionality.

Chapter 12

Figure C-14 shows an Ecosystem Map for the eStore. Notice that the basic systems from the scenario are pretty obvious in this Ecosystem Map. In addition, the business data objects and their direction of flow between the systems have been labeled.

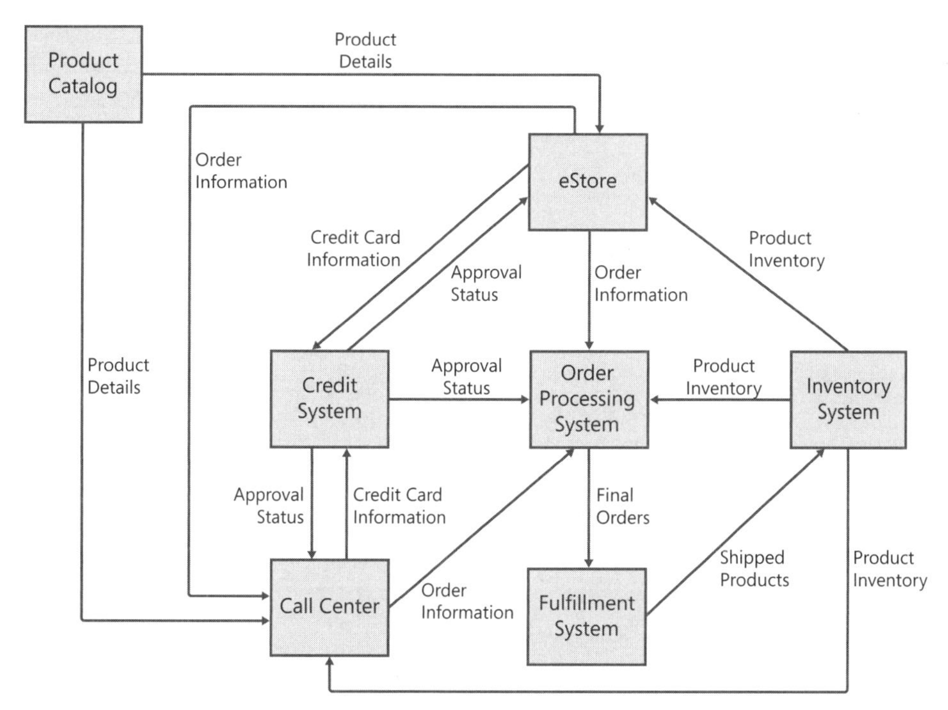

FIGURE C-14 An Ecosystem Map for the eStore.

The following are a few example questions to ask, generated from the draft Ecosystem Map:

- It seems that the inventory system does not integrate to the product catalog system and the integration happens in the eStore and the call center only. Is that correct?
- How are shipping and tax calculated on an order? For example, there might be a system to calculate taxes or shipping that needs to be discovered.
- Is there anything missing? It never hurts to ask! You might identify systems you knew nothing about.

Chapter 13

The L2 System Flow in Figure C-15 shows the system steps for processing orders for shipping.

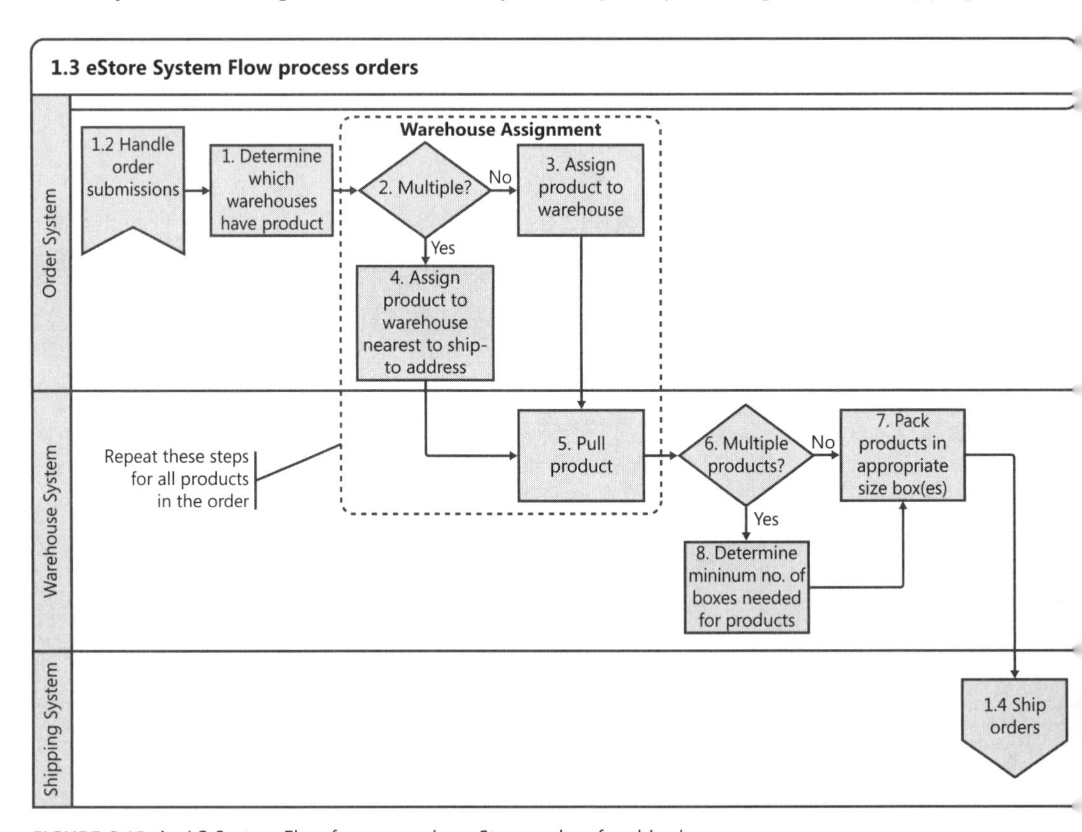

FIGURE C-15 An L2 System Flow for processing eStore orders for shipping.

Chapter 14

The UI Flow in Figure C-16 includes all the main screens identified by the scenario and creates the most important transition lines. The UI triggers are labeled on some of the transition lines because the trigger is not obvious. For example, the transition line leading from the cart to the decision to check that there are items in the cart is labeled, because it is not immediately obvious that this is the checkout navigation path.

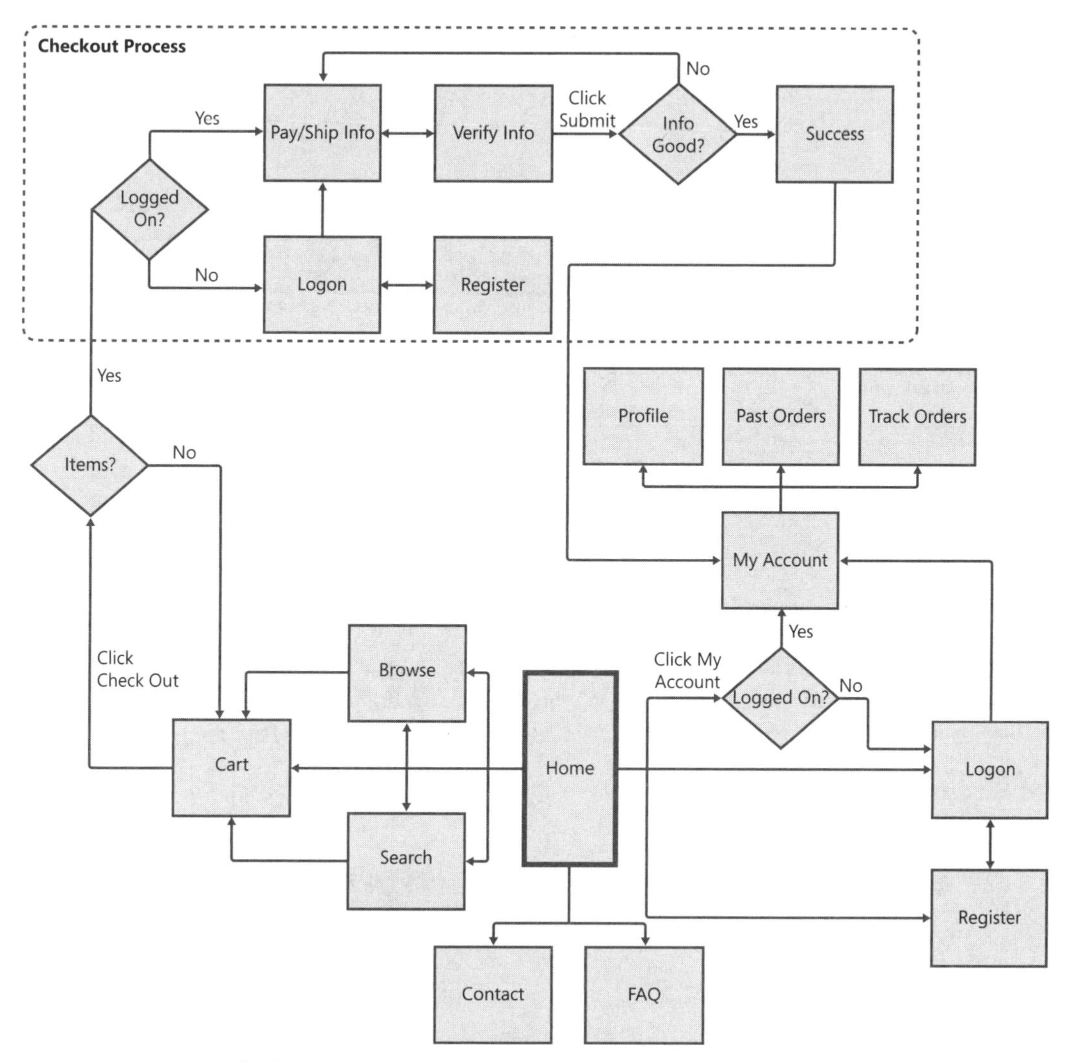

FIGURE C-16 A UI Flow for the entire eStore.

Chapter 15

Figure C-17 shows the UI element table for the color selector search result filter.

<table>
<tr><th colspan="3">UI Element: Color Filter</th></tr>
<tr><th colspan="3">UI Element Description</th></tr>
<tr><td>ID</td><td colspan="2">ELMT_0048</td></tr>
<tr><td>Description</td><td colspan="2">Color selector to filter products by color</td></tr>
<tr><th colspan="3">UI Element Displays</th></tr>
<tr><th>Precondition</th><th colspan="2">Display</th></tr>
<tr><td>Always</td><td colspan="2">A grid of all possible values of <product.color> for available products and pink is selected by default
Color
View all</td></tr>
<tr><th colspan="3">UI Element Behaviors</th></tr>
<tr><th>Precondition</th><th>Action</th><th>Response</th></tr>
<tr><td>Colors not selected</td><td>Select one color</td><td>System highlights color selected. System filters search results to show only products where <product.color> is the selected color.</td></tr>
<tr><td>Color(s) selected</td><td>Select an additional color</td><td>System highlights color selected. System filters search results to show only products where <product.color> is any of the selected colors. All other selected filters are also applied.</td></tr>
<tr><td>Color(s) selected</td><td>Select a highlighted color</td><td>System removes highlighting from selected color. System removes filter for that color.</td></tr>
<tr><td>Always</td><td>Select "View all"</td><td>System removed highlighting from all colors. System shows products where <product.color> is any color.</td></tr>
</table>

FIGURE C-17 A Display-Action-Response table for the eStore search product color filter.

Chapter 16

A complete Decision Table would not fit in the book, so the Decision Table shown in Figure C-18 has been simplified. Notice that in the case in which a gift card that does not have sufficient funds is selected for payment, two outcomes are valid and the order in which they are applied is specified.

Decision Table	Rule 1	Rule 2	Rule 3	Rule 4	Rule 5	Rule 6	Rule 7
Conditions							
Customer chooses to use saved payment method	Y	Y	N	N	N	N	N
Payment method is valid	Y	N	—	—	—	—	—
New payment type	—	—	Credit Card	Credit Card	Check	Gift Card	Gift Card
Credit card type	—	—	Contoso	A. Datum	—	—	—
Sufficient funds available	—	—	—	—	—	Y	N
Outcomes							
OC001 Use payment method on file	X	-	-	-	-	-	-
OC002 Give option to edit payment method on file	-	X	-	-	-	-	-
OC003 Obtain card number & 3-digit security code	-	-	X	-	-	-	-
OC004 Obtain card number & 4-digit security code	-	-	-	X	-	-	-
OC005 Obtain account info, DL#, and address	-	-	-	-	X	-	-
OC006 Use gift card	-	-	-	-	-	X	1
OC007 Select payment method for remaining balance	-	-	-	-	-	-	2

FIGURE C-18 A Decision Table for the rules for applying eStore payment methods.

Chapter 17

To create the Decision Tree for the scenario, think about the order of decisions that are made. The very first decision that must be made is whether or not the customer has a payment method that is saved to his profile. The possible choices are that the customer either has a method saved or he does not. After you have identified the choices, you then determine what possible new decisions or outcomes follow from these choices. For example, if the customer does have a payment method, the new decision is to determine whether the payment method is valid. As you continue to identify decisions, choices, and outcomes, you should come up with an ordered Decision Tree similar to the one shown in Figure C-19.

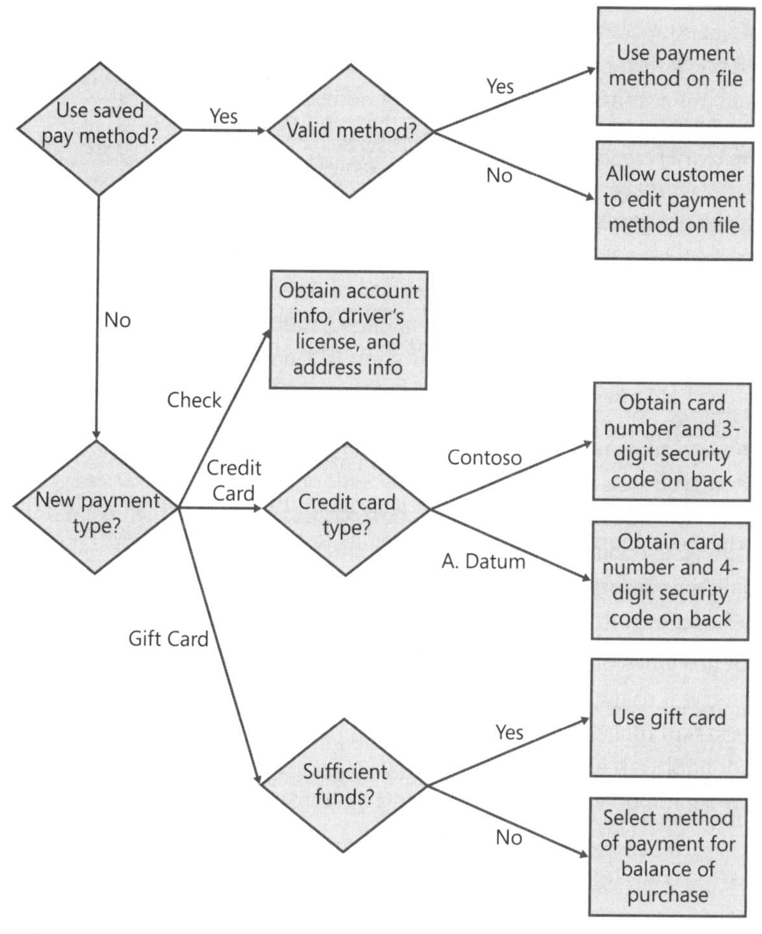

FIGURE C-19 A Decision Tree for the rules for applying eStore payment methods.

Chapter 18

Figure C-20 shows a System Interface Table for the interface between the inventory system and the eStore. There are many interfaces, but you only need to describe the details for the product inventory data transfer. The figure shows a reference to a System Flow for error handling; in a real project, you would need to look up the exact flow number and reference it here. In this case, only two fields of the Product object should be transferred: the SKU as an identifier, and the number of products available. There are no special rules to override for these fields.

System Interface			
Source	Inventory System		
Target	eStore		
ID	SI002		
Description	Inventory System updates the eStore with product inventory to show availability		
Frequency	Once per day at midnight		
Volume	All products, approximately 500 products		
Security Constraints	None		
Error Handling	Refer to System Flow 1.1 for error handling		
Interface Objects			
Object	**Field**	**Data Dictionary ID**	**Validation Rule**
Product	SKU	DD001	
Product	Quantity available	DD001	

FIGURE C-20 A System Interface Table describing the interface between the inventory system and the eStore.

Chapter 19

There is extraneous information provided in the scenario, but a good analyst needs to filter through the information to identify what is relevant to the model. For example, the business objectives do not directly lead you to objects in the BDD, nor do the fields of an address. However, the list of functionality should help you identify a few objects, such as customer, order, and item. The user list makes it clear that there are companies with customers as well as customers who don't belong to companies. Figure C-21 shows the BDD. Notice that addresses are attached to items and not to the order, because a customer can ship items in one order to different addresses.

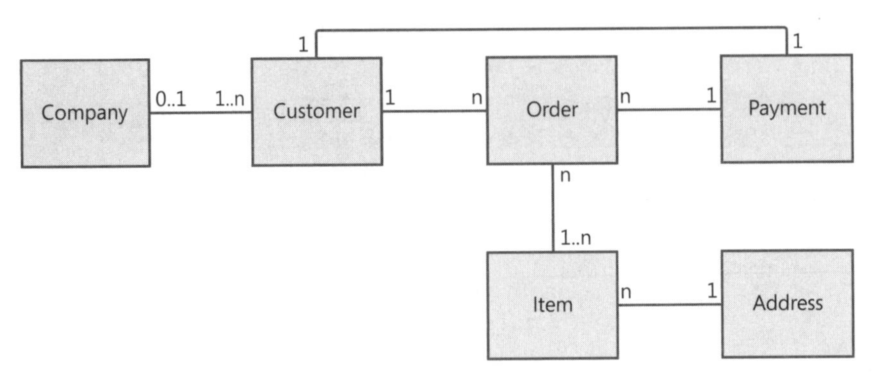

FIGURE C-21 The BDD for eStore business data objects.

Chapter 20

The obvious business data objects for the scenario include Cart, Order, and Product. A first set of processes to consider would be Create Cart, Confirm Order, and Maintain Products. The obvious entities are Shopper, Product Manager, and Order Fulfillment. When you start to place those on a diagram, more processes become obvious. Figure C-22 shows a first draft of the DFD.

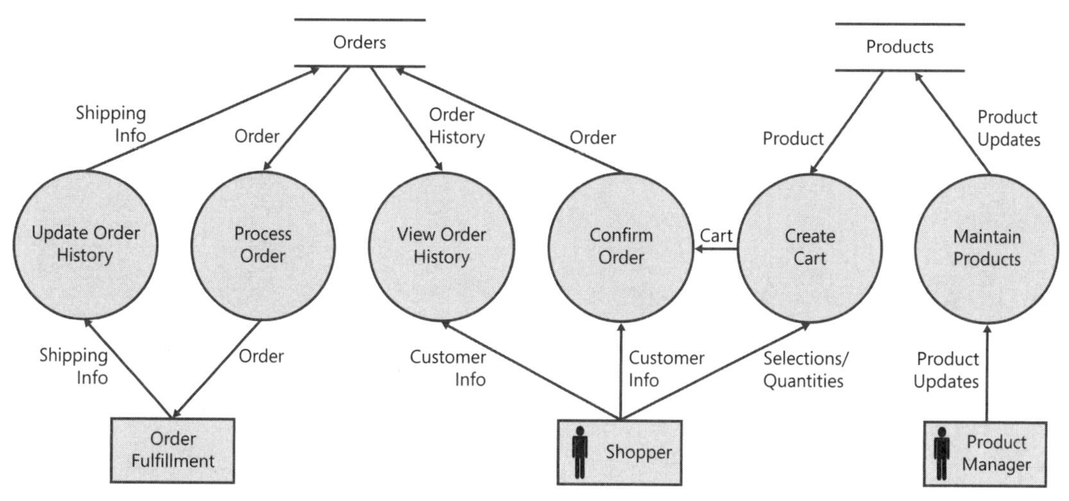

FIGURE C-22 A Data Flow Diagram (DFD) for the eStore.

Chapter 21

Using the information from the scenario, and inferring additional information, a Data Dictionary as shown in Figure C-23 can be created. The Discount Price and In Stock fields are both calculated fields.

ID	Business Data Object	Field Name	Description	Data Type	Valid Values	Length	Unique Values?	Required?	Default Value	Calculation
DD01	Product	Cost	How much the item costs the eStore to purchase or manufacture	US currency format: ($999,999.99)	0.00... 999,999.99	10	No	Yes	$100.00	N/A
DD02	Product	List Price	Display price of the item in the eStore catalog	US currency format: ($999,999.99)	0.00... 999,999.99	10	No	Yes	$120.00	N/A
DD03	Product	Discount Price	Discount price available to premium customers	US currency format: ($999,999.99)	0.00... 999,999.99	10	No	No	N/A	0.80 * List Price, rounded up to the nearest cent
DD04	Product	SKU	Code used to identify each unique product	Alphanumeric	Any combination of 10 letters and digits	10 digits	Yes	Yes	9999999999	N/A
DD05	Product	Quantity	Number of products for this SKU currently in stock	Integer	0...999,999	8 digits	No	Yes	0	N/A
DD06	Product	In Stock	Indicates whether a product is in or out of stock	Boolean	True, False	N/A	No	Yes	FALSE	Quantity > 0

FIGURE C-23 A Data Dictionary for the eStore accessory business data object.

Wherever possible, inferring information is a good technique that can save time. Always confirm that the inferred information is correct. The types of things inferred in this exercise answer based on past experience include the data types, valid values, and field lengths for all of the fields. Also inferred was how the value for in-stock is set in the calculation field, and a suggestion was made as to what should happen with rounding the discount price.

You might need to elicit information for additional properties. In general, you should elicit information about all of the necessary and recommended properties. However, if you are short on time or if information exists elsewhere, you can limit the Data Dictionary to a core set of properties.

Chapter 22

The object that requires a State Table is the Cart object. A first set of states for the Cart object might include "drafted," "finalized," "priced," "completed" (shipping and payment gathered), "confirmed," "assembled," "shipped," and "received." The draft State Table is shown in Figure C-24. It might change further throughout the project as more is learned, but it is close to complete.

	Target State							
Initial State	Drafted	Finalized	Priced	Completed	Confirmed	Assembled	Shipped	Received
Drafted	no	User chooses to checkout	no	no	no	no	no	no
Finalized	no	no	Taxes and discounts calculated	no	no	no	no	no
Priced	User edits order	no	no	User enters valid shipping and payment information	no	no	no	no
Completed	User edits order	no	no	no	User confirms purchase	no	no	no
Confirmed	Factory cannot fulfill order	no	no	no	no	Factory built	no	no
Assembled	no	no	no	no	no	no	Factory shipped	no
Shipped	no	no	no	no	no	no	no	Order arrived
Received	no	no	no	no	no	no	no	no

FIGURE C-24 A State Table for the eStore Cart business data object.

Chapter 23

The obvious object that requires a State Diagram is the Cart object. Figure C-25 is the corresponding State Diagram from the provided State Table.

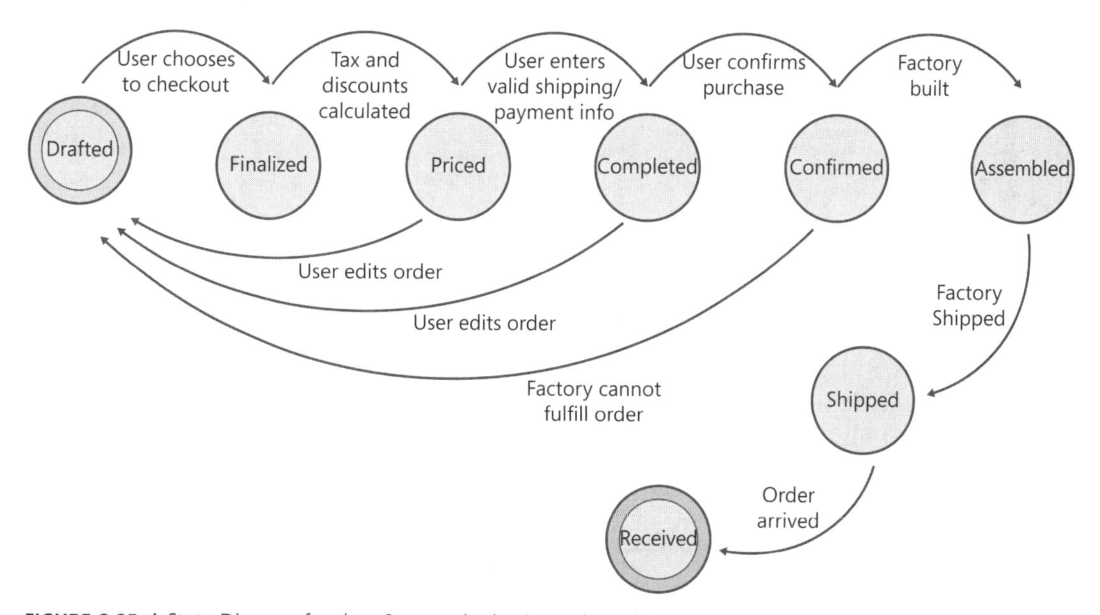

FIGURE C-25 A State Diagram for the eStore order business data object.

Chapter 24

Figure C-26 is the Report Table for the mockup report.

	Element	Call-Handling Report
Top-Level Elements	Unique ID	REP003
	Name	CSR Call-Handling Times
	Description	This report shows the number of support help calls answered per CSR and the average time it took each CSR to resolve the issues.
	Decisions Made from Report	Which CSR should be promoted each quarter?
	Objective	Business Objective 3 - Increase employee retention rate to 80%.
	Priority	3 of 5. See Objective Chain 003.
	Functional Area	Sales
	Related Reports	N/A
	Report Owner	Call Center Director
	Report Users	Call Center Director and Director's Assistant
	Trigger	User requests report
	Frequency	Generated on demand. Accessed on the third Friday of every month
	Latency	Data should be real time
	Transaction Volume	Each day roughly 30 calls are added to the report
	Data Volume	On average, the report returns 300 calls
	Security	Only Director and Director's Assistant can view
	Persistence	All settings are saved between report executions
	Visual Format	Matrix with CSR names as rows, Dates as rows, Number of Calls per Day and Average Call-Handling times as columns.
	Delivery Format	Displayed in application and emailable as an Excel file. Within the application, the user can scroll to see the data that does not fit on the screen.
	Interactivity	The CSR names can be expanded and collapsed to show or hide the call dates per CSR. Default to expanded.
	Drilldowns	N/A
Field Elements	Filtered By	System preset filter <call.date> = current month. User can select a different month from the 12 months.
	Grouped By	System preset grouping by <CSR.name>, then by <call.date>, then by all calls
	Sorted By	System preset sort by <CSR.name> alphabetically, then <call.date> chronologically
	User Input Parameters	N/A
	Group Calculation	Total number of calls for filtered month by date and by CSR Average Call-Handling Time by each date and CSRs = sum(individual call-handling times for date)/number of calls for date Average Call-Handling Time by month and CSRs = sum(individual call-handling times for month)/number of calls for month
	Calculated Fields	N/A
	Displayed Fields	<CSR.name> <Call.date> Count of calls Average Call-Handling Time Average Call-Handling Time should be rounded to 2 decimal places.
	What If	N/A

FIGURE C-26 A Report Table for the eStore call-handling report.

Chapter 25

The scenario describes a greenfield project whose characteristics include an extensive user interaction, a customer-facing system, analytics and reporting components, workflow automation, business process automation, and web app characteristics.

You will definitely need to create a Business Objectives Model and Objective Chain to prioritize requirements. KPIMs might be helpful because the current processes are manual. You can use KPIMs to ensure that the business does not lose any overall operational efficiency in taking orders with the new system. A Feature Tree will be helpful to communicate the full set of features for the executive team. And an RMM is going to be critical to map requirements back to Process Flows and business objectives to minimize scope creep, because this is a new system implementation.

You might create an Org Chart to identify the internal users of the system, and you will definitely need to create Process Flows to show how users will complete orders in the new system. An Ecosystem Map will be necessary for showing how the eStore interacts with other existing systems such as order fulfillment. System Flows can show the automated interactions that occur after orders are submitted. UI Flows and DAR models are critical for ensuring that the users can easily use the new website. BDDs and Data Dictionaries will be helpful for documenting the major pieces of business data such as customer and order, and their fields.

Additionally, a Roles and Permissions Matrix, State Tables, State Diagrams, Report Tables, DFDs, and Use Cases might be helpful. A Roles and Permissions Matrix will be helpful if you recognize that there is a security model for internal users. If primarily external users are accessing the UI and they all have the same permissions, this model might not be helpful. State Tables and State Diagrams can be used to represent the different states of orders that go through a defined workflow. Report Tables can be used to document the requirements for the reports the owner is requesting. Use Cases can further describe the users' interactions in the system. You might need a DFD to describe the flow of data that shows up in the reports.

The relevant project characteristics and their recommended models, as well the final models selected, are shown in Figure C-27.

	Objectives	Business Objectives Model	Objective Chain	Key Performance Indicator Model	Feature Tree	Requirements Mapping Matrix	People	Org Chart	Process Flow	Use Case	Roles and Permissions Matrix	Systems	Ecosystem Map	System Flow	UI Flow	Display-Action-Response Model	Decision Table	Decision Tree	System Interface Table	Data	Business Data Diagram	Data Flow Diagram	Data Dictionary	State Table	State Diagram	Report Table
Greenfield		L	L		L	L																				
Extensive user interaction									L	M	L				L	L										
Customer-facing									M	M	M				L	L										
Business process automation				L				L	L	M	M										L		L			
Workflow automation									L		L										L			L	L	
Web app													L	L	M	M					L		L			
Analytics and reporting									M								M	M			L	L	L			L
Selected models for scenario		**x**	**x**	**x**	**x**	**x**		**x**	**x**	**x**	**x**		**x**	**x**	**x**	**x**					**x**	**x**	**x**	**x**	**x**	**x**

FIGURE C-27 Project characteristics and recommended models for the eStore implementation project.

Chapter 26

A few of the models that can be used in this scenario are Process Flows or Use Cases, DAR models, and Data Dictionaries. You might use the proposed models together in the following ways:

- The Process Flows can be used to document the primary actions the eStore supports.
- Each step of the Process Flows can then be tied to one or more DAR models to ensure that the user interface is easy to navigate and use.
- A BDD defines the business data objects. Each of those has fields defined in a Data Dictionary.
- DAR models will also be used in conjunction with the Data Dictionary so that all of the data requirements are captured on a screen and in the underlying storage system.
- You can use the Data Dictionary to determine which business data objects have states that impact the eStore and require State Diagrams.
- An RMM can map the Process Flows to DAR models to requirements.

Glossary

Numbers & Symbols

7+/–2 See *Miller's Magic Number.*

A

activity diagram A model used to visually describe complex flow, often used to supplement Use Cases. Uses symbols similar to those used in Process Flows but shows user actions and system responses in the same diagram. See also *Process Flow; Use Case.*

actor See *user.* Note that systems are not actors.

affinity diagram A diagram that simply organizes items into related groups. A good way to quickly structure large amounts of information into smaller groups during elicitation. Often used in brainstorming sessions and works well if you apply Miller's Magic Number to it.

approach The type of process followed to implement a project.

B

bounding model A model that can be created with a high probability of capturing all the information for that model. The RML bounding models are the Business Objectives Model, Org Chart, Ecosystem Map, and Business Data Diagram. See also *model.*

business or "the business" A shorthand way of referring to the business stakeholders. See also *business stakeholder.*

Business Data Diagram (BDD) The RML data model that shows the relationships between business data objects from a business stakeholder's or customer's perspective. Shows the containment ("has a") relationship between objects as well as the cardinality of the set (many-to-many, many-to-one, one-to-one, and so on).

business data object Any conceptual piece of data that is of significance to the business stakeholders. Consists of fields and/or other business data objects.

business object See *business data object.*

business objective Measurable target that specifies how to determine when the business problem is solved.

Business Objectives Model The RML objectives model that defines and relates business problems, business objectives, product concepts, and success metrics. Used to identify the value of a project.

business problem An issue preventing the business from achieving its goals.

business process A set of activities a business user performs. Can be described in a Process Flow.

business rule A requirement that represents a conditional statement that modifies a functional requirement, including but not limited to when the function is available and who is allowed to execute the function. Contains words such as "if," "when," and "then." See also *requirement; functional requirement.*

business stakeholder A person (or group) who will be using the software or who has an interest in the benefits the software provides and who usually works for the company or organization producing the software. It is one type of stakeholder. See also *stakeholder.*

business user A person who will be using the software and who usually works for the company or organization producing the software.

C

cardinality The number of instances of a single business data object that can be related to another business data object.

class diagram A UML diagram describing a system's structure through system classes (Eriksson, Hans-Erik, and Magnus Penker. 2000. *Business Modeling with UML*. New York, NY: Wiley). See also *Unified Modeling Language (UML).*

collaboration diagram A UML diagram describing the interactions between a set of software objects (Eriksson and Penker 2000). See also *Unified Modeling Language (UML).*

component diagram A UML diagram describing the relationships between technical components of a system (Eriksson and Penker 2000). See also *Unified Modeling Language (UML).*

cross-functional process flow See *Process Flow.*

customer A person external to the company or organization implementing the software that will use the software as part of obtaining or consuming products or services that the company or organization provides.

D

data See *business data object.*

Data Dictionary The RML data model that describes the fields of any business data object in the system.

Data Flow Diagram (DFD) The RML data model that shows the flow of information through a solution and the processes that transform the business data objects.

data object See *business data object.*

Decision Table The RML systems model that describes all possible combinations of a set of conditions and their corresponding outcomes, represented in a grid.

Decision Tree The RML systems model used to represent relevant combinations of conditions and their corresponding outcomes in a tree format.

design How the requirements will be implemented in the solution, including the user interface.

diagram A visual representation of organized information.

Display-Action-Response (DAR) model The RML systems model that documents the ways a system displays a screen and how it responds to the actions a user can take.

E

ecosystem The full set of solution components in an organization; can include hardware, software, people, and data.

Ecosystem Map The RML systems model used to show the relationship between all systems in the solution ecosystem. See also *ecosystem.*

element Any component of a model.

entity relationship diagram (ERD) A database design model that is used to show the relationships between conceptual or physical data as they are stored in the database.

F

feature A short-form description of an area of functionality that the solution will ultimately include to meet the business objectives. It is a collection of requirements that is used to articulate and organize the requirements.

Feature Tree The RML objectives model that shows all of the system features organized into logical groups in a tree structure.

functional requirement A behavior or capability that the solution can provide irrespective of any qualifiers.

G

goal Qualitative statements about what the business stakeholders are trying to achieve. Similar to business objectives, but they are qualitative statements instead of measurable statements.

I

Information Technology (IT) The group of people who typically implement software projects that are designed to service users internal to the company.

K

key performance indicator (KPI) A quantifiable measure of the success of a business activity or of progress toward a goal.

Key Performance Indicator Model (KPIM) The RML objectives model that associates KPIs to business processes to evaluate the performance of the processes. See also *KPI*.

M

map A type of diagram that shows a whole picture of how elements relate.

matrix A grid structure that captures model details as the intersection of rows and columns.

methodology A system of methods, principles, and rules followed in performing some activity or discipline.

Miller's Magic Number A reference to work by cognitive psychologist, George A. Miller, indicating that humans can only process seven plus or minus two items simultaneously (Miller, George A. 1956. "The Magical Number Seven, Plus or Minus Two: Some Limits on Our Capacity for Processing Information." *Psychological Review* 63, 81-97).

mind map A way to structure information that supports rapid organization of the information. Useful during brainstorming activities when the information will be elicited in spurts and not in a particular order.

model A visual representation of information related to processes, data, and interactions within and surrounding the solution being developed.

N

non-functional requirement Any requirement that is not a functional requirement (including business rules). See also *requirement*; *functional requirement*.

O

object See *business data object*.

object diagram A UML diagram often used with class diagrams to describe instances of objects in a class diagram (Eriksson and Penker 2000). See also *class diagram*.

<*object.field*> notation The standard notation used in this book to reference data fields in a precise manner, where *object* is a business data object from the Business Data Diagram and *field* is a data field from the Data Dictionary.

Objective Chain The RML objectives model that measurably links features to business objectives by using objective factors and objective equations.

onion model A template of circles to show stakeholders and their relationships to each other and the product being developed. (Alexander, Ian. 2005. "A Taxonomy of Stakeholders: Human Roles in System Development," International Journal of Technology and Human Interaction, *http://easyweb.easynet.co.uk/~iany/consultancy/stakeholder_taxonomy/stakeholder_taxonomy.htm*)

operation An individual function in the system. Can be conceptual or an actual physical element in the user interface.

OPSD Objectives, people, systems, and data categorization of RML models.

ordered Decision Tree The most common type of Decision Tree, used if there is an implied order in which the decisions are made. Uses directed arrows to signify the order of the decisions and outcomes. See also Decision Tree; unordered Decision Tree.

Org Chart The RML people model that shows the structure of all people in an organization. Used to help identify all possible users, stakeholders, and subject matter experts from whom requirements should be gathered.

P

people Any group of stakeholders.

persona An example of a user that contains the user's background information and motivations for using the system.

process A set of activities performed for a specific purpose or to achieve a specific outcome.

Process Flow The RML people model that describes a business process that will be executed by people. Shows the activities performed, the sequence in which they are performed, and the different decisions that are made to achieve a desired outcome. Process Flows can use swim lanes to show the various people who perform activities in the Process Flow. See also *swim lane*.

product concept The vision of the actual solution that the business chooses to implement in order to meet the business objective. Typically described as a short description of the product with a list of high-level features.

project A temporary endeavor undertaken to create a unique product, service, or result (Project Management Institute (PMI). 2008. *A Guide to the Project Management Body of Knowledge (PMBOK Guide) – Fourth Edition.* Newtown Square, PA: Project Management Institute, Inc.).

prototype A working mockup of a user interface that is used to elicit and clarify requirements. Can be low fidelity (wireframe drawings) or high fidelity (an interactive experience for the users).

R

Report Table The RML data model used to describe report requirements in a structured way. Includes how data is displayed and how output is formatted, and can include drilldown views and manipulation and interaction requirements.

requirement Anything the business needs to have implemented in the solution. This can include functional requirements, non-functional requirements, business rules, and design. See also *functional requirement*; *non-functional requirement*; *business rule.*

requirements architecture The organization of requirements information; includes how you structure the requirements as well as the model-to-model relationships and model-to-requirements relationships.

Requirements Mapping Matrix (RMM) An RML objectives model that maps requirements and business rules to a model so that the requirements are grouped in a more easily consumable way. Most commonly maps Process Flow or System Flow steps to requirements and business rules.

Requirements Modeling Language (RML) A visual language to model requirements; comprised of objectives, people, systems, and data (OPSD) models. Designed and used specifically for the purpose of modeling requirements. See also *OPSD.*

RML See *Requirements Modeling Language.*

role See *user role.*

Roles and Permissions Matrix The RML people model used to define the types of roles and their associated permissions for executing operations in the system. See also *user role.*

S

sequence diagram A UML diagram describing a sequence of messages sent between objects (Eriksson and Penker 2000).

solution A full implementation for solving a business problem. Can include hardware, software, business processes, user manuals, and training. See also *business problem.*

stakeholder An individual with an interest in the outcome of the project. IT, business, and customers are all types of stakeholders. Can be involved in, affected by, and/or influence the outcome (Wiegers, Karl E. 2003. *Software Requirements, Second Edition.* Redmond, WA: Microsoft Press). See also *business stakeholder; technical stakeholder; customer.*

state A short-form description of a stage in a business data object's life cycle that influences behavior of the system.

State Diagram The RML data model that shows all possible states of a business data object plus the single-step transitions between states in the solution. See also *state.*

State Table The RML data model that shows all possible states of a business data object, plus the single-step transitions between states in the system, represented in a grid. See also *state.*

statechart diagram A UML diagram showing the states of a system (Eriksson and Penker 2000). Similar to an RML State Diagram.

subject matter expert (SME) A person who is an expert about a topic related to the solution. A SME can be IT, business, or customer stakeholders.

success metric A business objective that will actually be measured to determine whether the project is successful; can also be an additional measure that is related to the solution. See also *business objective.*

swim lane A grouping in a Process Flow, System Flow, or UI Flow that divides the diagram into several sections to visually communicate the entities performing the steps.

swim lane diagram See *Process Flow.*

system An implementation that can include hardware, software, and business processes to solve a business problem.

System Flow The RML systems model that describes the activities that systems execute automatically. Shows the activities performed, the sequence in which they are performed, and the different decisions that are made to achieve a desired outcome. System Flows can use swim lanes to show the various systems that perform activities in the System Flow.

System Interface Table The RML systems model that describes the communication between two systems from the business point of view, including what information has to be transferred, how much, and how often.

T

table See *matrix*.

team or "the team" The full set of people engaged to execute a project, including the analysts, the business stakeholders, and the technical stakeholders.

technical stakeholders The implementation team that is actually producing the software or configuring the system. Usually refers to database designers, architects, software developers, and testers.

technical team See *technical stakeholders*.

traceability The mapping between all instances of two types of objects, comparing the relationships to ensure full coverage of one by the other.

traceability matrix See *Requirements Mapping Matrix*.

transition The movement of a business data object from one state to another.

U

UI element Any entity of a UI that has display or behavior attributes (such as a button, a display table, an image, or a check box). See also *user interface*.

UI Flow An RML systems model that shows how a user will navigate between screens in a user interface. See also *user interface*.

Unified Modeling Language (UML) A language used to visually specify the design of object-oriented software systems (Object Management Group. 2007. "OMG Unified Modeling Language Specification." *http://www.uml.org/#UML2.0*).

unordered Decision Tree Decision Trees without directed arrows; used to simplify a set of decisions when there is no implied order. See also *Decision Tree; ordered Decision Tree*.

Use Case The RML people model that describes the interactions between a user and a system. Describes what the user needs to do, what he is trying to accomplish, and how the system responds when using the software.

use case diagram A UML diagram describing relationships between Use Cases (Eriksson and Penker 2000).

user A person who directly uses a system to achieve a goal.

user interface (UI) Screens in a software system through which a user communicates with the system.

user interface design requirement A requirement that represents how the system should look and how specific user interface elements should behave.

user role A name for a collection of users who share common functions and access to a system.

user story An agile approach to capturing requirements. Contains a name, description of what the user is trying to accomplish, and acceptance criteria that are used to determine when the user story has been properly implemented by the software.

V

validation The act of checking requirements to ensure that they are needed to fulfill the business objectives.

verification The act of checking requirements to ensure that they will result in a functional solution.

W

wireframe A mock-up of a screen used to show what a system's user interface will look like. Can be low fidelity (sketches or block diagrams) to encourage the audience to think about components and functions rather than look and feel, or can be high fidelity (screen shots) to show the audience what the screen will actually look like after the solution is developed.

Index

C

D

E

F

G

H

I

J

K

L

M

N

O

P

Q

R

S

T

U

V

W

About the Authors

JOY BEATTY is a Vice President at Seilevel. Joy drives creation and implementation of new methodologies and best practices that improve requirements elicitation and modeling. She assists Fortune 500 companies as they build business analysis centers of excellence. Joy has provided training to thousands of business analysts.

Joy is actively involved as a leader in the requirements community, serving on boards of multiple industry organizations. She is currently on the International Institute of Business Analysis (IIBA) core team for updating *A Guide to the Business Analysis Body of Knowledge (BABOK Guide)*. She has presented at numerous requirements-related conferences and speaking events. Additionally, she writes about requirements methodologies in journals, white papers, and blog posts. Joy graduated from Purdue University with Bachelor of Science degrees in both Computer Science and Mathematics.

ANTHONY CHEN is President of Seilevel. Over the past 15 years, Anthony has worked with numerous Fortune 500 companies. He is responsible for the strategic growth of Seilevel and the development of innovative software requirements techniques, including Objective Chains; the Business Objectives Model; the Objectives, People, Systems, and Data classification (OPSD); and RML.

In addition to his business and innovation leadership, Anthony has written extensively on software requirements techniques, experiences, and ideas. Some of his writing can be found on the Seilevel blog. He earned Bachelor of Science degrees in both Electrical Engineering and Microbiology from The University of Illinois, and a Master of Science in Medical Microbiology and Immunology from Texas A&M University.

You can contact us by leaving a comment on the Seilevel blog (*http://www.seilevel.com/blog/*), emailing us at RML@seilevel.com, or joining our conversation on Twitter @seilevel.